Prince, Musical Genre, and the Construction of Racial Identity

TRACKING POP

SERIES EDITORS: JOCELYN NEAL, JOHN COVACH, ROBERT FINK, AND LOREN KAJIKAWA

RECENT TITLES IN THE SERIES:

Prince, Musical Genre, and the Construction of Racial Identity
by Griffin Woodworth

Owning My Masters (Mastered): The Rhetorics of Rhymes & Revolutions [Online Resource]
by A.D. Carson

The Bastard Instrument: A Cultural History of the Electric Bass
by Brian F. Wright

Tracks on the Trail: Popular Music, Race, and the US Presidency
by Dana Gorzelany-Mostak

Here for the Hearing: Analyzing the Music in Musical Theater
by Michael Buchler and Gregory J. Decker, Editors

Queer Voices in Hip Hop: Cultures, Communities, and Contemporary Performance
by Lauron J. Kehrer

Critical Excess: *Watch the Throne* and the New Gilded Age
by J. Griffith Rollefson

Soda Goes Pop: Pepsi-Cola Advertising and Popular Music
by Joanna K. Love

The Beatles through a Glass Onion: Reconsidering the White Album
edited by Mark Osteen

The Pop Palimpsest: Intertextuality in Recorded Popular Music
edited by Lori Burns and Serge Lacasse

Uncharted: Creativity and the Expert Drummer
by Bill Bruford

I Hear a Symphony: Motown and Crossover R&B
by Andrew Flory

Prince, Musical Genre, and the Construction of Racial Identity

Griffin Woodworth

University of Michigan Press
Ann Arbor

Published in the United States of America by the
University of Michigan Press
First published May 2025

A CIP catalog record for this book is available from the British Library.

Library of Congress Cataloging-in-Publication Data

Names: Woodworth, Griffin (Griffin Mead), 1972– author. | Michigan Publishing (University of Michigan), publisher.
Title: Prince, musical genre, and the construction of racial identity / Griffin Woodworth.
Other titles: Tracking pop.
Description: Ann Arbor : University of Michigan Press, 2025. | Series: Tracking Pop | Includes bibliographical references (pages 305–322) and index.
Identifiers: LCCN 2024058182 (print) | LCCN 2024058183 (ebook) | ISBN 9780472077342 (hardcover) | ISBN 9780472057344 (paperback) | ISBN 9780472222148 (ebook)
Subjects: LCSH: Prince—Criticism and interpretation. | Music and race—United States—History—20th century. | Sex in music. | Sex role in music. | Rock music—United States—History and criticism.
Classification: LCC ML420.P974 W68 2025 (print) | LCC ML420.P974 (ebook) | DDC 781.66092—dc23/eng/20241218
LC record available at https://lccn.loc.gov/2024058182
LC ebook record available at https://lccn.loc.gov/2024058183

DOI: https://doi.org/10.3998/mpub.6047957

This book will be made open access within three years of publication thanks to Path to Open, a program developed in partnership between JSTOR, the American Council of Learned Societies (ACLS), University of Michigan Press, and The University of North Carolina Press to bring about equitable access and impact for the entire scholarly community, including authors, researchers, libraries, and university presses around the world. Learn more at https://about.jstor.org/path-to-open/

Authorized Representative: Easy Access System Europe, Mustamäe tee 50, 10621 Tallinn, Estonia, gpsr.requests@easproject.com

To Heide, who has seen me through all stages of this manuscript,
and to Colette and Gilbert, who are both younger than this project.
I love you with my entire heart.

Contents

Digital materials related to this title can be found on the Fulcrum platform via the following citable URL: https://doi.org/10.3998/mpub.6047957

Illustrations

Acknowledgments

I would like to thank my graduate professors at UCLA (where this project began as my Ph.D. dissertation) including Robert Fink, Mitchell Morris, Philip Brett, Robert Walser, and Susan McClary. I would also like to thank my colleagues in the Society for American Music, the American Musicological Society (those are two different things), and the International Association for the Study of Popular Music, who have helped me refine this project over many iterations. The list of scholars who have offered me support and guidance over the years is too long to fit on this page, so I will mention just a few: Loren Kajikawa, Stephanie VanderWel, Steve Waksman, Brian Wright, Andy Flory, Michaelangelo Matos, Jon Copeland, Olivia Mather, Caroline O'Meara, Glenn Pillsbury, Louis Niebur, Philip Gentry, and Ross Fenimore, THANK YOU for your help and friendship. Last but not least I want to thank my family for their love and support—Heide, Colette, and Gilbert Woodworth, George and Carrol Woodworth, Zoe Woodworth and Jacy Fitzpatrick, Will and Marietta Storlie, Heather and Bruce Christman, Drew, Tanner, and Rylee Christman: I love you all, and thank you. And of course, a heartfelt "thank you" to Prince Rogers Nelson, whose music has inspired and challenged me since I first heard it when I was twelve years old, and who is the greatest musician and performer I have ever seen.

Research and writing of this book was supported by the Office of Sponsored Awards and Research at the University of South Carolina, Upstate, including the Course Reallocation Award, the Research Initiative for Summer Engagement (RISE) award, and the Scholarly Start-Up Package. Chapter 5 of this book is revised from the article "Prince, Miles, and Maceo: Horns, Masculinity, and the Anxiety of Influence," originally published in *Black Music Research Journal* 33, no. 2 (Fall 2013): 117–50.

Introduction

He dared to fight for what was rightfully his: his freedom, wrapped up in words and music he created.

—Beyoncé Knowles-Carter[1]

Paisley Park, a white aluminum-clad complex in Chanhassen, Minnesota, served as Prince's business headquarters, recording and rehearsal complex, and sometime residence from some months before its official opening date on September 11, 1987, until his untimely passing on April 21, 2016.[2] In addition being Prince's private sanctum, Paisley Park was also host to many public and semi-public parties over those years, making the complex a gathering place for followers of Prince's music, a community that identified itself as "fams" (short for "family members") rather than "fans" (short for "fanatics"), a term that Prince reportedly disliked. One series of Paisley Park events that Prince hosted during the mid- to late 1990s was known as "Love 4 One Another" (L4OA) which is also the name of a charitable organization that Prince founded for which the parties served as fundraisers (as well as the name of Prince's official website from 1997 to 1999).[3] These L4OA events were not publicized in the press but instead were announced via a semi-secret telephone list that one could join by inquiring with employees at Prince's New Power Generation retail store, which existed in the Uptown neighborhood of Minneapolis from 1993 to 1996 (after the NPG store closed, that clipboard-and-pen contact list behind the counter was replaced by an email distribution list).[4] From 2001 to 2006, after the NPG retail store had closed and the Love 4 One Another website shut down, Prince's public Paisley Park events were announced and ticketed through his official online community, the NPG Music Club. After shuttering the NPGMC and retreating from his official online presence, the last iteration of Prince's public concert series, Paisley Park after Dark, was organized by Prince's former bandmember and longtime friend Kirk Johnson sometime in the early 2010s. With no official website, Paisley Park after Dark events were announced through social media outlets, including Facebook and Twitter, and this series has continued even after Prince's passing.[5]

Attending events at Paisley Park during any of these eras required a certain amount of faith: Prince fams would get short notice (if any) before a Paisley Park event; events typically started late at night and often stretched until past dawn; fams had to wait in long lines in Minnesota's extreme weather before doors would open; ticket prices varied widely and often had to be paid in cash; and, once inside, fams were not guaranteed a live performance or even Prince's presence in the building. Sometimes Prince and his band would perform, but sometimes the event would feature another band or artist whom Prince wanted to promote, a DJ spinning dance music, a showing of unreleased video footage, or some combination of these things. Prince fams in the Minneapolis metro area would simply queue up at the appointed time outside Paisley Park, having stowed their cameras and cellphones in their cars (owing to a strict no-recording-devices rule inside Paisley Park that remained in place even after his passing), pay whatever fee was being charged at the door—sometimes nothing, sometimes $7, sometimes as much as $60—and hope for an appearance from the artist himself. Consequently, these events could often leave fams feeling frustrated. Yet on those occasions when Prince did play, the intimacy of having a small and dedicated audience in his own private venue allowed the artist to stretch and experiment. On these occasions, he often revealed himself artistically in ways that he did not or could not in an arena concert for the greater public. I want to begin this book by discussing one such evening.

On Saturday May 2, 2015, Prince hosted a Paisley Park after Dark party under the title "Dance Rally 4 Peace," which I myself attended. Prince's organization had announced this event in advance through social media, and the digital flyer instructed attendees to "wear something gray," a reference to Freddie Gray, whose death on April 19, 2015, while in Baltimore police custody had galvanized the Black Lives Matter movement and sparked riots in the city of Baltimore that were ongoing at the time (several days later, Prince gave a benefit concert in Baltimore similarly titled the "Rally 4 Peace").[6] That night, after a short DJ set, Prince took the stage with his three-piece rock band 3rd Eye Girl and played a set that avoided his big hits, delivering instead the kind of thought-provoking and improvisatory performance that dedicated Prince fams cherished. Several days later, Prince uncharacteristically released a forty-one-minute live audio recording of that evening's concert on the online platform SoundCloud. Though that link no longer functions, the recording was quickly downloaded by many fams (the time markers to which I will refer in the analysis that follows come from that recording).[7]

In his Dance Rally 4 Peace concert at Paisley Park, which stretched across midnight from May 2 to 3, Prince constructed a six-song set out of four deep-cut album tracks and two cover songs. This set seemed designed both to arouse moral outrage and encourage community healing over the issue of racial disparities in the police's use of violence, which was capturing national headlines. Prince opened with the up-tempo rock song "Chaos and Disorder" from his 1996 Warner Brothers album of the same name, allowing the song's title, angry lyrics, fast tempo, and distortion-saturated guitar timbre to express the collective anger over Freddie Gray's death. Prince followed with the song "Dreamer," a minor-mode guitar rocker from his 2009 album *Lotusflow3r* whose lyrics focus on the theme of race, weaving together the assassination of Martin Luther King Jr. with images of police surveillance in Black neighborhoods. Prince then injected a lighter-hearted moment by covering Tommy James's classic-rock hit "Crimson and Clover," though this song was not included in the SoundCloud recording, presumably for copyright reasons. Prince's fourth and fifth songs that night were also rockers: "Guitar," from the 2007 album *Planet Earth*, and the instrumental "Plectrumelectrum," from his 2015 album of the same name, after which he left the stage and returned, sans backing band, for a meditative solo encore covering the Waterboys' 1985 single "The Whole of the Moon" (a song that some writers have speculated was originally inspired by Prince).[8]

It was during the second song, the Martin Luther King Jr.–inspired "Dreamer," that Prince created the most thought-provoking segment of the concert, a choice that may have stemmed from the thematic connection between that song and the problem of anti-Black police violence that Freddie Gray's death had brought to the fore. The song is a mid-tempo, cowbell-infused rock stomp based on an E natural-minor ostinato played by the bass and rhythm guitar that moves between the flat third and fourth and then the tonic and flat seventh (G–A–E–D–E, see example 1).

Example 1. Prince, "Dreamer," bass ostinato

In the album version, Prince spends nearly the entire second half of this song on a guitar solo, but in his performance that night in 2015 Prince truncated his guitar solo and added a five-and-a-half-minute keyboard solo between the second and third verses, answering the aggression of his distorted rock guitar with the introspection of subdued keyboard timbres. Prince's keyboard solo was primarily in the Lydian mode on E, which created a tension against the underlying E-Aeolian groove of the bass (E-Lydian includes the major third, G♯, and the raised fourth and seventh degrees, A♯ and D♯, whereas E-Aeolian has the minor third G-natural, the perfect fourth A-natural, and the lowered seventh D-natural). While this modal tension may have gone unnoticed by many concertgoers that night, Prince also gave the keyboard solo an obvious dramatic narrative arc by using a timbral conflict between different keyboard sounds. Prince began his keyboard solo with a detuned electronic timbre (at 19:06 in the concert recording released on SoundCloud) before adopting the familiar domestic sound of an acoustic piano timbre (at 19:42). This piano section of the solo began on—and returned numerous times to—the melodic cell D♯–G♯–A♯, emphasizing the two pitches of the Lydian mode that are most dissonant with the underlying E-Aeolian bass groove. After this modal jazz–influenced piano solo, Prince then switched to a flute timbre (at 21:51), with which he continued to solo in the E-Lydian mode, placing special emphasis on the raised fourth scale degree (A♯) for the first sixteen bars of the "flute" solo, which extended the motivic centrality of the dissonant E–A♯ tritone that he had begun with the piano solo.

For all the harmonic tension that Prince emphasized with these modal keyboard melodies, the most obvious sonic conflict that Prince set up was a timbral dissonance between the two keyboard sounds: throughout the piano and flute subsections of his keyboard solo, Prince gradually introduced an aggressively buzzy, resonant synthesizer timbre that became the musical drama's sonic antagonist. This new synth timbre was similar to the detuned sound with which he began the solo, insofar as both were obviously synthetic, mechanical sounds. But unlike the earlier timbre, this new sound was pitched, allowing it to augment the harmonic-melodic tension that the piano and flute had already introduced. Prince deployed this new resonant synth timbre first in unison with the piano solo, for twelve bars beginning at 20:40, then in sporadic unison with the flute solo, for twelve bars beginning at 23:20, and again for seven bars from 24:43 until the end of the keyboard solo at 25:03, after which Prince returned to his guitar and delivered the song's concluding spoken-word third verse.

This new synth timbre introduced a distinctly threatening element into the keyboard solo. With the piano and flute timbres, Prince remained within the realm of mimetic familiarity, giving listeners highly realistic simulations of acoustic instruments that would not be out of place in a modern jazz ensemble. Even as he played melodies that modally conflicted with the bass ostinato, he did so within a historically familiar soundscape: by using a repetitive and harmonically static bass ostinato to support modally derived solo lines played by acoustic instruments (piano and flute), the result was similar to the modal-jazz style of Miles Davis, an artist with whom Prince shared a mutual admiration and influence.[9] However, with the synthetic timbre that interrupted the piano and flute solos Prince introduced an element of threat that went above and beyond the modal tension of the Lydian E–A♯ tritone (and which stepped beyond the influence of modal-jazz into fusion-jazz). Intruding as it did into the familiar sound of the piano and flute solos, the buzzing artificiality of its non-imitative electronic timbre made it sound foreign and jarring, a quality that I propose be considered a type of dissonance: timbral dissonance. In addition, it was louder in dynamic and used a buzzy, resonant filter sound, which rendered it both more alien and more aggressive than either previous timbre. "Resonance" is a feature of the tone-shaping filters that are part of the three-stage synthesis process whereby a narrow range of frequencies just below the filter's cutoff are fed back into the input and thereby boosted.[10] The particular filter cutoff frequency that Prince had chosen for this resonant synth timbre was in the upper-mid range and was powerful enough to produce a secondary oscillation, giving it a particularly synthetic, buzzy, vibrating sound that would not have been out of place in a science fiction movie soundtrack. Indeed, the resonance of the timbre that Prince used had precisely the quality of "auditory roughness" that scholars of music perception associate with affective tension, a quality that comes across as aggressive, and this particular timbre bore a sonic resemblance to the sound of a distorted electric guitar.[11]

All three times that this resonant synthetic timbre entered into the keyboard solo, it was in unison with one of the imitative timbres—first piano (at 20:40) and then flute (at 23:20 and 24:43)—and in each instance Prince continued the solo as though the familiar, imitative timbre were trying to shake off the mechanical timbre or flee a pursuer. During the twelve bars (at 20:40) when the resonant synth timbre doubled the piano timbre, Prince ended the phrase with a rapid ascending arpeggio on the piano that was not doubled by the resonant synth sound, and the fact that this was the very last melodic gesture that he played before pausing the solo (to switch from the piano to the flute timbre) gave it an air of desperation, as though the piano were trying to break free of a pursuer. Prince ended the flute section of the solo with a similar gesture toward freedom. When the resonant synthetic timbre first began doubling the flute, for twelve bars beginning at 23:20, the flute seemed unable to break free: whenever the flute played the melodic cell D♯–E–D♯–C♯ (over a tonic E in the bass) the resonant synth timbre would double it; even when Prince rhythmically displaced this melodic cell, which he did at the start of the third four-bar phrase (by delaying the motive's entry by one beat, from the expected pickup to the "and" of beat 1, at 23:44), the resonant synth remained doggedly in unison. After this twelve-bar phrase, the flute seemed to escape by playing a series of tone-clusters (at 23:57). However, both the resonant synth timbre and the D♯–E–D♯–C♯ motivic cell returned in the end, like an idée fixe—or a pursuing police siren. It was this timbre and melodic cell with which Prince ended the keyboard solo at 25:03, at which point he left the audience hanging with a grand pause so long that some thought the song had ended and began to cheer (only to be corrected by the reentry of the drum-and-bass ostinato seconds later).

The rhetorical effect that Prince created by inserting a long silence at the conclusion of the keyboard solo was to make it seem as though the resonant synthetic timbre had caught up to and stopped the flute. This impression was heightened by the lyrical content of the third and final verse that followed, which connected the timbral-motivic narrative of the keyboard solo with the intersection of race, space, and policing that was on everyone's mind that night. Specifically, the lyrics to the third verse of "Dreamer" describe a character being stopped by the police while a helicopter circles the neighborhood, an example of the type of racialized police surveillance and intervention that—as the attendees that night were well aware—had recently ended the life of Freddie Gray and many other young African American men that year.

By creating a melodic and timbral narrative in which a threatening technological force—portrayed by the resonant synth timbre—followed and ultimately stopped an improvised modal-jazz-style melody played on familiar and, in the case of the flute, vulnerable-sounding acoustic timbres, Prince provided his audience with a potent metaphor for the fear and powerlessness that a young Black man might feel while driving late at night in a policed urban neighborhood. Indeed, Prince sonically transported his audience to that place, allowing us—the Paisley Park community of fams—to feel and contemplate what African American people have known since Reconstruction: the mortal danger that exists at the intersection of race, economic class, and urban policing. Prince moved on to other songs after "Dreamer," but the effect of that keyboard solo lingered. And when Prince had the audience chant the words "Baltimore, peace forever more" during his encore song in the early hours of that Sunday morning, it felt like a benediction.

Prince's concert that night is one example among many of how he made musical and performative decisions that did cultural work by connecting and commenting on issues of personal identity and national politics. Throughout his career, Prince's work was often politically charged but rarely politically explicit: consider how the graphic sexuality depicted in the lyrics of his 1984 song "Darling Nikki" inspired Tipper Gore to found the PMRC (Parents Music Resource Center), which became one of the major salvos of the 1980s "culture wars."[12] Prince's deliberately provocative but otherwise apolitical song thereafter came to represent a rebellion against Reagan-era cultural conservatism without the artist's ever having revealed his own political leanings. In fact, I am not aware of Prince ever endorsing or attacking a politician by name, with the possible exception of the rockabilly silliness of "Ronnie, Talk to Russia." In a similarly indirect though *non*-sexual fashion, the Dance Rally 4 Peace event poster's coded reference to Freddie Gray, and Prince's entreaty for peace in the city of Baltimore, gave attendees a shared political framework in which to experience the evening, despite the fact that Prince mentioned neither Freddie Gray nor Black Lives Matter that night. It was only later, when he released the single "Baltimore," that Prince mentioned Michael Brown and Freddie Gray by name in his lyrics. This implicit framework of racial justice inflected the songs Prince performed that night, allowing the keyboard solo in "Dreamer" to speak for him. By sonically placing attendees within a narrative of race, space, and police surveillance constructed through musical rhetoric rather than linguistic signification, Prince was able to take a very particular kind of experience—being racially profiled by law enforcement—and render it universally understandable. Specifically, during the keyboard solo of "Dreamer," Prince used the timbral dissonance between familiar, imitative sounds (piano and flute) and a threatening, mechanical sound (the resonant synth) to stand in for the experience of a young Black man being followed and stopped by the police. Though I can only speak for myself as a middle-aged, white academic, sharing this collective musical experience with the rest of the attendees that night brought me to a deeper understanding of the problem.

Throughout his career, Prince's music has done many kinds of cultural work, owing in part to his enigmatic public persona and changeable musical style, an approach that, as scholars Stan Hawkins and Sarah Niblock have argued, allowed him to "open up a special space for reconfiguring norms and attitudes," especially those surrounding categories of personal identity such as "ethnicity, sexuality, social class and gender."[13] Scholars, journalists, and fans alike have all written compellingly about how Prince's music broke down stereotypes in all of these areas and more, and in the years since Prince passed away there has been a deluge of articles debating his legacy. Many journalists made the argument for remembering Prince as a champion of sexual liberation, queer sexuality, and nonbinary gender identity.[14] Other writers focused on Prince's importance in the history of Black music, and still others made the case for remembering Prince as a philanthropist, a facet of his career that was only publicly disclosed after his death.[15]

Yet as Hawkins, Niblock, and other scholars have identified, there is a consistency at the core of Prince's work: despite the mutability of his image and sound, and despite the ways he mixed and played with identity signifiers, Black identity and Black music remained at the core of his work. As Hawkins argued, "Prince's derivations of musical style remain unambivalent. In effect, it is in the constant reiteration of rhythmic configurations, timbres, textures, call-response and grooves that his African American consciousness becomes his sonic trademark."[16] The idea of Prince's artistic consistency underpins this book, in which I have chosen to focus on the tireless work that Prince did throughout his career to break down stereotypes of Black masculinity. What I encountered at Prince's Dance Rally 4 Peace, as in many Prince concerts and recordings, was an artist whose work spoke to a universal audience while at same time giving specific attention to issues of racial justice. Indeed, the manner in which he used synthesizer timbres to create an immersive narrative about race in the United States put Prince in the company of several notable Afrofuturist musicians of the 1970s. As I have argued elsewhere, funk and jazz-fusion musicians including Bernie Worrell (of Parliament-Funkadelic), Stevie Wonder, and Herbie Hancock used the then-new technology of synthesizers to create timbral dissonance between familiar, imitative timbres and "uncanny" synthetic sounds, a technique that allowed them to create immersive narratives (e.g. "Chocolate City," "Living for the City," and "Vein Melter") that dramatized and protested against the economic and political injustices faced by communities of color during the Nixon administration.[17] These artists were foundational influences on Prince's work as well as canonic figures in the history of Black music, and it is my conviction that Prince's music and career must be understood within that history. This is not to downplay the contribution that Prince's music made in the fields of gender, queer, and postmodern theory, but rather to argue for a "both and" approach to Prince's work that recognizes the plurality of its effects while rooting it in African American traditions. As the legal scholar Twila Perry has argued, Prince had a talent for engaging a universal audience while simultaneously speaking to the particulars of African American identity, a talent that she contextualizes using W. E. B. DuBois's concept of double consciousness.[18] Though Perry's argument focuses on the mid-nineties period, when Prince was fighting with Warner Brothers over the ownership of his work, I believe that her argument holds true in the larger arc of his career: DuBois's concept of double consciousness, a cornerstone of Black literary and cultural theory, provides an apt metaphor for understanding why Prince's music can address multiple vectors of identity and yet simultaneously retain a core message of Black liberation.

In the late 1980s, after Prince achieved mainstream popularity with the *Purple Rain* album and movie, there were those who accused him of losing touch with the Black community, of abandoning his roots and selling out to the white rock mainstream. Notable among these was the music and culture critic Nelson George, who wrote the following in his 1988 book, *The Death of Rhythm and Blues*: "The two greatest black stars of the decade, Michael Jackson and Prince, ran fast and far both from blackness and conventional images of male sexuality (and their videos got on MTV)."[19] George displays a nuanced appreciation of Prince's work, and in the passage from which this quote is taken he was making a larger point about the intersection of racial and gender representation in the American music industry, in which context an androgynous self-presentation was the price of crossover success for many Black male artists (e.g., Little Richard). But on another level, I think that George was unfairly attacking Prince in accusing him of not being Black and/or manly enough, which assumes that there is a correct way to be either of those things. Prince was particularly stung by this criticism at the time, according to Prince's then-manager Alan Leeds, especially since it coincided with a decline in Prince's album sales and the concurrent rise of hip-hop as the new cutting edge of Black music.[20]

The central thesis that this book sets out to demonstrate is that Prince's music was, at *every* point in his career, deeply and consistently informed by the history and techniques of Black expressive culture. Pursuant of this goal, my principal analytical method is to focus on the ways that Prince mixed and manipulated musical genres that are indexed to racial identities, e.g., "white" rock and "Black" funk. This stylistic fluidity was one aspect of Prince's magpie-like skill at mixing different signifiers of identity, and it was made possible by his virtuosic musical talent and tireless work ethic: an autodidact, Prince learned to play piano as a child, then added guitar, bass, drums, and voice during his early teens, all the while listening to and absorbing the diverse musical genres to which he was exposed. In order to capture this mobility and explore its ramifications in the realm of identity politics, I have structured this book so that each chapter analyzes Prince's use of a different musical idiom: chapter 1 focuses on his use of rock guitar, chapter 2 on new-wave synthesizers, chapter 3 on funk drumming, chapter 4 on gospel and funk vocal techniques, and chapter 5 on R&B horns. By tracking Prince's transformations of instrumental and vocal idioms derived from specific musical genres, and by considering how these genres serve as vectors of historical meaning and sociocultural identity, we can read Prince's works as reconfigurations of the categories of identity in Western society, particularly the category of race.

Prince, from Minneapolis

Prince was born and raised in Minneapolis, Minnesota, the son of Mattie Shaw and John L. Nelson, both of whom had separately migrated from the rural South, and both of whom identified as African American.[21] Prince's parents were jazz musicians, though his mother ceased performing to raise the children, and Prince demonstrated a gift for music at a young age, teaching himself to play piano despite his father's strict rule against touching the elder Nelson's instrument. Prince's home life was turbulent: after his biological parents divorced, he did not get on with his new stepfather and went to live at his father's house but was kicked out after being caught breaking curfew, and eventually came to live at the home of Bernadette Anderson, a family friend from their Seventh-day Adventist congregation. Prince's biographers often point to this instability as an explanation for Prince's shy, aloof nature, as well as his intense drive to create and succeed.

That drive to succeed came in handy for Prince as a teenager in the highly competitive music scene of North Minneapolis, one of the city's historically African American neighborhoods. Prince was fortunate enough to grow up with a cohort of talented young musicians that included many of the players who would populate his later bands: André Cymone (née Anderson), with whom Prince shared a bedroom as a teenager and who would be the bassist in his first backing band, the Revolution; Morris Day, Jimmy Jam, Terry Lewis, and Jerome Benton, whom Prince went on to produce as the Time; and Sonny Thompson, bassist in Prince's later backing band the New Power Generation.[22] Prince and these peers benefited from the knowledge of their elders, many of whom had participated in the city's vibrant jazz scene. This included Prince's father, whose jazz combo, the Prince Rogers Trio, was the source of Prince's given name. It also included Jim Hamilton, a jazz pianist who offered a music business course at one of the high schools that Prince attended, Minneapolis's North High, in which Prince and his peers absorbed practical lessons about navigating the contemporary music industry.[23]

Despite Hamilton's practical advice on how to book and promote their own shows, Prince and his cohort had a difficult time finding venues at which to play due to the de facto segregation of the Minneapolis music scene. Minneapolis was and is a majority white city with a strong Scandinavian heritage, and, whether from indifference or outright racism, white club owners did not give African American musicians many opportunities for paying gigs, a fact that was true in the jazz scene before and after WWII and that had not substantially changed even by the 1970s.[24] As a result, Prince and other young Black Minneapolis musicians bounced between a small number of venues where they honed their skills in friendly but intense battle-of-the-bands competitions.[25] The small size of the African American market in Minneapolis also meant that, growing up, Prince and his peers did not have the benefit of a full-time R&B-formatted radio station.[26] In the 1960s and '70s, Minneapolis's sole rhythm and blues–formatted commercial radio station, KUXL, was a low-powered 1,000-watt station that only broadcast from sunup to sundown, and as a result Prince and his friends of necessity listened to Top-40- and AOR-formatted stations.[27] Nonetheless, there was a vibrant Black music community in Minneapolis even through the musically segregated 1970s, and Prince was exposed to jazz music through his father and to funk from his elder half-brother, Charles Nelson, who was a devotee of James Brown's music.

A corollary of Minneapolis's dearth of outlets for Black musicians, both in terms of live venues and radio stations, was that Prince and his peers absorbed the "mainstream" rock influences of the day. This included both the Top-40 soft-rock music of artists like Joni Mitchell and Maria Muldaur, the former of whom was a particular favorite of Prince's, as well as stalwarts of 1970s AOR format, hard rock, and progressive rock stations such as Santana, Led Zeppelin, and Grand Funk Railroad, alongside the few African American artists whose music crossed over into mainstream popularity, including Sly and the Family Stone and Stevie Wonder.[28] As Prince described his rock radio listening habits, "'The old KQ [KQRS 92FM] after midnight, that was the bomb station. I'd stay up all night listening to it. That's where I discovered Carlos Santana, Maria Muldaur, and Joni Mitchell. Was I influenced by that? Sure I was. Back then I always tried to play like Carlos [Santana] or Boz Scaggs.'"[29] This exposure to mainstream rock and pop music was not unique to Prince's experience, but was a feature in the musical life of most Black Minneapolis musicians of the time: as journalist Andrea Swensson points out, "black artists had an added incentive to stay up to date on all the Top 40 hits by popular white artists of the day so they could get gigs playing for the Twin Cities' predominantly white audiences, especially in the 1970s."[30] This wide and multiracial mix of genre influences that Prince and his cohort absorbed—jazz, soft rock, hard rock, R&B, and funk—provides context for the stylistic mobility of Prince's later career, and for his unwillingness to accept any boundaries around his identity, musically or otherwise.

When Prince signed his first record contract in 1977, he demonstrated a strong desire to maintain stylistic freedom and avoid being pigeonholed into a single genre based on his race. One of the chief reasons that Prince chose to sign with Warner Brothers Records, over the other two major labels who offered him contracts, was that they allowed him to be his own producer, though even they insisted that Prince—only eighteen years old at the time of signing—have the oversight of an experienced executive producer for his first album.[31] Prince was clear-eyed about how the racially segregated structure of most American record companies could affect his creative freedom vis-à-vis musical genre. Warner Brothers executive Marylou Badeaux recalled:

> Prince was very concerned about being labeled a black artist or being segmented into the black department. . . . He said to us, "I'm not an R&B artist. I'm not a rock 'n' roller. I'm an artist and I do a wide range of music. If I deliver you rock 'n' roll, don't come back to me and say I can't do it because I'm black." He didn't want to be perceived as a black artist.[32]

According to Prince's then-publicist Howard Bloom, Prince was "the first black artist with the potential to become a major white audience superstar since Jimi Hendrix," yet this potential was hindered by the fact that record executives and radio programmers alike were reluctant to promote music by Black artists that was stylistically in the rock genre.[33] As biographer Alex Hahn reports, Bloom encountered "significant resistance from Warner Bros. when he tried to change this perception" of Prince as a soul or funk artist.[34] As late as 1984, there were so few examples of successful Black rock guitarists in the American recording industry that Prince grew tired of being compared to Jimi Hendrix, despite the implicit compliment: when asked by *Rolling Stone*'s Neal Karlen what he thought about the comparison, Prince replied, "It's only because he's black. That's really the only thing we have in common. He plays different guitar than I do. If they really listened to my stuff, they'd hear more of a Santana influence than Jimi Hendrix."[35] Prince expanded on this in his first televised interview, which aired on MTV in 1985: "I was brought up in a black and white world, and—yes, black and white, night and day, rich and poor, black and white—and I listened to all kinds of music when I was young, and when I was younger I always said that one day I was going to play all kinds of music and not be judged for the color of my skin but the quality of my work, and hopefully that'll continue."[36]

This goal was not easily achieved, and Prince experienced difficulties releasing and promoting music that confounded the racially marked genre categories upon which the record labels and radio formats of the time were built. For an African American artist such as Prince, coming up in the music industry of the 1970s meant that stylistic choices had economic ramifications linked to racial identity: they determined which markets his record label would or would not promote him in, what radio formats would or would not play his music, and the type and amount of press coverage he would receive. As such, Prince had to decide carefully upon his musical idioms: would he use a horn section like the R&B and funk acts of the day, such as James Brown, Parliament-Funkadelic, or Tower of Power? Or would he center his songs around the sound and heroism of the distorted electric guitar, the flagship instrumental idiom of AOR bands that he loved, such as Led Zeppelin and Grand Funk Railroad? Would he use the kinds of polyrhythmic dance grooves popular in discotheques of the late 1970s, or straight-ahead, on-the-beat rock drumming? Would he sing in a soul- or disco-style, high-falsetto vocal range or a rock-style, chest-voice shout? Would he use traditional keyboard instruments like piano and organ, or experiment with newer synthesizer technology? For Prince, all of these creative decisions and more were freighted with genre rules that included expectations about the skin color of the artist.

Throughout his career, Prince used his musical choices to fight back against this racially segregated structure of the American music industry by strategically deploying, mixing, and transforming different instrumental and vocal idioms that were associated with musical genres that the industry held to be mutually exclusive based on race. In one sense, Prince, like Jimi Hendrix and Funkadelic's Eddie Hazel before him, defied the conventional wisdom of the music market simply by being an African American guitarist who played in a recognizably "rock" idiom. Though Prince, like Hendrix, was accused of betraying his African American identity by crossing over into rock (never mind that it was Black artists who had invented rock 'n' roll back in the 1940s), in fact he titrated the idiom of rock guitar through other musical practices and aesthetics common to the Black Atlantic, for example combining it with the melodic gestures of gospel music, the rhythmic techniques of funk drumming, and the aesthetic of Afrofuturism. Prince was not whitewashing his music with the guitar antics of hard rock; instead, he was drawing on his fluency in multiple idioms to create a musical experience that resisted static categorization and, as Perry argued (following W. E. B. DuBois), spoke simultaneously to universal audiences while retaining its particular meanings within the Black tradition. It was Prince's fluency in multiple musical idioms—made possible by the demographic peculiarities of his hometown of Minneapolis as well as by his versatility as a musician—with which he safeguarded his own creative agency while celebrating and expanding the categories of identity to which he belonged.

Analytical Methodology, or Prince: The Moving Target

When Prince officially joined the social media platform Twitter in 2013, the first "selfie" he posted was a picture of purple smoke, a sly admission of his feint-and-dodge approach to the media.[37] During his lifetime, Prince was a moving target for journalists and scholars, changing his sound and image from project to project and rigidly controlling the media's access to him, making the job of writing about him rather like catching smoke. In one infamous profile, British journalist Barney Hoskyns, frustrated with Prince's refusal to grant him a one-on-one interview, claimed that there was no *real* Prince: "I did not seriously expect to make Prince's acquaintance for the very good reason that Prince does not exist. He avoids me because he is a void. . . . We project him like a holograph."[38] Compounding the challenge posed by Prince's puckish media manipulations are the diversity of styles and the variety of media in which he worked, which stretch from funk to rock to electronica to hip-hop, and across studio recordings, music videos, movies, interviews, live performances, and even an interactive CD-ROM video game. This breadth of analytical material has attracted scholars from numerous fields, creating a body of Prince scholarship rich in analytical approaches. While a full survey of the scholarly literature on Prince is beyond the scope of this book, I must begin by specifying those analytical approaches that I am using, and those that I am not.

As a musicologist, I do *not* draw a distinction between "historical" and "popular" musicology: my root philosophy, which aligns with Joseph Kerman's conception of "critical" musicology, is that *all* music can be read as a historical and cultural document.[39] This "reading" is an interpretive act that combines two necessary components: musical analysis, or close reading—paying attention to fundamental aspects of music such as melody and harmony, tone color and dynamics, rhythm and form—and meta-musical information gleaned from the study of history, culture, technology, and other relevant areas. It is this extra-musical consideration that distinguishes the critical-musicological approach from "positivistic" methods that explain music primarily through music-theoretical analysis. I hold to the position, articulated by Frankfurt school theorist Theodor Adorno, that music concretizes the social and historical realities of its place and time and models the interior subjectivity of composer and/or listener—what Adorno referred to as music's "experiential content," or what critical theorist Richard Leppert, writing about Adorno, called the "historicity of time in music."[40] The question of how to move between the microscopic consideration of musical details (e.g. pitch, rhythm, and form) to macroscopic questions of identity, society, and culture is answered, for me, by Lawrence Kramer's concept of "hermeneutic windows." In Kramer's conception, music is part of a hermeneutic circle in which "meaning" is neither wholly immanent in the musical work nor projected onto a musical object by the interpreter, but rather emerges in the dialogue between the two.[41] The "hermeneutic window" between musical text and interpretive act can be opened by a number of things: Kramer mentions lyrics, musical allusions, and structural tropes, and I posit that hermeneutic windows can also be opened by historical and biographical data, and by concepts or metaphors borrowed from other areas of the humanities such as critical race theory and gender theory.[42]

Scholars in the field of popular musicology have developed a number of interdisciplinary approaches that open such hermeneutic windows, which musicologist Derek Scott has divided into seven overlapping categories: "film, video and multimedia; technology and studio production; gender and sexuality; identity and ethnicity; performance and gesture; reception and scenes; and the music industry and globalization."[43] I will briefly review Scott's list as a way of outlining my own methodology in this book. The first area, "film, video and multimedia," is *not* part of my approach. This branch of pop musicology, which derives from the study of film music, often exhibits a struggle between "whether the image or the music dominates," whereas I keep recorded music as my primary object of analysis at all times and do not incorporate analytical concepts from film- or television-music studies.[44] I am not concerned with Prince's visuality per se, and when I do discuss scenes and images from Prince's movies and music videos in this book, as I do at the start of chapter 3, I use them only as hermeneutic windows into the music and not as analytical objects in their own right.

The second approach on Scott's list, technology and studio production, *does* play a large role in my methodology. Tim Warner points out that "pop musicians tend to work directly with sound rather than any form of notation," and this was true for Prince, who used the recording studio as his primary compositional tool and by his own admission never learned to read music notation.[45] As such, studying the technologies with which Prince made his musical sounds is equally important to harmonic or structural analysis, and in several of my chapters I explore how Prince used specific pieces of production technology such as Oberheim synthesizers (chapter 2), Linn drum machines (chapter 3), and Varispeed tape-recording (chapter 4). Furthermore, as Albin Zak argues, the timbral effects that pop music producers commonly use, such as guitar distortion and vocal reverb, have rhetorical impacts that allow the sounds "to stand as symbols suggesting dialogues and resonances beyond the boundaries of the track."[46] Using timbre in this dialogic way was a key part of Prince's work, as I discuss in chapters 1 and 2, and, therefore, understanding his use of music technology is central to my exploration of how Prince used timbre as a vector of meaning.

The third, fourth, and fifth areas that Scott lists—gender and sexuality, identity and ethnicity, and performance and gesture—are at the very core of my analytical methodology.[47] Throughout his career, Prince manipulated musical and visual signifiers of racial and gender identity, and his performative decisions both onstage and on record constructed models of subjective interiority that undermined stereotypes of Black masculinity in American society. As such, every chapter in this book draws upon critical race theory and gender theory, and I have approached this from an "intersectional" perspective that I will discuss in the next section of this introduction.

Sixth on Scott's list, "reception and scenes"—a branch of popular musicology that focuses on how specific communities of listeners use and interpret particular musical artists or genres—is *not* a significant part of my methodology.[48] My research did not include any quantitative data-gathering among Prince's community of listeners, and the musical interpretations in this book are solely my own. Having said that, my methods do include some *qualitative* fieldwork—both journalistic and ethnographic—that I use to open hermeneutic windows into the songs that I analyze. As a Minneapolis resident from 1995 to '99 and again from 2005 to '16, I attended many Prince concerts; though I approached most of them purely as a fam, on some occasions I engaged my ethnomusicological training to write field notes, and this book includes some thick description of concerts I attended, such as the one with which I began this introduction. I also include insights from formal interviews that I conducted with musicians and production assistants who worked closely with Prince, such as keyboard player Matt Fink and synthesizer technician Roger Dumas (chapter 3), and saxophonist Eric Leeds and trombonist Mike Nelson (chapter 5). However, the songs themselves remain my primary objects of analysis, with the fieldwork serving only as a source of themes and concepts that inform those analyses.

Lastly, I use the seventh of Scott's areas, "music industry and globalization," only as a point of departure. In his early career, many of the decisions Prince made about musical genre references—the instrumentation and stylistic idioms he chose to employ—were informed by his struggle to escape the racially segregated structure of the music industry, and I will return to this topic later in the introduction and in chapter 1, on Prince's use of the rock guitar idiom. However, I do not analyze Prince's business decisions or career from a music-industry-studies perspective, and when I do bring in industry specific information—such as sales figures or record label contracts—it is to contextualize the performative decisions he made on record and onstage, i.e., as yet another hermeneutic window into the music, my primary object of analysis.

Intersectionality in the Study of Prince

Having positioned myself within the larger field of musicology and the subfield of popular music studies, I must also discuss how my methodology relates to those of other pop-music scholars specifically working on the music of Prince. In the time since I began my academic study of Prince, the prevailing analytical trends have shifted from the postmodernist cultural studies of the 1980s and 1990s to the intersectional approaches of the 2010s and 2020s. Prince rose to fame during America's postmodern moment, and his penchant for deconstructing and reconfiguring identity signifiers—the biracial musical influences, religious symbolism, androgynous gender play, and polymorphous sexuality—seemed perfectly suited to that moment, pushing all the hot-button issues of America's nascent culture war.[49] Media studies scholar Lawrence Grossberg argued that a lay postmodernism was endemic among the generation who came of age in the era of MTV and Reagan, and Andrew Goodwin specifically included Prince among a cadre of artists whose music enacted a postmodern "structure of feeling."[50] The earliest scholarly studies of Prince analyzed his work through this postmodern lens: Anne Danielsen argued that Prince's multiplicity of styles and images was a celebration of postmodern surface and a rejection of Romantic-authentic ideals of depth and history, while Robert Walser argued that Prince was engaging in poststructuralist deconstruction of gender and sexuality.[51] As late as 2017, cultural theorist Nancy Holland argued that by destabilizing and deconstructing the "dualistic hierarchies of race, gender, and sexuality," Prince's work was fundamentally postmodern, pointing toward a world beyond these categories.[52]

Though my own work is indebted to these scholars, postmodernist analytical concepts such as pastiche, bricolage, and blank parody don't sufficiently uncover what I believe to be the central cultural work of Prince's music, which I see not as rejecting Cartesian dualities of identity per se but rather as celebrating Black identity in a way that resisted the specific, intersecting hierarchies of power that have historically limited that identity—including male/female, straight/queer, and secular/sacred—with the white/Black hierarchy at the center. In her liner notes to the 2020 re-release of Prince's *Sign o' the Times* album, critical theorist Daphne Brooks points out that the Reagan administration in the 1980s enacted policies specifically designed to "slow the brakes on multicultural liberation movements" and to restore "racial, gender, and sexual identity hierarchies in America," and she goes on to argue that Prince's music, through its diversity and inclusivity, "posed a pointed, symbolic challenge to the peril in which black and brown folks, poor folks, queer folks, [and] women . . . found themselves."[53] In other words, what appeared at the time as a poststructuralist insurrection against the Cartesian epistemology of Western thought is better understood as a grassroots liberation movement for a number of minority groups whose common well-being was threatened by public-policy decisions, with African American people at the center of the fight.

In the 2000s, scholars working in the fields of critical race theory, gender theory, American studies, and performance studies created a body of scholarship that addresses the intersecting hierarchies of power that artists from marginalized groups have faced in the American entertainment industry, an approach generally referred to as "intersectionality." First proposed by legal scholar Kimberlé Crenshaw, the concept of intersectionality grew out of her desire to bring feminist theory and critical race theory together as a corrective to what she called "single-axis" conceptions of discrimination—based on gender *or* race—that reproduced marginalization of one group even as they were used to fight against the oppression another.[54] In the years since she coined the concept, scholars have expanded intersectionality to include other vectors of identity, and applied the concept to analyzing many types of cultural texts, including music.[55]

Surveying the work of scholars like Daphne Brooks, Emily Lordi, Shana Redmond, and Gayle Wald, we can see that the work of these intersectional scholars shares several analytical methods and theoretical concepts that are highly relevant to the study of Prince. Though I wrote the bulk of this book before I discovered this literature, my approach happily overlaps with several of the methods that they use. The first thing that these scholars share is the goal of expanding the scope of "rock history" to include more women of color while challenging the implicit biases of the field that prioritize the work of white heterosexual male artists. Gayle Wald's study of Sister Rosetta Tharpe; Daphne Brooks's studies of Beyoncé Knowles and of Amy Winehouse; Emily Lordi's study of Aretha Franklin and Nina Simone; and Shana Redmond's analysis of Janelle Monáe's work all serve as correctives to what Brooks described as the "sexed up, necrophilic dalliances of white (musical) masters and the (always) black (most often) men that they admire and desire, consume and cannibalize" and who "continue to hold center stage in the critical imaginaries of performance studies and rock music histories alike."[56] While the historiographic project of reimagining the rock canon is not explicitly part of this book on Prince, the challenge that Wald, Brooks, and others have posed to rock history's (cis, het) white male bias is a challenge that Prince took on. Early in his career, Prince fought against the racial segregation of the American music industry that excluded African American artists from the rock genre, as I discuss in chapter 1.[57] Throughout his career Prince promoted the work of female collaborators and forebears: this included bandmates like Wendy Melvoin and Lisa Coleman; studio engineers like Susan Rogers; artists that he produced such as Apollonia Kotero, Carmen Electra, Mayte Garcia, Támar Davis, and Bria Valente; and older female artists who influenced him such as Joni Mitchell and Chaka Khan. In the musical analyses included in this book, I unpack how Prince's manipulations of musical genre worked against the systemic racial and gender biases within the American music industry and society at large.

The second thing that these intersectional scholars have in common is a tendency to foreground the issue of work and its ownership, focusing on the performative agency that their subjects display—the artistic decisions as well as the sheer labor—as a way of uncovering how marginalized artists have resisted the stereotypes and corporate structures that would limit their agency and exploit their work. Lordi, for example, discusses how Beyoncé Knowles, like Prince, defined her early public persona in terms of a "spectacular work ethic," and that this image was both a comment on the historical inequities faced by Black women in the American workplace and a corrective to stereotypes of Black women's "essential" or "natural" talent that recentered "her genius in her performative choices."[58] Work and ownership were central themes in Prince's career, both in his songs—examples include "Let's Work" from 1981's *Controversy* album and "The Work, Pt. 1" from 2001's *The Rainbow Children*—and in his business decisions. In the later 1990s, for example, when Prince fell out with Warner

Brothers over what he perceived as limitations the label was imposing on his creativity, Prince appeared with the word "slave" written on his face, framing his fight for ownership of his work as a matter of freedom from racialized corporate slavery.[59] While my book does not explore Prince's business dealings, I do center my analyses of Prince's music on the question of how he used his performative agency. This includes his choices of musical genre and style, stage costuming and other sartorial decisions, choreography and gesture, and I argue that he used these performative decisions to fight for creative and financial freedom within an industry seemingly designed to limit the autonomy of artists of color and to take ownership of their labor.

A third commonality among intersectional scholars is their tendency to focus on embodiment as a particularly important type of performative agency (and this corresponds to the fifth pop-musicological approach surveyed by Scott, "performance and gesture"). By considering "embodied" parameters excluded from traditional musical analysis—such as choreography, costuming, timbre, audience interaction, and performance venue—Redmond, Brooks, Wald, and others unpack how performers from marginalized groups have reclaimed their bodies from hegemonic representations, and also how they reconfigured performance spaces and audience interactions as models of social change.[60] Prince was a master at using live musical performance as a model for social change, as I demonstrated in my analysis of his Dance Rally 4 Peace. Moreover, Prince was an exhaustively physical artist who carefully curated his own body onstage, in print, on film, and on television. My musical analyses in this book detail how he used embodiment to construct diverse and often oppositional constructions of Black masculinity, from the polymorphic perversity of his *Dirty Mind*–era stage costumes, to the doe-eyed androgyny of his *Lovesexy* album cover, to the hyper-macho chains-and-guns outfits of his *Love Symbol* album. By using such visual imagery as a hermeneutic window, my analyses unpack how Prince communicated physical embodiment in his recorded music, using harmonic syntax, melodic gesture, vocal timbre, and rhythmic development to construct diverse models of sexual pleasure and gender identity within the context of Black musical identity, and this issue of musical embodiment factors into every musical analysis in this book.

A fourth commonality that emerges from the intersectional analyses of Brooks, Lordi, Redmond, and Wald is how marginalized artists mix and move between multiple genres, idioms, and forms as a method of carving out space for themselves and their listeners in a hostile world, a strategy that rests upon the code-switching, multi-genre virtuosity of these performers.[61] The tactics of mobility, multiplicity, and fusion were among Prince's chief performative tools and are at the center of my analytical methodology. When Lordi argues that Black female artists like Aretha Franklin and Nina Simone "use multi-generic virtuosity to turn the condition of lacking any hospitable expressive system into a performative claim to *multiple* expressive homes," she could just as accurately have been describing Prince.[62] Brooks makes this connection in her liner notes to the *Sign o' the Times* reissue as she catalogues the many musical idioms that it mixes, including "crushing guitar chords . . . majestic gospel flourishes . . . synth-pop futurity . . . and Beatles-esque pop," as well as "jazz sensibilities" and "sweet folk and soul turns," an eclecticism that she later encapsulates within the phrase "the sounds of blackness that refuse to be named or contained."[63] Throughout his life Prince was an avid music listener, and his musical gifts in combination with his competitive nature drove him to quickly absorb new styles that he heard.[64] Consequently, Prince's songwriting incorporates a great variety of genre influences, from gospel to funk, folk to rock, psychedelic to symphonic, swing to Latin jazz. By exploring how he mixed and moved between multiple musical genre-idioms, I argue that Prince both created space for his own stylistic eclecticism in the music industry—no small task in itself—and gave his listeners space to experience subjectivity free from Western hierarchies of power by constructing alternative models of racial, gender, sexual, and religious identity within his work.

One corollary to the genre mobility that intersectional scholars often discuss is the issue of "crossover." A music industry term for artists or songs that are popular with multiple audience demographics, in practical terms "crossover" is most often discussed in terms of racial, ethnic, or religious identity, as when artists cross over from "Black" musical genres such as R&B into the dominant "mainstream" genre of pop, or from sacred gospel to secular pop or R&B. Such crossover acts are fraught with issues of cultural appropriation, commodification, and "authenticity," and artists from marginalized communities have often faced criticism for pursuing the approval of "mainstream" (read *white*) audiences. Gayle Wald points out that African American gospel artists who crossed over into secular R&B or pop were often portrayed as sellouts who "jeopardized African American musical tradition" by commercializing it, and her focus on the performative choices of such crossover artists is a corrective to such "quagmires of authenticity."[65] Similarly, Emily Lordi, in her study of female soul singers, argues that focusing on the artists' performative decisions to mix different genres shifts the definition of musical genre away from "a static object that one might steal, own, or buy" toward a definition that foregrounds the performer's agency, defining the soul genre instead "as a set of stories and techniques that one might use."[66] As I mentioned earlier, after achieving crossover success with his *Purple Rain* album and movie in 1984, Prince received criticism on the grounds that he had abandoned his African American audience and/or his own Black identity. Prince was certainly a crossover artist who enjoyed popularity with African American *and* white audience demographics, but seeing this as a dilution or sellout of his Black identity reduces that identity, and Black musical genres, to fixed, static objects. The corrective that I make is to define the genre-based idioms that Prince used as collections of performative techniques which I describe in specific musical terms; then, using close musical analysis, I show Prince's agency in the way that he deployed those techniques.

Fifth and lastly, the intersectional scholars whom I mentioned often use the concept of outsider identity or difference, discussing how their subjects turn marginalization into a critical tool. For example, Emily Lordi discusses the critical power that Black artists have historically derived from marginal status, pointing out that the author James Baldwin "figures black exclusion as the source of superior expressive skill, or what we might call performative swagger."[67] Daphne Brooks condenses this discourse of reclaiming the trauma of racial discrimination as a critical tool into a concept that she names "Afro-alienation": "In what I call "Afro-alienation acts," the condition of alterity converts into cultural expressiveness and a specific strategy of cultural performance. Afro-alienation recurs as a trope that reflects and characterizes marginal cultural positions as well as a tactic that the marginalized seized on and reordered in the self-making process."[68] This concept is highly relevant to the study of Prince, who has used the topoi of difference, mystery, and strangeness often in his work. Prince grew up Black and poor on the north side of Minneapolis and experienced racial taunts and physical bullying at a young age, during a period when he was bussed to a majority-white elementary school.[69] Prince had other experiences growing up that marked him as "different" even within his own community: he was small, shy, and suffered from childhood epilepsy, experiences that likely left psychological marks into adulthood.[70] In his autobiography, Prince touched upon the topic of difference and how important he felt that it was to his creativity, writing, "Those considered 'different' R the ones most interesting 2 us," and later, "Hidden

Places, Secret Abilities. A part of oneself that is never shown. These r the necessary tools 4 a vibrant imagination & the main ingredients of a good song."[71] My analytical approach in this book is neither biographical nor psychoanalytic. But themes of difference loom large in Prince's work, and several of my musical analyses explore Prince's use of alienation-effects in his music, specifically chapters 2 (on his use of synthesizers) and 5 (on horns). From his reclusive and misunderstood character "The Kid" in the semi-autobiographical *Purple Rain* and its sequel, *Graffiti Bridge*, to his musical explorations of ambivalence and alienation in songs like "Controversy," "Lady Cab Driver," "I Would Die 4 U," or "Strange Relationship," Prince repeatedly engaged in Afro-alienation acts, constructing and occupying subject positions that stood at a critical distance from stereotypical constructions of Black and male and heterosexual identity in American society.

To sum up: the issues of gender and sexuality, identity and race are the central hermeneutic windows that I use in my interpretive analyses of Prince's music, and I approach these issues from an intersectional perspective. My chief methodology is close musical analysis with a focus on how Prince's compositional and performative decisions—in particular his virtuosic, code-switching fluency in multiple genre-idioms—placed stereotypes of identity (Black, male, heterosexual, religious) at a critical, alienating distance. By close-reading songs from Prince's oeuvre in this way, my goal is to show how Prince worked to liberate himself, his fellow artists, and his listeners from the limitations that the music industry and American society placed around marginalized identity groups, thereby expanding rock's canon beyond cis, het white men making secular music.

Genre, Idiom, and Black Music

Because stylistic multiplicity was one of Prince's chief tools in his fight for freedom, musical genre and the related concepts of style and idiom are key parts of my analytical methodology. Few terms have been fretted over as much as "genre" and "style" in the literature of popular music studies; in this book, I am using the terms interchangeably, as in common parlance, rather than placing one hierarchically above the other, and I *am* using the term "idiom" as a sub-concept of genre/style. Specifically, I use both "genre" and "style" to refer to the large-scale categories into which musical works and artists are sorted by the music industry, listeners, and the artists themselves, categories that are discursively constructed and whose defining characteristics are not fixed but rather develop through iteration and can change over time.[72]

Musical genres/styles are particularly useful analytical tools because they are themselves hermeneutic windows that connect observable musical details to extramusical considerations of identity, culture, and commerce. As popular-music scholar Keith Negus argues, the concept of musical genre operates in three discrete spheres: "the organization of music companies, the creative practices of musicians, and the perceptions of audiences."[73] Regarding the "organization of music companies," musical genre is a marketing category that reflects the economic interests of record companies and retailers, broadcasters and their advertisers, and the other corporate interests that we generally refer to as "the music industry." Within "the creative practices of musicians," genre or style refers to the collection of material practices and performative techniques—what Philip Tagg refers to as the "parameters of musical expression," David Brackett calls "style traits," and I refer to as *idioms*—that musicians and producers draw upon in the creation of pop songs.[74] These traits or idioms—which include but are not limited to instrumental and vocal techniques, production technologies, repertoire choices, instrumental timbres, texture, rhythm, tempo, melodic gestures, and harmonic progressions—can be observed and objectively quantified, as research into automated music-genre recognition algorithms has demonstrated, and as such they form the basis of much of the musical analysis in popular music studies.[75] In terms of "the perceptions of audiences," genres are subjective, discursively constructed categories that reflect the identities of the artists and fans in that genre community due to shared semiotic codes and/or cultural values that operate through the material practices of that genre, though not in a fixed "homologous" sense but rather a changeable, iterative one.[76] By providing a bridge between these three spheres—music's objectively observable phenomena; the subjective, sociological issues of identity and community; and the commercial interests of the music industry—genre provides a tool for linking elements of musical style with hermeneutic considerations of identity, an analytical method that Tagg refers to as the "hermeneutic-semiological model."[77] As Susan McClary argued, "genuine social knowledge is articulated and transmitted by means of shared procedures and assumptions concerning music," and the explication of "social knowledge" encoded in Prince's music is a primary goal of this book.[78]

With each of the songs I analyze, I begin with an observable characteristic that connects the song to a genre—some call these "style traits" or "genre markers," while I am using the term "idioms"—and use it as a hermeneutic window through which to connect musical sound with cultural identity. In the strictest sense, a musical idiom refers to a technique or gesture that is distinctively suited to a particular musical instrument; for example, the way a pianist can simultaneously play a chord in the left hand and a melody in the right hand is *idiomatic* to keyboard instruments. However, instruments and their idioms also serve more generally as genre markers or style traits: in his 2003 article "Reading the Instrument," Steve Waksman (following Paul Théberge) points out that "different genres of music have different instrumental identities, such that rock might be considered guitar music, while analog synthesizers conjure new wave, digital sequencers are linked to techno, banjos are identified with bluegrass, and saxophones most commonly represent jazz."[79] Further, instrumental and vocal idioms signify meanings even beyond the taxonomic: Waksman goes on to argue that musical idioms—which he calls "the techniques embedded in a given instrument"—also mediate social relationships and cultural values, and that by paying attention to the specific ways that instruments are used we can discover how artists have chosen to "reinforce dominant modes of social organization or . . . confront them, to reinscribe dominant social relations, or to open new alternatives."[80] Prince was most certainly an artist who used musical instruments—including his voice—as tools with which to confront the dominant modes of social organization. By picking up the electric guitar and playing it in not one but two different idiomatic ways associated with the rock genre (hard-rock virtuosity and punk-rock simplicity) he claimed a position for himself in a genre—rock—from which the structural racial bias of the American music industry would have excluded him. By being an early adopter of polyphonic synthesizer technology, Prince disrupted the taxonomic function of horns as a marker for Black genres such as disco and funk—striking another blow against the racialized structure of the American music industry—while simultaneously adapting the horn idiom to the synthesizer, preserving its semiotic function for those fluent in the code and thereby creating a new genre-space for Black identity. As the chapters to come will show, at every step of his career Prince mixed and transformed musical idioms—and the genres that they mark—in his fight against racism and any other "mode of social organization" that would place limits around him or his listeners.

My investigation of Prince's work is based on the assumption that there *is* such a thing as Black music, as Olly Wilson and other scholars have argued, but that this fluid category does *not* correspond to the objectified conception of "Black" musical genres and tastes enforced by the American music industry.[81] What defines the multi-genre-spanning category of Black music, as Wilson and Samuel Floyd have argued, is the persistence of certain cultural values and aesthetic practices from the West African diaspora, immaterial things that survived the Middle Passage when specific repertoire, instruments, and languages did not.[82] Yet there is no essential or deterministic connection between cultural identity and musical style: as with any semiotic signifier, the relationship between musical idioms (signifier) and cultural values (signified) are arbitrary and learned. No one is born knowing how to slap funk bass any more than they are born knowing how to dance the minuet; rather, techniques and meanings circulate among members of a community and change over time. As musicologist Susan McClary argues in her discussion of musical conventions, "none of them counts as anything more than artificial constructs human beings have invented and agreed to maintain—in particular contexts, for particular reasons, to satisfy particular needs and desires."[83] Black music is plural, malleable, and syncretic; not a collection of objects but "a set of stories and techniques that one might use," in Lordi's words, and these stories and techniques have given rise to different genres and performance practices in different communities at different times.[84] It is precisely this plurality and changeability that Prince explored throughout his career: in defiance of the structural racism embedded in the American media industry, his work demonstrates over and over that there is no one way to make Black music.

As many writers have argued, notably Nelson George, Keith Negus, David Sanjek, and Reebee Garofalo, race is a central tension in the American music industry, and musical genre is the arena in which this tension plays out.[85] Negus wrote in 1999 that "the major companies and their labels have come to deal with black music in separate divisions," a business practice formalized in the 1960s and '70s that segregated genres such as rhythm and blues into "separate formally defined corporate entities."[86] In their 1985 report on race in the music industry, the NAACP put it even more plainly, stating, "The record industry is overwhelmingly segregated and discrimination is rampant. No other industry in America so openly classifies its operations on a racial basis."[87] As a Black man working in this industry, Prince was centrally focused on overcoming racial segregation and its attendant stereotypes throughout his career. Prince was keenly aware of the structural racism that stood in his way, as biographer Alex Hahn wrote: "Prince had a sophisticated understanding of the quandary he faced. Throughout the 1970s, music executives both perceived and fostered a highly segregated industry. It was an article of faith that white consumers would gravitate towards so-called album-oriented rock . . . while blacks would favor funk stars. . . . Only very rarely . . . were African-American artists viewed by record companies as viable rock acts."[88]

As I will demonstrate in this book, the principal weapons Prince used in his fight for Black liberation were his virtuosity on multiple instruments and his fluency in multiple genres. In each of the chapters that follows, I focus on how Prince used specific instrumental or vocal idioms, each one linked to a particular musical genre that is, in turn, embedded within the racialized structure of the music industry. In chapter 1, I focus on Prince's use of the electric guitar, the most iconic instrument in the rock genre. Despite the fact that the rock guitar idiom had been invented by African American artists in the 1940s and '50s, by the time Prince entered the music industry in the 1970s the distortion-saturated guitar heroism of album-oriented rock had become the de facto soundtrack of young white suburban American men. Yet a new style of rock called "new wave" was emerging from the American underground in the late 1970s and early '80s, with values—amateurism, simplicity, irony, and camp—that challenged the virtuosity, complexity, and machismo of hard-rock and progressive-rock genres. My analyses of Prince's songs "Bambi" and "Jack U Off" show how he played these two value-systems against each other—mixing and moving between hard-rock guitar virtuosity and punk-rock guitar simplicity—as a way of claiming a space for himself as a Black rock guitarist in an industry that did not, at that time, allow for the existence of such a thing.

In chapter 2, I explore how Prince used the new-wave *keyboard* idiom to create his distinctive "Minneapolis sound." Prince adopted synthesizers when the first polyphonic analog models were being introduced, and this ability to play multiple notes simultaneously, combined with the timbral mutability of analog synthesis, allowed Prince to use synthesizers as (among other things) a replacement for horn sections, which were a common idiom in Black musical genres of the 1970s like disco and funk. I begin the chapter by demonstrating how Prince's use of synthesizers adapted and defamiliarized the horn idiom, thereby disrupting one of the genre markers on which the industry's racial segregation depended, while preserving that idiom's rhetorical role within the music. Yet Prince's use of synthesizers was much more than a just timbral substitution: as I show in my analysis of the songs "Dirty Mind,"

"Controversy," and "Automatic," Prince constructed a cyborg persona that used the "uncanny" power of synthesizers as an Afro-alienation act. Specifically, Prince used the keyboard synthesizer to construct an androgynous cyborg persona that flipped the macho funk topos of the "sex machine" on its head, retaining the techniques that link funk to Black identity while disrupting the racist construction of Black male hyper-virility.

In chapter 3, I delve into Prince's approach to rhythm, specifically the funk drumming idiom, and how he used it to push against racial stereotypes. Rhythm is the musical parameter most closely associated with discourses of racial difference: while there are demonstrable links between funk drumming techniques and cultural values from the African diaspora, as Alexander Stewart argues, there is also a dangerous constellation of stereotypes attached to "African rhythm" in the white Western imagination, as scholars such as Kofi Agawu and Ronald Radano have pointed out.[89] In this chapter, I use Radano's concept of "hot rhythm" as a way of collectively understanding these stereotypes, and analyze how Prince's music from the mid-1980s worked against them.[90] During this period, Prince forged a signature style that translated the polyrhythms of funk onto drum machines while simultaneously stripping the instrumental texture to an ascetic austerity. In my analysis of the song "When Doves Cry" I explore how this minimalist approach worked against the stereotypes of "hot rhythm"—such as violence, sexuality, and a cyclical model of temporality—and show how Prince used the texture to enact the complex and conflicted interiority of the song's main character. I then analyze the song "Anotherloverholenyohead" from Prince's 1986 album *Parade*, in which Prince put his signature stripped-down funk style into dialogue with an avant-garde orchestral sensibility to construct a cosmopolitan model of Black identity.

In chapter 4, I explore Prince's use of two specific vocal idioms in his work, one from the gospel genre and the other from funk, and argue that both are rooted in the cosmology of the historical Black church. Several musicologists have interpreted Prince's use of the high falsetto voice as a deconstruction of heteronormative gender and sexual identities, especially in his high "ecstatic" screams.[91] As I argue in my analysis of "When Doves Cry" and "Kiss," however, Prince's use of the falsetto is deeply informed by the gospel musical genre and must be understood within the model of "sacred sexuality" used by previous generations of R&B and soul singers such as Little Richard, Ray Charles, Aretha Franklin, or Al Green. As such, I argue that Prince's falsetto voice functions as a vector of religious and racial identity, which complicates readings of Prince's falsetto voice as a tool of gender or sexual deconstruction. The second vocal persona that I explore in chapter 4 is a deep, booming basso-profundo that I am calling Prince's "prophetic" voice. As I argue, Prince often used this voice in Afrofuturistic contexts—songs whose lyrics combined techno-futurism, ancient Egyptian iconography, space travel, and Biblical references—that conveyed a cosmology rooted in African American religious and musical traditions. This chapter culminates with a close reading of the song "Family Name" from Prince's 2001 album *The Rainbow Children*, in which I show how Prince deployed techno-futurist tropes of Armageddon, along with funk and gospel tropes of vocal transcendence, to symbolically enact racial justice for America's sin of slavery.

In chapter 5, I return to the topic of Prince's use of wind and brass instruments that I raised in chapter 1, focusing on the reemergence of the R&B horn idiom in Prince's later albums such as *The Rainbow Children* (2001), *N.E.W.S.* (2003), and *Musicology* (2004). As musicologist Doug Miller argued, the saxophone played a central role in the history of Black popular music, and the use of horns—wind and brass instruments—is a clear marker for many African American music genres from 1920s jazz through 1940s R&B, 1960s soul, and 1970s funk.[92] Prince's decision to avoid using horns in his 1970s and early 1980s recordings speaks to the continued strength of this sonic association, and this made it all the more surprising when he integrated saxophone into his band on the *Purple Rain* tour and then continued expanding the role of horns in his music for the rest of his career. Using Harold Bloom's theory of influence, I argue that Prince used horns to work out his "anxiety of influence" with regard to his musical patrilineage.[93] Prince had a difficult relationship with his own father, a musician who played in a fusion of jazz and R&B styles, and he also had to contend with the influence of equally domineering musical "fathers," including Miles Davis and Maceo Parker (saxophone player to James Brown). In my musical analyses of "Housequake" and "Sexy M.F.," I show how Prince used the R&B horn idiom in songs where he was also deconstructing the heteronormative model of masculinity. Yet as it turned out, this was just the first step in Prince's journey with horns and with patriarchy: in his later career, Prince grew more interested in the jazz genre, mixing it with R&B and funk references; coincidentally, he also moved away from gender bending and towards a more traditionally masculine self-presentation. As I argue, Prince's allusions to the jazz canon placed Duke Ellington,

Charlie Parker, and Miles Davis alongside funk forefathers like James Brown and George Clinton, a move that closed the rift between "high" and "low" Black vernacular genres. At the same time, Prince's musical evocations of masculinity progressed from the androgynous trickster of "Housequake," through the conflicted misogynist of "Sexy M.F.," and finally arrived at a sense of peace with his role as a patriarch on post-millennial projects like *The Rainbow Children* and *N.E.W.S.*

This book ends with an epilogue in which I discuss three unexpectedly revealing projects that Prince undertook in the last years of his life: He began his first ever solo tour sans backing band, 2016's Piano & a Microphone tour; he opened his Paisley Park recording complex (sporadically) for public tours; and he began cowriting his autobiography. These projects were surprising, given Prince's cultivated aura of mystery and longstanding refusal to discuss his past. Taken together, they suggest a late-career turn toward retrospection. Prince structured his Piano & a Microphone shows biographically, playing songs in chronological order from his earliest albums, and sharing anecdotes about his childhood and his development as a songwriter. Similarly, Prince began his autobiography talking about the foundational influence that his mother had on his creativity and personality. While music journalists had already mined Prince's musically rich yet emotionally tumultuous childhood as context for his later work, these were the first times that Prince had spoken directly about his own life. Rather than representing a sea-change in his attitude toward privacy, however, I argue that this newfound self-revelation was the logical next step for an artist who had long fought to control every aspect of his own work. Indeed, opening up his Paisley Park inner sanctum for public tours gave Prince the opportunity to curate his own museum, an operation that has expanded since his passing. I conclude this book by discussing what these three interconnected projects say about Prince's legacy and how he may have wanted us to view it.

In closing, I want to clarify a few things that this book is *not*. First, this book is not a biography. There are many biographies of Prince already in print, and I have relied on several of them for salient details about Prince's life and milieu, including one by Minneapolis journalist Jon Bream, two by former Prince fan magazine editor Per Nilsen, and one by journalist Alex Hahn. I have also used archival information gleaned from the Minnesota Historical Society, whose Minneapolis Music Collection was an invaluable resource for corroborating dates and gaining an understanding of the professional community in which

Prince spent his formative years.[94] Yet I am not using these biographical and archival resources for the sake of chronicling his life or psychoanalyzing him, and I reject the idea that pop music is intrinsically autobiographical. Rather, in keeping with my hermeneutic-semiological model of analysis, I use biographical and archival details as windows between the musical and social worlds, providing context for interpreting how Prince's musical decisions constructed different models of identity.

Second, this book is not a comprehensive survey of Prince's career, nor is it chronological. Prince was a prolific artist who released thirty-seven studio albums in as many years (from 1978 to 2015), wrote numerous songs released by other artists, and recorded countless hours of unreleased music that he locked away in his famous vault and which his estate has begun to release posthumously. Trying to discuss all of Prince's music—or even all of his studio albums—in the space of one book would necessitate either giving the scantest analytical attention to each individual song or else writing the longest of all monographs. Instead, I have analyzed a handful of songs in each chapter to illustrate how Prince used and transformed musical genre idioms and to what effect. As such, genre-idiom serves as the main organizing principle in this book rather than historical chronology, and though I present each chapter's musical examples more or less in historical order, taken as a whole this book jumps back and forth in time.

Third, this book is not an attempt to decode what Prince "really meant" by any of his songs, and I make no claims that my hermeneutic interpretations of Prince's music are ones that he explicitly intended. This is not to say that I believe authorial intent is irrelevant and that my interpretations are nothing more than projections, but rather that I have taken a middle path between the extremist poles of the "authorial fallacy" debate, as described by music theorist Ethan Haimo. At one extreme, treating the composer's intentions as the only source of validation for a musical analysis would set an impossible bar for any writer of music criticism, and especially one studying an artist as private as Prince; at the other extreme, rejecting information about the composer's personal life or cultural milieu as irrelevant to a putatively "pure" and "objective" musical analysis is an untenable position given that all music-analytical methodologies are based on historically and/or culturally specific values, and therefore "the very act of choosing an analytical method often presupposes the . . . invocation of historical, stylistic, or biographical assumptions."[95] By using facts from Prince's biography, observations from live performances, interviews with Prince's collaborators, and concepts from critical race theory, gender theory, and music industry studies, I am attempting to ensure that my analytical readings show relevant connections between the sounds themselves, the life of the composer, and his world. Conversely, by grounding my book in musical analysis, I am attempting to show that the cultural work Prince did wasn't communicated solely through his words, image, or personality but rather came through in the music itself.

As an extension of my belief in the relevance of authorial intent, I have limited myself to analyzing only studio recordings that Prince officially released under his own name during his lifetime. Throughout his career Prince fought for control over his music, both inside the recording studio—by acting as his own producer—and outside, by fighting for ownership over his master tapes. Prince carefully curated his own catalog and made definitive decisions about which songs should be released and which should not. For example, biographer Per Nilsen reported the existence of an unreleased song called "Moonbeam Levels" from the *1999* album sessions that the artist chose never to include on any of his official releases; sound engineer Susan Rogers related her frustration when Prince chose not to release the song in the 1980s, and the issue remained contentious even after Prince's death, when the Prince estate chose to release the song as a bonus track on a posthumous greatest hits compilation, over the objections of some of Prince's family members.[96] I have chosen to respect Prince's definition of the boundaries of his own body of work partly because it presents a useful way of limiting my own project and partly because I want to respect his intentions regarding the musical message he put out into the world. The one exception that I make is my use of some bootleg recordings of songs that Prince also released officially. Comparing the officially released versions of a song with live concert recordings, rehearsal tapes, or alternate studio takes is the pop-music equivalent of Beethovenian sketch studies, and these types of bootlegs help us get closer to understanding Prince's compositional and performative decision-making process and therefore to uncover a clearer hermeneutic window.

By presenting my musicological readings of Prince's work, I am by no means claiming to have uncovered the singular truth in the songs I examine. Rather, I am making an argument about the cultural work that Prince's music did in the context of American identity politics. Mystery was always part of Prince's image, and when journalists asked him about the "meaning" of any given song he always demurred, which I believe showed both a trust in the listener's ability to hear his message in the music and a desire to create space for listeners to bring their own meanings. As such, I hope that this book will honor Prince's intentions, and that the interpretations I put forward will spark still more research and discussion about the work of this artist, whom I consider to be among the most consequential in postwar American history.

ONE | Confrontation, Crossover, and Rock Guitar

On Friday October 9, 1981, Prince and his band were living what should have been the rock 'n' roll dream. On the eve of releasing his fourth album, *Controversy*, Prince had been invited to open for the Rolling Stones on the Los Angeles stop of their 1981 North American tour in support of their *Tattoo You* album. By that time, Prince had made a name for himself on the soul singles chart but had not yet established a following with mainstream rock listeners, having not yet cracked the top ten on the *Billboard* Hot 100. In terms of touring strategy, Prince had spent nine weeks as the opening act for Rick James's *Fire It Up* tour in 1980, playing for predominantly African American audiences; his first tour as a headliner, the 1980–81 *Dirty Mind* tour, had enjoyed modest success playing to new-wave audiences in predominantly white clubs, but this tour lasted only a month and included just twenty shows.[1] Gaining access to the Rolling Stones' mainstream rock audience should have been a godsend, with more than 90,000 people in attendance at the LA Memorial Coliseum over two days (Friday and Sunday, October 9 and 11) and many more listening to live coverage of the show on from Los Angeles's two album-oriented rock stations.[2] Prince was the first opening act, followed by two white blues-rock bands—the J. Geils Band and George Thorogood and his Delaware Destroyers—before the Stones took the stage around sunset.[3]

Unfortunately, the show did not prove to be a triumphant introduction to the rock audience for Prince: so vehemently was he booed, and so enthusiastically did the audience throw garbage at his band, that the whole thing went down in rock legend as the "Prince Rolling Stones boo" incident. The hostility of the crowd surprised even the seasoned road veterans in Prince's band, including his guitarist, Dez Dickerson, who described their second Rolling Stones opening performance, on Sunday October 11, in his memoir:

> I saw something appear in the air in front of me. . . . When it drew near enough for me to see what it was, I recognized it as a large sandwich bag. What was amazing was what the bag contained—obviously bad, grey-colored raw chicken parts. . . . I knew at that moment, we were in for a whopper of a day. . . . Not long after, as Prince was at his microphone singing, I saw a FULL, 5th-sized bottle of Jack Daniels come flying out of the crowd at Prince's head. . . . He moved his head slightly to the right just in time to avoid being hit. . . . Seconds later, [bass player] Mark Brown . . . was the target of a full gallon plastic jug of orange juice that hit his bass and just exploded everywhere.[4]

Dickerson shrugs off the negative reception as just another example of the uphill battle faced by any opening act, but Prince's booing that day was singular: neither George Thorogood nor the J. Geils band received that level of audience vitriol. There was clearly more at stake, and music journalists quickly identified race as the issue. Prince was the only Black artist playing on that concert, and despite the guitar-heavy onslaught of his touring band, Prince included two disco-influenced songs at the end of his five-song set, specifically "Uptown" and "Why You Wanna Treat Me So Bad?," the former of which had been a top-twenty hit on the *Billboard* Disco Top 100 chart during the previous year. Robert Hilburn, writing about the incident in a 1982 *Los Angeles Times* article, chalked the negative reaction up to the racial segregation of radio formats:

> Rock-oriented radio stations avoid playing records by black artists, even if the records have a rock slant, because they feel rock fans associate any black artist these days with the dreaded disco. . . . Though the almost exclusively white audience at the Stones show listened to the nostalgic strains of Jimi Hendrix records during intermission, many near the front of the stage hurled paper cups and shouted obscenities when Prince began playing.[5]

Music historian Alice Echols used the Prince Rolling Stones "boo" incident to illustrate the racial appropriation at the center of rock history: how a genre invented by African Americans had been so mainstreamed in American society that Black musicians had ceased to be recognized as legitimate participants in the style.[6] When the Rolling Stones played Altamont in 1969, it was an African American audience member, Meredith Wilson, who was murdered by thugs; ten years later at the LA Coliseum it was an African American *performer* who was attacked.

But was Prince's booing by the Rolling Stones audience simply the result of racism? Was the crowd's hostility due solely to the fact that this was a Black artist whose only hits to date were on the soul or disco charts playing rock music in front of a predominantly white audience that had assembled to hear the best-known white rock band then touring? There is one circulating bootleg recording of Prince's second and final opening performance for the Rolling Stones (October 11, 1981), and on it one does not hear unremitting booing. In fact, Prince was received politely for his first two songs, the hard-rock number "Bambi" and the Beatles-esque "When You Were Mine," and one can even hear the bootlegger comment "Say, this is okay" during the former. Nor does one hear the most vociferous booing only during the two disco songs at the end. Instead, the biggest boos were elicited by a quirky song called "Jack U Off" that Prince and his band played smack in the middle of the set. This was the song the band played when the garbage-pelting got to its worst level: on the bootleg recording, one can clearly hear the bootlegger say, with awe in his voice, "Look at all the trash," just as the song's guitar solo begins.

What made "Jack U Off" different from the two other guitar-based rock songs that Prince played at the beginning of the set was that it did not display the virtuosity and heroism of the hard-rock genre, and instead showed the values of amateurism, simplicity, and confrontation that were identified with the growing punk rock/new-wave underground. Biographers and journalists have often written about Prince's incorporation of punk influences as the X factor that helped him to gain the attention of rock critics in the early 1980s: one reviewer called Prince's style "a combination of Little Richard and Lou Reed," while another suggested that Prince was more punk than the Knack or the Dead Kennedys.[7] Many of those same writers also pointed out that Prince's hometown of Minneapolis had a vibrant underground punk scene in the 1970s and that Prince's launchpad, the First Avenue nightclub, was a venue that supported underground bands. But if the Rolling Stones audience's response was any indication, playing new-wave-influenced rock to a blues-rock crowd was no better a crossover strategy than playing disco was. Either Prince was on a suicide mission that day, or he was playing a long game.

As music scholars John Covach and Theo Cateforis have pointed out, between 1979 and 1982 there was a growing tension between the older style of blues-based hard rock exemplified by the Rolling Stones and the emergent style of new-wave rock. This was precisely the period during which Prince released his most overtly new-wave-influenced albums, 1980's *Dirty Mind* and 1981's *Controversy*. Listening to Prince's guitar solos during these years, one hears an artist playing in two very different styles—hard rock and punk/new wave—with two very different sets of values. Was Prince simply expressing the different sounds of his native Minneapolis, as some have argued? And what was he gaining from his excursion into new-wave territory that outweighed the risk posed by abandoning the familiarity of the R&B and hard-rock genres?

The electric guitar is the most iconic instrument in the history of rock music, and as music scholar Steve Waksman has argued, it has been a locus for debate over the racial, sexual, and gender identity of rock.[8] When Prince entered the music industry in the 1970s, guitar rock was the de facto sound of the suburban white American male, and the conventional wisdom among journalists and biographers is that Prince's decision to integrate the rock guitar idiom into his otherwise R&B-oriented style was the stroke of genius that allowed him to "cross over" into the mainstream while also setting the template for the racial and genre mixing of 1980s pop. But his career as a guitar hero was not as linear as biographers portray it. Prince *had* included hard-rock guitar songs on his first two albums—"I'm Yours" on 1978's *For You* and "Bambi" on 1979's *Prince*—but didn't get traction with rock critics until his third and fourth albums, which took a distinct turn away from hard-rock and toward new-wave rock influences. Then again, for all the critics who praised Prince's blend of new wave and R&B on 1980's *Dirty Mind* and 1981's *Controversy*, Prince didn't have a top-ten single on the mainstream pop chart until his fifth and sixth albums—1982's *1999* and 1984's *Purple Rain*—which included the arena-rock-style guitar songs "Little Red Corvette," which hit number six on the Hot 100, and "Let's Go Crazy," which reached number one. To understand the multiplicity of guitar styles that Prince used, we must complicate the dominant narrative of his career as a guitarist by asking: what *kind* of rock guitar did Prince bring into his music, at what time, and why? If Prince crossed over because he played rock guitar, did it matter what *kind* of rock guitar it was, hard rock or new wave? And if Prince's innovation was indeed the combination of new-wave and funk influences, did this marriage come out of his experiences in the Minneapolis music scene, with its strong underground music community? As the analyses in this chapter demonstrate, what we can hear in Prince's guitar playing is an artist hedging his bets between old and new styles, and in so doing exploiting the growing tensions in the American rock mainstream in order to sidestep the snare of racial determinism endemic to the music industry.

Race and the Music Industry

In the late 1970s and early 1980s, when Prince was beginning his career, the music industry remained stubbornly segregated by race, with the "rock" genre on the white side of the color line.[9] What came to be called rock 'n' roll was invented by African American artists in the 1940s and 1950s, when guitarists like Sister Rosetta Tharpe, T-Bone Walker, B. B. King, Muddy Waters, Ike Turner, Chuck Berry, and Bo Diddley pioneered the overdriven electric guitar idiom.[10] Despite this, the rock genre was recoded as "white" due to the popularity among baby boomers of Anglo-American stars like Elvis Presley, the Beatles, and the Rolling Stones, to the point that by the late 1960s Black artists were squeezed out of that genre with the token exception of Jimi Hendrix.[11] In his biography of Hendrix, Charles Shaar Murray summed up the conundrum of Black rock artists at the dawn of the 1970s: "A black rocker is anathema, considered ludicrous, demeaning and—worst of all—inconvenient. Black rock falls right through the cracks in the Anglo-American cultural continuum. Hard rock is not included in the spectrum of styles which constitute the black pop mainstream; all of which makes it hard for a black rocker to get signed to a major record company or to get any significant degree of radio exposure."[12]

This state of affairs continued through the 1980s and '90s, as ethnomusicologist Maureen Mahon demonstrates, when Black artists working in the rock genre found themselves shut out of existing media outlets: "The black chart, black music, and sounding black enough have become commonsense music industry concepts that place black rock musicians in [an] intractable position. . . . Black and rock had become mutually exclusive and . . . those artists who put the two together risked falling through the cracks."[13]

This genre-based racial segregation was built into the structure of the recording and broadcast industries. At the major record labels, "mainstream" pop and rock music had larger promotional budgets, while genres like R&B and disco were relegated to separate, "Black music" departments, usually with fewer staff and smaller budgets.[14] FM radio was similarly segregated: the AOR radio format, which had replaced the "freeform" FM stations of the 1960s, targeted the young, white, male demographic with a mix of hard rock, heavy metal, and progressive rock that included hardly any Black artists.[15] In the 1970s and '80s, Black radio stations had to contend with advertisers' negative perceptions of African American middle-class buying power, and as such both the older R&B-formatted stations and the newer "urban" format tended to earn lower advertising revenue, while at the same time white-owned "contemporary hit radio" stations, a format similar to Top 40, siphoned away listeners and advertising dollars from R&B and urban formats alike.[16]

This separate-but-unequal dichotomy in the music business meant that record executives and radio station managers had an economic disincentive to promote either unproven Black artists in the mainstream market or rock-oriented artists in the African American market, which meant that Black artists who recorded rock didn't get promoted in either, a state of affairs that continued well into the 1990s.[17] The nascent field of rock criticism also contributed to the marginalization of Black artists within the rock canon by portraying the Black contributions to rock 'n' roll as a kind of raw material that had to be refined by a subsequent generation of white artists. As Daphne Brooks argues, when influential critics like Robert Christgau and Greil Marcus lionized early twentieth-century African American blues artists such as Robert Johnson as *precursors* to the British blues-rock explosion of the 1960s, they buttressed a roots-and-shoots narrative in which the work and suffering of older Black artists yielded "white pleasure in the hands of celebrated 'inheritors': Keith Richards, Eric Clapton, Duane Allman, and Dylan."[18] Thus, despite the fact that African American artists had invented the electric blues and rock 'n' roll guitar idioms, and despite the defining role that Hendrix played in the rock counterculture of the late 1960s, by the 1970s rock music and rock guitar were firmly established as mainstream "white" music.

There were in fact *many* influential Black rock guitar virtuosi who had careers in the 1960s, '70s, '80s, and '90s, but because of the music industry's structural racial bias they tended not to be marketed in the rock genre. In his 1996 book *Funk*, historian Rickey Vincent argues that there is an unbroken Black rock lineage connecting 1940s electric-blues pioneers like Muddy Waters, 1950s rock 'n' roll originators like Chuck

Berry, 1960s Black rock and funk bands such as the Isley Brothers, Jimi Hendrix, and Sly and the Family Stone, 1970s funk and fusion bands like Parliament-Funkadelic, Mandrill, Earth, Wind & Fire, and the Ohio Players, Prince in the 1980s, and 1990s metal and punk artists like Living Colour and Bad Brains.[19] But with the token exception of Hendrix (and, later, Prince and Living Colour) Black guitarists were not often promoted in the "mainstream" rock market and only grudgingly to the pop market. As a result, many chose to "dispose of their rock riffs and guitar solos" and play guitar within the idioms of funk, soul, jazz fusion, or smooth jazz in order to gain radio airplay on urban-formatted stations.[20]

Prince in the early 1980s was precisely the kind of Black rocker who could have fallen through the cracks of the American music industry. In his 2019 memoir, Prince's longtime musical collaborator Morris Day described his first impressions of Prince when they met in high school as "[a] guitarist who, at fifteen, had absorbed all of Eric Clapton and thrown in Jeff Beck for good measure. Later I learned [he'd] even studied cats that influenced Hendrix—Johnny Guitar Watson and Buddy Guy."[21] Prince himself reminisced about listening to rock guitarists on Minneapolis's KQRS in his formative years: "The old KQ after midnight, that was the bomb station. . . . Back then I always tried to play like Carlos [Santana], or Boz Scaggs."[22] To be sure, "rock" was not the only genre that influenced Prince's guitar-playing: oft-cited early influences include R&B and funk guitarists like Jimmy Nolen of James Brown's band, Ernie Isley of the Isley Brothers, and Eddie Hazel of Parliament-Funkadelic, and in his later career Prince absorbed the influence of jazz guitarists such as George Benson. Furthermore, guitar was *not* Prince's only instrument: a musical polymath, Prince was a keyboard player before he was a guitarist, and also developed spectacular abilities as a vocalist, drummer, and bass player. His mastery of these different styles and instruments gave Prince other, "safer" career options besides rock: he could easily have marketed himself solely as an R&B, funk, or jazz guitarist, or as a vocalist and keyboard player instead. Yet Prince proved unwilling to dispose of his rock riffs, to borrow Vincent's phrase.

Prince included rock guitar numbers on *all* his early albums, at the risk of running afoul of the music industry's segregated marketing practices, and he foregrounded his own guitar playing onstage. In his first touring band, Prince chose both to play rock guitar himself and to feature a second Black man on lead electric guitar next to him, Dez Dickerson, who had years of experience on the Midwestern rock-ballroom circuit. According to Marylou Badeaux, an executive in the

Black music department at Warner Brothers who worked with Prince for many years, Prince wanted to avoid any stylistic restrictions on his musical output, especially those stemming from the music industry's genre-based racial segregations: "Prince was very concerned about being labeled a black artist or being segmented into the black department. He said to us, 'I'm not an R&B artist. I'm not a rock 'n' roller. I'm an artist and I do a wide range of music. If I deliver you rock 'n' roll, don't come back to me and say I can't do it because I'm black.'"[23] In fact, Prince chose to sign with Warner Brothers over the other major labels in part because they allowed him to produce his own albums and made a commitment *not* to "pigeonhole him into the R&B department," as Badeaux confirmed in her memoir.[24] Yet even with such supportive executives, the odds were stacked against an African American artist who wanted to move beyond the genre boundaries of Black music, and Prince's decision to foreground his rock guitar-playing amounted to a mission statement.

My goal in this chapter is *not* to try and summarize or define Prince's particular style of guitar-playing (his "idiolect" in Richard Middleton's terminology).[25] Prince's guitar-playing is complex and multifaceted, incorporating idiomatic elements of rock, R&B, soul, funk, disco, and jazz, and I hope future scholars will generate a body of literature that explores these myriad influences. Rather, my goal in this chapter is to discuss only how Prince used *rock* guitar idioms in his early career. The story about Prince and the guitar that we assume we know is that, facing a segregated musical landscape, he fused "Black" R&B and funk with "white" rock guitar so successfully that he created the cross-racial paradigm of 1980s pop. But given the structural segregation that was mapped onto musical genre in the 1970s and '80s, playing rock guitar was more likely to be detrimental than beneficial to music-industry success for a Black artist such as Prince. My goal is to complicate this assumed narrative by considering, as the Rolling Stones boo incident suggests, that there was more than one way to play "rock" guitar in the late 1970s. Specifically, I argue that Prince used two divergent rock-guitar idioms in his early music, hard rock and new wave, and that he exploited the slippage between them—their different semiotic meanings and aesthetic values—as a way of disrupting the binary logic by which the music industry excluded Black artists from the rock genre writ large. After characterizing these two styles in his work, I will consider the question of *why* Prince chose this strategy, looking first at the possible influence that Minneapolis new wave bands may have exerted on Prince, and second, at the extramusical associations that Prince may have gained from punk/new wave, especially pertaining to representations of gender and sexuality.

Prince's Hard-Rock Guitar Style: "Bambi"

As a representative example of one of Prince's early rockers, consider the song "Bambi," which Prince used to kick off his performance for the Rolling Stones audience on that October weekend in 1981. Prince included at least one hard-rock guitar number on both of his first two albums: "I'm Yours" from his 1978 debut album *For You* and "Bambi" from his 1979 self-titled sophomore album. Neither of these songs was released as a single: Warner Brothers had chosen instead to release more disco-influenced songs as singles from Prince's first two albums—"Soft and Wet," from *For You*, reached number twelve on the *Billboard* soul singles chart but only ninety-two on the mainstream Hot 100 singles chart, while "I Wanna Be Your Lover," the highest-charting single from *Prince*, hit number one on the soul chart and number two on the dance chart but only number eleven on the Hot 100—so it's plausible that the majority of the Rolling Stones audience would have had no inkling of who Prince was, due to his lack of AOR radio airplay.[26]

"Bambi" has many of the stylistic markers of late-1970s hard rock. The main timbre that you hear throughout the song is distorted electric guitar. It has the rich, fuzzy high-end saturation of an overdriven tube amplifier, and it would remind any guitar aficionado of the sound of a Marshall stack, the preferred sound of British blues-rockers and of Hendrix, although Prince was most likely using a Mesa-Boogie amplifier at the time, the same model used by Carlos Santana.[27] Prince sings his lead vocal in the kind of steely falsetto scream used by hard-rock singers such as Robert Plant, and while he doesn't completely avoid a pure falsetto register that might remind listeners of gospel music or disco (during the verses), he mitigates this by *not* using any backup singers or multitracked vocals, avoiding the kind of call-and-response gestures that would signify soul or R&B.

Harmonically, the song uses the minor-sounding Dorian mode—common in heavy metal music—instead of the major-sounding Ionian or Mixolydian modes more common in pop music.[28] Its root progression stays strictly within the C♯ Dorian tetrachord of C♯–D♯–E–F♯ (with the chorus centered on C♯ and the verse on F♯), and when Prince's vocal melody enters during the verses it oscillates between G♯ and A♯, filling out the C♯ Dorian scale. The rhythm guitar plays power chords, a hard-rock/heavy-metal technique that includes only the root and fifth of a chord and relies on the upper partials provided by the distortion to pad out the harmonic landscape.[29]

The song's rhythm signifies hard rock as well. The song is at a medium tempo, around 90 beats per minute—not a tempo for dancing—and Prince uses a straight-ahead rock beat, avoiding the kind of interlocking polyrhythms that would mark the song as funk or disco (the kick drum plays on beat 1, the snare drum on 2 and 4, and cowbell—a staple of hard-rock drums—plays straight quarter notes to mark the tempo). The only hint of syncopation is in the chorus, where the main guitar riff anticipates beat 3 of each measure, which gives the chorus a sense of rhythmic propulsion and urgency but stops short of inviting the audience to dance (see example 2).

Example 2. "Bambi" chorus

The most potent signifier of any hard-rock song is a catchy lead-guitar melody, and Prince does not disappoint. First, there's the main riff: repeated four times per chorus, it consists of a scorching but simple line that descends from E to C♯ with a flourish, and is played at high pitch and high volume, and with high distortion. Even more telling is the extended guitar solo that comes at the end of the song, after the last chorus and before the fade-out (mm. 81–96). The solo is sixteen bars long—double the length of the other sections—and in it, Prince shows a canny mastery of hard-rock guitar heroism. The solo has a dramatic arc of struggle and triumph in the C♯ Dorian mode, which Prince sketches out in seven gestures (see examples 3 and 4).

In gestures 1 and 2 of the guitar solo (example 3), Prince introduces the pitches of the C♯ Dorian mode: gesture 1 provides C♯, E, and F♯, with the flat seventh, B, provided by the pickup in m. 80; the D♯ second scale

Example 3. "Bambi" guitar solo, gestures 1–4

degree is supplied by the rhythm guitar, and then gesture 2 gives us G♯ and A♯. Then, in the third gesture, Prince gives us a firm cadence on C♯, a descending pentatonic figure in a very high register that moves from the fifth to the tonic of C♯ Dorian. In gestures 1 to 3, Prince pounds the C♯ tonic home eight times in four bars and, having set up his base camp, so to speak, the subsequent gesture (4) sounds as though it represents the first attempt at summiting a mountain. On the downbeat of m. 89, he leaps up to a high B but is only able to hold it for a bar (example 3); failing to attain the high C♯ tonic, Prince slides back down two octaves plus a third to G♯, with increasingly frantic flurries of notes on the way down. But after this symbolic failure in gesture 4, the protagonist does not return to the safety of his low C♯ base camp and instead sets out again to summit the high C♯ peak (example 4). In gesture 5, Prince's guitar melody moves doggedly upward from E with heavy, plodding quarter-note steps that are so shaky with vibrato they become indetermi-

Example 4. "Bambi" guitar solo, gestures 5–7

nate in pitch as they go up (see m. 92, example 4). Finally, mustering his strength with a whammy-bar dive-bomb, Prince makes his final attempt at the summit on the downbeat of m. 93. Not only does he achieve it, he soars above it, playing a triumphant F♯ for two bars before cadencing on high C♯. This high F♯ is only eight semitones from the very highest note on the guitar—assuming that Prince was playing one of the two guitars he was most often photographed with at the time, a Les Paul Studio or a Hohner copy of a Fender Telecaster, both of which have 22 frets—making the journey of the guitar-protagonist both metaphoric and literal, as Prince has traversed nearly the entire guitar neck. After this triumphant climax, gesture 7 is a victory lap, an extended mediant-to-tonic cadence from E to C♯ (m. 95–6, example 4).

This guitar solo in "Bambi" displays the values audiences would expect in a hard rock or early heavy metal guitar solo: it uses minor-sounding modal harmony, it features bent notes and pentatonic riffs (recalling the blues origins of hard rock), and most importantly, it demonstrates virtuosity. Prince expresses this virtuosity not only in the speed and precision of his guitar playing, but also in its rhetorical teleology: by establishing both a tonic home base and a high-C♯ goal he creates a narrative of initial failure, struggle, and ultimate triumph—a hero's journey. It's not a *huge* journey—Prince never tries to escape into a different key area, for instance—but it is enough to show that the hero has struggled and then mastered the C♯ Dorian mode. This was a song that the Rolling Stones audience listened to politely, even cheering. Yet they did not embrace it: "Bambi" never appeared on the Top 40 charts or on AOR radio, having been passed over as a possible single by Warner Brothers. In 1981, Prince as a hard-rock hero was a nonstarter, and had he continued recording guitar songs only in this hard-rock vein he may have fallen victim to the racial-genre segregation that Murray, Mahon, Vincent and others described. How, then, did Prince use rock guitar to cross over?

Prince's New-Wave Rockabilly Guitar Style: "Jack U Off"

By contrast, the guitar-centered songs that Prince released on his third and fourth albums—songs like "When You Were Mine," from *Dirty Mind*, and "Ronnie, Talk to Russia" and "Jack U Off," from *Controversy*—have very different stylistic markers from the AOR hard-rock sound of "I'm Yours" and "Bambi." I'll discuss "Jack U Off," from the 1981 album *Controversy* and the song that got Prince his biggest boos from the Rolling Stones audience, as a representative example of this new-wave rockabilly style.

"Jack U Off" immediately establishes a very different stylistic profile from Prince's earlier guitar-rock songs: the harmony, melody, and structure of the song all convey an exuberant simplicity reminiscent of 1950s rock 'n' roll. The rhythm *is* made for dancing, but it's not disco: the tempo is an extremely fast 216 beats per minute, and it features swung eighth notes, giving it a retro, jump-band feel that's reinforced by the boogie-woogie pattern played by bass and rhythm guitar (see example 5). Furthermore, the song's chorus features backup singers whose close-harmony style is reminiscent of 1940s or '50s vocal-harmony groups, intensifying the retro feel of the song. Prince uses simple, major-mode harmony throughout and limits himself to just the dominant and tonic chords. The vocal melody and guitar hook are identical, with a simplistic antecedent-consequent phrase structure that makes it sound like a playground chant. Adding to the sense of simplicity, the song has only four structural units—verse, chorus, bridge, and guitar solo—which are distinguished by the presence or absence of the rhythm instruments and backup singers.

The guitar solo is notable for its simplicity and retro, 1950s rockabilly feel, in marked contrast to the hard-rock heroism of Prince's earlier guitar-rockers. Like "Bambi," the guitar solo in "Jack U Off" is sixteen bars long and uses a richly distorted guitar timbre, but the similarity stops

Example 5. "Jack U Off" vamp

there. Where "Bambi" sketched out a hero's journey from struggle to mastery over the Dorian mode, the "Jack U Off" guitar solo has a nested, symmetrical, open-and-shut structure comprised of two eight-bar halves that are each subdivided into four-bar question-and-answer gestures (see example 6). In the antecedent "question" phrases (mm. 101–104 and mm. 109–112), Prince plays a simple, repetitive triplet-based riff followed by a

Example 6. “Jack U Off” guitar solo

descending melodic gesture. In the consequent "answer" phrases (mm. 105–108 and mm. 113–116), Prince plays a variation on the song's quarter-note hook (the same melody used to sing the words "I'll jack you off" in the chorus) followed by a descending cadential gesture (a chromatic scale in the first phrase, and a mediant-to-tonic glissando in the second phrase). In addition to the simplicity of the solo's nonnarrative symmetrical structure, Prince is using a constrained pitch palette: every note that he plays can be reached using an extended box-position finger pattern with the first finger on the fifth-fret A. Thus, even though Prince is playing fast notes, he is *not* displaying the kind of technical virtuosity that defines the hard-rock / heavy-metal guitar idiom. In fact, Prince allows himself to be technically imprecise in his playing, especially in the second "question" gesture where he seems to be hammering on a couple of notes without really bothering to press the strings down properly. Where the solo in "Bambi" had a heroic climax, "Jack U Off" has none; where "Bambi" demanded Prince use the whole guitar neck from the first to the sixteenth fret, and advanced techniques of left-hand hammer-ons and whammy-bar dive-bombs, "Jack U Off" doesn't even require him to move his left hand, and even then he lets his fretwork get sloppy.

Another important stylistic marker occurs at the beginning of the solo (mm. 101–102), when Prince bridges his first finger across the top two strings and slides back and forth in a chromatic lower-neighbor gesture between the fourth and fifth frets. This is an instantly recognizable reference to the style of Chuck Berry and, along with the boogie-woogie bass line and the swung eighth notes, places this song firmly in the retro rockabilly subgenre. Rockabilly might not be the first thing that comes to mind when we think of new wave or punk rock, but it was an important component of the New York underground movement of the 1970s. Both British and American punks were inspired by it: think of the greaser, leather-jacketed look of the Ramones, or the Chuck Berry licks copped by Johnny Thunders of the New York Dolls ("Personality Crisis") and by Steve Jones of the Sex Pistols ("God Save the Queen"). The iconoclasm of the punk movement was predicated, in large part, on a return to 1950s and '60s garage-band basics, and as the term "new wave" replaced the word "punk" in America the genre became a catchall for a number of substyles, including rockabilly.[30] Ironic though this may seem, by looking back to the musical and visual styles of the post-WWII boom years of rock 'n' roll, new-wave rockabilly groups were actually looking forward, reclaiming the looks and sounds of the past as a way to remake rock as a rebellious, fun dance music rather than the bloated, virtuoso concert music that progressive and hard rock had arguably become. One new-wave rockabilly band in particular, the Stray Cats, had a big influence on Prince, who saw their show on June 1, 1981, when both their bands were playing in London for the first time. Guitarist Dez Dickerson remembered, "Prince was visibly impacted by the band [the Stray Cats], as well,—I could always tell when an artist had made an impression on him. This style-heavy presentation would serve as a confirmation to us that we were right in the thick of a New Wave of artists who would be making a global impact."[31] Immediately upon returning to Minnesota from that London trip, Prince holed up in his home studio and recorded all of the *Controversy* album by himself that same month.[32]

The fact that the song "Jack U Off" angered the Rolling Stones audience so much shows the schism between hard rock and new wave values in that historical moment. In 1981 new wave was only just beginning to push its way onto AOR radio playlists, so while Prince's retro-rockabilly new-wave style wasn't the dreaded "disco," it also wasn't the specific rock idiom that the Rolling Stones' audience craved. Furthermore, Prince mixed his rockabilly guitar with the kind of androgyny and sexual provocation that harkened back to punk-adjacent artists like David Bowie, Marc Bolan, and the New York Dolls. Indeed, "Jack U Off" had a homoerotic subtext to its lyrics: as bassist Mark Brown succinctly put it, "In terms of street lingo, where I come from, guys don't jack girls off."[33] Fast tempo, aggressive rockabilly guitar, gender-bending fashion, and homoerotic lyrics: Prince was playing the tensions between mainstream hard rock and new-wave punk for all they were worth. In retrospect, the surprise is not that he was booed, but that he was unprepared for that reaction.

In the span of two years, from 1979 to 1981, Prince's forays into the "rock" genre had shifted from the safe but anonymous hard rock of "Bambi" to the new-wave amalgam of rockabilly and glam we hear on "Jack U Off," and the question that I will explore for the remainder of this chapter is what could have motivated Prince to make this change, given the strong negative reaction that it earned him from the mainstream rock audience. As the *Los Angeles Times*'s Robert Hilburn pointed out in his 1982 profile, neither Prince's new-wave rock styled songs nor his Rolling Stones opening slot helped him reach the rock audience: "Prince's new album [*1999*] has entered the pop charts nicely, and the single is a hit on pop, dance and black music charts. But neither is on the list of Top 50 records on *Billboard* magazine's check of rock radio playlists."[34] If Prince's goal was to court the mainstream rock audience—already a risky proposition given the music industry's genre-racial segregation—why dabble in new wave at all instead of sticking with the established hard-rock style? I want to consider two interrelated answers to this question. First, Prince's decision to blend post-disco funk with new-wave rock may have been an organic expression of his Minneapolis roots, given the progressive, cross-genre booking policies of the influential nightclub First Avenue. Second, regardless of where he was from, Prince's decision to embrace the new wave genre garnered him something more than just a stripped-down, retro-inspired guitar style: it also gave him a frisson of danger and gender transgression—call it punk fairy dust—that helped him break out of the false binary opposition between "Black" and "white" musical genres.

New Wave: The Minneapolis Connection

Journalists and biographers have long taken it for granted that Prince's success as a crossover artist had *something* to do with coming up in Minneapolis, a city where the market for Black music was so small that its only gospel- and R&B-formatted radio station, KUXL, was still on the AM band (at 1570) and went off the air at 8:30 p.m. Indeed, it was not until 1978 when Minneapolis got its first R&B-formatted commercial FM station, KMOJ, and even then it was limited by a paltry broadcast power of only 10 watts until 1984, when it increased to 1,000 watts.[35] There is logic to this assumption—one is shaped by the culture in which one grows up, and Prince was most certainly influenced by the North Minneapolis musical milieu in which he first cut his teeth, as Andrea Swensson has documented.[36] Yet the argument that Prince blended rock and funk because he grew up in a city with limited opportunities for Black musicians minimizes his agency and overlooks the calculation that he put into the specific musical idioms that he employed—hard-rock guitar heroism at one moment, new-wave retro-rockabilly at another. To evaluate this assumption more deeply, then, let's consider the specifics of Prince's place within the larger Minneapolis music community of the late 1970s.

Minneapolis was always considered a "flyover" in the music and media industries, being equally distant from the power centers on both coasts, but in the 1960s and '70s there was enough work for pop musicians to eke out a living touring the Midwest ballroom circuit. Minneapolis had nightclubs, music stores, and booking agencies that supported these local musicians, as well as the national touring acts who came through town. These musical institutions tended to cater to the genre preferences of their particular communities, despite the fact that all the musicians from the period that I interviewed made it clear that no group was *just* a top-40 band, or just an R&B or rock band. North Minneapolis is a historically African American neighborhood, and the Northside had its own clubs like the Fox Trap and the Capri that tilted towards jazz, R&B, and funk music. The University district—Dinkytown and the West Bank, populated largely by college students—was known for blues bars like the Cabooze, the Flame, and the Triangle Bar.[37] The downtown Minneapolis business district boasted the most lucrative nightclub scene, where the rock clubs, discos, and theaters booked national touring acts and only the most popular local rock and, less frequently, R&B bands.

Outside of this established musical ecosystem, a new-wave rock scene was bubbling up in Minneapolis in the 1970s, as in cities across America, with underground bands exploring alternatives to what they perceived as the bloat and pretension of AOR rock and disco alike. Locally, this movement was led by the band Suicide Commandos and their frontman, Chris Osgood, who hung out with a community of like-minded musicians at the Oar FolkJokeOpus record store and played at venues scattered around Minneapolis including Duffy's, the Longhorn, and First Avenue's 7th Street Entry. As they soon discovered, there were similar underground music scenes in cities across the nation, and by establishing a space for underground music in Minneapolis, Osgood and his associates were able to host punk/new-wave bands including the Ramones, Talking Heads, the Police, and Richard Hell and the Voidoids when they first toured through Minneapolis.

This underground music scene was mostly separate from the established R&B and rock scenes but for a few Minneapolis venues where funk and punk musicians crossed paths, one of which—First Avenue—would become famous as Prince's launchpad. The venue that eventually became First Avenue first opened as a rock club called the Depot in 1970.[38] Its name soon changed to Uncle Sam's in 1972, when it became part of a national chain run by American Events Management, and through the 1970s AEM ran it as a disco club with some live performances by rock bands.[39] As the "death of disco" dawned in 1979, the original owners, along with manager Steve McClellan, took back control of the club and shortened the name to Sam's, and on New Year's Eve of 1981 the club finally changed its name to First Avenue and 7th Street Entry, in which form it has continued into the twenty-first century.[40] McClellan was adventurous, booking up-and-coming local acts alongside established touring bands, in genres from mainstream rock to post-punk to reggae and funk, and this eclectic approach created a scene that brought together musicians and fans from many disparate musical communities. Furthermore, McClellan opened the venue's smaller second room—7th Street Entry—which became ground zero for the local punk community, especially after other clubs supporting underground bands such as Duffy's and the Longhorn closed. McClellan nurtured the careers of local punk bands like the Replacements, Suicide Commandos, Hüsker Dü, as well as funk/R&B acts like Prince and Alexander O'Neal.

First Avenue was not the only place where musicians of different genres and races came together, as I learned from my interviews; working musicians tended to rent rehearsal space in the same few facilities around town, and there were a few music stores that brought in everybody, most notably the Knut Koupée guitar store. Located at Twenty-Eighth and Hennepin in the Uptown neighborhood, Knut Koupée was situated next door to a musician's referral service and across the street from West High School, making it a hang out both for working musicians and wannabes. The luthiers on staff gained a national reputation, servicing the guitars of touring rock giants like the Who and Eric Clapton and making custom instruments for local bands like Chameleon, Fairchild, and the Suicide Commandos.[41] Knut Koupée nurtured both the local punk scene—Chris Osgood taught lessons there—and the local funk and R&B scene as well. It was also the place where Prince bought his guitars, and when he became successful, where he had his custom Cloud guitars built.

Given the common support that institutions like First Avenue and Knut Koupée gave to musicians working in the different style communities of the day—R&B/funk, mainstream AOR rock, and punk/new-wave—it is almost irresistible to see this as a contributing factor to Prince's decision to mix these genres. Knut Koupée and First Avenue were common hangouts for musicians Black and white, mainstream and underground, and Prince frequented both of those spaces. Yet correlation is not causation, as the axiom goes. The musicians I interviewed who were around the Minneapolis scene at the time all said the same thing: *yes*, these were places where musicians from different neighborhoods all hung out, but that did not necessarily lead to collaboration or cross influence. Chris Osgood explained,

> It's not like The Replacements were opening for Prince. Much has been made about the punk and funk, you know. . . . People recast it

> in a way that looks like there was a lot more brotherly love and interface than there really was. We coexisted and the things were going on simultaneous to each other, and right next to each other, but interfaces were infrequent rather than frequent. That's the truth. It's not like we were running in and out of each other's scenes. We were stealing each other's girlfriends, stuff like that, but . . .[42]

In the early 1980s, funk bands and punk bands all aspired to play at First Avenue, but when they did, it was on separate nights or on separate stages. Musicians were certainly aware of the other scenes in town, but there was little if any musical interaction.[43] This separation was especially true for Prince, a kid from the Northside who kept to an insular circle of musicians—many of whom he had known since high school—even after he became famous. The exceptions to this were the musicians he met through his first manager, Owen Husney, including Bobby and David Rivkin and Matt Fink, all of whom were Jewish teenagers from St. Louis Park who played R&B music. One of the few musicians Prince did hire in an open audition was Dez Dickerson, another Black guitarist from the Midwest who played hard rock. As Dickerson recalls, the main influence he and Prince shared was (white mainstream rock band) Grand Funk Railroad, and their ambition was to be "more of a multiracial Rolling Stones than a stereotypical R&B group. He had spoken often of my playing Keith to his Mick."[44] Prince didn't hire bandmembers from the underground scene, nor did he play at the Longhorn or Duffy's. His guitar heroes included Mark Farner, Boz Scaggs, and Carlos Santana rather than Ron Asheton, Johnny Thunders, or Steve Jones. Prince has admitted that he was influenced by the rock music he heard growing up, but that meant the hard-rock he heard on the local AOR station KQRS, *not* Minneapolis's underground punk rock.[45]

What Prince Gained from New Wave

While it may be disappointing to some Minneapolis music aficionados to let go of the idea that Prince's punk-funk crossover was an organic result of his association with First Avenue and Knut Koupée, doing so recognizes Prince's agency and foregrounds the performative choices that he made. As Emily Lordi demonstrates, Black artists have often been portrayed as "natural" entertainers, a stereotype that erases the intellectual decision-making and sheer labor that goes into crafting a musical act.[46] Recognizing the artists' performative decisions and hard work are correctives to this, and as such we should view Prince's decision to incorporate the simplicity and confrontation of punk/new-wave guitar (as well as the virtuosity and heroism of hard-rock guitar) into the framework of R&B/funk as a calculated decision that was predicated on the multi-genre fluency that he gained through laborious practice.

This shifts the question of Prince's punk/new-wave influence from one of location (where did he hear it) to one of motivation: what did he gain from his decision to incorporate new-wave influences into his music? Prince's early decision to incorporate hard-rock guitar heroism (e.g., "Bambi") is easier to understand, given the racial segregation structured into the music industry. In the late 1970s, hard rock was the dominant style on AOR radio, and fans and radio DJs displayed an antipathy that bordered on vitriol towards Black-identified genres like disco and funk, as evidenced by the violent Comiskey Park "disco demolition" night. As critics like Dave Marsh point out, the anti-disco backlash showed both the lingering racial segregation of American musical tastes and a macho rejection of the perceived effeminacy of disco culture.[47] By positioning himself as a rock guitarist in the blues-rock AOR mold early in his career, with the songs "I'm Yours" and "Bambi," Prince was staking his claim on the mainstream side of the rock vs. disco schism. Prince may have even shared the rockist, anti-disco sentiment at the time: in July 1979 he and his backing band recorded an unreleased guitar rocker titled "Disco Away" that featured lyrics satirizing the dance club scene.[48] In his early press interviews, Prince made it clear that he had no love for disco, dismissing its reliance on producers rather than musicians, a standard rockist criticism of disco. He said to one journalist, "To me disco was always *very* contrived music."[49] He went on to denigrate the producer-driven nature of disco music in a 1981 *New York Rocker* interview, saying, "A lotta records today are producers' records. . . . I don't believe in any act, really, which had to rely on a producer. What happens if the cat dies? There you go, there goes your sound—you obviously didn't have one."[50]

But despite his mastery of hard-rock guitar heroism, and despite these verbal attempts at distancing himself from the disco genre, Prince had not been accepted as a hard-rock artist. AOR radio didn't play "Bambi" or "I'm Yours," and neither were these songs hits with his Black listeners. Reviewing a late 1979 show, *Right On* writer Cynthia Horner said, "I have to admit that hard rock isn't very appealing to his primary audience, young black teens. He needs to define his concept more fully because he crosses so many musical barriers that he's too difficult to categorize."[51]

Given the binary division between racially marked musical genres—the Black vs. white, disco vs. rock dichotomy—punk/new wave offered Prince a stylistic third option, allowing him to disrupt the binary opposition. As *Rolling Stone* critic Barry Walters put it, "it was either funk or die, or take your chances with New Wave."[52] In 1979, new-wave artists began scoring pop hits by combining the guitar-based instrumentation and back-to-basics ethos of punk/new wave with disco's synthesizers and dance rhythms, such as Blondie's "Heart of Glass," which hit number one on the Hot 100 that year.[53] Take his chances with new wave, then, is precisely what Prince did.

Prince's decision to switch from hard-rock guitar heroism to new-wave, garage-rock simplicity, which lasted for the span of two albums (*Dirty Mind* and *Controversy*), did not result in immediate hits on the Hot 100 pop chart or acceptance by the mainstream rock audience, as the Rolling Stones boo incident highlights. But like the multi-generic virtuosity that Emily Lordi identified in Nina Simone's career, Prince's mixture of different musical idioms was a survival strategy that allowed him to claim a space for himself—and, by extension, the marginalized members of his audience—outside of those delineated by the music industry.[54]

In particular, Prince's two-album turn to punk/new wave gave him tools to disrupt the hierarchies of power (racialized and gendered) that intersected in Western constructions of Black masculinity, or what writers Andrew Shin and Barbara Judson called "the straitjacket of black virility."[55] The garage-rock simplicity and avant-garde semiotics of new wave gave Prince the means to interrupt the chain of signifiers by which Black male sexuality had been made a fetish object by British blues-rock artists of the 1960s, appropriated, and eventually erased from the hard-rock genre by the 1970s. As Daphne Brooks argued, the dominant narrative of rock history is based on the sexualization and appropriation of Black identity insofar as it "threatens to recycle the racial and gendered biases of cultural appropriation debates plaguing pop culture since the rise of minstrelsy."[56] Steve Waksman, drawing on the postcolonial theory of Frantz Fanon, puts this issue into an even broader historical context: just as nineteenth-century colonizers projected their feelings of "lack" onto Black colonized bodies, so too did 1960s rock fans project fears and desires of Black phallic potency onto the bluesmen whose guitar music inspired the rock genre, and onto Jimi Hendrix, who suffered under the weight of his image as a buck-wild, Black sex machine (and whose amplifier-humping act at the 1967 Monterey Pop Festival Robert Christgau once described as a "psychedelic Uncle-Tom routine").[57]

Hendrix cast a long shadow over Prince's rock career, and we can see in Prince's early hard-rock-style songs a similar linkage between guitar heroism and an over-the-top performance of heterosexual masculinity. As Steve Waksman and Charles Schaar Murray have argued, linking guitar virtuosity to performances of hyper-virility (e.g. the Monterey Pop act) ultimately became a trap for Hendrix, as they played into the stereotypes of unrestrained Black male sexuality held by the predominantly white rock audience.[58] By veering into punk/new wave, Prince accessed a different guitar idiom, one that allowed him to use speed and aggression *without* the heroic virtuosity that stood for heteronormative male potency in the minds of AOR rock fans. At the same time, punk/new wave allowed Prince to access a construction of masculinity and sexuality based on the androgyny and gender-fluid sexuality of artists like David Bowie, Marc Bolan, and David Johansen.

The semiotic freedom that Prince got from new wave's androgyny also allowed him to avoid another stereotypical construction of Black male sexuality, which is effeminacy. A generation earlier, Black rock 'n' rollers like Little Richard had used effeminacy as a tool to defuse the threat that Black male heterosexuality held for a society still terrified of miscegenation. Richard himself explained, "That's the reason I started wearin' makeup, so that they wouldn't feel threatened when I was in the clubs, around the white girls."[59] In the context of the 1970s, however, Prince's androgyny—like Bowie's and Bolan's—*was* threatening in its mixture of femininity and aggression, and even more so for his explicit discussions of taboo sexual subjects in songs like "Sister" and "Head." Circa *Dirty Mind* and *Controversy*, Prince still displayed a voracious sexuality onstage, but both the subject and the object of that sexual desire came unmoored from the heterosexual masculine/feminine dichotomy. And where contemporary disco artists like Sylvester proudly used androgyny as a signifier of gay identity, Prince demanded to be heard as a lover of women, while musically demanding to be heard as a rock guitarist and not just a disco singer. Prince didn't use androgyny to slide himself from the masculine to the feminine side of the Cartesian poles; instead, he interrupted the visual signifiers by which he could be identified as male or female, while using the simplicity, speed, and aggression of new wave's rockabilly guitar style to scramble the main musical signifier of machismo, which was the virtuoso guitar solo. Of course, Prince did not totally avoid being perceived as effeminate or gay—comedians from Eddie Murphy to Jamie Fox have mined Prince's androgyny for jokes—but my point is that Prince was trying. New-wave semiotics gave Prince tools that previous generations of Black rockers had lacked, and he used them to refuse both the binary choice between funk/disco dance rhythms and rock guitar, *and* between the dominant constructions of Black masculinity as either sexual savage or effeminized buffoon.

Conclusion

Not only did new wave provide Prince with a third option beyond the music industry's Black/white and disco/rock binaries, it also proved to be a commercially advantageous move for an emerging artist at that moment, given the brief flowering of commercial success new-wave artists enjoyed between 1979 and 1981. The term "new wave" has been used to denote different things at different times, as Theo Cateforis points out: in England, it was initially used to describe the Sex Pistols and other groups in what came to be called the original "punk" movement of 1976–77.[60] These bands had some commercial success in England but none in America, and this first wave of "punk" quickly sputtered out; worse, it was linked to antisocial behavior and un-airable obscenities, and the American record industry viewed it as mainstream poison. However, the musical rebellion that punk represented took hold among musicians and rock critics who were growing tired of mainstream AOR rock as well as disco. Adding to this was the global recession and the bursting of the disco bubble, both of which contributed to a massive slowdown in record sales across the industry. Suddenly the grassroots popularity and back-to-basics aesthetic of underground bands seemed like a viable alternative, both to rock critics and to record label executives who needed to find "rock" artists with low production costs that it could market to mainstream listeners.[61] All it took was the rebranding of underground punk rock as "new wave" for major labels to go on a signing spree, and by 1981 skinny-tie-wearing bands like Blondie, Talking Heads, Elvis Costello, Joe Jackson, and The Knack started showing up on both AOR and Top 40 pop radio playlists.

Yet this popularity proved fleeting—new-wave album sales were not sufficient to pull the record industry out of its slump—and by 1982 major labels and radio programmers had largely moved on from new wave. Prince's two new-wave-themed albums directly correspond to that style's brief music industry heyday, with *Dirty Mind* released in 1980 and *Controversy* in 1981. These albums are full of references to new-wave modernism, including retro-rockabilly guitar, vaguely political lyrics like those in "Ronnie, Talk to Russia," and techno-futurist synthesizers. Furthermore, Prince's changing production aesthetics mimicked the AOR/new-wave dichotomy: for his first two albums Prince used the full technological arsenal of the Record Plant in Sausalito, California, spending on one album nearly the entire budget that Warner Brothers had promised him for five. By contrast, Prince recorded *Dirty Mind* and *Controversy* at his home studio in Minnesota for virtually nothing. Though Warner Brothers balked at the explicit lyrics and lurid, gender-bending photos on these albums, the fact that they released them anyway speaks to the powerful allure that cheap production costs and new-wave aesthetics held for the major labels in that moment.

The period spanning these two albums was also a time when Prince's management team was pursuing crossover marketing strategies for the artist. Prince's then-publicist, Howard Bloom, wrote a now-famous memo on how best to break Prince into the mainstream charts, advocating a biracial touring strategy:

> The task is to hold his black audience while aggressively pursuing the rock and new wave audience. . . . I'd suggest booking him two dates in each market: a date as second act on the bill to a major black headliner like Cameo, Parliament, etc and a date at the local New Wave dance club. The idea is to go after the black and rock audience simultaneously. Neither date will conflict with the other.[62]

Though Prince did not implement this two-venue-per-city recommendation, he nonetheless split his tour performances between Black and white audiences.[63] For example, after spending the bulk of his *Dirty Mind* tour opening up for the well-established funk artist Rick James in large theaters, Prince did his next tour as a headliner, playing smaller theaters and rock clubs.[64] This was not an intuitive move from a business perspective: as a headliner he had less drawing power than Rick James, and by striking out on his own he was reaching fewer people with his new sound. Had he been committed to breaking into the mainstream audience with a mainstream sound, he could have gotten an opening slot for a more established, white rock act. In fact, he turned down just such an opportunity opening for the Rolling Stones: after the two disastrous opening slots he played in October 1981, Prince declined the additional string of tour dates that they had offered him.

Prince and his management seemed to be counting on the cachet that new wave had among taste-making rock writers as a new, modern movement within rock. Prince's management carefully booked him into certain hip clubs in some cities, such as the Roxy in New York, where Mick Jagger first saw Prince. These weren't just any small clubs; they were part of a growing circuit of so-called "rock discos," clubs that may have begun as either DJ-centered dance clubs during the disco boom or live rock clubs but, when popular taste shifted at the start of the 1980s, began playing new-wave records precisely because they mixed the energy and artiness of punk with the dance rhythms of disco.[65]

By 1982, the honeymoon was over between major labels and skinny ties: the industry-wide sales slump continued, and new wave lost the interest of both the major labels and the taste-making rock critics, who abandoned the genre when it went commercial. Prince similarly backed away from his punk/new-wave style after 1982, returning to a soaring, heroic hard-rock guitar style on the albums *1999* and *Purple Rain*. He also moved back to his profligrate recording habits, tracking several albums at Sunset Sound in Los Angeles before moving into his own 48-track Paisley Park recording facility, custom built in Chanhassan, Minnesota. To be sure, Prince retained some of the semiotic gender play of new wave, but he more or less abandoned the simplicity and anti-virtuosity of the retro-rockabilly guitar style as well as punk's deliberately rough recording aesthetic.

Prince's dabblings with the punk/new-wave genre seem to have been a means to an end, something that helped him avoid "falling through the cracks" of a segregated music industry in which his earlier hard-rock sound was too rock for Black radio but too Black for rock radio. The blend of disco dance rhythms and punk-rock guitar with which new-wave artists like Blondie scored crossover hits provided Prince with a recognizably rock idiom in which he could gain traction with influential critics while remaining true to his own stylistic plurality. Furthermore, new wave's gender fluidity allowed Prince to be perceived by critics as an exciting new rock artist without pandering to the two predominant sexual stereotypes of Black masculinity—effeminized or hyper-virile—with which previous generations of Black rock artists like Little Richard and Jimi Hendrix had to contend. To be sure, Prince took new wave's lesson of semiotic play to heart: new wave's mix of futurism, historical retrospection, and androgyny continued to inform his later work, becoming core elements of his identity as a performer. But the new-wave genre was one that Prince was quick to leave, along with rockabilly guitar and wearing underpants and legwarmers onstage, once he had gained a foothold with the rock audience. As an example of how decisive a shift this was, think about the soaring, virtuoso blues-rock style of guitar playing that Prince deploys throughout his seminal 1984 song "Purple Rain," an arena-rock anthem if there ever was one. As Minneapolis journalist Jon Bream revealed in a 2011 article, this was a song that Prince had first offered to none other than Stevie Nicks, former member of Fleetwood Mac, one of the biggest mainstream rock bands of the 1970s—who demurred—before he recorded and released it himself.[66]

TWO | Cyborgs, Sex, and Synthesizers

In pop music history, many cities are associated with particular "sounds"—for example, the Detroit sound of Motown in the early 1960s with its symphonic approach to rhythm and blues, or the 1990s Seattle sound with its combination of heavy metal guitar and the do-it-yourself outsider ethos of punk rock. In the early 1980s, Minneapolis was one such city, and for a time the "Minneapolis sound" dominated both *Billboard*'s Hot Black Singles and mainstream Hot 100 pop singles charts. The "Minneapolis sound" emerged from the funk and R&B scene on the city's predominantly African American Northside, and it went on to exert a huge influence on the sound of R&B and pop nationally in the mid-1980s.

Though precise definitions of the 1980s "Minneapolis sound" vary, most Minneapolis musicians would agree that it is based in the funk genre, it incorporates elements of new-wave rock, and that synthesizers play an essential role. In his liner notes to a compilation of late-1970s Minneapolis funk and R&B, writer Jon Kirby describes the nascent Minneapolis sound as "a slick, black, technologically advanced genre fusion" that was partly the result of "the full embrace of synthesizers by the region's plastic-ticklers."[1] This local trend intensified after Prince's breakout success with *Purple Rain* in 1984, as musicians flocked to the city in an effort to capitalize on the Minneapolis sound. A 1988 *Washington Times* article by David Mills captured this milieu: "The Twin Cities were crawling with Prince clones in the wake of 'Purple Rain.' And yes, some got record deals. Exotic Storm is often cited as a band that got signed expressly because it had the Prince look, the Prince sound—that nasty, synth-driven funk groove—and because it was based in Minneapolis."[2] The fact that Minneapolis was crawling with record label scouts highlights the fact that, for a time, Prince's brand of "nasty, synth-driven funk groove" ruled the airwaves. Janet Jackson's 1986 *Control* album was produced in Minneapolis by former Prince associates Jimmy Jam and Terry Lewis, and Minneapolis artist Alexander O'Neal topped the R&B charts in 1987 with several synthesizer-driven songs also produced by Jam and Lewis. Prince's engineer/producer David Z. Rivkin and former bassist André Cymone produced hits for the Jets and Jody Watley, and Paula Abdul's chart-topping 1988 album *Forever Your Girl* contained several songs cowritten and produced by Prince associate St. Paul Peterson.[3] Artists unconnected to Minneapolis began emulating this synthesizer-driven, funk-influenced pop sound, and by the mid-1980s the charts were thick with Minneapolis-sounding songs by non-Minneapolis artists, including Ready for the World's 1985 crossover hit "Oh Sheila," Phil Collin's 1985 hit "Sussudio," and George Michael's 1987 hit "I Want Your Sex." Even as Prince burnished his reputation as a rock guitar hero, his city's synthesizer-driven sound dominated the musical *zeitgeist.*

Prince was an accomplished keyboard player who began teaching himself to play on his father's piano at seven or eight years of age, long before he picked up any other instrument. Prince reportedly spent hours at the keyboard seeking comfort and escape from a tumultuous childhood, especially after his musician father left the family—and his piano—behind.[4] When Prince began his professional career—recording demos in Minneapolis with the backing of his first manager, and then recording his first album in California after being signed to the Warner Brothers label—he gravitated to the new polyphonic synthesizers that were entering the market.[5] On his first two albums he used synths alongside more common keyboard instruments like the Hohner Clavinet and the Fender Rhodes electric piano, but with 1980's *Dirty Mind* Prince began to rely almost exclusively on the novel timbres that he was coaxing out of his Oberheim and ARP synthesizers with the help of Minneapolis synth guru Roger Dumas. Prince built the title tracks of both 1980's *Dirty Mind* and its 1981 follow-up, *Controversy*, around prominent synthesizer riffs, and by the time he released his 1982 album, *1999*, he was using synthesizers to the exclusion of traditional electro-acoustic keyboards: only two of *1999*'s songs contain any electric piano or organ at all.

Prince was by no means the first pop musician to exploit the power of synthesizers: by the late 1970s, synths had been adopted by artists in a variety of genres, from the virtuosic solos of progressive rockers like Keith Emerson to the disaffected simplicity of new-wave artists like Gary Numan and the Human League.[6] Nor was Prince the first African American artist to bring synthesizers into the funk or R&B genres: Stevie Wonder, Herbie Hancock, and Bernie Worrell of Parliament-Funkadelic were all early adopters who used Minimoog and ARP Odyssey synthesizers to create burbling basslines and spooky solos that expressed the joys and traumas of urban Black life in the early 1970s.[7] And Prince was by no means the sole creator of the Minneapolis sound, as Kirby's *Purple Snow* compilation shows: Minneapolis funk artists like Lipps, Inc., Mind & Matter, and Flyte Tyme all incorporated electronic keyboards into their music, and the funk sounds emanating from clubs like the Nacirema, the Taste Show Lounge, and The Way Community Center—where Prince and his contemporaries cut their teeth on the city's predominantly Black Northside—were punctuated by synthesizers throughout the later 1970s.[8]

The innovation in Prince's early 1980s synthesizer work was how he used the transformative power of synthesizers—their timbral mutability and newfound polyphonic capacity—to adapt and defamiliarize funk and R&B while at the same time using technology's nexus of pleasure and danger to create an uncanny cyborg persona that alienated and undermined stereotypes of Black masculinity. Analog synthesizers were powerful tone-creation tools when they entered the commercial market in the 1970s, but they had technical limitations and negative cultural associations that made them a hard sell for many musicians and audiences. Sounds had to be programmed by hand, and the first analog synthesizers were monophonic, capable of producing only one pitch at a time. Synthesizers also threatened the traditional model of music production by replacing the sounds of acoustic instruments and eliminating the jobs of the musicians who played them. This power to disrupt and alienate was precisely what Prince exploited in his music. Firstly, Prince used synthesizers to disrupt the racially segregated genre structure of the American music industry, where white-identified rock music was idiomatically associated with the sound of distorted electric guitar and Black-identified genres like funk and R&B were marked by horns. Secondly, Prince used synthesizers to exploit the technological trope of the uncanny, in a way similar to Daphne Brooks's concept of "Afro-alienation acts," by creating musical narratives about cyborgs and sex that disturbed "cultural perceptions of identity formation" even while they made audiences dance.[9]

Prince was not the first funk artist to adopt synthesizers, but his sound was markedly different from forebears like Stevie Wonder, Bernie Worrell, and Herbie Hancock, and from Minneapolis contemporaries like Flyte Tyme, Herman Jones, or the Lewis Connection. Per Nilsen, past editor of the fan magazine *Uptown* and Prince's chief biographer, described Prince's version of the Minneapolis sound as follows:

> The arrangements are sparse and predominantly synth-based. Prince uses the synth as the main instrument, playing chords, fills, and lead lines, showing that synths were for more than making weird sound effects or playing solos. His technique of layering synths and incorporating fluid synth lines, often replacing traditional horn lines, became known as the "Minneapolis sound."[10]

Using synthesizers to create not only monophonic lead and bass lines but also *chords* was perhaps the most novel aspect of Prince's sound, and it was the result of a happy historical accident: Prince began his recording career at the same time that the first *polyphonic* synthesizers, capable of playing multiple notes simultaneously, entered the commercial market. By making it possible to play four-note chords and harmonized melodies in addition monophonic solos and bass lines, Prince had a tool with which he could fill out the middle ground of his funk arrangements without hiring a horn section. Furthermore, the sonic mutability of analog synthesizers allowed Prince to create timbres that fulfilled the function of other instruments without directly mimicking their sounds, allowing Prince to exploit the uncanny valley between familiar and foreign.

In a 1978 interview with his hometown newspaper, Prince all but admitted to adopting synthesizers as a means of avoiding horns.

> We originally planned to use horns, but it's really hard to sound different if you use the same instruments. By not using horns on the record, I could make an album that would sound different right away. So I created a different kind of horn section by multi-tracking the synthesizers and some guitar lines. I got hip to Polymoogs . . . when I was here working at Sound 80. I liked them a lot. I was trying to get away from using the conventional sound of pianos and clavinets as keyboards, as the main keyboards, so I thought I would try to use that [synthesizer] as the main keyboard on a few songs—and it worked.[11]

Prince had good reason to seek out a different sound in 1978, given the music industry's structural racism. At that time, the five major-label record companies assigned the development and marketing of "Black" musical genres like R&B, soul, funk, and disco to separate departments or subsidiary labels, moving Black artists into the pop department only after they had demonstrated significant sales potential to mainstream (read: white) audiences.[12] Idiomatically, the presence of a horn section was a powerful marker of Black genres: harkening back to the 1960s popularity of Stax Records' "Memphis sound" and James Brown's early funk, horns remained central in Black musical styles of the 1970s, including the funk of Parliament-Funkadelic, the funk-jazz of Earth, Wind & Fire, and the soul produced by Al Bell, Isaac Hayes, and Norman Whitfield.[13] At the same time, the fuzzy sound of an overdriven electric guitar had, despite its origins in the R&B genre, been so thoroughly appropriated by Anglo-American rock artists that it had become "a privileged signifier of white male power and potency."[14]

Given this racialized genre segregation, it's easy to interpret Prince's decisions to avoid horns and foreground rock guitar as calculated appeals to the AOR audience. Yet promoting himself solely as a rock artist would have meant "falling through the cracks" of a music industry unwilling to promote an unknown Black artist on mainstream rock radio *or* an unknown rock artist on Black radio, as discussed in chapter 1.[15] What Prince needed was a new sound that was neither horn nor guitar—an unmarked third term—that he could use to disrupt the semiotic dichotomy of Black R&B versus white rock, and synthesizers gave him that.

In the late 1970s synthesizers were still sufficiently new that they did not have firmly established musical roles or cultural meanings—technology theorists Pinch and Trocco called them "liminal objects"—yet they carried a frisson of science fiction's apocalyptic danger.[16] In his early career leading up to *Purple Rain*, Prince leveraged this liminal power in order to carve out a new space for himself—and his audience—within the racially segregated landscape of the American music industry. On his first two albums, Prince used the earliest polyphonic synthesizers in a way that was idiomatically similar to how a 1960s R&B band or a 1970s funk band would have used horns, as I will show in my analysis of the song "Soft and Wet," while at the same time defamiliarizing the R&B horn idiom, disrupting the sonic-racial binarism. Yet this was just a first step: synthesizers were more than a timbral disguise for Prince, and after these first two albums he explored bold new uses of the technology. As I will discuss, analog synthesizers could be used to create both previously unheard new timbres and passable imitations of existing instruments, and this combination of novelty and familiarity gave them an uncanny power. On a career-defining string of albums from the early 1980s—encompassing 1980's *Dirty Mind*, 1981's *Controversy*, and 1982's *1999*—Prince used synthesizers to construct a disruptive, anti-Freudian cyborg identity, an act of "Afro-Alienation" that he used to defamiliarize and critique stereotypes of Black male identity and gendered tropes of technology in Western society.[17]

Synthesizers: Transformative Technology

In order to understand how Prince used synthesizers we need to first understand how analog, aka "subtractive," synthesis worked, and synthesizers' place in the American music industry at the time. Analog synthesizers entered the commercial music market in 1970, when American manufacturers Moog and ARP released the first models that were inexpensive and portable enough to appeal to working musicians (the Minimoog and the 2600, respectively).[18] Popular musicians were by this time well accustomed to electric keyboards such as the Fender Rhodes piano and Farfisa electric organ, and the early use of synthesizers owed something to the established performance practice of these earlier keyboards. Yet the increased sonic mutability that defined analog synthesizers exacerbated a latent tension in electronic keyboard technology between familiar, imitative timbres and novel, previously unheard sounds.

What set synthesizers apart from older keyboards was an entirely electronic three-stage signal pathway that gave users tone-creation powers previously unavailable outside of academic electronic-music laboratories. In the first stage, a circuit called a voltage-controlled oscillator (VCO) transforms wall current into a soundwave whose pitch varies with the voltage of a second current from a keyboard controller (the control voltage). In order to add richness to what would otherwise be a thin-sounding waveform, all early synthesizer models used *two* oscillators fed by the same control voltage: analog VCOs were manually tuned, and the paired VCOs would create a waveform rich with microtonal interference and upper harmonic partials even if they were tuned to the same pitch. Furthermore, each VCO could also be set to produce one of several different waveforms, from a simple sinusoid oscillation to a more complex sawtooth or square/pulse waveforms, adding another source of timbral richness.

In the second stage, this aggregate soundwave passes through one or more voltage-controlled filter (VCF) circuits, each of which attenuates a selected frequency range (hence the term "subtractive synthesis"). In the third stage, a voltage-controlled amplifier (VCA) determines the output volume. Analog synthesizers also contained two other circuits—a low-frequency oscillator (or LFO) and an envelope generator—that added more expressive control by altering the control voltage going to any of the three main circuits (VCO, VCA, or VCF). The LFO is an extra oscillator with variable speed and depth; by feeding this alternating current into the control voltage of another circuit (rather than the audio signal), the user could add trills or pitch vibrato (by oscillating the control voltage of the VCO), dynamic vibrato (by oscillating the VCA), or sweeping changes in tone like that of a wah-wah pedal (when applied to the VCF). Lastly, the envelope generator creates a multistage "envelope" that changes the control voltage over time (attack, sustain, decay and release is the typical four-stage configuration), allowing the user to give shape to the dynamic or frequency profile of each note. For example: when applied to the VCA, an envelope generator allows the user to mimic the variations in loudness that notes have when played on an acoustic instrument; when applied to the VCF, it can change a frequency filter from low to high, creating a "wah" sound in the same way that a brass player can do with a plunger mute.

Because they could only produce one note at a time, early analog synthesizers didn't replace existing electro-acoustic keyboards and instead took their place alongside them in a working keyboard player's rig. Much as the modern trap set represents an assortment of different drum practices that coalesced over time, the 1970s keyboard player's "rig" was a collection of keyboards, each with a different sound and history. Here, for example, is Matt Fink, the first keyboard player whom Prince hired, describing his rig at the time he entered Prince's touring band:

> In those days you'd have your Minimoog, and then you'd have your Fender Rhodes piano, and you'd have your organ, and then usually you had your string machine of some kind. At first I started out with an Elka string machine, and then from there I bought a Freeman. . . . And then I got the [ARP] String Ensemble too, later. . . . I kept swapping out gear and upgrading. . . . [Later] I brought the [Hohner] Clavinet in . . . I was still 20 years old at the time, and [Prince] hired me to be in the group after I auditioned in November of 1978. So I went into that with my Minimoog and my Rhodes and all that equipment.[19]

As Fink mentions, the monophonic Minimoog synthesizer (or its ARP 2600 competitor) took its place alongside several other instruments in any working keyboard player's arsenal, becoming part of an already well-developed performance practice. One element of this practice that particularly shaped the way synths were used was that players used electric keyboards both as imitations of familiar-sounding instruments and as sources of new, unfamiliar timbres. The older electro-acoustic keyboards—electric piano, electric organ, and the so-called string machine—were first marketed as portable, electrified imitations of difficult-to-transport acoustic instruments (the piano, organ, and string orchestra, respectively). The Fender Rhodes and Hohner Clavinet were mallet-action keyboards with electromagnetic pickups: the Rhodes, which used metal tonebars, was introduced as a piano substitute during World War II; Hohner brought its mallet-and-string-action Clavinet to market in the 1960s to capitalize on the Baroque music revival's vogue for harpsichords. The original Hammond organ was marketed to churches as an affordable imitation of a pipe-organ (where it became an important part of gospel music), and the 1954 advent of transistors allowed cheaper, lighter electric organs like the Vox and Farfisa to flood into many other pop genres. The "string machines" that Fink mentions were simply another class of electric organs whose oscillators were set to mimic the smooth waveform and legato dynamic envelope of bowed stringed instruments; these were in a sense proto-synthesizers, with the advantage of multi-note polyphony—owing to their fixed-pitch design, which used twelve oscillators pre-tuned to the chromatic scale, and divide-down circuit architecture—but with the limitation of a thin-sounding timbre and no advanced filters or envelope controls.

Though introduced as imitations of their acoustic namesakes, keyboard players coaxed their electric pianos, organs, and string machines into producing innovative new sounds. Before he became famous for his Monster Moog synthesizer solos, progressive rocker Keith Emerson added overdrive to his Hammond B3 organ to get an aggressive, distorted sound.[20] The Hohner Clavinet, with its strings and electromagnetic pickups, produced a timbre so similar to an electric guitar that many players ran its output through guitar-effect pedals, leading to innovative sounds like the wah-Clavinet featured on Stevie Wonder's "Superstition." Similarly, players exploited the bell-like treble tone of the Fender Rhodes electric piano by running it through stereo effects like phasing or flanging, creating the shimmering piano-cum-glockenspiel sounds featured on songs like Minnie Riperton's "Loving You."

This tension between mimetic imitation and novelty informed the way that players used the new synthesizer keyboards that they added to their rigs in the early 1970s. Indeed, the question of what synthesizers were *for*—imitating preexisting sounds or creating new ones—was present from the very birth of the analog synth. The inventor of the VCO himself, Don Buchla, believed that the technology should *not* be used to imitate preexisting sounds, and he didn't even include a keyboard controller on his famous Buchla Boxes.[21] Nonetheless, the relative ease with which brass, woodwind, and stringed-instrument waveforms could be reproduced meant that analog synthesizers made the sounds of orchestral instruments available at a fraction of the usual cost, and commercial music producers were quick to exploit this potential. For instance, with an envelope generator on the VCA circuit, one can easily set a fast but soft attack, fast and loud decay, no sustain, and immediate release to emulate a pizzicato string sound; by setting the envelope generator to a fast and loud attack with a rapid decay and release (but at higher volume levels) one can simulate the sharp stab of a brass instrument; and by using a flat volume envelope and a light low-frequency oscillation on the pitch one can create a close facsimile of an electric organ sound. This kind of imitative synthesis became common enough among working keyboard players that manufacturers built and marketed certain models of synthesizer, like the ARP Solina, that were specifically aimed at users who wanted synthetic violin, woodwind, and brass timbres.[22]

When the Oberheim company introduced the first true polyphonic synthesizers in 1975, it became possible for a synthesizer to replace, rather than just augment, one or all of the instruments in a keyboard player's rig.[23] For an artist like Prince, who preferred to record by himself rather than hiring studio musicians, and who was searching for a new sound that distinguished him from the traditional timbres of R&B, this was a perfect solution. After an initial period of writing and recording with the proprietor of Moon Sound Studios in Minneapolis, Prince gained the support of a management company run by Owen Husney and began recording demos at the larger Sound 80 Studios. There, he gained access not only to a twenty-four-track mixing console (handy for Prince's overdub-heavy, one man band *modus operandi*) but also to an Oberheim Four-Voice synthesizer, owing to the presence of a consulting engineer named Roger Dumas. Dumas, a former employee of the ARP company, opened the first full-service synthesizer retailer in Minneapolis—Roger Dodger Music—and subsequently supplied Prince with many new models of synthesizer into the late 1980s.[24] When Prince signed his major-label contract and began recording his first album at the Record Plant in California, he continued using Oberheim polyphonic synths and the programming knowledge Dumas had given him.

The main innovation of the Oberheim polyphonic synthesizer was its keyboard controller, which could drive up to eight separate synthesizer modules (or SEMs) by routing the control-voltage from each key to a different module based on the order in which the keys of a chord were depressed. This meant that each multi-voice Oberheim was really just a number of monophonic synths (four or eight) built onto a single chassis (or, in later models, soldered onto the same circuit-board) and sharing a single keyboard. Each SEM unit had its own dedicated controls—two VCOs, one LFO, one VCF, and two ASR envelope generators—allowing the user to assign each separate pitch in a chord to a separate timbre (though later models allowed users to control all the SEMs at once), and each SEM also had its own audio output, making it easy to record and mix each voice on a separate track.[25] Furthermore, after 1976 the Oberheim Four-Voice offered a rudimentary memory bank called the "programmer"—an item that Dumas remembered Prince buying—that allowed users to save four timbres per SEM (sixteen in total), making this and subsequent Oberheim models more practical for live performance.[26] Prince used the Four-Voice and successive Oberheim models, including the 1979 OB-X, the 1981 OB-Xa, and the 1983 OB-8, on the road until 1984 or '85, according to Matt Fink, making them a defining part of his sound.[27]

Though Oberheim's brute-force approach to creating polyphonic synthesizers was eclipsed by later innovations such as digital frequency-modulating synthesizers like the Yamaha DX-7 and sampling keyboards like the E-Mu (both of which Prince purchased, according to Dumas), its introduction of polyphony was the proverbial shot heard around the world in the recording industry.[28] When Fred Wesley, longtime arranger and trombonist in James Brown's band, realized that Prince recorded his first album entirely by himself with the help of synthesizers, he heard it as a death-knell for horn and string players in the music industry—"Synthesized horns, synthesized strings, and percussion. The real bad thing about the album was that it was very funky and sounded very good"—and he was not wrong.[29]

This first part of Prince's career, when he developed and gained fame with his Minneapolis sound, coincided with the specific period in synthesizer history when analog models still dominated the industry and polyphony was first being introduced. This was a time when synthesizer timbres still had to be programmed by hand, and as such, the timbral decisions that Prince made on his Oberheims convey meaning just as much as the melodies and harmonies he played with them. In addition to its polyphonic capacity, Prince was attracted to the Oberheim for two reasons, according to Roger Dumas. First, Dumas's memory was that Prince preferred "relatively pure tones" that he could get without too much programming of the filter or dynamic envelopes.[30] The Oberheim's oscillators offered rich timbres that were easy to program with minimal effort: instead of the triangle, square, and sawtooth waveforms options of ARP and Moog keyboards, Oberheim oscillators offered just sawtooth or pulse-wave options, the latter of which featured a variable pulse-width control that gave the pulse waveform greater timbral variability.[31] Second, Dumas remembered that Prince liked the programmability that the polyphonic Oberheim's four separate SEMs offered:

> As far as programming synthesizers for Prince, [Prince] always wanted to have something that was not referential . . . He wanted to have something different, which is why he chose programmable synthesizers . . .
>
> . . . We would set up this Oberheim Four-Voice with a slightly different sound on every one of the [SEM] modules. And he wanted it to sound like an ensemble, but not an ensemble of horns. . . . I'm sure he listened to a lot of James Brown, and knew that he wanted that effect, but not that instrument.[32]

As the above quote indicates, Dumas remembers Prince approaching the synthesizer with the goal of sounding different, which entailed avoiding overtly referential sounds such as horns. Dumas also points out that Prince exploited the Oberheim's unique multi-timbral brand of polyphony, treating the instrument more as a section of related timbres than as a single unified sound like a keyboard instrument. And while Dumas's memory is that Prince did not want imitative sounds, it is interesting that as renowned a horn arranger as Fred Wesley *did* hear Prince's arrangements as "synthesized horns, [and] synthesized strings."[33] With this lacuna in mind, let us consider one of the first songs that Prince recorded using synthesizers, "Soft and Wet." How does the tension between imitative and new sounds play out in the song, and how does Prince's use of the synthesizer compare to what a traditional horn section would have provided?

The Synthetic and the Organic: "Soft and Wet"

"Soft and Wet" was among the first batch of songs that Prince recorded, first at Moon Sound studio in 1976, then at Sound 80 in 1977, and in its final album form at the Record Plant in Sausalito, California, in 1977. The two demo versions of the song (from Moon Sound and Sound 80) are available as bootlegs, and the arrangement and synthesizer timbres are remarkably consistent with the officially released album version, a fact also attested by Dumas, who worked on "Soft and Wet" with Prince at Sound 80.[34] In this song, we can hear both the influence of the R&B horn idiom and also the germinal seed of the uncanny technological trope that came to dominate Prince's early 1980s work. Prince mixes familiar and unfamiliar timbres, mining the mimetic tension inherent in synthesizers to defamiliarize the timbral markers of R&B.

On first listen, "Soft and Wet" is typical of funk-influenced pop music of the period. The song is strophic with a repeating chord progression. The sections consist of regular four- and eight-bar phrases, and the groove is made up of instrumental ostinati that interlock to form a danceable polyrhythmic groove. The instrumentation, too, is typical, up to a point: the rhythm section includes bass, drums, and rhythm guitar, and Prince uses a Hohner Clavinet keyboard treated with an envelope-filter effect, similar to what Stevie Wonder used on "Higher Ground." But while these background timbres are familiar staples of late 1970s R&B/funk, the middle- and foreground instrumentation are not. Horns and electric guitar are notably absent; in their place, Prince uses three different electronic keyboards: a polyphonic Oberheim synthesizer (likely a four- or eight-voice model), a monophonic synthesizer for the solo (likely an ARP Pro Soloist), and a string machine–type electric organ. It is these electronic keyboards that occupy the space that would have otherwise been filled by horns and lead guitar, and Prince uses their timbres to create a dialectic between familiar, mimetic sounds, and sounds that are foreign and potentially threatening.

As with many pop songs, instrumentation is the chief way that Prince marks the song's structure: the rhythm section plays the same ostinato throughout, while Prince adds synthesizer motives—each with a distinctive timbre—to differentiate the vamp, verse, and bridge/solo sections. The first synth motive, which enters in measure 1 (Synth A, example 7), is an ascending pentatonic riff played on an Oberheim synthesizer.[35] Its two oscillators are tuned in parallel fourths, with the instrument's outputs panned to the far left *and* right of the stereo spectrum at high vol-

Example 7. "Soft and Wet," introduction / vamp

ume. (This motive is present in both demo versions and the album version of the song.) The second synth motive (Synth B, example 7) answers the first with a falling gesture at a much softer volume and in the center of the stereo field, using an Oberheim timbre whose two oscillators are detuned to a dissonant interval relative to each other, making its pitch content difficult to discern. (This second synth motive is absent from the earlier demos and only appears on the Warner Brothers version.) These two motives form a call-response gesture that structurally marks the vamp sections between each verse. The song does not have a recurring chorus section (the only contrasting sections are a bridge/solo at 1:07 and an outro at 2:38) and therefore the Synth A/B call-response motive takes the place of a chorus, making it structurally prominent.

Prince uses two older electronic keyboards alongside the Oberheim synthesizer: a string machine, and an ARP Pro Soloist. During the song's second verse (at 0:42), the legato sound of the string machine enters. This Synth C motive (example 8) is a monophonic line that pads the high-treble register: with its thin, tinny timbre, slow attack, and long sustain, Synth C is easy to recognize as an ARP Solina string ensemble like the one Prince's keyboard player Matt Fink mentioned. Rounding out the list of electronic keyboards, Prince uses a monophonic ARP Pro Soloist synthesizer to deliver a virtuosic solo during the bridge/solo section (at 1:32).[36]

Example 8. "Soft and Wet," verse 2

These four electronic keyboard parts are played using distinct synthesizer timbres with different degrees of familiarity or unfamiliarity relative to the pop-music idioms of the late 1970s. String machines, such as the one Prince used to create the Synth C part, were well established in disco, funk, and new-wave rock, where they tended to be used for harmonic padding (e.g. the Bee Gees' "Nights on Broadway") or legato melodies (e.g. Parliament-Funkadelic's "Tear the Roof Off the Sucker" or Joy Division's "Love Will Tear Us Apart"). Thus, Synth C would likely have been familiar to Prince's audience in both timbre and idiom, despite its uncanny artificial timbre, which resembles a violin in its envelope but lacks the rich upper partials and multi-stage dynamic shaping of a real violin.

The other three synth timbres featured in "Soft and Wet" are idiomatically harder to place, occupying a gray area somewhere between the function of electric organ and horn section. The ARP Pro Soloist timbre that Prince uses in the keyboard solo (Synth D, example 11) would likely have been familiar to fans of rock and funk alike. Introduced in 1972, the ARP Pro Soloist was a monophonic analog synthesizer favored by progressive rock keyboardists like Tony Banks for virtuosic solos (e.g. Genesis's "Cinema Show"), and also used by R&B, jazz-fusion, and funk artists such as Billy Preston, Herbie Hancock, and Bernie Worrell for solos and basslines.[37] What identifies it as a true synthesizer is its fat, mellow, high-frequency profile—rich in upper partial tones—that contrasts the thin tinny timbre of the string machine; this, combined with a slight phase-shifting effect, is a hallmark of the two-oscillator design

Example 11. "Soft and Wet," synthesizer solo (second bridge)

Example 12. "Soft and Wet," synth solo play-out

Example 13. "Superstition," chorus play-out (concert pitch)

of analog synths. The relatively simple dynamic envelope and smooth waveform, combined with an after-touch vibrato effect, are particularly characteristic of the ARP Pro Soloist model, which was one of the earliest synthesizers to include preset imitative timbres, one of which—the "French Horn" setting—matches the sound of Prince's Synth D.

The solo that Prince plays using the Pro Soloist idiomatically blends a hard-rock guitar or progressive-rock keyboard with an R&B horn. On one hand, Prince opens the solo with a slow, lyrical passage that grows out of Prince's falsetto vocal line, and he winds down the solo with a near-quote of the slow trumpet motive from Stevie Wonder's "Superstition" (example 12 and example 13), putting listeners in mind of a horn section. (This winding-down gesture is absent from the earlier demo recordings and appears only on the Warner Brothers version.) On the other hand, the twelve-bar solo climaxes with a display of virtuosity that would have been at home in a progressive-rock keyboard solo or a hard-rock guitar solo. The gestures of this solo—descending arpeggiated chords played in fast, sixteenth-note triplets followed by rapid scalar runs in thirty-second notes—call to mind the classical keyboard or violin idioms that inspired progressive-rock and heavy-metal musicians of the era, who drew upon the prestige and rhetorical power of classical virtuosity.[38] Using the synthesizer solo this way—part trumpet, part virtuoso guitar or electric organ—was relatively familiar in the 1970s, given the prominent place that funk artists like Stevie Wonder had given to ARP synthesizers as solo instruments. Yet it points toward the disconnection of timbre from instrumental idiom: Prince used an imitative timbre—one that his own keyboardist Matt Fink described as a "flutey, horn-type tone"—to play arpeggios and scales that could scarcely be played on a flute or French horn, but which would sound (and feel) natural when played on an organ, violin, or electric guitar.[39] It is this idiomatic slipperiness, the synthesizer's ability to move between lyrical, horn-like passages and the virtuosic intricacy of an organ toccata or heavy-metal guitar solo—all the while using a timbre that sounds like an electronic simulacrum of a French horn and flute—that gave synthesizers their uncanny power.

If the ARP Pro Soloist synthesizer and string machine timbres hint at a disconnection of timbre from instrumental idiom (but were nonetheless familiar to listeners), Prince's Oberheim synthesizer timbres widen the disconnect. The two Oberheim patches that Prince used are timbrally foreign, even harsh sounding, while the lines they play are recognizably indebted to the function of a horn section. In contrast to the relatively imitative timbre of the ARP Pro Soloist that Prince used for the Synth D part, the two timbres used for Synth A and B sound uncanny or mechanical. Synth A has a brass-like dynamic envelope, but from there Prince defamiliarized the sound. Perhaps the most characteristic aspect of a brass instrument's timbre—its brassiness—comes from its dynamic envelope, which has a sharp attack that quickly attenuates to a slightly lower sustain volume and stops immediately when the player releases the note. Prince gave Synth A precisely this profile using the Oberheim's ASR envelope generator; however, Prince tuned the synthesizer's two oscillators a fourth apart, giving the Synth A riff a foreign quality, evoking medieval plainchant or the Western compositional trope of parallel fourths as shorthand for Asian exoticism. Also, the oscillators are set to a noisy waveform that sounds like a sawtooth, and the resonant filter is run through an ASR envelope generator in such a way that tone moves rapidly from dark to bright after the attack of each note, adding a subtle "mwee" effect.[40] The result is a timbre that combines traces of multiple instruments—it is growly and rich in its upper-partial tones, like a distorted guitar; it has a strident, brassy dynamic attack and a vowel-like filter shape, like a muted trumpet—yet is obviously artificial and foreign owing to its waveform and parallel-fourth tuning.

The Synth B timbre is a similar blend of familiar and foreign. The two oscillators are detuned by an interval something like a wide major second or a narrow minor third (I have notated it as a parallel whole step in example 7). The waveform of the oscillators sounds hollow, devoid of the upper partials that confer richness and warmth, and there is no audible envelope-shaping on the filter or amplifier circuits, giving each note an unnatural dynamic uniformity. Furthermore, there is a low-frequency oscillator on the pitch, giving every note a wide, slow vibrato. By itself, LFO vibrato is often used by keyboard players to give timbres a more organic feel because it imitates the vibrato that a string or wind player might add to a note; but when combined with the parallel dissonant interval of the two oscillators, the LFO vibrato destroys the illusion that a human being could ever play it on an acoustic instrument. Though the riff that Prince plays on the Synth B timbre is a simple descending pentatonic fill that any organ player might throw in at the end of a measure (it moves from tonic to flat seventh to dominant, A♭–G♭–E♭), the parallel dissonance, unnatural vibrato, and cold, hollow-sounding waveform give the timbre a mechanical quality that defamiliarizes the melodic gesture, taking what might have been a common funk riff—the "response" of a call-and-response pattern—and making it sound like a robotic simulacrum of horns.

To better understand why Prince's Synth A and B motives resemble a horn section, we need a provisional definition of the "horn section" idiom. At the risk of flattening the differences between R&B, soul, and funk, we can identify some general patterns in horn arrangements by looking back to the foundational 1960s work of the Stax Records Memphis Horns and at James Brown's horn arrangements.[41] In this repertoire, horns had several important functions. In the musical foreground, horns often introduce important melodic hooks during the introduction section, play solos, and perform prearranged soli (a harmonized melodic line played by a group of horns) during a bridge section. In the middleground, horns deploy a vocabulary of short, repeating melodic "riffs" and isolated rhythmic "shots" or "stabs" to create countermelodies and call-and-response rhythmic interactions with the other instruments; and in the background, horns can provide long sustained "pads" that add harmonic support without overshadowing the vocals, in the same way that a string section might also provide background padding in a soul recording.[42] What governed the deployment of these techniques, according to musicologist Rob Bowman, were the principles of addition and contrast. In Stax arrangements, horns typically vary their vocabulary to mark the different sections of a song, for instance by playing a riff during the choruses but padding during the verses. Horns would then create a sense of narrative progression through accretion, such as by remaining tacet during the first verse, adding a riff to the second verse, and augmenting that riff with additional shots and pads during subsequent verses.[43]

These are all techniques that we hear performed on electronic keyboards in "Soft and Wet." Prince used the Solina string ensemble to provide background padding (Synth C, example 8), the Oberheim to fill out the middle-ground with hooks, riffs (Synth A and Synth B, example 7) and stabs, and the Pro Soloist for a foreground solo (Synth D, example 13). The Oberheim's Synth A and Synth B riffs provide a characteristic call-and-response pattern, with Synth A's upward pentatonic query answered by Synth B's downward cadential gesture. Furthermore, Prince used these synthesizers to give the sections structural contrast and to create narrative progression via the use of additive texture, as any R&B/funk horn arrangement would do. The Oberheim's two riffs, Synth A and Synth B, differentiate the song's verses from the introduction and interstitial vamp sections, which are otherwise identical but for the vocals. Prince then adds layers on top of this: the Solina string ensemble adds padding to verses 2 and 4, creating structural differentiation and forward momentum. This momentum culminates in the song's bridge and solo: these are the only sections that move to a different harmonic area (the relative minor) from the verse and vamps, and Prince creates a sense of mounting excitement by adding one- and two-note synthesizer shots and a two-voiced cadential riff at the end, both played by the Oberheim's Synth A timbre (example 9). This two-note polyphony makes the analogy to a horn section even clearer, and Prince plays this section twice, once underneath the bridge vocals and then again underneath the Synth D solo. Finally, Prince caps the song with a syncopated two-bar riff, in two-voiced harmony, repeated over the outro by the Oberheim's Synth A timbre (Example 10). The effect is structurally analogous to the two-bar horn riffs that repeat over the fade-out of earlier soul and funk songs like Wilson Pickett's "Midnight Hour" or James Brown's "Out of Sight."

Example 9. "Soft and Wet," bridge

Example 10. "Soft and Wet," coda

What Prince has accomplished with his electronic keyboards is to take the vocabulary of horn shots, riffs, pads, solos, and soli familiar from two decades of R&B, soul, and funk music and render them unfamiliar or alien with the use of technology. In particular, the two Oberheim voices that Prince uses in the song (Synth A and B) combine familiar with foreign qualities. As I have argued, Prince used these voices in an idiomatically similar way to an R&B or funk horn section, and the timbre of Synth A has the characteristically sharp attack envelope of a brass instrument. Yet this is where Prince's defamiliarization began: while Synth A has a brassy envelope, its parallel-fourth tuning and mechanical-sounding waveform render it uncanny, a mixture of familiar and artificial. Prince goes even further with the Synth B riff: though Synth B behaves idiomatically like a horn, Prince gives it a hollow sounding mechanical waveform and detunes its two oscillators to a dissonant interval, rendering it almost musically unrecognizable.

Synth B blurs the line between musical motive and sound-effect, a fact which makes it easy to dismiss from an analytical perspective, yet it is an insistent germ, a moment that performs in miniature the cultural work that Prince was doing by defamiliarizing the idioms that he had inherited. The Synth B motive's descending 1–♭7–5 gesture is not one of the song's more important melodic hooks; it's an unremarkable funk riff, and it feels like an afterthought owing to the fact that Prince did not include it in either of the two demo versions he recorded. Yet Prince's antiphonal placement of Synth B in response to Synth A means that, for all its denatured sound, it still reads as a transformation of a call-and-response R&B horn riff: familiar, but rendered almost unrecognizable by the power of the machine.

Throughout "Soft and Wet," Prince gives us familiar landmarks of R&B—falsetto vocals, a polyrhythmic groove, the burble of the wah-Clavinet, even the silky glide of the ARP Solina string ensemble and Pro Soloist keyboards—but defamiliarizes the landscape by introducing unfamiliar, strange-sounding polyphonic synth timbres. The antiphonal lines of Synth A and B function like horns but sound like something else, as though Prince had taken an early 1970s R&B or funk band and quietly replaced two of its members with robots. These synthetic timbres have horn-like dynamic envelopes but are otherwise strange and novel, constituting a combination of the familiar and the foreign that simultaneously invites attention and denies identification. To make a historical comparison, where guitarists like Jimi Hendrix and Muddy Waters combined their technical skills with the newest advances in guitar technology to create new sounds that were based upon, but sonically distinct from, older forms of the blues, Prince's proficiency as a keyboard player and his interest in the latest advances in music technology allowed him to create a new sound by defamiliarizing an older R&B/funk idiom, that of the horn section.[44]

In "Soft and Wet," the dynamic between familiar and unfamiliar that I am reading in the synthesizer timbres is subtle, and indeed one can easily hear the Synth A and Synth B timbres not as uncanny simulacra of the R&B horn idiom but as an update of it. The popularity of "Soft and Wet" suggests that listeners may have heard it that way: the song was a hit on the Black singles charts, reaching number 11 in 1978, though it climbed no higher than 92 on the "mainstream" Hot 100 singles chart. But Prince's technological defamiliarization of the R&B horn idiom shows the germinal beginnings of the Afrofuturism and "Afro-alienation" acts that would blossom over his next five albums. On *Dirty Mind* and *Controversy*, Prince's use of synthesizers grew bolder as he pared down his use of traditional instrumentation, losing the lush textures of late-1970s disco and R&B in favor of a stripped-down sound that foregrounded the ARP Omni and Oberheim OB-X synthesizers. To be sure, the way that Prince deployed these synthesizers continued to resemble the R&B horn idiom—with pads, riffs, stabs, solos, and soli—but his choice of timbres moved further away from anything recognizable or mimetic. By the time Prince recorded his album *1999*, he was exploring the intersection between human and machine in earnest, treading the same thematic territory as artists like Gary Numan and Devo, a move that led writers to describe Prince's music with hybrid genre names like "new-wave R&B," and "punk-funk."[45] Having discovered the potential of synthesizers for defamiliarizing the genres to which the music industry was intent on assigning him (e.g. R&B, funk, and/or disco), Prince quickly began exploring the synthesizer as a tool for building a new musical identity, one that defamiliarized stereotypes of Black masculinity by using topoi of computers, robots, and cyborgs.

Synthesizers, Afro-alienation, and the Uncanny

As synthesizers became more prevalent on the American pop charts in the late 1970s, anxiety over this new technology began to surface, and tracing this anxiety to its root will help us understand how Prince leveraged it as a source of power. Some musicians were so threatened by the ability of synthesizers to imitate acoustic instruments—and thereby replace them—that the New York chapter of the American Federation of Musicians issued a (short-lived) ban on synthesizers in recording sessions.[46] But underneath this economic argument lay a more gut-level, emotional rejection of synthesizers. Severing the physical connection between musical sounds and the physicality of traditional electro-acoustic instruments meant that synthesizers tickled Freudian fears of emasculation even as they promised empowerment for their users. As the seventies bled into the eighties, anti-synthesizer rhetoric portrayed synthesizers as unmusical devices that diminished the manliness or heterosexuality of their users. Yet this rhetoric was just the latest iteration of a latent technophobia that runs deep in Western culture, one which Prince was able to harness.

Anti synth sentiment was so common and so vitriolic that some hard-rock bands, including Queen and Boston, printed disclaimers in their album notes attesting that those recordings included no synthesizers.[47] This makes sense given the importance that hard-rock/heavy-metal fans and musicians placed on the virtuoso prowess of a lead guitar player, which enacts the power of an idealized masculinity.[48] Against this standard, synthesizers seemed like a cheat—a push-button machine operated with little effort—that violated the masculinist tenet of hard work and earned rewards. As musicologist Simon Frith argues, the backlash against synthesizers and drum machines in the 1980s was informed by a lingering romantic ideology in which "technology" opposed nature, truth, and community. According to Frith, the anti-synth arguments went like this: by eliminating the physical demands of instrumental playing, synthesizers "emasculate" the act of music-making, rendering it unnatural or dead; by making sounds unconnected to a recognizable sound-source, synthesizers are "somehow false or falsifying"; and by standing between the artist and the audience, technology interrupts the "old-fashioned model of direct communication" upon which folk- and rock-music ideals of authenticity are built.[49] Even as certain pieces of music technology became naturalized over time—the electric guitar, for instance—synthesizers were, to a 1970s rock audience, the epitome of all things inauthentic: lazy, effeminate, and soulless. Even the one type of rock that enthusiastically embraced synthesizers, progressive rock, had to overcome their feminizing stigma, which it did by invoking the athletic struggle, phallic imagery, and classically influenced virtuosity of heavy metal musicians.[50]

In the late 1970s, the two musical genres that were perhaps *most* implicated in this discursive linkage between synthesizer technology and emasculation were disco and new-wave music. If hard-rock musicians and their audiences were afraid of humans being replaced by machines in the recording studio, the rise of Eurodisco and new-wave synth-pop embraced this possibility. Starting with Eurodisco, many dance music producers used synthesizers and drum machines to streamline their studio productions (which, anecdotally at least, diminished the work available for session musicians).[51] Meanwhile, artists like Devo, Gary Numan, and the Human League swapped their guitars and live drums for synthesizers and drum machines as a way to express the disaffection of modern life, a move that distinguished what became known in

America as new wave, or synth-pop, from the post-punk milieu out of which it arose.

Eurodisco and new wave not only sounded synthetic but also hinted at sexual difference, mixing themes of mechanicity and sexuality in ways that deviated from the (white) cis-gendered, heterosexual male mainstream of American rock culture. For example, Donna Summer and Giorgio Moroder's disco hit "I Feel Love" used synthesizers and drum machines to create a model of endless sexual pleasure—a libidinal plateau, lacking the single-climax structure of a virtuoso solo—that violated the phallic model of rock music, according to musicologist Robert Fink.[52] Moreover, Summer's panting, fragmentary vocal style, combined with Moroder's fully synthetic musical texture, suggested that the sexual object of "I Feel Love" was not a proper woman, but rather an amalgam of synthetic parts—an insatiable female robot, or what Andreas Huyssen calls a machine-vamp—that violated the boundary between human and machine.[53]

Meanwhile, new-wave synth-pop pioneers like Kraftwerk, Gary Numan, and Devo crafted personas that were emotionless and androgynous while using synthesizers in simplistic, anti-virtuosic (read *un-macho*) ways. By using a one-finger playing style, combined with heavy repetition and flat dynamics, they eliminated the heroic toil-and-triumph that male musicians in the hard- and progressive-rock genres depended upon, and instead depicted nervous sexual dysfunction and/or alienating technological dystopias.[54] For example, in his 1979 song "Cars," Gary Numan uses a monotone, nasal singing style and simple, repetitive synthesizer riffs to portray a character who, alienated from people and attracted to technology, only feels safe in his car.

In both disco and new wave, this confluence of synthetic timbres, repetitive musical structures, and outsider sexuality—disco's hedonistic dance floor futurism and new wave's nervous dystopian androgyny—garnered backlash from the rock press. Rock critics in the "disco sucks" movement argued that the repetitive beat and simple structures of disco betrayed a lack of talent and a vulgar commercialism.[55] These critiques of disco were intertwined with homophobic and racist rhetoric, a fact that music historian Tim Lawrence attributes to the unease that the white male radio DJs and rock critics felt about the growing influence of gay and African American artists and club DJs.[56] New-wave or synth-pop bands fared little better in the eyes of rock critics and fans, who dismissed new wave with epithets like "Brit-fag" and "blow-wave" music.[57] In a 1982 sociological survey, American college students predominantly associated new-wave music with outsider or deviant identities, using descriptors like "repetitious," "exotic," "strange" and "kinky."[58] That same year, a *Creem* album reviewer summed up the anti-synth prejudices of many rock fans by writing, "You can't coax much in the way of emotion out of a Yamaha CS15 as compared to (author's prejudice) a Rickenbacker."[59] Even synth manufacturer Bob Moog questioned the way disco and new-wave artists were using synthesizers: in a 1981 interview, Moog dismissed the synth playing in Numan's "Cars" as "simple," and hinted that the all-synth instrumentation of Summer and Moroder's "I Feel Love" was "more show biz than music."[60] The anti-technology prejudice in American rock journalism was clear: electric guitars, technological though they may be, merely enhanced the talents that a man had worked to possess, but synthesizers yielded unearned sonic power that was stripped of human emotion, and their users were emasculated automatons.

This rhetorical association of synthesizers with soulless mechanicity and sexual deviance is emblematic of the ambivalence with which Western culture has always greeted technological change. Building on Freud's theory of prosthetics, theorist Klaus Theweleit argues that the rhetoric surrounding new technology remains neutral or positive when that technology enhances our natural abilities—like laser eye surgery or, presumably, electric guitars—but turns sharply negative when it replaces human workers' physical or intellectual labor—like robotic assembly-line workers or artificial intelligence—or when it encroaches upon our own biological reproduction, as with "test-tube babies."[61] In his analysis of Fritz Lang's *Metropolis*, technology theorist Andreas Huyssen makes a complementary point about the gendering of technology, arguing that artistic representations of robots became overwhelmingly female and sinister during the industrial revolution, a time when industrial machinery was automating the labor of factory workers, reducing men to cogs in a larger machine or replacing them outright.[62] The advent of the information age saw the same pattern repeated in white-collar industries: as cyborg theorist Jack (then Judith) Halberstam points out, Alan Turing's initial theories of computing and artificial intelligence brought him the harsh scrutiny of the American government who held thinking machines in the same suspicion that it did homosexuals and communists.[63]

This fear of technology emasculating workers—violating the boundaries of the bourgeois self, penetrating, fragmenting, and even replacing male bodies—is one that early psychologists labeled "the uncanny."

In common parlance, "uncanny" refers to a situation where an imperfect simulation of life causes a person to experience a discomfiting swing between attraction and revulsion. In its original coining, by psychologist Ernst Jentsch, the "uncanny" described a primal uncertainty over whether an apparently living thing is truly alive or if a supposedly dead object might become animate, a feeling engendered by such things as waxwork figures or mechanical automatons.[64] Freud elaborated on Jentsch's theory, focusing his analysis on a horror story in which a young man was repulsed by the discovery that the object of his desire was a robotic automaton masquerading as a woman, a discovery made more horrible by the removal of the automaton's eyes (an event that Freud linked to castration-anxiety).[65] Though Freud and Jentsch are irrelevant in modern psychology, their concept of the uncanny has proven durable, in part because of its relevance to robotics and digital animation: the "uncanny valley," a term coined by roboticist Matsumoto Mori, has become a common-parlance term for the instinctive revulsion that users feel when confronted with a robot or digitally animated character that is meant to imitate a living human but is not sufficiently lifelike.[66]

This idea of the uncanny, and the history that it encapsulates, helps us understand the power that lay at Prince's fingertips when he began experimenting with synthesizers in the late 1970s, in his demo sessions at Sound 80 in Minneapolis and his first Warner Brothers album sessions at the Record Plant in Sausalito. At that time, synthesizers were starting to engender a backlash rooted in the fear that technology would replace American workers and effeminize rock music, a fear itself rooted in the uncanny. This conflation of technological mimesis—i.e., synthetic imitations of "organic" musical instruments—with the loss of livelihood, selfhood, and manhood has a long history in Western literature and cinema, embodied most famously in the cyborg femmes fatales of Fritz Lang's *Metropolis* and Ridley Scott's *Blade Runner*; significantly, a poster of *Metropolis* hung in Prince's video editing room at Paisley Park during his lifetime (and remains there as of this writing). This uncanny quality made synthesizers toxic in the eyes of some musicians and fans but was nonetheless a source of power: progressive rockers like Keith Emerson wrestled with that power onstage as a performance of heroic masculinity, while new-wave artists like Gary Numan allowed it to infuse their entire personae with an aura of transhuman mystique.

Using synthesizers meant that Prince was invoking the anxiety engendered by this uncanny power. But rather than following the model of either progressive rock—with its heroic mastering of technology—or new wave, with its self-abnegating techno-dystopia—Prince blurred these two positions together to create a third, a hybrid, cyborg persona that matched his sound. The first step in creating this cyborg persona was his choice of synthesizer timbres. As I have discussed, Prince used synthesizers in ways that idiomatically resembled preexisting instruments—such as strings and horns—but with timbres that had obviously electronic qualities, such as buzzing sawtooth waveforms, detuned oscillators, or automated filter envelopes. By combining familiar and novel elements within the same tone Prince used the uncanny to create an alienating distance between listeners and the musical idioms they were familiar with, as we heard in "Soft and Wet."

The next step in Prince's engagement with synthesizers—and in his project of personal and musical liberation—was treating stereotypes of gender and sexuality with the same uncanny, alienating power that his synthesized sounds had already treated R&B/funk horn idioms, a strategy that resembles both the cyborg theory put forward by Halberstam and Haraway and Daphne Brooks's concept of "Afro-alienation acts."[67] Prince was already known for his hybrid musical style, which, as I argued in chapter 1, combined hard rock and R&B, genre influences that—within the context of America's segregated music industry—represented a hybrid racial identity. Prince added another axis of hybridization by embodying both masculine and feminine subject positions in his songs and visual presentation. Prince "defied ideals of heteronormativity," according to Stan Hawkins and Sarah Niblock, "by not acting out his masculinity in the 'right way.'"[68] This often involved multiple and conflicting constructions of gender: Prince did not simply adopt a feminine or androgynous mode of gender presentation, but instead used *both* macho constructions of masculinity *and* non-heteronormative ones in which he made himself the object of a sexualized male gaze.[69] On the one hand, Prince's lyrics often portrayed women as sex objects, and onstage, he often accompanied his macho guitar virtuosity with over-the-top phallic displays: one reviewer dismissed his 1981 *Dirty Mind* tour performance as "BLAMBLAMBLAM push up push up thrust thrust thrust," followed by "willie-on-a-Stratocaster wanking."[70] On the other hand, Prince enacted the polar opposite of this kind of machismo, using synthesizers to play non-virtuosic riffs, and wearing androgynous stage attire to project a campy, sexually ambiguous subject position: discussing his *1999* tour performances, *Rolling Stone*'s reviewer described him as a student of Mae West's "high camp and low-rent vamping," and *NME*'s reviewer called him a "trans-sexual flasher."[71]

In addition to Black/white and masculine/feminine hybridities, synthesizers allowed Prince to add a third axis of hybridization to his musical persona: human/machine. This science-fiction trope of robots and cyborgs had already been exploited by early new-wave synthesizer artists like Gary Numan and Devo, but Prince used it to subvert racialized gender constructions, a strategy that resembles Daphne Brooks's concept of "Afro-alienation acts," as I will discuss later in this chapter.[72] As my analyses of "Dirty Mind" and "Controversy" will show, Prince used uncanny synthesizer timbres in the context of funk—a genre rooted in African diasporic cultural values—to depict characters with robotic identities and non-heteronormative sexualities, a strategy that allowed him to defamiliarize the "sex machine" stereotype of Black male sexuality, placing it at a critical remove from audience identification.[73] Prince built an image that shocked the sexual sensibilities of bourgeois America with lyrics that touched upon oral sex, homosexuality, and even incest, with stage costumes that frequently included high heels, women's underpants and not much more, and a sound that used synthesizers both to defamiliarize R&B/funk idioms and to depict the robotic heart of the singer himself.[74] Though this man/machine cyborg identity may have escaped reviewers at the time, it is precisely the emancipatory quality of cyborgs, as theorized by Donna Haraway, that allowed Prince to create an alienation effect that defamiliarized musical, racial, and sexual stereotypes, and thereby helped him remake American pop music in his own image.[75]

Like a Sex Machine

On his third, fourth, and fifth albums, Prince expanded both his use of synthesizers and his sexual provocation, building a persona that was half man and half (sex) machine. There is a long tradition in blues, R&B, and funk of using machinery as a metaphor for male sexual power: one need only think of a few examples—Robert Johnson's "Terraplane Blues," Chuck Berry's "Maybellene," or James Brown's "Sex Machine"—to realize the well-trodden pathway down which Prince could have traveled.[76] Indeed, Prince *did* use such a metaphor in a song on the *1999* album, "Little Red Corvette," planting the topos in the listener's mind (though he turns this metaphor on its head in the subsequent song "Automatic," as I will discuss later). Yet in numerous songs from this time period Prince constructed male identities whose relationships to technology diverged sharply from the car-as-phallus cliché. Let us consider two songs from this period, the title tracks from his 1980 album *Dirty Mind* and 1981's *Controversy*. In both songs Prince identifies himself with the musical machine, linking his own sexuality to machinic qualities of tireless repetition. But Prince disrupts the boasting machismo of such metaphors by portraying his cyborg as sexually alienated or dysfunctional, placing the stereotype of Black-man-as-sex-machine at a critical distance.

"Dirty Mind" and "Controversy" both have austere arrangements built of non-imitative synthesizer timbres and not much else ("Dirty Mind" features an ARP Omni 2, according to Prince's then–keyboard player Matt Fink, while "Controversy" most likely features the Oberheim OB-X).[77] Both songs use a rhythm section of acoustic drums and clean, non-distorted electric guitar; "Controversy" has the slightly expanded palette of a second, distorted guitar line and an electric bass. But in both songs, it is the synthesizer that delivers both the main melodic hook, chordal padding, and bass line, thus dominating the high, middle, and low frequency spectra. It is in this context that Prince's persona as a sexually ambiguous cyborg takes shape.

In both songs, the synthesizer bass is the element that connects the main character's body to the power of the machine, and in both the synth-bass timbres are overtly synthetic, with buzzing, non-imitative waveforms. In "Dirty Mind," the bass plays an eighth-note pulse on the tonic (C) that overlays the kick drum, and sounds like a fast, robotic heartbeat (see example 14). In "Controversy," a conventional electric bass provides the machinic quarter-note tonic-drone heartbeat, and a louder synthesizer timbre adds rhythmic punctuation at the end of each four-bar phrase (see example 15). As cultural theorists Roland Barthes and John Mowitt have pointed out, the musical beat is a place where the internal, physical rhythm of the heartbeat is interpolated into the cultural realm of musical notation and performance practice.[78] As such, Prince's use of a synthetic-organic drumbeat-cum-heartbeat is a significant choice that communicates the cyborg hybridity of his central character.

The ARP Omni 2 that Prince used in "Dirty Mind" was itself a hybrid instrument that ARP had created to get into the polyphonic synthesizer market. According to Roger Dumas, the ARP Omni was technically not a true synthesizer, but rather a modified electric organ: "The Omni was the String Ensemble with an ARP filter on it. . . . So they put one of these [resonance filters], one filter only, on the ARP Omni, and ran the entire String Ensemble sound through it. So, it's like you had

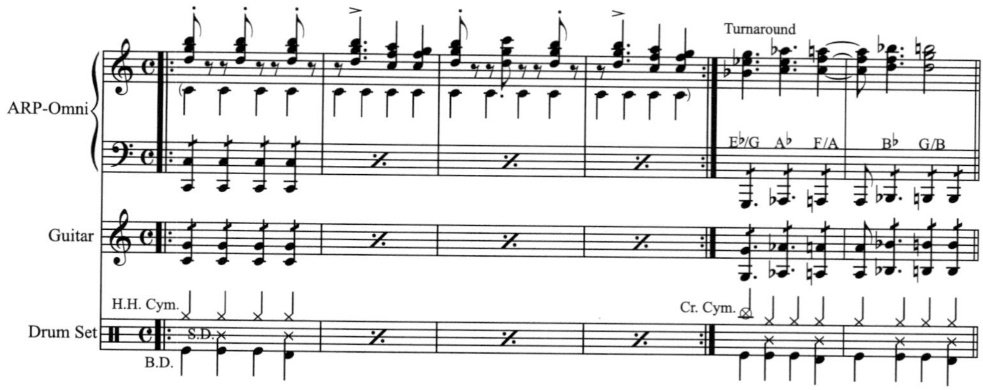

Example 14. "Dirty Mind," verse / vamp ostinato and turnaround

an organ that you could play polyphonically, and the entire output ran through this filter."[79] Matt Fink, the keyboard player in Prince's band at the time, describes the Omni in similar terms, as a hybrid of the familiar and the new:

> The Omni was meant to be sort of a hybrid. . . . You could mix in that string vibe with that polyphonic synth vibe and then it became kind of this . . . original-sounding tone unto itself. . . . If you listen to, like I said, the song "1999" or "Dirty Mind," that Omni tone is the main part, and it has that mixture of the ARP String Machine with that polyphonic synth side, which is sort of . . . hard to describe, unless you hear it. It's unique, it doesn't sound like anything else, really.[80]

Where Oberheim had created their polyphonic synths by putting multiple synthesizer modules under the control of a single keyboard interface, ARP's and Moog's first polyphonic "synthesizers" were really just modified electric organs, with twelve oscillators tuned in a chromatic scale (with a frequency-divider circuit to create the lower octaves) instead of the twin voltage-controlled oscillator design of a true analog synthesizer. The only difference between an ARP Omni or Moog Polymoog keyboard and the imitative sounds of older string machines was the addition of a synthesizer-style resonant filter (VCF) and ADSR envelope generators.

The ARP Omni and Omni 2 keyboards became part of Prince's trademark sound from *Dirty Mind* to *Purple Rain.* As Fink described, the Omni could be used in two different modes—as a regular string machine plus keyboard bass (the two functions separated by range) with dedicated attack-and-release dynamic envelope controls, or as a "synthesizer" with the oscillator output routed through a separate voltage-controlled filter and ADSR envelope generator—and these two modes could be employed simultaneously, with a slider control determining the mix between the string machine and "synth" outputs. This hybrid circuitry gave the Omni the power to juxtapose novel filter and envelope effects on a more familiar, imitative string sound. On "Dirty Mind," Prince relied on this uncanny power. Prince played the synth-bass eighth-note pulse in octaves, using a timbre that sounds like a blend of the Omni's string-machine and synth outputs. It has the rich high-frequency spectrum that comes from a resonant VCF filter (as well as a shimmer quality that comes from the Omni's built-in phasing effect), yet its dynamic envelope has the slower, legato attack of a string machine—the loudest part of the note is *not* its anacrusis—which makes it sound like a throb rather than a pluck. The combination of Prince's uncanny timbral choice—simultaneously imitative of a bowed string-bass and mechanical-sounding (from its high-frequency filter resonance)—with its rhythmic function as a heartbeat creates a strong musical juxtaposition of the machine and the body.

In "Controversy," an electric bass sets the quarter-note pulse, but it is the synth riff whose timbre dominates the low frequency spectrum (see example 15, OB-X left hand). Using the Oberheim OB-X, which has essentially the same signal pathway as its predecessors (the 4- or 8-voice) but with a single set of controls for all four SEMs, Prince built a bass timbre using the two oscillators set to richly grained waveforms (either sawtooth, pulse-wave, or a blend of both) and slightly out of tune with each other. The ADSR envelope controlling the VCA circuit (i.e., the dynamic envelope) has a rapid attack and very little decay, with a loud sustain and fast release, giving it a full-on sound with little dynamic variation. Its most arresting feature is its filter envelope (the keyboard's second ADSR envelope generator, set to control the resonant filter), which Prince used to generate a wide filter sweep. Specifically: each time the synth bass plays, the filter—which is set to a high-mid-range cutoff with added resonance at that frequency—rapidly opens on the first note and closes again on the second, producing an effect analogous to opening a plunger mute on a brass instrument or making a compound vowel sound like "wah-cow." This filter envelope gives the synth bass an anthropomorphic quality, as each riff seems to move and breathe as it is played despite its obviously artificial timbre. Incidentally, Prince would have had to record and perform the left- and right-hand

Example 15. "Controversy," verse / vamp ostinato

OB-X parts separately: the OB-X did not have an "after-touch" function that would have allowed an automatic filter-sweep to kick in after a note was released. This meant that the keyboard player covering the bass part would have to have one hand on the keys and the other hand on the filter cutoff slider to create the distinctive "wah-cow" filter sweep, and this is precisely what you can see keyboardist Matt Fink doing in the music video for "Controversy." As with the bass pulse in "Dirty Mind," the "Controversy" synth bass makes a strong connection between the musical heartbeat of the song—the kick drum—and a machinic identity, yet one that sounds, thanks to the filter sweep, alive.

These synth basses dominate the texture of their respective songs with timbres simultaneously mechanical and animate. The eighth-note drone in "Dirty Mind" hums and pulsates like an assembly-line heartbeat, while the bass-synth filter-sweep riff in "Controversy" sounds like a vowel sound vocalized by a robotic larynx. As in "Soft and Wet," Prince has combined mechanical timbres with a hint of imitative familiarity: the ARP Omni timbre in "Dirty Mind" is at root a string emulation playing a bass ostinato, while the envelope and filter-sweep of the OB-X bass riff in "Controversy" call to mind the low honk of a baritone saxophone or an electric bass played with a wah-wah effect à la Bootsy Collins. In both songs, the keyboard bass fulfills a mimetic role, playing the part of a piano left hand or electric bass, yet Prince has subjected these sounds to a process of alienation. They are, in a word, uncanny:

alive yet inorganic, familiar yet strange, attractive but at the same time slightly repulsive, and they are linked directly to the body—the kick-drum heartbeat—of the song's protagonist.

Prince also uses synthesizer timbres to provide the middle-ground harmonic padding in "Dirty Mind" and "Controversy." Structurally, each song has two main units: the verse and vamp sections, with the tonic bass drone, and a contrasting section of harmonic movement that serves as a turnaround or chorus. In "Dirty Mind," this is a two-bar turnaround in which the bass drops down to the dominant and ascends chromatically to the seventh, while the harmony makes a series of dominant and mediant moves that resolve back to the tonic (see example 14). The contrasting section in "Controversy" is a full chorus, and it too begins with a sudden harmonic move, though to the submediant this time. Unlike in "Dirty Mind," Prince uses the chorus of "Controversy" to provide conflict: the OB-X plays a descending vi–V–IV chord progression, while another synthesizer part plays an ascending motive in unison with the guitar and the lead vocals (see example 16). The Oberheim timbre that Prince uses for the chordal padding of "Controversy" is most audible during this chorus, and it has a rich two-oscillator waveform (it sounds like at least one of the oscillators is set to the more artificial-sounding pulse-wave form) with wide vibrato. This vibrato would have been produced with the Oberheim's LFO, which had a limited number of waveforms—sinusoidal, square wave, and triangular wave—all of which were perfectly regular. The vibrato renders each note more expressive but at the same less human: the ADSR dynamic envelope may remind us of a brass instrument, with its loud, rapid attack-and-decay, but the mechanical oscillation is too perfect to be played by a human. In both songs, the contrasting sections provide momentary motion, but neither brings about lasting harmonic change, and the robotic tonic drone always returns.

In addition to the bass drones and chordal padding I've already described, Prince uses synthesizer to play the main melodic riffs of "Dirty Mind" and "Controversy" (example 14 and example 15). Both motives have an "uncanny" mix of idiomatic familiarity and timbral mechanicity. Furthermore, both motives are characterized by harmonic frustration, to the extent that each riff makes a cadential gesture toward another key that is defeated by the relentless tonic drone of the synth bass. In "Dirty Mind," the main synth motive is played on a timbre that blends the ARP Omni 2's string-machine and synth sounds: it has the legato, imitative sound of the string machine, but

Example 16. "Controversy," chorus

the synthesizer output provides a faster and louder attack, making the timbre sound like a hybrid with the sharp attack of a piano followed by the softer sound of a string section. Melodically, this motive consists of three C chords with added seventh and ninth (see the right hand of the Omni part in example 14), followed by a second-inverson Fadd9 that doesn't properly resolve (it moves to a C chord with an added eleventh), played in a two-bar clave pattern whose rhythmic rotation blunts any sense of cadential closure. This motive's C7add9 chord is pregnant with harmonic conflict: the high B (7th) pulls our focus towards the upper tonic, while the D (9th) spells a G chord with C in the bass, suggesting that the V chord is struggling to assert itself against the relentless pull of the tonic triad. However, this motive unfolds as a string of incomplete resolutions: the 7th *doesn't* resolve up to the tonic (it moves downward as the harmony shifts to the subdominant), and the dominant G triad never fully emerges. Prince avoids even a plagal cadence, leaving the F suspended as IV attempts to move to I. Prince repeats this motive over and over during the verses and vamps, engendering a sense of continually denied cadence.

The main hook of "Controversy" is also based on an un-resolved seventh (see example 15, OB-X right hand) and is played with an even more uncanny timbre. In its antecedent phrase, the motive moves from the fifth to the flat seventh twice, and though it has a brief stop on the tonic in the middle, its off-beat rhythmic placement robs this tonic of any cadential finality. The motive's consequent phrase is a Memphis-horns style pad-and-stab: Prince plays a two-fingered chord (C♯–A) which he slides up a step and then back down (creating an F♯min–B–F♯min harmonic motion as heard with the bass), and then concludes with a distinctly horn-like sixteenth-note "stab" on the F♯min harmony. Despite—or perhaps because of—its glissando slide, this motive's ending back on the tonic triad reinforces the ineluctable pull of the F♯ synth-bass drone. Prince uses the OB-X for this right-hand melody with a distinctly imitative timbre: the ADSR envelope has a brassy shape (fast attack and decay, loud sustain and fast release), and there is an expressive LFO audible on the longer notes. Furthermore, the OB-X's portamento feature that Prince used for the F♯m–B slide reinforces the mimetic similarity to horns, especially with the motive's idiomatic brass stab tacked on the end. However, the timbre's waveform is aggressive and electronic, owing to the twinned out-of-phase oscillators and rich upper partials of the sawtooth setting, and the LFO produces a mechanically perfect vibrato, both of which defamiliarize the brass-like quality of this timbre with an uncanny mechanicity.

While "Dirty Mind" and "Controversy" are suffused with elements of funk and soul—interlocking ostinati, Afro-Caribbean polyrhythm, and especially Prince's use of his falsetto vocal range—the austere and synth-dominated instrumental texture, insistent mechanical bass pulse, and repetitive, unresolved synthesizer hooks give these songs a dystopian ambiance similar to new-wave music of the period. Where pioneering new-wave artists like Gary Numan used synthesizers to portray robotic or alienated principal characters (e.g., "Are 'Friends' Electric?" and "Cars"), Prince went further by linking his main character's sexuality to the songs' robotic, mechanical qualities.[81] "Dirty Mind" portrays a subject who's controlled *by* his machine-like sex drive—a drive that turns on automatically when the female object is around—rather than being *in control* of it. Throughout the song Prince sings in a light falsetto, in stark contrast to the low, insistent pulse of the bass synth. His lyrics use the passive voice (e.g., "it happens every time") and portray a man in thrall to his own desire, which is in turn under the control of the female object. This desire remains musically unsatisfied: the major seventh in the main synth riff never resolves up to the tonic, and the harmonic motion of the turnaround moves through a cycle of fifths and thirds without ever resolving its aching G/C sonority. The only instance where the singer approaches anything like a climax is during the bridge (at 2:38 in the album version): as the bass drone sinks downward by half step, the harmony moves from B♭ major down to the same G/C triad (dominant over tonic). Prince's vocals (multitracked in harmony) become strident, and his lyrics insistent, but even this impassioned wail fails to resolve the G/C harmony or halt the pulsation of the synth bass. Ultimately, the male protagonist remains within the machine, bounded below by its robotic throb and above by the ache of the main motive's unresolved harmony. It is as though the song's main subject has himself become a machine driven by a ceaseless flow of sexual desire, with no goal or destination in sight.

In "Controversy," Prince also portrays an ambivalent male subject with a robotic sexuality (though sexuality is only one of several identity topics that Prince touches on in this song). The lyrics pose a series of invasive questions concerning the protagonist's race, religion, gender, and sexuality (e.g., "Am I black or white, am I straight or gay?"), portraying a main character dominated by relentless questions from the press (the cover art of the album *Controversy* shows Prince framed by newspaper headlines). While the robotic bass drones away, Prince's falsetto voice sounds by turns abject and defensive (never heroic) as he mirrors back the desires that are being thrust upon him—as when he sings, "Was it good for you, was I what you wanted me to be?" Furthermore, this falsetto vocal melody doubles the antecedent phrase of the OB-X's right-hand synth motive (which is in turn doubled by the electric guitar), reinforcing the principal character's robotic identity. All the while, the bass riff provides a relentless counterpoint, one that is both mechanical in its rhythmic regularity yet also alive with its throbbing filter-sweep, over which the main motive's aching harmonic tension never resolves.

In one sense, Prince's metaphor of machinery for sexuality is unremarkable. There is, in American pop music, a long history of comparing the masculine sex drive to a machine, as in the automotive sexual metaphors of Robert Johnson's "Terraplane Blues" and Chuck Berry's "Maybellene," or James Brown's barely metaphoric "Sex Machine." Yet this trope—and these songs—reinforce heteronormative sexuality by portraying the male sex drive (or the woman herself) as a machine under the command of the male subject. What is remarkable in Prince's work is the way that he links technology—realized through mechanical-sounding synthesizer timbres and repetitive beats—with non-heteronormative, anti-patriarchal male sexuality. *Dirty Mind* and *Controversy* are marked by sexual excess and a variety of "inappropriate" sexual object choices including oral sex, incest, and masturbation. In the two title tracks I have discussed, Prince portrays male subjects with non-heteronormative sexual identities in the sense that they are robotic and mechanical, first because their sexuality is externally controlled or programmed, and second because their sexuality is constructed as an endless flow without climax or resolution. This conjunction of technology and non-heteronormative sexuality clearly conveyed some power or meaning to Prince's music, but what was it?

The answer lies in the nexus of machinery and sexuality embedded in the concept of the "uncanny." First, the Freudian/Jentschian concept of the uncanny revolved around a sexual attraction that violated the human-machine boundary. Second, Freudian/Lacanian theory often employs the metaphor of a machine to describe the instinctual drives of the id, and Freud's definition of the uncanny includes people in the grips of automatic or instinctual behavior, whom he likened to robotic automatons. As I have argued, both "Dirty Mind" and "Controversy" portray a male character who is uncanny in the sense of violating the human-machine boundary and also in the sense that he is under the control of his (instinctual/programmed) sex drive. In both songs Prince foregrounds the uncanny quality of his synth timbres—both the main motives and the electro-mechanical bass pulse—and makes a clear connection between these synthesized sounds and the song's protagonist, portraying him as a sexualized human-robot hybrid. Indeed, like Summer and Moroder's "I Feel Love," Prince creates an uncanny tension by juxtaposing a mechanically produced groove with a breathy, high-pitched singing voice that lyrically begs for love. *Rolling Stone* reviewer Ken Tucker picked up on this in his review of *Dirty Mind*: "In his favorite musical trick, the artist contrasts a pumping, low-toned drum sound with a light, abrupt guitar or keyboard riff pitched as high as his voice (which is often double-tracked to emphasize its airiness)."[82] Third, these songs musically construct a male subject who violates the Freudian Oedipal stage by refusing to attach to the so-called "mature" sexual object choice (i.e. discrete heterosexual procreation), and who instead experiences an unresolved continuum of sexual desire and pleasure. In both "Dirty Mind" and "Controversy," the interaction between the synth bass drone and main motive creates an unresolved harmonic tension between tonic and seventh (among other things). If we hear these synthesized sounds as elements that enact the interior subjectivity of the main character, and if we follow Susan McClary's argument that tonal harmonic motion works as a mechanism for "arousing and channeling" erotic desire, then it follows that the main character of these songs is suspended in a perpetual state of pleasure and/or desire that never reaches its "proper" Freudian resolution (either cadentially or sexually).[83] The throb of the synth bass and the harmonic ache of the main synth motive neither rest nor climax, suggesting that the subject's sexual desire is an automatic or instinctual drive, flowing without control or resolution.

"Dirty Mind" and "Controversy" were both well received by the rock press, and their two albums performed well on the *Billboard* 200 album chart (reaching numbers 45 and 21, respectively), avoiding the kinds of anti-synthesizer backlash that affected both disco and new-wave artists at the time. Perhaps one of the reasons that Prince's linkage of synthesizers and non-heteronormative sexuality inspired admiration rather than vitriol from rock critics was the fact that Prince also displayed prodigious talent as a guitarist—onstage he was the lead guitarist, not the synth player—using the trope of virtuosic guitar solos that was the bread and butter of hard rock, including the phallic display of the guitar neck. Indeed, on the *Dirty Mind* tour Prince gave some of his synthesizer-based songs a more macho, guitar-oriented focus by adding virtuoso guitar solos (by either himself or Dez Dickerson) and simulating masturbation with his guitar neck (you can see an example of this in the final performance scene of the movie *Purple Rain*).[84]

Yet perhaps what critics and audiences were responding to in "Dirty Mind" and "Controversy" was *precisely* the pleasure of the machine, and the philosophy of anti-Freudian sexual emancipation. On both of these albums, Prince used the lyrics and album jackets to elaborate a philosophy of polymorphous hedonism as spiritual and political liberation, a philosophy that *Rolling Stone* magazine was quick to point out in its favorable reviews of *Dirty Mind* and *Controversy*.[85] I argue that Prince's musical construction of a robotic main character dominated by a ceaseless flow of desire was doing cultural work analogous to that of the French theorists Gilles Deleuze and Félix Guattari, who aimed to debunk Freud's outdated model of the unconscious.[86] Their concept of "desiring-machines" undercuts Freud's view that sublimating the inappropriate desires of the id (during the Oedipal phase) is the central fact upon which the modern bourgeois self is built. In their book *Anti-Oedipus*, Deleuze and Guattari argue that desire is a productive force requiring no singular or unitary object. In their theory, the subconscious is a machine fueled by desire, desire expressed through an endless series of couplings in which parts of a person couple with other objects (e.g., sexual organs, hands and tools, ears and music) to form temporary productive nodes.[87] This understanding of the self is fragmentary, contingent, and without borders: the unconscious is a machine fueled by the flow of desire, and people are connections of parts that interface with one another, nodes in an ever-shifting nexus of organic machinery and an ever-flowing ocean of productive desire. As Klaus Theweleit points out, this understanding of the self represents a liberation from—and a threat to—the bourgeois understanding of the self as a separate and bounded entity.[88]

In this context, we can see that Prince's "Dirty Mind" and "Controversy" enact modes of being that are sexually liberating (and/or threatening) precisely because of, not despite, their machine-like qualities. The synth bass does *not* enact phallic pounding toward a climax, but rather a stream of electric desire flowing without resolution. Prince's protagonists are *not* macho heroes who bend technology to their wills, but rather organic-mechanical hybrids whose sexual identity is subsumed in the desiring-machine of synthesizer drones and motives. Furthermore, Prince built this desiring-machine on a chassis of historically Black musical idioms—R&B horns, funk bass, soul's falsetto vocals—linking this uncanny man-machine hybrid to African American identity, but in a manner markedly different from the boastful macho clichés used by previous generations of blues and funk artists.

"Automatic"

Robots, sex, and freedom continued to be major themes in Prince's work, and it was with *1999* that Prince made the definitive statement of both his techno-sexual vision and his synthesizer sound. All but one of the album's eleven songs prominently use synthesizers, and several songs have themes of dystopian alienation and/or characters in the grips of uncanny automated sexuality. The title track features one of Prince's best-known synth riffs, played by the ARP Omni 2, and millenarian lyrics that link biblical revelation with technologically mediated Armageddon, portraying sex as a last-ditch rebellion against death. On the song "Little Red Corvette" Prince uses the old car-as-sex metaphor—and a lushly dark ARP Omni 2 chord progression—but reverses the typical gender roles, turning what might have been a macho boast into a warning about voracious female sexuality. "Lady Cab Driver" continues the car/sex association, but this time using the car as a symbol of urban alienation, with a repetitive monophonic synthesizer motive that depicts the male character's compulsive, unfulfillable sexual desire. In "Let's Pretend We're Married," Prince's lyrics portray a character numbly using sex as a palliative to loneliness while, at the same time, the music uses a rapid bass synthesizer pulse to portray the protagonist's uncontrollable desire. Perhaps the album's most alienated protagonist is the one in "Something in the Water (Does Not Compute)," in which Prince sings about computational disorder over a hollowed-out musical texture that features a synthesizer timbre so detuned that the main motive sounds almost aleatoric. But the song I want to focus on is "Automatic," a track in which Prince depicts a sexualized automaton in a dystopian musical landscape.

In "Automatic," Prince portrays a robotic male character whose emotional and sexual responses are preprogrammed and under the control of an unnamed lover, using both lyrics and synthesized timbres to depict this character's uncanny identity. As with "Dirty Mind" and "Controversy," Prince defamiliarizes the R&B/funk horn idiom and traditionally gendered portrayals of technology, creating an alienating distance between the listener and the intersecting stereotypes of Black masculinity and heteronormative sexuality. There are three elements that Prince uses to accomplish this. First, Prince harmonically constructs a dystopian-futurist soundscape and establishes his main character's robotic sexual identity using lyrics and motives. Second, Prince uses synthesized timbres to defamiliarize the R&B/funk horn idiom and add a sense of the uncanny, just as he did in the earlier songs that I've analyzed. Third, Prince structurally stages a confrontation between his male robotic main character and a female robot, and this conflict creates a sense of sexual confusion that alienates the listener from both the heteronormative sci-fi trope of male technological dominance and the racial stereotype of the Black-man-as-sex-machine.

Prince puts the listener in a harmonic landscape that is both tense and static, which, combined with an instrumentation dominated by synthesizers, creates a sense of dystopian futurism. Prince bases the song on the E♭-mixolydian mode (with some use of the flattened third), with barely any harmonic motion in the song: the bass only moves between tonic and flat seventh, and the chords rotate among just three E♭ variants (E♭7add11, E♭, and E♭add9). These chords are spiked with dissonance: during the verse, a polyphonic electronic keyboard plays chordal stabs on an E♭7add11 chord (see Synth A, example 17), emphasizing the dissonant 3–♭7 tritone built into the mixolydian mode. During the chorus, a separate synthesizer timbre plays whole-note pads that move from E♭7add11 through the tonic triad to E♭add9, as heard against the bass (Synth C, example 18), motion that highlights the major-second dissonances of scale degrees 4 against 5 and then flat 7 against 1. This tense harmonic landscape—dominated by tritone and major-second disso-

Example 17. "Automatic," verse 1

(*continued*)

nances, and unrelieved by any root harmonic motion—remains largely unchanged for the entire nine and a half minutes of the song's duration, and because it is dominated by non-imitative, artificial-sounding synthesizer timbres, the overall effect is dystopian and futuristic.

Against this tense harmonic backdrop Prince portrays an uncanny, robotic main character. In the verses, the lyrics depict a man whose reactions to his love object are automated: he neither controls nor, by the sound of it, particularly enjoys these reactions, with lyrics like "Every time you leave me, I die. . . . I'm just an addict. . . . If you cry, me cry, boo-hoo." Prince punctuates each of these lines with the refrain "It's automatic," and begins each chorus with the phrase "A-U-T-O-matic, just tell me what to do," all of which suggests the same kind of instinctual behavior that Freud equated with the uncanny.

Sonically, Prince portrays this main character as robotic by juxtaposing his voice onto an angular guitar motive and mechanical-sounding synthesizer timbre. During the sixteen-bar verse sections, Prince begins each four-bar phrase of his vocal melody with a short rhythmic motive of six straight eighth-notes (plus a pickup). Prince sings this motive with little emotion, no rhythmic syncopation, and little pitch variation outside of toggling between the fifth and third scale degrees, a singing style that strongly resembles the robotic (and overwhelmingly white-identified) vocal style of new-wave artists such as Devo.[89] Prince also adds an uncanny sheen to his voice by double-tracking it, with an inconsistent interval between the two voices (sometimes they are in unison, sometimes the second voice sings a drone note, occasionally a major-second dissonance).

During the verse sections, Prince uses this rhythmic motive to juxtapose his robotic singing voice onto an angular guitar motive and artificial-sounding synthesizer timbre. In the first bar of each four-bar phrase, the vocal melody is in rhythmic unison with a guitar motive that is equally robotic, though in a different way (see example 17, guitar). Beginning on the same note as the vocal melody (scale degree 5), the guitar plays an angular downward-then-upward minor arpeggio (fifth, tonic, then flat third) followed by a chromatic neighbor-note-motion between the minor- and major-mode versions of the third scale degree. (Prince plays this guitar motive in the first and third bars of each four-bar phrase of the verse, adding a final tonic note to the second statement to give it a call-and-response symmetry.) This neighbor-note gesture is notable for its almost-but-not-quite similarity to the normal guitar idiom of *bending* scale degree three from minor to major: by failing to play this most basic blues gesture correctly—i.e., the "blue note"—the guitar motive sounds awkward and robotic, an unsuccessful simulation of bluesy authenticity. This pattern continues during each eight-bar chorus section as well—the guitar plays its awkward, angular melody while the vocals emotionlessly intone the lyric "A-U-T-O-matic" (in rigid root-fifth-octave three-part harmony this time), all on the six-eighth-note rhythmic motive—which reinforces the identification between these two motives and the main character's robotic identity.

During the verse sections, Prince also adds a synthesizer sound to give this voice-guitar motivic nexus an uncanny timbral sheen. Specifically: in the second half of each verse (the third and fourth four-bar phrases), Prince echoes the angular guitar motive on a hollow, mechanical-sounding synth (see Synth B, example 17). Because they share the same rhythmic motive, and because the synth and guitar play the same pitch content, these three sounds—voice, guitar, and synth—all become juxtaposed during the verse and chorus sections. As they do, their robotic qualities reinforce each other: the flat affect of the vocals, the herky-jerky arpeggio and failed blue-note of the guitar melody, and the hollow artificiality of the synth timbre all coalesce, giving a strong sense that the main character is a robotic-organic hybrid. Furthermore, by using nested call-and-response phrase structure (the guitar motive's four-bar antecedent-consequent structure is echoed in alternate measures, by

Synth B, only in the second half of each verse), Prince subtly signals this man-machine hybrid's Black identity by using one of the most definitive melodic gestures in African diasporic music, according to Olly Wilson.[90]

In "Automatic," as in "Dirty Mind" and "Controversy," Prince uses his ARP Omni 2 and Oberheim OB-X (or OB-Xa) synthesizers in ways idiomatically similar to R&B/funk horns, but he defamiliarizes that idiom by choosing non-imitative timbres. This is the second element that Prince uses to portray the song's protagonist as uncanny and robotic.[91] One synthesizer provides rhythmic "stabs" on an Eb7add11 chord during the verses (Synth A, example 17); a second synthesizer timbre plays the song's main melodic riffs (Synth B, examples 17 and 18); and a third synthesizer timbre plays long, sustained harmonic "pads" during the chorus (Synth C, example 18). Yet where these three types of gesture—stabs, riffs, and pads—would have sounded familiar if played by wind and brass instruments or synthesizer imitations of them, Prince's choice of timbres gives them an uncanny sheen. The rhythmic stabs (Synth A) and melodic riffs (Synth B) sound as though they were recorded using the ARP Omni 2: both have a thin, single-oscillator waveform, wide LFO vibrato, and slow attack envelope, sounding like a cross between a violin emulator and a pipe-organ. As discussed earlier, the ARP Omni 2 was a hybrid instrument (not a true analog synthesizer, but a type of electric organ), and Prince's decision to use it here is significant. With the Oberheim synthesizer at his command, Prince could have crafted an entirely novel timbre for these parts *or* a passable approximation of a brass sound, but instead he chose the Omni's mechanical simulation of orchestral strings, further defamiliarized with un-stringlike envelope shaping, to replace a horn section. In so doing, Prince accessed the combination of familiarity and (mechanical) strangeness that defines the uncanny valley.

Where the ARP Omni 2 timbres (Synth A and B) create a sonic disjunction in the listener's unconscious (Are these strings or horns? Do I *like* them, or are they creepy?), the third, Synth C timbre (which plays whole-note padding during the intro and chorus sections, see Example 18) is even less imitative, and ratchets up the tension around the main character's robotic sexual identity. According to keyboardist Matt Fink, Prince created this timbre on an Oberheim OB-X or OB-Xa, owing to its fat, two-oscillator waveform that is rich in harmonic partials (a far cry from the thin, single-oscillator waveform of the ARP Omni 2 string-machine timbres).[92] Synth C's other defining feature is an LFO pitch-vibrato that is so wide it nearly obscures the tonal center of the

Example 18. "Automatic," Intro and Chorus (vocals tacet during intro)

notes, like a broken-down calliope. Taken together with the fact that Synth C plays long, sustained pads that are often dissonant (moving from E♭7add11 to E♭7 to E♭9), this Synth C timbre sticks out like an industrial robot in a cyborg factory, creating a sound that aurally signifies the main character's increasing mechanicity while simultaneously obscuring the R&B/funk horn roots of its harmonic-padding gesture.

This Synth C timbre underscores the main character's full conversion into a sex robot. At 2:12, during the last verse of the song's verse-chorus structure (before the extended coda section), Prince sings the most sexually explicit *and* subservient lyrics of the song, offering to "go down on you all night—it's automatic." This offer turns the blues/R&B sex-machine metaphor on its head (pun intended): instead of the traditional car-as-phallus/car-as-woman braggadocio, which, Ken McLeod argues, is based on "controlling a woman as one controls technology," Prince portrays *himself* as a piece of technology under the woman's control, tirelessly giving but not receiving sexual stimulation (something like a mechanical vibrator).[93] As Prince sings these lyrics, he layers the Synth C harmonic padding from the chorus onto the Synth A stabs and Synth B riff that normally accompany the verse sections. Adding Synth C to this verse not only increases the harmonic tension, rhythmic density, and overall volume level, but it also creates a kind of identity-slide away from the organic and toward the mechanistic. This is because the electronic artificiality of Synth C's non-imitative Oberheim timbre (which is louder in the mix than the uncanny string-synth sounds of Synth A and B) pulls the listener backward through Mori's uncanny valley diagram, away from "human likeness" and toward "humanoid robot," as though the main character's remaining humanity is dissolving into the machinery of his desire.[94]

Prince builds on this sense of identity dissolution during the song's six-minute, free-form coda section. This section begins with a breakdown at 3:30, when Prince drops out all instruments except the drum machine, bass, and Synth B intro/chorus riff. The coda then unfolds in eight-bar phrases as Prince recombines fragments of the verse and chorus sections: instrumental riffs float in and out, starting and stopping without any obvious cadential goal. This subtractive/additive structural technique is common in soul, funk, disco, and modern electronic dance music (Mark Spicer calls it "accumulative form"), and it entrains the listener to expect a stream of small moments of pleasure—e.g., the entry of a new instrument—rather than the typical single-climax harmonic resolution that, as Susan McClary argues, represents the phallocentric model of heterosexual pleasure undergirding Western tonality.[95] In short, Prince creates the same type of "desiring machine" that he had done in previous works like "Dirty Mind," enacting a non-object-oriented, anti-Freudian model of sensual pleasure based on repetition, in which the song directs libidinal energy not along a single path toward a single (human, female) object, but in multiple directions toward multiple, fragmentary objects of desire.[96] Furthermore, as in his earlier songs, Prince links this anti-Freudian model of sexual pleasure to technology through the use of synthesizer timbres: not only is this coda section dominated by the uncanny/mechanical timbres of Synths A, B, and C, Prince also introduces several electronic sound effects as the coda unfolds.

Within the pleasurable ebb-and-flow of the coda's "accumulative form," Prince stages a confrontation between male and female robots that upends the traditional science-fiction narrative of male technological dominance in the same way that the third verse already upended the blues/R&B techno-phallic trope. This begins with Prince's male character delivering a seduction monologue (starting at 4:00) in which that character's subjectivity—already established as a human/robot hybrid—becomes increasingly fragmentary and disintegrated. Prince's monologue begins with rhymed couplets, declaimed in a sultry low voice that contrasts the emotionless monotone of the preceding verses, making clear his amorous intentions (a brass bed is rolled onstage during this section of the music video, providing a clear hermeneutic window into the sexual subtext of the song at this moment). However, Prince undercuts the smoothness of this seduction in two ways: first, his lyrics stop making linear sense and begin meandering from one topic to the next, including torture and insanity, and he periodically interrupts himself with the rhetorical question "Can you hear me?" Second, Prince electronically processes his voice and adds sci-fi sound effects that illustrate his increasingly disjointed lyrics. At 4:00 and 4:42 he double-tracks his voice using variable-speed pitch-shifting, creating an unnaturally high-pitched doppelgänger whose voice is both androgynous and robotic; the effect is uncanny in the purest sense, with Prince's "natural" voice juxtaposed onto the electronically processed one. Also, starting at 4:53 and continuing until 5:30, Prince moves his voice slowly back and forth between the left and right sides of the stereo field, combining instability of pitch with instability of location. Prince's robotic subjectivity, like the robot HAL at the end of *2001: A Space Odyssey*, seems to be devolving into fragmented images and questions. Prince augments this with sound-effect text-painting: at 4:38, just as Prince's character intones the words "don't torture me," a synthesizer plays five half-note bursts of semi-pitched white noise that sound like a dental drill (in the music video, Prince recoils from this noise as if struck, falling onto the bed). At the end of the monologue (around 6:28), Prince uses another semi-pitched electronic noise to create a warning alarm followed by a doppler-effect aircraft takeoff noise, mimetic sound effects that illustrate Prince's final line ("Fasten your seatbelts, prepare for takeoff"), and which are accompanied in the music video by the sight of Prince, stripped to the waist and tied to the brass bed frame, being rotated around and around by female bandmembers Wendy Melvoin and Jill Jones.

After this liftoff sequence, a female robot-voice delivers a response to the male character's seduction monologue (beginning at 6:42), and this is when the simmering tension between male and female characters erupts into its final conflagration. This is not the first moment in

"Automatic" when the listener hears a robotic female voice—she sang the song's vocal hook of "A-U-T-O-matic" in harmony with the male singer during each chorus—but it is the first time she has spoken on her own. Her voice sounds simultaneously human and synthetic—an uncanny cyborg hybrid—owing to its monotone declamation and electronic processing. It is double-tracked and panned to the far left and right sides of the stereo spectrum, filtered to eliminate some of its high-frequency range (making it sound tinny, as though transmitted over an analog telephone) and treated with a time-based effect (such as phasing or delay) to put the left and right voices slightly out of phase with each other. In keeping with the automaton theme, the female robot does not say anything *new,* but rather answers the rhetorical questions that Prince's character posed during his seduction monologue: where Prince said, "Stop me if I bore you," the female cyborg replies, "With you I am never bored." By parroting back such reassurances the female robot seems like an instance of the Stepford wives subservient cyborg trope, but that ends when the female robot answers the male character's rhetorical assertion "don't torture me" (4:37) with "I'm going to have to torture you now" (6:53). Prince turns up the dramatic tension of the female robot's monologue by increasing the rhythmic density and harmonic tension: he adds a new drum-machine layer consisting of pounding eighth-notes on the low toms and kick drum, and just as the female robot intones her "torture" line he reintroduces the wobbly Synth C timbre with its dissonant chord progression (example 18).

The "torture" line concludes the female robot's monologue, after which, Prince enacts a musical techno-sexual confrontation. Over the next minute (from 6:56–7:50) Prince juxtaposes three sounds: a guitar solo, the sound of a robotic female voice moaning, and the synthesizer's spaceship-liftoff sound effect. The guitar solo uses the macho, phallic tropes of hard-rock virtuosity—including scalar runs and soaring high notes—yet the robotic female moaning is mixed so loudly that it partly drowns out the guitar's attempts at a heroic melodic climax. The crying voice is processed using the same uncanny effects as the female robot's monologue but with even more multitracked moaning voices added. The effect is overwhelming: overlapping cries float in and out at multiple points in the stereo field, forming a robotic wailing wall. Lastly, the synthesizer's swirling takeoff sound, which punctuates this episode at several points, adds textural density and science-fiction text-painting.

This musical confrontation creates confusion and disidentification on a number of levels. First, the robotic cries confront the listener with the question of whether the sexual object in question is a living woman or instead a castrating automaton, as in Freud and Jentsch's theory of the uncanny. Second, the cries confuse pleasure and pain: are these moans of sexual ecstasy, tortured agony, or both? Third, the gender dynamics are ambiguous: the robotic crying partly drowns out the heteronormative pleasure of the guitar solo, *but* both the song and music video make it unclear whether we are meant to hear the cries as emanating from the male or the female character. (At this point in the music video, Prince's two female band mates whip him with a belt as he writhes, tied, on the brass bed.) If this is a robotic battle of the sexes, who has won? Is the male character being tortured, as the female robot promised, or has the male robot turned the tables with his guitar solo (and if so, is the guitar an instrument of torture or of pleasure)?

Once this confrontation is finished (at 7:50), the coda's "accumulative form" resumes for another minute and thirty seconds but without any more vocals. This winding-down section leaves the listener in a fragmented landscape made from disembodied parts of the groove—drum machine ostinato, synthesizer riffs, and bass. By leaving the conflict unresolved, Prince suggests that the main character's identity is similarly unresolved. Instead of a clear victory—human male guitarist triumphing over synthesized femme fatale, or conversely, robotic Stepford wife liberated from human servitude—the song's characters dissolve into a morass of organic and synthetic body parts, a hybrid of human and robot, male and female, pleasure and pain. Heteronormative subjectivity itself has broken down, and in its place is an anti-Freudian model of identity where desire is satisfied through momentary connections between fragmented parts (rather than by channeling the listener through a harmonic teleology toward a single melodic climax), and where organic and synthetic sounds and bodies become juxtaposed.[97]

This unresolved conflict confounds the typical way that technology gets gendered in science fiction. Literary theorist Andreas Huyssen has pointed out that in science-fiction literature and movies, technology tends to be gendered "female" in ways that reinscribe heterosexual male power and privilege, and that these depictions often function to assuage mainstream anxiety about the changing role of technology in industrial society. The two most common tropes of feminized technology are the compliant sexual slave, as in *The Stepford Wives*, and the threatening robotic femme fatale, like the "false Maria" from Fritz Lang's *Metropolis*, whose voracious sexuality threatens to castrate and destroy men, and whose ultimate defeat reinscribes the power of men over both technology and women.[98] In "Automatic," Prince could have stuck with one of these two tropes, portraying the female character as either a subservient or vengeful robot, and it probably would have made his male audience feel more comfortable with the new synthesizer technology he was using. But instead Prince leaned into the uncanny cyborg persona: not only did he use his synthesizer timbres to replace traditional acoustic keyboard timbres and defamiliarize the R&B horns idiom, he also crafted a musical narrative in which *both* his male and female characters had hybrid-robotic identities and *neither* of the two emerged as the clear winner, thus offering up an alternative, anti-Freudian model of gender and sexual identity within the context of a Black musical idiom.

By using synthesizers to push listeners into the uncanny valley while at the same time creating narrative uncertainty around gender and sexual identity, Prince was harnessing the liberatory power that gender theorists Jack Halberstam and Donna Haraway have ascribed to cyborgs, and doing so within the larger context of what Daphne Brooks has called "Afro-alienation" acts.[99] Where cyborgs—human-machine hybrids—are commonly used as figures of either pathos or horror in science-fiction literature, Halberstam and Haraway use the cyborg trope to resist and rethink categories of the self that were once thought immutable. Specifically, by violating the boundary between human and machine, the figure of the cyborg demonstrates how identity categories like gender and race can also be seen as artificial constructs.

The cyborg personae and their unresolved conflict that Prince staged in "Automatic" retain an element of uncanny threat (as do the synthesizer timbres he chose), and this uncertainty is a wedge that prevents the listener from identifying too closely with either character. This element of disidentification, or alienation, is a key part of Brooks's "Afro-alienation acts." As Brooks argues, Afro-alienation is a trope or performative strategy in which Black performers combine sociopolitical marginalization with artistic experimentation to forge resistant, self-actualized, and/or liberated identities.[100] Two key elements connect Prince's synthesizer work to Brooks' concept: first, the artists Brooks surveys (nineteenth-century Black performers) tended to use hybrid genres, blending "Victorian magic, religious, classical, and secular song, . . . drag performance, . . . musicals, spiritualism, and modern dance" in a way that is directly analogous to Prince's generic blend of hard rock, new wave, R&B, and funk.[101] Second, Brooks argues that Afro-alienation acts tend to work by subjecting stereotypes of Black identity to an anti-realist or alienation effect so as to enable audience critique, a strategy that echoes both the Brechtian V-Effekt and DuBoisean double-consciousness.[102] This is precisely what Prince did in "Automatic": Not only did synthesizers allow Prince to add mechanical strangeness to otherwise familiar musical idioms, thereby accessing the uncanny, they also opened up the science-fiction trope of cyborgs, a trope that allowed Prince to defamiliarize the stereotypical "sex-machine" construction of Black male sexuality, placing it, too, at a critical remove from audience identification.

Conclusions—The Passing of the Minneapolis Sound

The innovation of the Minneapolis sound was in its technologization of funk/R&B music, and in the early 1980s Prince staked his career on this fusion. By building the interlocking groove of funk songs with synthesizers and a drum machine, Prince retained the structural and rhythmic framework of R&B and funk while defamiliarizing the horn idiom, which was at that time a principal timbral marker of Black musical identity. In an industry structured on the assumption that Black and white audiences had separate musical tastes, this technological mediation may well have been the move that allowed Prince and the Minneapolis sound to break open the mainstream charts to Black artists in the 1980s.

Prince went further by taking a common technological trope from the history of blues/R&B music—the sex machine—and stripping it of its macho narrative of male domination. In "Automatic," as in "Dirty Mind" and "Controversy," Prince used repetition, fragmentation, and uncanny synthesized timbres to portray himself as a cyborg, a juxtaposition of flesh and machine whose ceaseless flow of desire and polymorphous sexual object-choices enact an anti-Freudian identity. Further, Prince upended the science-fiction trope in which phallic power is reinforced by defeating a feminized technological threat, instead constructing male and female cyborg identities in which power and pleasure flowed more freely.

The fact that Prince constructed these cyborg identities within the context of an African American musical idiom is significant because it gives his cyborg gender liberation a distinctly Afrofuturist slant. American society remains imbued with the (racist) fear of miscegenation, a terror which stems from projecting the fantasy-fear of voracious sexuality and hyper-potent virility onto the racial Other. In this light, Prince's main contribution to the topos of technophobia in Western thinking may have been his decision *not* to contain and defuse the uncanny threat of synthesizer technology by feminizing and dominating it, but instead to lean into the uncanny qualities of the cyborg (and the synthesizer) and thereby place intersecting stereotypes of race, gender, and sexuality at an alienating distance. Prince neither dominates female sexuality nor defeats the technological threat; rather, he interpolates those elements into his own musical subjectivity as an African American man without losing that identity: synthesizer riffs form a funk groove in which the main character lives, while the lyrics portray both male protagonist and female antagonist as hybrids in a ceaseless flow of desire in which neither character ultimately dominates the other. In so doing, Prince transcends both the racist stereotype of the Black man as sex machine and the tragic antebellum reality of Black men as dehumanized robotic workers. If Prince's use of synthesizers to subsume the role of a horn is on one level a deferral of racial signifiers—i.e., as a way of sounding less Black while still honoring Black music—and if the science-fiction trope of robotic women functions as a deferral of men's Freudian castration anxiety, then Prince performed a neat hat trick. By using synthesizers to build an anti-Freudian subjectivity that is simultaneously an intersexed and biracial cyborg, Prince played Western society's fear of female sexuality *and* male workers' fear of technological replacement against America's fears of Black male sexuality, holding both constructions at a critical distance and thereby liberating himself and his listeners from stereotypes of both race and sex that American society attaches to Black men.

Prince's synth-funk "Minneapolis sound" arguably reached its full flowering with the album *1999*, though it featured on his subsequent album, 1984's *Purple Rain*, to a lesser extent. Prince changed his sound drastically after that, and over the course of his next few albums his use of the cyborg trope also diminished. Perhaps this owed purely to his artistic wanderlust or the need to distance himself from all the Minneapolis-sound-alikes on the radio, but it may also reflect a decreasing tension around technology in post-industrial American culture. By the late 1980s, synthesizers were no longer threatening and new, and had become a routine part of the mainstream American recording industry. Digital advances in synthesizer technology had all but eliminated the need for musicians to laboriously create their own timbres, a development which, several historians have argued, made synthesizers cheaper and easier to use while diminishing their power as tools for exploring new identities.[103] As Roger Dumas put it, the switch from analog synthesis to digital keyboards with preset sounds was "the death of serious synthesis, and the birth of synthesis for every man."[104]

At the same time, the sociopolitical landscape of the United States was changing. The threat of thermonuclear war that had hung a mushroom cloud over the American imagination began to dissipate with the thawing of the Cold War. While never partisan in his politics, Prince had released numerous songs with explicit antiwar messages over the years; the imagery of bombs and mushroom clouds had come up in his lyrics numerous times, and it is not difficult to imagine that part of the power that Prince's novel synthesizer idiom had tapped into was America's fear of the bomb. Another technological fear that began to ebb in the late 1980s was the fear of computers. As cultural theorist William Covino points out, François Lyotard's cautionary identification of the "computerization of society" stopped being a subject of scholarly debate and became a fait accompli during this period.[105]

Given the link that Andreas Huyssen has pointed out between society's fear of new technology and the (gendered) expression of those fears in art and literature, it seems likely that, after glasnost and the digital revolution, the uncanny threat that synthesizers represented may simply have dissipated, leaving Prince's synth-funk style sounding dated and defanged. New styles were ascendant in Black music of the late 1980s and early 1990s, most notably sample-based hip-hop. While electronic keyboards remained important elements in Prince's timbral arsenal, his reliance on the uncanny cyborg trope and his version of the Minneapolis sound more or less disappeared after 1985, returning only as a nostalgic echo on his 2009 album *MPLSound.*

THREE | Symphonic Funk and "Hot Rhythm"

Following the blockbuster success of 1984's *Purple Rain*, Warner Brothers gave Prince carte blanche to create his second feature film, and the movie that Prince delivered could not have been more different from its predecessor.[1] *Under the Cherry Moon* tells the tale of two African American hustlers—Christopher Tracy and his sidekick Tricky, played by Prince and Jerome Benton, respectively—who make their living as expatriates hustling wealthy society ladies on the French Riviera until the transformative power of love causes Tracy to mend his ways. In contrast to the new-wave look of *Purple Rain*, Prince modeled *Under the Cherry Moon* on 1930s screwball comedies: the movie's costumes, production design, and cinematography hearken back to the art-deco glamour of Hollywood's golden age, an inspiration that led Prince to release the movie in black and white.[2]

Under the Cherry Moon was a box office failure for Warner Brothers, grossing only $10 million in its 1986 run and earning mostly negative reviews, a disappointing performance compared to the nearly $70 million gross of *Purple Rain*.[3] But what critics and audiences may have missed at the time was that Prince was engaged in a larger project of cultural deconstruction aimed at stereotypes of Black male identity.[4] As biographer Dave Hill pointed out several years after the film's release, "Prince . . . makes the most of the incongruity created by these culturally alien infiltrations into a formula-genre where blacks had previously existed only as freaks, menials and Uncle Toms."[5] Placing two working-class Black characters within the film conventions of a 1930s-style comedy of manners allowed Prince to put African American vernacular culture into conversation with upper-class Anglo-European culture, a conversation that Prince used to demonstrate the fluidity and plurality of Black identity.

One scene in particular showcases Prince's character Tracy's ability to code-switch between European high culture and African American street culture. The scene (entitled "Down to Our World" on the DVD release) takes place at an upscale restaurant to which the film's rich, Anglo-European ingenue Mary Sharon has invited Tracy and Tricky for the stated purpose of introducing them to "the finer side of life." Tracy and Tricky initially play along, wearing tuxedos and speaking French to the waiter, but later upend the dinner with acts of linguistic and musical *détournement.* This begins with a joke, at Mary's expense, based on the lexicographic differences between African American Vernacular English and British English: Tracy writes the phrase "wrecka stow" on a napkin and demands that Mary make sense of it. After laughing at her attempts, and her protestations that the phrase is merely gibberish, Prince reveals its meaning—"record store"—by asking, very slowly and in an exaggerated Black dialect, "If you wanted to buy a Sam Cooke a'bum, where would you go?"

According to two of Prince's collaborators at the time, this scene was written by Prince himself and not the movie's screenwriter Becky Johnston: St. Paul Peterson recalled being given the "wrecka stow" test in real life by Prince, and Susannah Melvoin suggested that Prince had conceived of this joke years earlier.[6] Prince clearly had a specific effect in mind: the joke is an act of code-switching that gently mocks its white audience while showcasing the Black characters' multicultural fluency, and in this it recalls the trickster archetype of African American folklore upon which literary theorists Houston Baker and Henry Louis Gates Jr. based their theories of Black vernacular creative resistance.[7] Furthermore, it references the singer Sam Cooke, who was among the first African American soul artists to achieve crossover success with Anglo-American audiences and play at the formerly all-white Copacabana club in New York, a model of sophistication and cultural mobility that Prince was clearly evoking in *Under the Cherry Moon.*[8]

The scene's subsequent musical number further illustrates the African American characters' code-switching ability, this time musically. Taking an enormous portable stereo from beneath the table, Prince's character interrupts the restaurant's quiet violin and piano trio with a diegetic performance of his funk song "Girls and Boys." The movie signals the success of Prince/Tracy's musical mobility when the restaurant's patrons get up to dance. Though the song and party are soon shut down by the arrival of the film's antagonist, the point is clear: Black vernacular culture is mobile and its appeal multicultural, something which cannot as easily be said about European high culture.

This theme—the flexibility and mobility of Black identity—fits within Prince's career-long struggle against stereotypes of Black masculinity, and my focus in this chapter is how Prince deployed funk rhythm in this struggle. Specifically, Prince used funk rhythm in ways that celebrated its link to African-diasporic identity while simultaneously disrupting the stereotypes that the white Western imagination has projected onto that linkage, a discourse that ethnomusicologist Ronald Radano has dubbed "hot rhythm." Radano takes this term from white critical writing about early twentieth-century ragtime and jazz music: as Radano points out, these writers discursively conflated jazz and ragtime's *metric* difference—techniques like syncopation or cross-rhythm—with a biological conception of *racial* difference. Within this discourse, white writers constructed Black music as an evolutionarily primitive style compared to European music, a construction that reflects "white supremacist assumptions of a bestial Negro instinct" marked by violence, sex, and pounding drums.[9] As Radano demonstrates, this stereotype has informed public debate about successive genres of Black music from ragtime to hip-hop, regardless of whether the writer in question is praising or attacking that music, and throughout this chapter I use Radano's term "hot rhythm" to refer to this discourse in general.[10]

On one hand, there is a strong body of scholarship demonstrating how Black musical genres such as funk are informed by African-diasporic aesthetics. Scholars such as Eileen Southern, Olly Wilson, Samuel Floyd, Alexander Stewart, and Anne Danielsen have compellingly argued that rhythmic practices such as syncopation and triple-against-duple hemiola patterns (e.g., the *son* clavé pattern), common in many forms of African-diasporic music, derive from the multi-metric practices of West African music.[11] These authors in turn rely on a strong body of ethnomusicological literature, in particular the work of Richard Waterman and John Chernoff, that shows the practical similarities between African American musical aesthetics and those of the West African countries from which enslaved African people were predominantly brought to the United States.[12]

On the other hand, the white colonialist fantasy-fears of African rhythm that fuel the discourse of "hot rhythm" are so pervasive that they insinuate themselves into even the most well-intentioned critical and scholarly discussions of Black music. Two aspects of this discourse have been particularly sticky. First, from the earliest writings on ragtime and jazz, many music journalists who noted the rhythmic difference of Black popular music described that music as mindlessly violent and sexual.[13] For example, consider white America's response to rock 'n' roll music, née rhythm and blues, in the 1950s: concerned white citizen and covert KKK member Asa Carter infamously opined, "It appeals to the base in man, [and] brings out animalism and vulgarity," making plain the slippage between rhythmic difference, African American racial identity, violence, and sex that existed in the minds of many white Americans.[14]

Second, musicologists often construct African and African-diasporic musics as *temporally* different from Anglo-European music, with the idea that African-derived music is built on an essentially cyclic experience of time rather than the linear teleology of Western modernity. This position derives from the observation that many West African musical styles are based on the layering of repetitive rhythmic patterns rather than on harmonic teleology or melodic development, a quality that is shared with numerous groove-based musical genres created by African American musicians. The trouble begins when writers link the use of such cyclical rhythms to the prelapsarian fantasy of African identity as an Edenic refuge from the clock-punching, goal-oriented grind of Western industrial society, a stereotype that, Radano argues, proposes Black identity as an escape from "modernity."[15] Musicologist Kofi Agawu, a staunch critic of this position, points out that the literature of ethnomusicology portrays this perceived circularity of African music as a lack, "the absence of the kind of narrative curve that one typically encounters in Western melodies and forms of the nineteenth century."[16] Echoing Radano's argument, Agawu demonstrates that the assumed opposition between circular and linear temporality in African and Western music is a fiction, and argues that this selective focus on African circularity stems from underlying racial ideology. (Musicologist Robert Fink has extended Agawu's critique into the discussion of African American pop music genres such as funk, as I will discuss.)[17]

Because of the systemic racial bias of the American music industry of the 1970s, these stereotypes of "hot rhythm"—of Black music as essentially rhythmic, sexual, violent, and lacking in narrative teleology—were a defining backdrop to Prince's early career. From the beginning, Prince was aware that race was a factor that could limit his mobility in terms of musical genre and the pop-music marketplace.[18] Initially, he chose a hypersexual image for himself as a way to gain traction within an industry that expected that of him as a Black artist. According to

Prince's former guitarist Dez Dickerson, Prince conceived this onstage persona after receiving a lackluster response to their first show at the Roxy Theater in Los Angeles, when he told his band, "I've decided, I'm going to portray pure sex."[19] Over the course of his next six albums and associated tours, Prince wrote sexually explicit lyrics, wore revealing (and often gender-bending) outfits, and mimed sex acts onstage, such as simulating masturbation on his guitar neck with a specially modified guitar that "ejaculated" onto the audience by spraying water through a tube.[20] As biographer David Hill argued, some in the African American community viewed Prince's use of explicit sexuality as a capitulation to white stereotypes of the hypersexual Black man, a sentiment echoed by music critic Nelson George, who called several of Prince's songs "overt examples of quite disgusting immaturity."[21] I would argue that Prince's sexual subject position was subtler than these writers gave him credit for, imbued as it was with a sense of polymorphous gender play, but even Prince himself acknowledged the validity of this critique in later years, admitting in one interview, "We've all used shock value to sell things. . . . I used shock to get attention."[22]

After achieving crossover success with 1982's *1999* album and 1984's *Purple Rain*, Prince began dialing back his hypersexual image, yet the association between funk rhythm, the body, sexuality, and violence—-i.e., the "hot rhythm" stereotype—dogged him throughout his career. By 1984 the bikini-briefs-and-legwarmers look was long gone, and by 1986 even the regency ruffles of his famous *Purple Rain* outfits had been replaced by double-breasted suit jackets. Neither of the two albums that immediately followed *Purple Rain* contained any profane lyrics; on the contrary, one song from *Around the World in a Day*, "Temptation," featured the voice of an angry god condemning Prince's character for the sin of lust. In the movie *Under the Cherry Moon*, Prince insisted that his character, Tracy, die at the end, a decision that—according to Prince's then-publicist Howard Bloom—showed Prince's desire to symbolically kill off his own salacious image.[23] Yet even after all this, audience expectations of Prince's lustful persona continued to weigh on him: Prince structured his 1988 *Lovesexy* tour performance as a two-act sin-and-salvation trajectory (the first act devoted to his older, more sexually explicit hits, the second filled with his spiritually minded *Lovesexy* material), and made clear his intentions by announcing, "The first set I did because you expected it of me. The second half I do because this is where it's at."[24]

Another, perhaps more lasting, way that Prince combated this expectation of hypersexuality—and the racialized stereotypes of funk rhythm attached to it—was through a kind of strategic cosmopolitanism. As moral philosopher Anthony Kwame Appiah argues, cosmopolitanism provides an ethical "rubric" for living in our increasingly urbanized and globalized world, and it relies on a sort of dynamic tension: the cosmopolitan person maintains the value of their own nation or culture of origin while also respecting the "legitimate difference" of other nations and cultures, adopting "a sense of family and tribe that [is] multiple and overlapping."[25] As I will show in this chapter, a "multiple and overlapping" model of identity is precisely what Prince used funk rhythm to construct. Consider again the example of *Under the Cherry Moon*: with the clout he commanded after *Purple Rain*'s success, Prince could have conceivably gotten a green light for any film project he wanted. What he chose was to go to France, and the story he chose to tell showed the mobility and flexibility of Black music and identity. This decision placed Prince in a tradition of African American writers and artists—W. E. B. DuBois, Josephine Baker, James Baldwin—for whom the expatriate experience provided a space outside of American structural racism in which they could fashion new critical tools and/or artistic personae. Starting in the immediate postbellum period, Black leaders such as Frederick Douglass and Booker T. Washington traveled to France to visit "the land of the egalitarian principles," an expatriate experience that was shared by later generations of African American men who came to France as soldiers during WWI and WWII, where they had "their first taste of true equality."[26] As scholars Walton Muyumba and Paul Gilroy have argued, these cosmopolitan (or trans-local) experiences helped create moral and critical resources in the fights against racism and fascism.[27] Muyumba argues that the expatriate experience forced African American writers Ralph Ellison, James Baldwin, and Amiri Baraka "to interrogate the meanings of blackness, [and] American identity."[28] In so doing, those writers looked to blues and jazz music as experimental tools with which to create a "cosmopolitan blackness" that was rooted in Black expressive culture but transcended racial essentialisms.[29] Indeed, many influential jazz composers traveled extensively overseas (e.g., Louis Armstrong, Duke Ellington, Charlie Parker, Dizzy Gillespie), and their music incorporated cross-cultural influences—as Gary Giddins and Scott DeVeaux have written, "wherever jazz landed, it developed a bond with local musical practices"—demonstrating just the kind of "multiple and overlapping" cosmopolitan identities that Appiah described.[30] Prince was treading this same path in the 1980s and '90s using funk rhythm as a flexible framework in which to construct a mobile and plural model of identity that was both unapologetically Black and coolly cosmopolitan.

As I will show in this chapter's musical analyses, Prince's experimental approach to funk rhythm—first stripping it down to the bone, then putting it in dialogue with European symphonic orchestration—allowed him to dismantle the "hot rhythm" stereotypes that have historically clung to Black music in the white Western imagination. Though I'm certain he didn't conceive of his project in these terms, my musical analysis of several of his songs from the mid-1980s shows that Prince was constructing modes of subjectivity that falsified the association of funk rhythm with mindless physicality and circular, non-teleological temporality, and that also demonstrated funk's cosmopolitan, multicultural mobility. Specifically, the two songs that I discuss, "When Doves Cry" from *Purple Rain* and "Anotherloverholenyohead" from *Parade*, both use funk rhythm to enact the conflicted interior psychological state of the songs' protagonists, which, I argue, works against the discursive construction of groove-based, African American genres of music as encoding an externalized sense of identity marked by violence and sex. Second, these two songs use a mixture of cyclic and linear rhythmic processes to create teleological narratives, undermining the stereotype of Black musical temporality as essentially cyclical. Third, in "Anotherloverholenyohead," Prince creates a sonic equivalent to the cosmopolitan Blackness of his characters in *Under the Cherry Moon* by incorporating symphonic orchestration into his funk groove in a unique and destabilizing way.

Funk Rhythm and Psychological Interiority in "When Doves Cry"

Though *Purple Rain* might be best remembered for Prince's sexed-up persona and searing guitar heroics, the album's first single was "When Doves Cry," a funk song that presented a melancholy and conflicted persona. In it, Prince constructed a spare yet polyrhythmic groove that worked against the discourse of "hot rhythm" in two ways. First, he radically stripped down the musical texture, which at times consists of little more than a two-bar drum-machine ostinato. This austerity made the rhythmic layers more easily legible, an important factor for a funk song aimed at rock radio, and allowed the subtle conflicts embedded within these polyrhythms to enact the conflicted interior psyche portrayed in the lyrics, a decision that worked against the stereotype of funk rhythm as mindlessly physical. Second, Prince used additive layering, or what Mark Spicer calls "accumulative form," to give the song a narrative teleology.[31] By using rhythm and texture to create a dramatic song form that included an exposition, rising tension, climax, and resolution, Prince subverted the stereotype of Black, groove-based musical styles as temporally cyclic.

Principal shooting for the movie *Purple Rain* wrapped on December 22, 1983, and by March 1984 Prince had already submitted the second draft of the soundtrack album to Warner Brothers, having prerecorded much of it at a live concert the preceding April.[32] Yet something was still missing, and Prince wrote "When Doves Cry" as a last-minute addition to both soundtrack and movie. Making room for this song on the film's soundtrack meant omitting two previously included songs and cutting the length of two more, not to mention last-minute film edits. Yet Prince insisted, and personally selected "When Doves Cry" as the album's advance single. These were not choices that Warner Brothers quickly supported: in addition to the expenses incurred by these last-minute changes, "When Doves Cry" was a radical departure from the rock-guitar sound of "Let's Go Crazy" and "Purple Rain," the next two singles released from the album. "When Doves Cry" includes no distorted electric guitar save for a short introductory cadenza; instead, it features a repeating two-bar drum-machine groove, around which Prince arranged pointillistic synthesizer lines and backing vocals, giving it a distinctly funk style. However much it differed from contemporary rock radio, though, "When Doves Cry" was also quite different from the funk and R&B songs on *Billboard*'s Black Singles charts at the time: while songs like Marvin Gaye's "Sexual Healing," New Edition's "Candy Girl," and Gladys Knight's "Save the Overtime (for Me)" also featured drum machines and synthesizers, Prince gave "When Doves Cry" a uniquely austere sound by omitting the bass guitar from the final mix, a radical decision given the central role that bass typically plays in the funk genre, and one that could have made the song a hard sell for Black radio.[33] Yet the song was an instant and huge crossover hit, earning the number-one spot on *Billboard*'s Black Singles, Dance, *and* Hot 100 charts, and maintaining its position on each for weeks.[34]

Prince's decision to give "When Doves Cry" a bare instrumental texture radically unlike anything else on the *Purple Rain* soundtrack or on Black or white radio was a decision that perhaps owed to the unique psychological weight that the song carried in the film. Biographers have speculated that the song was motivated by Prince's breakup with a longtime girlfriend and/or by his difficult relationships with his own parents, but the movie in which it appeared provides a more useful hermeneutic framework. In that context, one can hear the song's tense rhythmic groove, ascetic instrumentation, claustrophobic minor harmony, and ambivalent lyrics as a musical depiction of the main character's interior emotional battle.[35] In the movie, Prince's character, the Kid, struggles to establish trusting relationships with several women in his life, a struggle that is informed by his fraught relationship to his father, whose abusive behavior toward his mother the Kid witnesses and later emulates. Prince encapsulates this Freudian family drama in the lyrics to "When Doves Cry" with lines such as "Maybe I'm just like my father, too bold" and "Maybe I'm just like my mother, she's never satisfied." Robert Walser argued that Prince's struggle with and eventual triumph over his own patriarchal impulses in *Purple Rain* constructs a model of "de-Oedipalized" subjectivity that resists binary gender and phallocentric sexual desire, a model that is also manifest in the austere yet funky polyrhythmic groove of "When Doves Cry."[36] I would like to make a parallel argument: that Prince uses funk rhythm in this song in a way that resists the equation of Black identity with mindless, externalized physicality, and with circular, non-teleological models of temporality.

Broadly understood, the hallmark of funk rhythm is the coexistence of two or more conflicting rhythmic layers. In his seminal 1974 article on African-diasporic aesthetics in pop music, Olly Wilson pointed out that funk artists like James Brown used rhythmic displacement at multiple hierarchical levels, from simple syncopation to actual polyrhythm or polymeter, techniques that are "an Afro-American adaptation of the West African practice of multimeter."[37] Building on Wilson's observations, Alexander Stewart argued that the defining element of funk rhythm is the tension between duple and triple subdivisions of beat and/or meter (such as a hemiola pattern), a tension that comes from New Orleans second-line drumming, which in turn derives from West African polyrhythmic practices that persisted owing to the French-colonial history of that city.[38] Scholars like Anne Danielsen have gone on to codify numerous specific techniques that funk pioneers like Brown and Parliament-Funkadelic used, including the group emphasis on the first downbeat of each cyclic repetition of the rhythmic ostinato (the "One" in funk parlance) and the tendency for rhythmic density to change near the end of each cycle in anticipation of the following heavy "One."[39] In his work on electronic dance music, a popular genre directly related to funk and disco, music theorist Mark Butler used

Table 1. Linn drum machine two-bar matrix

	1	&	2	&	3	&	4	&	1	&	2	&	3	&	4	&
high-hat						X	X									
side-stick		X	X								X	X				
snare drum			X				X				X				X	
low tom														X	X	
mid tom		X			X					X			X			
bass drum	X			X					X			X				

Harold Krebs's 1987 theory of rhythmic dissonance to codify how the multiple, conflicting rhythmic layers of dance music work together, and in the analysis that follows I will also adopt Krebs's terminology.[40]

The most distinctive aspect of "When Doves Cry" is the manner in which Prince sketches a groove that is funky by all the metrics mentioned above yet maintains a spare, almost empty texture, allowing this groove to enact both a psychological complexity and a forward-leaning process of rhythmic development that work against the stereotypes of hot rhythm. In the analysis that follows, I will demonstrate two things. First, I will discuss how Prince constructs the song's basic groove out of multiple, conflicting rhythmic layers. Using Krebs's concept of rhythmic dissonance, I will show how these rhythmic layers push and pull against each other to enact not just a funky, danceable groove but also a model of complex and conflicted psychological interiority, one significantly enhanced by the song's austere instrumentation. Second, I will explore how Prince progressively elaborates this texture by adding new rhythmic layers as the song goes on, creating a model of temporality that mixes cyclical and linear time.

Prince constructed the basic groove of "When Doves Cry" using a drum machine by Roger Linn, most likely the LinnDrum model first manufactured in 1982 (see example 19). Working with only five of the machine's fifteen basic sounds, Prince built an asymmetrical two-bar ostinato that contains multiple, conflicting rhythmic strata yet sounds relatively empty in texture. The groove uses an eighth-note grid with a drum sound occurring on every eighth-note of each bar except for the very last one (see table 1). While this may seem rhythmically dense on paper, the eighth-note is a slower subdivision of the beat—what Danielsen calls a "density referent" and Krebs calls the "pulse layer"—than typical funk rhythms, which normally use a sixteenth-note grid.[41] Yet the groove is unmistakably funky: in addition to the conflicting metric layers, Prince's decision to leave an empty eighth-note on the "and"

Example 19. "When Doves Cry," Linn drum machine ostinato

of beat 4 is another common funk rhythmic technique, which Danielsen calls the "downbeat in anticipation," that adds emphasis by creating a vacuum effect that draws the listener's attention forward to the upcoming downbeat.[42]

There is considerable empty space built into the groove of "When Doves Cry." In addition to the less-dense eighth-note grid, Prince also ensured that no single drum timbre played more than two successive eighth-notes (see table 1). But perhaps the greatest contribution to the groove's openness comes from the bass guitar, or rather, Prince's omission of it. In funk, bass is often a primary vector for off-beat phrasing and movement at the sixteenth-note level; as Duane Tudahl describes it, funk bass "propels the song and usually adds a heavy dose of sexuality."[43] In example 19, I have transcribed two lines that the bass player in Prince's band at the time, Mark Brown, added to this song during live performances on the *Purple Rain* tour. These live basslines may or may not be the same as what Prince had originally recorded for the song (which has never been released even in bootleg form), but they nonetheless illustrate how a typical funk-bass pattern would have impacted the groove. Each funk bass line starts with a loud, long note on the downbeat (either right on the "One" or in anticipation), and then adds rhythmic elaboration in the second half of the bar by syncopating beats three and four and subdividing the rhythm into the sixteenth-note level. By eliminating such a typical funk bassline, therefore, Prince purposefully left the pulse layer or density referent at the slower eighth-note level.

Within this eighth-note rhythmic matrix, Prince created a groove that conforms to both Krebs's model of rhythmic dissonance and Danielsen's model of funk rhythm. The first criteria is the presence of multiple rhythmic layers that move according to different note durations—the "pulse level"—and two or more slower "interpretive levels."[44] In "When Doves Cry," the drum machine groove includes a pulse layer of eighth notes provided mainly by the high-hat cymbal and side stick, while the bass drum, mid-tom, and snare drum provide slower interpretive layers by moving in half-note or dotted-quarter-note durations.

The second criteria of a funk groove is some degree of metrical dissonance between these multiple layers, and Prince's groove provides this as well. The snare drum plays a backbeat on beats 2 and 4, a slower interpretive layer but one that's metrically consonant, in Krebs' parlance, and is typical of both rock and funk drumming. Against this dominant metrical pulse, Prince uses the kick and tom-tom drums to provide cross-rhythms that introduce tension and complexity into the groove. The kick drum plays a heavy downbeat on beat 1 of both measures, conforming to the funk principle of a heavy "One," but then anticipates beat 3—its normal position in a pop/rock context—by an eighth-note. This creates an asymmetrical 3+5 rhythmic pattern, a syncopation that simultaneously destabilizes the strong-beat 3 but also draws the listener's attention back to it by anticipation (one is keenly aware of beat 3 having arrived early).[45] Furthermore, this kick drum pattern introduces a momentary triple-against-duple polyrhythm when heard in relation to the snare drum on beat four, with which the kick drum creates an aggregate pattern of 3+3+2 that's equivalent to a *son* clavé. This constitutes what Mark Butler calls an embedded grouping dissonance, and it gives the groove its polyrhythmic quality.

On top of this syncopated kick drum, the mid-tom plays the same 3+5 rhythm but displaced one eighth-note after the kick drum. This rhythmic displacement dissonance pulls the listener's attention away from beat 1, subtly destabilizing what should, in the funk tradition, be the single most unified beat of the entire measure. The second note of the mid-tom's pattern then counterbalances the kick drum's anticipation of beat 3 by playing directly on that beat. This creates a dynamic experience of the strong beats, 1 and 3: both strong beats are played by one drum timbre or the other, yet beat 1 has an echo and beat 3 has an anticipation, a rotational manipulation in which the kick-tom pattern remains the same yet changes relative to which timbre is on the beat. In sum, the drum-machine groove is multilayered and polyrhythmic, giving the listener both a rotating pull-push experience of the strong beats and an implicit triple-against-duple rhythmic dissonance.

As Butler argues, dividing spans of time asymmetrically is a common rhythmic strategy that dance-music producers use to create variety, and one that links dance music to African-diasporic rhythmic values.[46] In addition to the asymmetrical kick-tom rhythm described above, which happens in every bar of "When Doves Cry," Prince also gave the drum-machine ostinato a two-bar asymmetry that functions like a call-and-response rhythmic cycle. Prince does this using two higher-pitched drum machine timbres–the high-hat cymbal and side stick—and a low tom-tom drum sound. Unlike the other rhythmic layers in the drum groove, each of these timbres plays two eighth notes in a row, and their rhythmic position changes from bar 1 to bar 2 of the cycle. In the first bar, the "crack" of the side stick sounds on beat 2 and the preceding eighth-note, while the "tic" of the closed high-hat plays on beat 4 and its preceding eighth-note, a pattern that reinforces the snare drum backbeats. In the second bar of the cycle, Prince shifts the side-sticks an eighth note later so that they play "two-and" instead of "and-two," removing the syncopation. Also in the second bar, Prince replaces the high-hat cymbal with the low-tom's lub-dub on "and-four" (a lower pitched drum that gives the second bar of the ostinato a consequent or cadential feeling). This two-bar asymmetry gives the drum-machine ostinato a cyclic call-and-response quality, thus adding another layer of syncopation to the groove at a higher hierarchical level.

As I have described, Prince used rhythmic grouping and displacement dissonance at multiple levels to give this two-bar drum-machine groove an unmistakably funky quality, and there is an element of sensual pleasure in this. But Prince constructed it in a way that puts the listener *inside* the body of the song's main character, inviting us to share his sense of interiority rather than engaging with his exterior physicality—to identify rather than to ogle. He does this by using the lower-pitched drums—kick drum, mid-tom, and low-tom—as a heartbeat. Cultural theorist John Mowitt, echoing Roland Barthes, argues that even electronic drums link musical rhythm to the human body, serving as a mechanical analog for the heart in a way that bridges the physical and cultural constructions of that organ.[47] When the kick/tom play their asymmetrical pattern ("one and—and three"), the alternation between the louder, lower-pitched kick and the quieter, higher-pitched mid-tom creates a heartbeat effect (strong-weak, strong-weak) that we hear twice per bar throughout the entire song. Prince reinforced this with the low-tom drum layer, which adds another "lub-dub" on the eight-notes "and-four" in the second bar of the ostinato. Heard as a heartbeat, then, these asymmetrical lub-dubs give the listener a feeling of occupying the main character's *interior* physical space.

Having drawn us into identifying with the main character in this way, the tension of the drum-machine groove (its rhythmic dissonances and asymmetries), combined with the comparative emptiness of its eighth-note grid, enact the internal conflict of the song's main subject. Consider the hermeneutic window provided by the movie's plot. At the point where Prince and his director, Albert Magnoli, inserted "When Doves Cry" into the movie, we see four intercut scenes: the present, in which the main character meanders alone through the Minnesota countryside; a previous scene of happiness between the main character and his girlfriend in that same idyllic landscape; and two previous scenes of trauma, one in which the main character's father strikes his mother, and another in which the main character strikes his girlfriend. These juxtapositions of sensuality and violence mimic the lyrical structure of "When Doves Cry," in which the verses reminisce about intense physical attraction and pleasure, but the choruses present the Freudian family drama in miniature, linking the main character's romantic conflict to his conflicting feelings of identification with his mother and father.

Within this hermeneutic frame, the dissonant rhythmic strata of the drum groove and its two-bar asymmetrical push and pull enact both sexuality and psychological tension. On one hand, we can easily map the sensual lyrics onto the interpenetration of rhythmic layers to form a musical picture of the steamy intertwining between the main character and his lover, precisely the kind of oversexed narrative that the discourse of "hot rhythm" would lead us to expect in a funk groove. On the other hand, Prince's lyrical and visual alternation between sensuality and psychological conflict invites us to hear the individual parts of the drum-machine groove as individual actors in the psychodrama unfolding onscreen and in the lyrics, or as competing impulses within the main character, or both. The austerity of the groove lends weight to this psychological reading by making it easier for the listener to distinguish the individual layers within the groove. As Mark Butler points out in his analysis of the drum groove in a James Brown song, "the marked timbral differences between the three drum sounds make it easy for the listener to 'tune in' closely to particular strands within the texture, while the interlocking rhythmic attacks enable an alternate focus on the composite rhythm."[48] In the case of "When Doves Cry," it is not just the timbral differences that make the drums easy to distinguish, but the relative emptiness of the eighth-note density referent and the lack of bass guitar.

The listener is thus free to interpret the groove in a number of different ways. One can focus on the heartbeat of the kick and mid-tom and hear their push-pull rotation as a symptom of the main character's internal conflict between tenderness and anger. Alternately, one can focus on the faster-moving layers (the side stick, high-hat, and low-tom) and the asymmetrical two-bar cycle they create, and hear in that cycle an echo of the Oedipal drama, with the higher-pitched high-hat sound in the antecedent bar representing the son's questioning of his identity and the lower-pitched tom-tom in the consequent bar marking the father's threatening answer. Or one's attention may drift among these different conflicting layers, drawn at one moment toward the snare drum's cracking transient on beat 2 and at another toward the low-tom's off-beat "lub-dub," and that drift itself can serve as an analog to the main character's internal confusion. Because of this interpretive openness, the rhythmic conflict built into the drum-machine groove is not simply sensual but also pensive, giving the listener an experience of psychological interiority that transcends exterior physicality. In sum, by offering the listener multiple pathways through the groove and making these different pathways so easy to pick out, Prince puts the listener in a contemplative space that mimics that of the song's principal character.

Rhythmic Development in "When Doves Cry"

So far, I have discussed how Prince used a repeating two-bar drum-machine ostinato in "When Doves Cry" to enact the main character's psychological interiority, a move that falsifies the stereotype of funk rhythm as hypersexual and mindlessly physical. But Prince was also using another rhythmic tool to dismantle the discourse of hot rhythm: accumulative form. Specifically, Prince used the drum-machine ostinato as the starting point for a process of rhythmic development, adding and subtracting other layers to produce a large-scale narrative, a move that contradicts the stereotype that African-diasporic musical genres encode an essentially cyclical experience of time. This stereotype is deeply embedded in the white Western imagination, and has led many writers to portray Black music as an escape from industrial modernity's relentless focus on linear clock time. As I mentioned earlier in this chapter, musicologists like Radano, Agawu, and Fink have already demonstrated how African and African American music employs linear teleology, even in the absence of melodic or rhythmic development, through the use of rhythmic and dynamic intensification over time (Spicer's "accumulative form").[49] Prince uses this technique at two different levels in "When Doves Cry": first, he adds and subtracts ostinati to differentiate the alternating sections of the song (e.g., verse and chorus); second, he adds new layers over time (both repetitive instrumental ostinati and non-cyclic vocal layers) to increase the rhythmic/textural density. Over the course of the song, Prince uses this textural accretion to develop a narrative structure of climax and resolution that augments the psychological complexity of the drum ostinato described above.

Prince creates a cyclic alternation between three different formal sections, which I will call the verse, chorus, and vamp, by adding and subtracting two synthesizer ostinati. The verses are the least dense of the three sections: Prince adds no synthesizer ostinati, so that the texture of the first verse includes nothing more than the drum machine ostinato and Prince's lead vocal melody. The vamp, an eight-bar section without any vocals that comes immediately before each verse, includes the drum machine and a simple two-bar synthesizer ostinato (labeled Synth 1 in example 20). The chorus is relatively busier in texture, as Prince added both a two-bar synth ostinato (Synth 2 in example 20) and a backing vocal part.

These two synthesizer ostinati (Synth 1 in the vamp and Synth 2 in the chorus) are short and simple—two bars long, made from eighth-notes played with a crisp, pointillistic articulation—but they add another layer of polyrhythm, deepening the song's portrayal of psychological complexity. Each has an antecedent-consequent phrase structure in which the first bar is rhythmically consonant but the second bar is syncopated, creating asymmetrical two-bar patterns similar to that of the drum machine. During the chorus section, the Synth 2 ostinato has running eighth-notes through its first measure, but in its second bar it omits the notes on beats three and four, creating a series of syncopations that anticipate the following downbeat (one-and-two-and-*rest*-and-*rest*-and). During the vamp sections, the first bar of the Synth 1 ostinato is also metrically consonant, playing eighth notes on "one, two-and-three," but in in its second bar Prince plays its second eighth-note a sixteenth early, creating a displacement dissonance that fragments the groove of the song into the sixteenth-note grid (at least momentarily). The met-

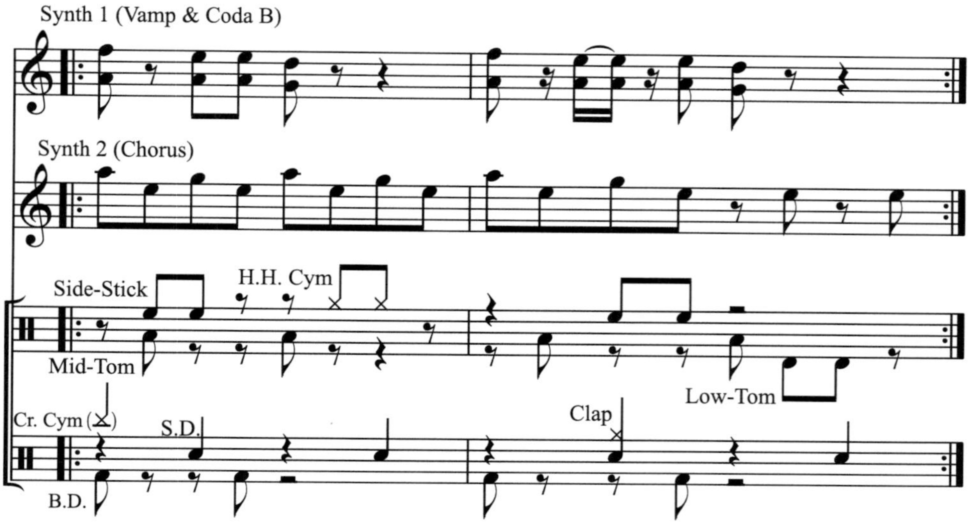

Example 20. "When Doves Cry," drum machine and synthesizer ostinati

ric dissonances introduced by these two ostinati conform to Stewart and Danielsen's models of funk rhythm, in which additional layers add momentary cross-rhythms that allow the listener to simultaneously experience the dominant metrical accent pattern and "virtual alternatives" to that pattern.[50] Furthermore, they do so without adding much more textural density to the overall groove, maintaining the ascetic quality and interpretive openness that Prince established with the drum ostinato and lack of bass, an openness that invites the listener to experience the rhythmic push-and-pull of the groove as an enactment of the main character's interior conflict.

By adding and subtracting these two synthesizer ostinati (Synth 1 and 2), Prince created a hypermetric structural cycle of vamp, verse, and chorus sections. In one sense, this reinforces the stereotype of cyclic temporality that white writers have attributed to groove-based, African-diasporic genres such as funk, a stereotype that Agawu, Radano, and Fink have debunked.[51] Yet this structural cyclicism is the backdrop for a linear rhythmic teleology, based on the technique of accumulative form, that culminates in two climactic moments (one during the final chorus and another during the song's extended coda). Prince used two rhythmic techniques to create this teleology: first, he added new synthesizer ostinati with each successive repetition of the verse and chorus sections, creating a buildup of tension that culminates in the song's third chorus. Second, he added non-repeating layers of backup vocals, contributing to both the third-chorus climax and an even bigger climax during the song's extended coda section.

In addition to the Synth 1 and 2 ostinati, Prince added two more synthesizer ostinati in successive repetitions of the verse and chorus sections to create a linear accumulation of rhythmic/textural density. (The song's overall form is: intro, vamp, verse 1, verse 2, chorus 1, vamp, verse 3, chorus 2, vamp, chorus 3, coda.) After the electric guitar intro that opens the song, the sections that follow gradually increase in density: starting with the vamp (which includes only the drum machine and Synth 1 ostinati), the texture remains austere through verses 1 and 2 (which include only drum machine ostinato and lead vocal), and then increases dramatically in the first chorus, whose addition of the Synth 2 ostinato *and* backup vocals make it the most rhythmically dense section up to that point. From this point on, Prince added new rhythmic layers to each repetition of these sections. In the third verse, Prince added the Synth 3 ostinato (example 21): this new layer is a four-bar cycle consisting of a near-constant string of metronomic eighth-notes similar to the Synth 2 ostinato (though without any syncopation or rhythmic dissonance). In the third and final chorus, Prince added the Synth 4 ostinato (example 22), which moves in whole and half notes, a much slower interpretive layer than any of the song's other ostinati.

Prince's addition of these two new synth ostinati gives the listener a sense of progression despite the cyclic repetition of formal sections, a cue that time is indeed moving forward, in contrast to the conception of groove-based music as purely cyclical. This culminates in the third and final chorus, in which the addition of the Synth 4 ostinato provides a sense of climax and resolution. Unlike all previous ostinati, Synth 4 consists of three- and four-note chords, and given the lack of bass guitar, its four-bar chord progression (Amin, Dmin/A, G, E7sus6–5) comes as

Example 21. "When Doves Cry," verse 3 synth ostinato

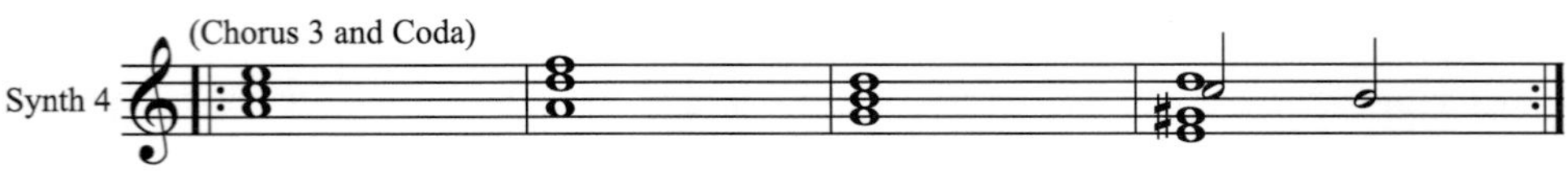

Example 22. "When Doves Cry," chorus 3 / coda synth ostinato

a harmonic revelation (see example 22). The song's vocal melody has been repetitive up to this point, moving between A and G (tonic and Aeolian flat seventh), and resolving to E or G♯ (dominant or harmonic-minor leading tone) at the cadences; this pattern has been the same from verse to chorus, making the lead vocal a de facto ostinato but for the changing lyrics. When Synth 4 enters, however, it recontextualizes that vocal melody as chord-tones within the Amin, Dmin/A, G, E7sus6–5 progression. The drama of this moment has as much to do with Synth 4's rhythmic characteristics as its harmony: the listener suddenly experiences the song's repetitive melody and two-bar drum and synth ostinati as parts of a larger, slower-moving whole, and at the same time they can mentally project this cycle backwards, respelling and reexperiencing the previous sections of the song in an instant. In this sense, the entry of Synth 4 contributes to the linear, climactic quality of the third chorus not despite but because of Prince's use of rhythmic cycles.

This climactic quality does not come solely from Prince's use of repeating ostinati, however. He also added non-cyclic layers of multitracked vocals, creating an accumulative form with two distinct climaxes: the first, discussed above, happens in the song's third chorus, and the second during the song's extended coda. During the chorus, the main vocal melody is comprised of four phrases, one per line of text, each made up of a two-bar antecedent and a two-bar consequent sub-phrase (see example 23). Every antecedent sub-phrase uses the same rhythmic motive of 1+1+1+2+1+1+2+2 (where eighth note = 1) on lines that include "how could you *just* leave me *stan*-ding" and "may-be I'm *just* like my *mo*-ther" (my italics indicate the longer, syncopated notes; see example 23). This yields an overall rhythmic scheme of A-B-A-C-A-D-E-F where "A" is the main rhythmic cell, and its high degree of repetition means that the "A" rhythmic motive serves as the chorus's hook. Adding to the repetitive quality, all the other rhythmic phrases (B, C, D, E, and F) are closely related to that hook, only differing by one or two eighth notes each (see example 23). Furthermore, the main melody of the chorus remains consistent over successive repetitions: there are some minor rhythmic variations in the second chorus, but the third chorus's main vocal melody is identical to that of the first.

As the song form unfolds, Prince introduces linear rhythmic development by multitracking this "main" melody and adding a new lead vocal track that provides increasingly elaborate antiphonal responses. This process happens primarily in the chorus sections, which are each sixteen bars long, divided into regular four-bar phrases. During the

Example 23. “When Doves Cry,” choruses 1 and 3 vocals

(*continued*)

choruses, Prince adds multitracked harmony vocals to the main melody, creating a choir that sings the hook-y rhythmic motive described above. Prince then fills in the rhythmic space around it by adding a new, antiphonal lead-vocal track that changes over time. This process begins gradually: during the first chorus, Prince's lead-vocal track interjects just two responses, one after the first four-bar phrase and one after the third (see example 23, top staff). These lead-vocal responses are syncopated, adding a new layer of rhythmic-displacement dissonance, but they are also quiet and relatively short, and thus don't overpower the main rhythmic motive sung by the backing choir. In the second chorus, Prince also restricts his lead-vocal responses to the spaces after the first and third phrases of the choir's main vocal melody, but this time the lead-vocal responses are longer and more rhythmically complex than in the first chorus, and Prince delivers them in two-part harmony, adding more rhythmic/textural density and raising the dynamic level.

This sense of growing tension explodes during the third, climactic chorus section, when Prince's antiphonal lead vocals introduce counter-rhythms so insistent that they threaten to overwhelm the dominant pulse of the meter (see example 23, middle staff). In this final chorus, Prince adds lead-vocal responses after all four phrases of the choir's main melody, as opposed to just the first and third phrases, as well as mid-phrase interjections that subdivide the second, third, and fourth phrases into two-bar call-and-response patterns, doubling the middleground rhythmic activity. Throughout, Prince matches the rising emotional tenor of his character's internal monologue with the increasing rhythmic dissonance of his lead vocal melody.

The first vocal response is similar to those in choruses 1 and 2, coming at the end of the first four-bar phrase and echoing a fragment of the first line of text ("world that's so cold") on a syncopated rhythm. However, Prince's lead-vocal responses to the second, third, and fourth lines of text all begin *before* the backing choir has finished declaiming the main melody lines, and are much more rhythmically active, blurring the roles of call and response and stealing focus from the main melodic hook. In the second four-bar phrase, Prince's mid-phrase interjection of "may-be" begins *before* the backing vocalists have finished declaiming the line "maybe I'm just too demanding," and delivers two displacement dissonances that anticipate beats 1 and 3 (while pushing upward melodically to a relatively high E). Prince's next lead-vocal interjection comes in the consequent half of this same four-bar phrase (on the line "maybe I'm just like my father, too bold"), with Prince's lead vocal declaiming the word "father" on strong-beat 3 (ahead of the backing choir), as if to associate the Freudian law-of-the-father with the on-beat metrical accent. The lead vocal ends this second four-bar phrase by interjecting three short, syncopated grace notes anticipating beats 1, 2, and 3, creating another displacement dissonance (these are higher notes, too, pushing against the high E which had been the song's pitch ceiling to this point).

On the third phrase of this last chorus, the backing choir begins with the line "maybe I'm just like my *mo*-ther," after which Prince's antiphonal lead vocal interjects a complex counter-rhythm that includes displacement dissonances and an implied triple-against-duple grouping dissonance. In the antecedent two-bar half of this phrase, the lead vocal begins on beat 4 of the measure with an anguished vocal timbre on a high F (breaking the previously established pitch ceiling of E) on the word "maybe"; Prince holds this last syllable over the barline, providing a syncopated lead-in to the downbeat that's common in funk (per Danielsen, the "downbeat in anticipation"). The lead vocal then echoes the rest of the line "I'm just like my mother" in a headlong rush that pushes rhythmically ahead of the beat as it sinks downward melodically from high F to the tonic A, making the whole second bar of the phrase into one long displacement dissonance. Prince also introduces a subtle sixteenth-note triplet-swing pattern at several points in this measure (see example 23), on the words "I'm just" and "mother." Whether or not he intended them as triplets, Prince's addition of these rhythmic grouping dissonances adds an emotional weight to those words that mirrors his anguished vocal tone on the word "mother": where the lead vocals had previously sung "father" directly on the strong beat, they now add counter-rhythmic spin to the word "mother," as though trying to escape the dominance of the on-beat metric accent, a Freudian family drama in rhythmic miniature. In the consequent half of this third phrase, Prince adds a rhythmic grouping dissonance (an implied sixteenth-note triplet on the downbeat of the second measure) and also leads the beat in several places, including another "downbeat in anticipation" that elides the barline between the third and fourth phrases of the chorus.

During the fourth and final phrase of this third chorus, Prince's lead vocal line is slightly less rhythmically active, providing a kind of winding-down after the excitement of the third phrase. During the antecedent half of the fourth phrase, the lead vocal continues to use syncopated displacement dissonances that lead the beat, including a virtuosic melisma on the word "why" that anticipates the downbeat with a melodic leap up to a C, the highest note in the song's vocal melody. In the consequent half of this last phrase, Prince's lead vocal melody ends its call-and-response interaction and delivers the last line in rhythmic unison with the choir: "what it sounds like when doves cry."

Throughout this last chorus section, Prince's interplay between the rhythmically repetitive main melody sung by the choir and the through-composed rhythmic dissonances interjected by the lead vocal enacts the main character's internal psychic tension. Although the main melody (sung by the choir) includes some embedded rhythmic dissonance, these have become regularized through repetition, and by the third chorus the listener experiences the main melodic hook primarily as an on-the-beat eighth-note pulse. Against this, Prince's antiphonal lead-vocal responses, with their phrase-by-phrase changes and virtuosic rhythmic manipulations, suggest a character searching for a way to escape or subvert the dominant eighth-note pulse and the paternal authority for which it stands. Prince's vocals trace a journey in this chorus section: from rhythmic conformity, on the line "world that's so cold," he grows more dissonant with his syncopation in successive phrases, reserving his greatest rhythmic dissonance—triple against duple grouping dissonance—for lyrics about his mother. In the end, however, Prince's character seems to acquiesce to the law of the father by coming back into rhythmic unison at the final sub-phrase of the chorus, rejoining both the dominant beat and the chorus of backup singers.

Whether or not we hear Prince's rhythmic improvisations in this third chorus as an escape from or a capitulation to the patriarchal domination with which Prince's character struggles in the movie, there are two conclusions that we can draw regarding the stereotypes of "hot rhythm." The first is that rhythm is the musical parameter with which Prince made the most compelling depiction of internal psychological tension. Far from the stereotypical associations that "hot rhythm" paints between Black musical rhythm and moral depredation, the violent pounding of fists, and/or sexual abandon, Prince used some of the most characteristic gestures of funk rhythm—the downbeat in anticipation, syncopated displacement dissonance, triple against duple grouping dissonance—with great subtlety to show the main character's psychological dialectic between resistance and capitulation to the patriarchy. This depiction of internal psychic struggle, rather than an external physicality dominated by either sex or violence, is precisely the opposite of what the discourse of "hot rhythm" would have us expect. It's also telling that the psychic struggle Prince depicts in this song represents a challenge to the constitutive role of violence in the formation of masculinity: where Freud's Oedipal struggle dictates that the infliction of patriarchal violence on the male child—the beating—is what internalizes the law of the father and with it the "proper" sexual and gender roles, Prince's lead-vocal interjections resist and question the primacy of the metrical layer, which is the ersatz rhythmic law of the father.

The second conclusion is that funk rhythm is not "essentially" cyclical in its temporality, nor does the presence of cyclical rhythms in the groove oppose or preclude linear teleology. Far from it, in fact: by establishing rhythmic cycles on the foreground, middle-ground, and background levels—the main vocal rhythm, the call-and-response sub-phrases, and the alternation of structural sections, respectively—Prince set up a system in which he could create a narrative of rising tension and climax by making relatively subtle rhythmic changes over time. By adding and subtracting different elements to the groove, Prince created a sense of structural progression from vamp to verse to chorus. By introducing and then deviating from this structural cycle, Prince gave the third chorus a sense of dangerous import. By setting up and then intensifying the antiphonal interaction between the rhythmically repetitive main melody of the chorus and the increasingly dissonant rhythmic responses of the lead vocals during the chorus, Prince brought the sense of climax to fruition in the third chorus.

Song-versus-Groove Tension in the Coda of "When Doves Cry"

The version of "When Doves Cry" that Prince's label released as a radio single fades out after that third chorus, lasting under four minutes. However, the album version is over two minutes longer, and its coda section is also worth examining for what it shows us about Prince's use of rhythm to create different modes of temporality. The chief difference between this two-minute coda and the preceding sections of "When Doves Cry" is that Prince suspends the cyclic alternation between vamp, verse, and chorus sections that he had previously established and instead allows the coda to unfold as one long extended jam, with no recurring hypermetric cycle of sections. Instead, Prince uses several of the song's preexisting ostinati to provide the bedrock groove of the coda, over which he layers seemingly improvised interjections from the voice, guitar, and synthesizer.

The cessation of the middle-ground structural cycle of vamp, verse, and chorus immediately puts the listener in a different relationship to the passage of time, which feels distinctly more cyclical owing to the repetitive, ostinato-based nature of the groove. Danielsen argues that this coexistence of formless, cyclical, groove-based sections within the more formally regularized verse and chorus structure of a pop song is a common feature in funk (especially Parliament-Funkadelic and the later work of James Brown), one that she explains with the idea of groove-versus-song tension.[52] She argues that the groove of a funk song—its repeating polyrhythmic ostinato—represents the "pure" state of funk, one that is akin to a Heideggerian state of "being" (in which the listener experiences the groove as the unfolding of an ever-changing same).[53] By contrast, she argues that the linear structure of verse and chorus sections—the pop song form—is an external imposition onto that pure groove, one that is demanded by the linear, teleological listening habits of Western listeners and the economic necessity of selling records. In light of Danielsen's theory, we can hear the two-minute coda at the end of "When Doves Cry" as a restoration of the "pure groove" after the necessities of a linear song structure have been met.

However, as Robert Fink has argued, Danielsen's Heideggerian song-versus-groove theory hews too closely to the racially biased perspective of groove-based music as an essentially cyclic alternative to linear temporality—a palliative for listeners wanting to escape the "time-is-money" ethos of modern life.[54] In other words, conceiving of a binary distinction between the pure groove and the linear song structure devalues the ways that funk artists create syntax and channel desire using rhythmic, textural, and dynamic processes. This is precisely what Prince did during the coda section of "When Doves Cry." First, Prince gave the coda an episodic structure through the addition and subtraction of different layers (both instrumental ostinati and non-repeating parts). Second, one of the non-repeating rhythmic layers that Prince added was a vocal motive which he treated to a process of durational diminution. Finally, Prince used both processes—the structural addition and subtraction of rhythmic elements and the developing vocal interjections—to create a large-scale narrative structure that includes a spectacular climax.

Despite the end of the song's verse-chorus structure, Prince gave the coda section an easily discernible episodic structure (comprising 10 eight-bar or 20 four-bar phrases) by adding and subtracting the song's rhythmic ostinati; specifically, the two-bar drum machine ostinato, the Synth 1 and 2 ostinati from the vamp and chorus, and the Synth 4 ostinato from chorus 3 (see table 2). As Butler points out, this is the same technique that electronic dance-music producers use to create a sense of narrative syntax in their loop-based music, although Prince recorded his instrumental ostinati live instead of using prerecorded loops (other than the drum machine's sequenced two-bar pattern), allowing for some harmonic and melodic variation.[55] In contrast to the song's preceding verse, chorus, and vamp sections, the coda finds Prince recombining the drum and synth ostinati in new ways. For example, in the coda Synth 4 enters first, and is joined eight bars later by Synth 1, a combination that did not occur during the proper song structure; later, Synth 2 joins Synth 4 while Synth 1 drops out, another novel recombination. Furthermore, Prince also added and subtracted some of the individual drum voices within the drum machine's two-bar ostinato. For example, the snare drum and crash cymbal drop out at the beginning of the coda, leaving an extremely sparse rhythmic texture; the snare drum reenters after eight bars, reestablishing the backbeat, followed by the crash cymbal layer after an additional eight-bar phrase has passed.

Prince's addition and subtraction of these preestablished rhythmic ostinati gives the coda a satisfying narrative structure (see table 2). The dropping-out that occurs at the beginning of the coda is a dramatic letdown after the intensity of the third chorus, and it destabilizes the listener's sense of the dominant metric accents (i.e., by dropping out the snare-drum backbeat and crash-cymbal downbeat). The next two eight-bar phrases progressively increase the polyrhythmic tension and intensity of the groove with the addition of more rhythmic elements (i.e., snare drum, synth 1, and crash cymbal). Having built the groove back up to full rhythmic density in the third eight-bar section, Prince leaves the groove unchanged for the three following eight-bar phrases (from mm. 122–145), letting the listener stew in the emotional ambiguity left over from the song's third chorus: is the principal character celebrating the resolution of his emotional dilemma, or is he still racked by internal, Oedipal tension? During this part of the coda, Prince creates a sense of rising action by adding through-composed layers of vocals and guitar that increase the textural density and dynamic level, leading up to a climactic section that begins at m. 146 (both of which I will discuss in more detail later). This climactic coda section (mm. 146–161) starts with another radical break in the texture, when all instrumental ostinati drop out except for a bare-bones drum machine groove of kick and tom-tom drums, after which Prince adds non-cyclical vocals and a synthesizer solo to create a climax (example 25). After this climax, the last sixteen bars of the coda serve as a narrative denouement, in which Prince brings back the synth and drum ostinati but allows the harmonic, rhythmic, and dynamic tension of the through-composed layers to wind down, ending with a reduced texture and a tonic cadence on the downbeat of m. 177.

Cyclic layers aren't the only rhythmic technique he uses, however: Prince also adds through-composed parts for voice, guitar, and synthesizer that contributed to the coda's narrative arc. The first of these layers is a guitar solo, which enters in the second eight-bar phrase of the coda (see table 2), at the same time as the Synth 1 and snare drum ostinati's reentry. This guitar solo contributes to the sense of forward temporal motion, but it's definitely *not* the climactic event of the coda: Prince keeps the dynamic level of the guitar solo well below the other elements

Table 2. "When Doves Cry" coda, textural changes

						Example 24							Example 25							
Measure #	98	102	106	110	114	118	122	126	130	134	138	142	146	150	154	158	162	166	170	174
Time	3:20	3:28	3:35	3:43	3:50	3:58	4:05	4:13	4:20	4:28	4:36	1:44	4:51	4:59	5:06	5:14	5:21	5:29	5:36	5:44
Backup Vocal		X		X	X		X				X	X	X		X	X	X	X		
Lead Vocal	X	X	X	X	X	X	X	X	X	X			X		X	X	X	X	X	
Guitar Solo			X	X	X	X	X	X												
Synth Solo														X	X					X
Synth 2																X	X	X	X	
Synth 1			X	X	X	X	X	X	X	X	X	X								
Synth 4	X	X	X	X	X	X	X	X	X	X	X	X				X	X	X	X	X
Crash					X	X	X	X	X	X	X	X								
Snare			X	X	X	X	X	X	X	X	X	X				X	X	X	X	
LM-1	X	X	X	X	X	X	X	X	X	X	X	X	X	X	X	X	X	X	X	

Table 2 legend: One column = 4 bars, *italics = cyclical ostinati*, **bold = through-composed melodies** in the mix, and doesn't display the kind of virtuosity that would make a guitar solo stand out in the context of a traditional rock or funk song.

The two other through-composed layers that Prince adds to the coda section—the vocal parts and synthesizer solo—contribute the most to the coda's (and the song's second) rhythmic and melodic climax. This process begins in the "rising-action" section of mm. 122–145 (the fourth, fifth, and sixth 8-bar sections of the coda), and reaches its climax in mm. 146–161 (the seventh and eighth 8-bar sections). Prince's lead vocal line makes a number of interjections during this time span—some wordless, some repeating fragments of previous lines—and though they give the impression of spontaneous outbursts of emotion, on closer examination they reveal very careful rhythmic placement. Each lead-vocal interjection includes a short rhythmic motive that Prince briefly develops (often through rhythmic diminution) before moving on, and the progressive intensification of these rhythmic interactions heightens the depiction of a conflicted interior psyche.

For example: during the rising-action section, Prince's first lead-vocal interjection comes during the guitar solo, at the pickup to the fourth four-bar phrase (example 24, m. 109). In his falsetto register, Prince sings a melismatic two-bar rhythmic and melodic motive (on the words "oh yeah") that begins on the "and" of beat 1 and stays consistently off the beat, creating a one-bar metric displacement with a downbeat-in-anticipation leading into the second bar. Furthermore, by starting this melody in m. 109, Prince elides the end of a four-bar phrase, thus creating a displacement dissonance both at the mid-level of the melodic phrase structure as well as at the micro-level of the groove. Prince then repeats this motive twice in the next four-bar phrase (in mm. 111–12 and mm. 113–14), creating two downbeat-in-anticipation elisions where the previous four-bar phrase had only one; at the same time, Prince adds two multitracked voices singing background harmony, increasing the textural as well as the rhythmic density. Prince then compresses three statements of that motive in the following four-bar phrase. Measures 115, 116, and 117 each contain one statement of the motive: the first two have their final notes clipped short, but the third does not, and this syncopated downbeat-in-anticipation elides the end of that four-bar phrase, returning the motive to its original rhythmic position relative to the phrase end. In sum, Prince's rhythmic rotation of this short motive uses displacement dissonances and a process of rhythmic diminution (repeating the motive more times in each successive phrase) to create a micro-structure that moves from exposition (mm. 109–110) to rising

Example 24. "When Doves Cry" coda, rhythmic development in vocal part (mm. 106–118)

action (mm. 111–14), climax (mm. 115–16) and closure (mm. 117–18), all within a ten-bar span of time that, owing Prince's use of downbeat-in-anticipation phrase elisions, links together four successive four-bar phrases (mm. 106–109, 110–13, 114–17, and 118–21).

After this and several other lead-vocal interjections during the "rising-action" section of mm. 122–145 (interjections that use repetition and variation of short motives, as described above, to create a gradual rhythmic intensification), Prince creates a climactic section in mm. 146–161. This begins with a textural break at m. 146 (at the start of the coda's seventh eight-bar phrase) when the snare drum, crash cymbal, and Synth 2 layers all drop out, leaving only the bass drum, side-stick, tom-toms, hi-hat, and Synth 4 ostinati. The remaining drum-machine ostinati are the off-beat, rhythmically dissonant layers of the groove, and without the on-beat accents provided by the crash and snare they destabilize the duple meter, creating a sense of expectancy. (Prince mitigates this somewhat by changing Synth 4's rhythm to straight quarter notes, although its volume level is very low relative to the drums). Prince answers that expectancy with a new, through-composed vocal layer that enters on the "and" of beat 3, functioning like a consequent rhythmic phrase to the asymmetrical drum-machine pattern (see example 25).

Just as with the vocal interjection in the rising-action section described above, Prince gives this climactic section (mm. 146–61) a distinctive form—exposition, rising action, climax, and resolution—by repeating the vocal melody with rhythmic variation (though he also interjected a synthesizer solo; see example 25). The vocal melody is four bars long and consists of an off-beat antecedent rhythmic cell that's repeated three times—a single chord, sung on "ah" for about a half note's duration, that anticipates beat three of the bar—followed by an on-beat consequent cell consisting of four quarter-note chords (see example 25, mm. 146–49). Rhythmically, the antecedent cell of the vocal melody forms a call-and-response pattern with the (reduced) drum machine groove—the drum machine plays low-pitched drum sounds on the first three eighth notes of the bar, and the choir's high-pitched "ah" answers on the fourth—and the syncopated nature of the "ah" extends the rhythmic displacement dissonance built into the drum-machine groove. Taken together with the minor-mode harmony and the sudden reduction in texture, this four-bar choral melody suggests a character crying out in psychic anguish.

After stating this choral "ah" melody once (the "exposition"), Prince interjects a synthesizer solo (the "rising action") and then brings the choral melody back a second time with rhythmic variation (the "climax" and "resolution,") at mm. 154–57. Rhythmically, he shifts the choir's antecedent cell onto the downbeat of each bar, making it consonant with the dominant metric pulse, and slows down the consequent cell from quarter-notes to half-notes. In between these phrases, Prince adds a virtuosic, through-composed synthesizer solo; the first four bars of this synthesizer solo take place in the absence of vocals, but the second half of the solo is juxtaposed against the varied return of the choral "ah" melody, and it is the combination of these two rhythmic layers that constitutes the song's second and final climax.

This eight-bar synthesizer solo moves at the sixteenth- and thirty-second note duration levels, making it by far the song's fastest rhythmic layer, and this drastic change gives the solo an intensely dramatic quality. According to keyboard player Matt Fink, Prince recorded the keyboard solo at a slower speed in the studio, allowing it to sound brilliantly fast at normal tape speed; according to several bandmembers, Prince intended to evoke a Baroque or Classical style as a friendly challenge to his bandmate Lisa Coleman, a classically trained pianist.[56] During the four-bar phrase when they overlap (mm. 154–57), the synthesizer ascends to its highest pitch in the piece on the downbeat of m. 158, at precisely the same moment when the lead vocal melody reaches its

Example 25. "When Doves Cry," climax of coda section (mm. 146–162)

melodic climax, an anguished high G sung in Prince's gospel-inflected falsetto register. The synthesizer's furious sixteenth- and thirty-second-note runs make the choir's half-note duration layer seem achingly slow by comparison, which has the effect of drawing out and intensifying this climactic moment, after which Prince resolves his melody downward with a few bars of wordless falsetto melisma (i.e. climax and resolution).

Admittedly, part of the climactic punch comes from traditional melodic means (ascending to a high pitch), but the moment would not be nearly as affecting without the rhythmic techniques that Prince employed. First, he subtracted rhythmic layers to create a structural "break" at m. 146 to focus attention on the new rhythmic layers he

(*continued*)

would add; second, he added an off-beat rhythmic layer (the choral "ah" melody) that extended the rhythmic displacement dissonance of the drum groove; third, he added the song's missing density referent (the sixteenth- and thirty-second note layer of the synth solo); and fourth, he juxtaposed this rapidly moving layer against the slower half-note layer of the choral "ah" melody, allowing listeners to experience the climactic cadence at the downbeat of m. 158 at two different speeds at the same time. Lastly, Prince marked the downbeat of m. 158 as a climax by bringing back the rhythmic ostinato layers that he had dropped out at m. 146 (Synth 2, snare drum, crash cymbal, and the original version of the Synth 4 motive). All of these techniques combine to make the downbeat of m. 158 feel conclusive, even triumphant, despite the fact that Prince did not change the harmonic context at all—the same four-bar harmonic ostinato continues in Synth 4 for the rest of the song. In sum: though the coda's climax does involve a melodic breakthrough, it functions as a climax only because Prince had carefully prepared the listener through a rhythmic—rather than a harmonic or melodic—process.

Stripping Down for Legibility

"When Doves Cry" used the rhythmic and textural techniques of funk to portray a character's interior psychological conflict, and in so doing made a potent argument against the musical stereotypes of "hot rhythm." As Agawu has pointed out, "the construction of African rhythm as complex, superior, but ultimately incomprehensible" continues to be perpetuated in scholarly writing about Black music.[57] Radano has detailed how this construction historically contributed to the (white critical) portrayal of African American genres such as jazz, funk, and hip-hop as having an infectious, "bodily affecting power" that conjures the figure of "Richard Wright's Bigger Thomas, a razor-wielding male beast whose violence was expressed musically as propulsive rhythm."[58] "When Doves Cry" is rhythmically propulsive, to be sure—the song uses many of the documented techniques of funk rhythm, including cyclically repeating rhythmic ostinati, multiple rhythmic layers at different density referents, and implied polyrhythmic or polymetric conflicts—but Prince used those techniques to depict a subjectivity that is eminently nonviolent and comprehensible. Although the song's lyrics hint at both sensuality and violence, Prince framed these events as memories, allowing the listener to experience the song's various rhythmic processes as analogues of the main character's interior conflict as he wrestles with ambivalent feelings of attraction towards his lover and identification with his father. The rhythmic dissonances and asymmetries that Prince built into the groove, the polyrhythmic interactions among the different layers, and the hypermetric structures that Prince created through rhythmic repetition and variation contribute to a melancholy, pensive mood—even in the midst of dancing—that is diametrically opposed to the kind of orgiastic or violent release posited by the discourse of hot rhythm.

Furthermore, Prince used funk rhythm in ways that increased the comprehensibility of the song's groove and structure. First, by radically stripping down the texture Prince increased the clarity of each remaining rhythmic layer, emphasizing the empty space between the notes as much as the notes themselves. Secondly, by using accumulative form to create a sense of linear narrative structure, Prince gave the song an easily legible verse-chorus form within a narrative structure of exposition, rising action, climax, and denouement, in contrast to the stereotypical misunderstanding of African-derived rhythmic practices as essentially cyclical. This is a funk groove that conjures a sense of interiority and *anteriority*: as the song mixes cyclical ostinati with linear, teleological narrative, so too does the character struggle with his memories of events in the past and his desires for the future. Prince created not just a polyrhythmic matrix but a poly-temporal one, using the building blocks of funk to fight against the primitivist fantasy of funk (and African rhythm) as an eternal present moment. In the end, perhaps Prince's last-minute decision to remove the bass from "When Doves Cry"—an instrument closely associated with the funk genre—was a subconscious mission statement, a signal to listeners that the song encodes a message of rebellion against assumptions of Black identity and its relationship to musical rhythm.

The austerity of its texture is a large part of why "When Doves Cry" is such an effective vehicle for Prince's exploration of psychological interiority. Rock critics had commented on Prince's "minimalist" or "stripped-down" funk style as early as 1980's *Dirty Mind* album, and "When Doves Cry" went a further step further in this direction.[59] Prince's 1986 album *Parade* found him again experimenting with radically austere textures on songs like "Kiss," achieving what a *Rolling Stone* reviewer described as a "a clean, diamond-hard style."[60] The thinner textures of Prince's music may have had the shock of the new for mainstream American audiences accustomed to the lush sounds of disco, AM radio pop, and the multitrack bloat of album-oriented rock in the late seventies, but Prince was by no means the first artist to reduce a band to little more than its rhythm section, nor was he the first Black artist to use funk rhythms to explore complicated emotions. In the postwar 1940s, bebop music cut swing jazz down to the bone, giving voice to a modernist impulse in Black America; at the same time, jump-blues stripped the big-band model down to its rhythm-section chassis and in so doing created the blueprint for rhythm and blues and rock 'n' roll.[61] In the 1970s, soul music producers such as Norman Whitfield and Gamble and Huff created relatively bare rhythm tracks—comprised of little more than drums, bass, and isolated stabs of guitar or strings—in which subtle metric conflict and a severe economy of notes depicted the economic and social problems affecting working-class African American communities in the Nixonian era of "benign neglect."[62] In the 1980s, Detroit techno artists used desolate yet funky drum-machine and synthesizer textures to portray humanity in a futuristic techno-dystopia. Around the same time, East-coast hip-hop artists such as LL Cool J and Run-DMC combined spare drum-machine beats with little more than their own voices, using strategies of "flow" and "layering" that Tricia Rose argues were hip-hop's affirmative response to the "profound social dislocation and rupture" facing working-class communities of color in early 1980s America.[63] This is a diverse and transhistorical list of examples, to be sure, but they are all the work of Black artists who used a stripped-down funk rhythm to sketch complex psychosocial landscapes, in contradiction to the white Western stereotype of funk rhythm as a place of untrammeled id and primitivistic hedonism.

Another aspect of such asceticism is that by reducing funk's textural density without sacrificing its multilayered polyrhythms, Prince and the other Black artists mentioned above were fighting the primitivist idea of "unknowability" in African-diasporic rhythm by making the code of funk rhythm easier to read. Ethnomusicologist John Chernoff has pointed out that one of the characteristic reactions Western listeners have upon encountering West African music is to emphasize its incomprehensible difference from European-derived music: "Western attitudes toward African music, whether affirmative or negative, are alike in emphasizing an awesome distance between Western and African sensibilities and in involving the topic of African music with the extremely ambivalent connotations of the word 'primitive.'"[64] In his theory of hot rhythm, Radano points out that Anglo-American listeners extended this quality of incomprehensibility to African American music as well: "Black music epitomized the outer limits of white common understanding to define the excesses to which both blackness and modernity, in all their uncertainty, were linked. The power and 'truth' of hot rhythm related above all to these qualities of intangibility and difference."[65] The discourse of hot rhythm thus portrays the polyrhythmic techniques of African-diasporic music as *essentially* incomprehensible to the white outsider.

By contrast, the stripped-down funk produced by Prince and other Black artists of the 1970s and 1980s worked against this stereotype of unknowability and excess in two related ways. First, by making the linear development of the groove more legible to listeners, stripped-down funk undercut the idea that cyclic and linear time are mutually exclusive. Second, by making it easier to hear the groove as a collection of gaps between precisely positioned notes, stripped-down funk worked against the stereotype of African-diasporic rhythm as a chaotic maelstrom of violent beating. To demonstrate these points I must delve briefly into the Western philosophical underpinnings of rhythm. As noted earlier, the repetitive quality of ostinato rhythms in funk music has led outsiders to ascribe an essential quality of cyclicism to that genre—and to Black music in general—that links it back to nature and the body within the Cartesian episteme of Western thought. In his concept of embodied metaphors (also called "image schemata"), philosopher Mark Johnson argues that our understanding of a "cycle" begins in our own bodies—from the repetitive rhythmic beating of our hearts and the cycle of drawing and expelling breath, to more complex cycles such as eating, digestion, and elimination (or arousal, intercourse, and orgasm)—and is reinforced by a host of external natural cycles such as sunrise/sunset and the seasons.[66] Similarly, the beating of a drum has an inescapable physical analogue in violence, as cultural theorist John Mowitt points out: a drum has a skin and a body, and the skin must be struck for the instrument to sound.[67]

By contrast, Western art-music since the Viennese classical era has been governed by the metaphor of linear progression through time, an idea that is mapped onto the moral career of the civilized citizen of a modern industrialized economy. As musicologist Karol Berger argues, informed listening to music of the classical era onward depends on the understanding that events occur in a preset order along a singular linear trajectory, a quality that Berger relates to the beginnings of Europe's industrial modern era around the same time.[68] Susan McClary amplifies this point in her discussion of tonality, arguing that the linearity of time in Western classical music depends upon the idea of self-motivation and delayed gratification, ideas that were part and parcel of modernity's clock-punching work ethic.[69]

Given this epistemological linkage of drums and ostinato rhythms with primitivism and the body, on the one hand, and of linear harmony and melody with industrial modernity and Protestant morality on the other, one can easily see why repetitive, groove-based genres of African-diasporic music get the short end of the philosophical stick time and again. Generations of African American composers and producers have fought against these stereotypes, from William Grant Still to Duke Ellington to Berry Gordy, yet many have done so by adopting the idiom of late-Romantic symphony orchestration as a means of asserting upward class mobility and/or assimilation into the European American mainstream.[70] What distinguishes Prince's mid-career funk and the work of fellow travelers like Run-DMC and the Belleville Three is their converse decision to *remove* layers, rather than adding them, and in so doing to cleanly expose the core rhythmic tensions that define the funk idiom. By choosing a sparse texture, these artists made it easier for listeners to recognize the individual rhythmic strata as well as the unfolding interactions between cyclic ostinati and linear processes, giving even the most inexperienced listener fluency and comfort with the funk rhythmic idiom. Furthermore, the textural emptiness of songs like "Papa Was a Rolling Stone," "Alleys of Your Mind," "The Message," and "When Doves Cry" mitigates against the drumbeats-as-violence metaphor that Mowitt identified by allowing the listener to hear the space between each percussive transient and thereby imagine themselves within the groove without fear of coming to blows. In short, stripping down funk made the idiom more accessible to white America, as evidenced by the 1980s proliferation of the Minneapolis sound amongst Anglo-American pop stars as well as the mainstream explosion of the EDM genre in the 1990s and 2000s. Prince's funk reduction was an important part of this mainstreaming: in "When Doves Cry," Prince cleared a space so that even a listener unversed in the codes of funk could hear the subtle interplay of rhythm, and the forward-moving accretion of rhythmic complexity, without the expectations of sex or violence that are the discursive baggage of "hot rhythm."

Symphonic Funk and the Black Cosmopolitan

In the wake of *Purple Rain*, Prince recorded less of the guitar-centered rock-funk hybrid that had become his hallmark and more of the stripped-down funk he had begun exploring with "When Doves Cry."[71] He also began experimenting with new timbres and textures, putting his ascetic funk into dialogue with other sound-worlds. Prince's next album, aptly titled *Around the World in a Day*, found the artist incorporating Middle-Eastern instruments such as darbouka, oud, and finger cymbals into his drum-machine rhythms.[72] After that came *Parade* and its accompanying movie *Under the Cherry Moon*, whose plot—African American hustlers on the French Riviera—allowed Prince to play Black street culture against European high culture to comic effect, as discussed earlier in this chapter. In creating its soundtrack, Prince combined the stripped-down funk of "When Doves Cry" with symphonic strings and a soupçon of jazz, creating a sonic analog for the Black cosmopolitanism depicted onscreen.[73] As I will show in this next musical analysis, Prince's song "Anotherloverholenyohead" (from *Parade*) extended the musical critique of hot rhythm that he had begun with "When Doves Cry."

As he had done in "When Doves Cry," Prince gave "Anotherlover" a drum-machine groove whose polyrhythmic layers portrayed the conflicted interiority of the movie's protagonist, yet whose ascetic, stripped-down quality made those rhythms both more legible and less threatening, in defiance of the stereotype of mindless physicality. Also, as he had done in "When Doves Cry," Prince combined linear and cyclic modes of temporality in the song's middle-ground rhythm, giving the lie to the stereotype of groove-based African American music as essentially cyclical and non-teleological. Where Prince took "Anotherlover" a step beyond the stripped-down funk of "When Doves Cry" was his addition of a symphony orchestra—the sonic emblem of European cultural identity—to his rhythmic palette as a means of enacting the onscreen interaction between Black vernacular and European high culture. By explicitly locating his movie's African American protagonists on the French Riviera and implicitly placing the European (by way of Hollywood) orchestral idiom inside that of funk rhythm, Prince created a sonic experience of Black cosmopolitanism that worked against hot rhythm even more boldly than his previous work. Prince's symphonic funk enacts the kind of cross cultural expatriate experience that historically helped African American people step outside of the racialized structures of American society and, once outside, recognize and fight against those structures, as I discussed earlier in the chapter.[74]

Symphonic Funk

One of the most pervasive discourses in Western music is the assumed superiority of Western art music over popular music, a discourse that has an inescapable element of colonialist white supremacy. One of the earliest discussions of jazz music in the white press built a metaphorical "house of the muses" in which harmony and melody enjoy pride of place in the main ballrooms while "jass" and other rhythmic musics intended for dancing were relegated to the basement, a metaphor meant to illustrate European symphonic music's superiority over the violent, sexual, and rhythmically focused music made by nonwhite cultures, summed up by the line "Rhythm is not necessarily music."[75] Paul Whiteman, the Anglo-American bandleader of the 1920s, popularized "jazz" with white audiences in part by using symphonic orchestral arrangements that all but banished improvisation; his commercial success as the "King of Jazz," and the emphasis he put on "elevating" jazz above its origins as dance music and into the concert hall, demonstrates how the discourse of European classical superiority has cast a long shadow over Black popular music.[76]

Since that time, many pop-music producers have used the trick of adding symphonic arrangements to their records as a way of appealing to a white middle-class audience, for whom the sound of violins, flutes, and French horns signifies bourgeois luxury and European cultural identity. Prince was certainly not the first artist working in the soul or funk genres to do so, either: over the decades, many African American artists have participated in the tradition of classicizing popular music (though certainly not in the sense of whitewashing its provenance as Whiteman did). Many of the producers at Motown Records incorporated symphonic strings, winds, and brass into their rhythm-and-blues music in the 1960s, and 1970s soul and disco music were epitomized by the sizzling string sound of producers like Barry White, Kenneth Gamble, and Leon Huff, to say nothing of the symphonic jazz music created by Duke Ellington in the 1930s and '40s or the many African American symphonic composers such as William Grant Still.

These artists combined blues, jazz, R&B, soul, and/or funk with the European symphonic idiom in diverse ways, to be sure, but the combination alone did not necessarily undermine the tacit privilege afforded to the European symphonic tradition—rather, it relied on the image of bourgeois luxury and upward class mobility that is indexed to the sound of European classical music and classicized pop-music arrangements. When Berry Gordy and the producers at Motown added strings to their recordings, the sound harkened back to pop crooners of the postwar generation who used orchestral arrangements—singers such as Nat King Cole, Frank Sinatra, or Perry Como—a sonic reference that arguably helped the Motown sound appeal to middle-class Americans across the racial spectrum.[77] Producers at Stax Records in Memphis, a label known for its gritty, less-is-more arrangements in the 1960s, began incorporating string sections in part to signal the label's financial success, again relying on the association of upward mobility with Europeanization.[78] During the late 1960s and early '70s, the high water mark for the Memphis recording industry, producers such as Isaac Hayes were using "symphony sized" string and wind sections, and deploying the strings in lengthy introductions and fade-outs that musicologist Roy Brewer describes as a deliberate form of "conspicuous consumption."[79] Producers of soul and disco also pursued this aesthetic of sonic luxury in the 1970s: the "Philadelphia sound" of Kenny Gamble and Leon Huff and Barry White's Love Unlimited Orchestra both relied on strings to add high-frequency sheen and sensuous countermelodies to songs such as "Mother, Father, Sister, Brother" and "Love's Theme," respectively, creating a style of African American pop music that symbolized opulence and luxury and that appealed to the emergent Black middle class.[80] Luxury and upward class mobility was not the only aesthetic for which African American producers used orchestral instruments, to be sure: Norman Whitfield's 1970s productions for the Temptations, such as "Papa Was a Rolling Stone," used orchestral instruments in an ascetically spare texture as a way to highlight the blighted urban landscape and social problems facing the African American community during that decade. Yet the way that funk, soul, and disco producers were able to use orchestral strings both to enact upper-class luxury and, by contrast, to cast urban blight into harsh relief rested on the tacit association of those orchestral sounds with the European American middle and upper classes.

Prince's soundtrack to *Under the Cherry Moon* depicts European luxury but sounds very different from the lush aesthetic of 1970s soft soul and disco, hewing closer to the psychological complexity and textural asceticism of producers like Whitfield, though without sounding like them. As with both of these models, *Parade* depends upon the Euro-American upper-class associations of the symphony orchestra, yet Prince's combination of African American funk rhythm with European-style orchestration challenges the tacit assumption that upward class mobility necessitates Europeanization. This is not to say that Prince's film and soundtrack are exempt from considerations of class consciousness or conspicuous consumption: the film is filled with palatial mansions and manicured gardens whose tuxedoed party guests are musically entertained by string quartets, and Prince's characters are grifters who aspire to enter (or at least pilfer) that economic stratum. However, Prince put these luxurious images at a distance by insisting the film be released in black and white, treating the sumptuousness of the French Riviera—the azure of the Mediterranean, the emerald green of manicured lawns, the gold and jewels bedecking the upper-class characters—with a Brechtian alienation effect.

Prince found analogous ways of complicating or distancing the luxurious connotations of the orchestral timbres that he used. The string arranger with whom Prince worked, Clare Fischer, was a Hollywood composer with an R&B/jazz background who had previously arranged music for both bebop pioneer Dizzie Gillespie and R&B/funk artist Chaka Khan. Yet despite his Hollywood pedigree, Fischer's string arrangements were very different from the neo-Romantic styles favored by most soundtrack composers. Furthermore, despite his association with 1970s funk and R&B artists, Fischer's string orchestrations avoided rhythmically static "sizzling" string padding and tonal countermelodies, skewing instead toward expanded or atonal harmonies and chromatic countermelodies, as well as rhythms that often contradicted the dominant pulse of the music. In fact, Fischer's most important influences, in his own estimation, were the modernist symphonic composers Béla Bartók and Igor Stravinsky, the large-scale jazz compositions of Duke Ellington, and the samba-infused jazz of the Brazilian composer Tom Jobim.[81] When I interviewed Fischer, I was struck both by his restless urge to use distinctive, nonstandard chord voicings and by his dissatisfaction with the standard backbeat pattern of most popular music, with its strong and consistent emphasis on beats 2 and 4, which he described to me as unimaginative and repetitive.[82]

This drive to avoid the rhythmic and harmonic cliches of both standard Hollywood and R&B arranging gives Fischer's orchestral arrangements an avant-garde flavor, and is arguably what drew Prince to Fischer's work. According to Prince's longtime recording engineer David Rivkin, "[Fischer's] string arrangements were weird because they went sort of sideways. They just cut across the track like there was a movie going on, but Prince wanted something dissonant, something weird, so I called Clare for Prince."[83] According to several sources, Prince's musical influences were expanding rapidly during the early and mid-1980s, and included the work of Duke Ellington and Igor Stravinsky—in particular, Ellington's *Diminuendo and Crescendo in Blue* and Stravinsky's *Firebird Suite*—composers who were also formative influences on Fischer's harmonic and rhythmic style.[84]

Prince's desire to keep his string arrangements at a distance extended to his hands-off working relationship with Fischer. When Prince hired Fischer to provide orchestral arrangements for his songs, he provided Fischer no instructions, imposed no limitations, and avoided even meeting with Fischer face to face: Fischer claimed never to have met Prince in person or set foot in the Paisley Park recording complex. The workflow was this: Prince would provide Fischer with demo recordings of songs for which he wanted orchestral arrangements; Fischer (or his son Brent) would transcribe Prince's recordings in musical notation on which Fischer *père* would overlay his arrangements; and finally, Fischer *père* or *fils* would conduct and record the orchestral recording of the arrangement at a studio in the Los Angeles area.[85] As if these measures provided insufficient independence, Prince would also (on occasion) take Fischer's recorded orchestral parts and transfer them via multitrack tape onto other songs entirely, juxtaposing Fischer's arrangements on songs for which Fischer had not originally written them, songs with different keys and tempos, and this was the case for the song "Anotherloverholenyohead."

"Anotherloverholenyohead"

"Anotherloverholenyohead" was the third single from *Parade*, released in July of 1986. The song rose only to number 63 on the *Billboard* Hot 100, though it performed better on the Dance Club Songs chart, where it reached number 21. This discrepancy in chart performance may reflect the song's complex, multilayered polyrhythms, which marked it as a dance song more than a pop song. The song occupies an important, though non-diegetic, place in the movie *Under the Cherry Moon*, in which it underscores the third-act rising action: Prince's character rushes to intercept his rich, Anglo-European love interest before she embarks for the marriage that her father has arranged for her, leading to the film's climax in which Prince's character is killed. Prince constructed the groove and the structure of "Anotherloverholenyohead" as a series of nested rhythmic and metric tensions, tensions that both complement the chase scene and, as with "When Doves Cry," enact the main character's conflicts (both internal and external). At the micro level, Prince employs the kind of stable, non-resolving metrical dissonances that, as Mark Butler argues, provide the polyrhythmic dynamism that animates contemporary dance music.[86] At the macro levels of hypermeter and song structure, however, Prince uses rhythmic/metric conflict to create a sense of narrative teleology that enacts the principal character's sense of internal conflict and provides an analog for the tension between African American and Anglo-European cultures that the movie depicts. In so doing, Prince creates a cosmopolitan model of Black musical identity, one that uses both cyclic and linear modes of temporality and that subsumes the conflict between European and African American musical idioms into the rhythmic/metric techniques of funk.

The first layer of rhythmic tension that Prince sets up is the drum ostinato itself (see example 26). The song begins with an eight-bar instrumental introduction featuring just the drum machine groove (minus its snare drum layer) and a guitar-synth, allowing the listener to clearly hear the groove's constituent layers. This drum-machine groove operates mostly at the eighth-note level (though technically has a higher density referent owing to a pair of recurring sixteenth-notes played by the kick drum), and it has a sparse, open texture similar to that of "When Doves Cry." As in "Doves," this two-bar drum machine

Example 26. "Anotherloverholenyohead," vamp and chorus groove

loop is asymmetrical and contains both metrical and anti-metrical layers, creating a dynamic and ambiguous sense of time. A tambourine sound provides the song's eighth-note pulse, which Prince groups into a stable 4/4 meter with a *loud*-soft, on-beat accent pattern. Prince also adds two slower interpretive layers—an on-beat high-hat cymbal (at the quarter-note level) and backbeat half-note snare drum (effectively at the half-note level)—that reinforce the 4/4 meter, just as in Harold Krebs's model of metrical consonance, and that conform to the common practice of rock and funk music.[87]

Against these metrical layers Prince places two anti-metrical interpretive layers—the kick and tom-tom drums (see example 26)—that create polyrhythmic embedded-grouping dissonances and give the two-bar phrase an asymmetrical shape, just as Butler describes. The kick drum plays an asymmetrical two-bar pattern: in the first bar it emphasizes the strong beats 1 and 3 (with an eight-note grace note before beat 3), reinforcing the 4/4 meter; in the second measure, however, it plays only beat 1 and the "and" before beat 2, creating a *són* clave grouping when heard in conjunction with the beat 4 snare drum (the same kick/snare clave pattern Prince used in the groove of "When Doves Cry"). In addition to the momentary tension created by this grouping dissonance, the kick drum's on-beat/off-beat two-bar cycle creates a regular pattern of expectation and frustration in which the kick conforms to the common practice of rock drumming (strong beats on 1 and 3) in bar 1 and then deviates from it in bar 2.

The tom-tom drums add an even more strikingly off-beat and asymmetrical interpretive layer (example 26). In the first bar of the cycle, the mid-toms play two pairs of eighth notes in which the first pair is shifted a sixteenth note after beat 1, the second is shifted an eighth-note ahead of beat 3, yielding a pattern—two eighth notes with a sixteenth rest in between—that destabilizes the dominant meter on beat 1 but reinforces it on beat 3. In the second bar of the cycle, the mid-tom plays in unison with the kick drum (on 1 and the "and" of 2) but Prince adds a high tom-tom drum on the "and" of beat 3, creating a 3+2+3 clave pattern in the toms that contrasts the 3+3+2 son clave pattern of the kick and snare, and provides a surprising fillip at the end of the two-bar pattern.

This polyrhythmic drum-machine ostinato, with its push and pull of metrical and anti-metrical layers and its two-bar asymmetry, provides a dynamic experience of meter marked by unresolved yet stable rhythmic dissonances. Indeed, it is the stable, repetitive nature of this metrical/anti-metrical tension that led Mark Butler and Robert Walser to argue against using the terms "consonance" and "dissonance" when discussing dance grooves.[88] Rather, they argue that this particular construction of meter is a defining feature of electronically produced dance music. Butler specifically points out that by generating ambiguity about the dominant metrical groupings, this technique allows listeners to have diverse experiences of temporality.[89] But regardless of whether we call it metrical dissonance or not, Prince programmed a drum loop that, without feeling cluttered or dense, uses cyclic asymmetry and embedded polyrhythms to create a tense rhythmic grid, one that requires interpretation on the part of the listener.

This metrical tension easily maps onto the conflicts in the song's text and the movie plot: in the song, the protagonist vacillates between attraction and anger toward his former lover, while in the movie the lead character is struggling to resolve his own internal conflict between love and greed while simultaneously fleeing his pursuers. Yet in addition to enacting these conflicts, the drum ostinato also serves an important purpose in the song's middle-ground, where Prince sets up a process of hypermetric tension and resolution. With its clearly delineated first and second bars, and the high-tom acting as a flag to let the listener know the two-bar pattern is about to restart, this drum-machine ostinato has a clear two-bar cyclical temporality. Yet Prince adds and subtracts several *three-bar* instrumental ostinati during the song's verses to create a larger sense of linear narrative.

Like most dance songs, "Anotherloverholenyohead" has a structure which cyclically alternates between verse (see example 27 and example 28) and chorus sections, and Prince differentiated those sections by adding and subtracting instrumental ostinati (as well as shifting the tonic from F♯ minor in the verses to A minor in the choruses). During the first two verses, the additional ostinati are three bars long, creating a hypermetric dissonance against the two-bar drum machine groove, which continues uninterrupted throughout the song, with the clarion sound of the off-beat high-tom clearly (circled in example 27) marking the end of that pattern. In contrast, all the pitched instruments and the lead vocal melody move in a repeating three-bar cycle during the first two verses. The piano plays a six-chord progression in half-notes that moves from the F♯ minor tonic through the relative major A and ends with a V–IV gesture in the key of A before falling back to F♯ minor (the chords are F♯min, E/B, A, Bmin, E, D; in A Major, this is vi–V6/4–I–ii–V–IV). Prince rhythmically marks the end of this three-bar harmonic cycle with an eighth-note anticipation of the F♯ minor downbeat that restarts the ostinato (circled in example 27), a momentary disruption of the steady half-note rhythm. Even if we ignore the clear syntax of the harmonic progression, the piano's rhythmic pattern makes the three-bar cycle clearly audible: after six stable half notes, the syncopated downbeat-in-anticipation (on the F♯min tonic) signals the uneven timespan of this cycle.

The vocal melody and bassline reinforce this three-bar hypermetric cycle during the verses, and they also add another layer of polyrhythmic tension to the groove. The polyrhythm comes from the fact that Prince has shifted the vocal melody and bass line in time relative to the stable half notes of the piano ostinato. Like the piano, the bass moves at the half-note duration level, and the vocal melody changes pitch with the bass every half note; however, both parts are shifted a sixteenth note ahead of the of the beat (i.e., their harmonic motion leads the beat), creating a consistent displacement dissonance against the piano's metrical half-note layer. Prince highlights this rhythmic tension by adding a harmonic one: in defiance of common bass-playing practice, Prince put the bass on the third of each chord while the lead vocal sings the root, creating a literally rootless feeling that enacts the emotional instability of the lyrics. Finally, Prince gave the bass a rhythmic flourish that marks

Example 27. "Anotherloverholenyohead," verse 1 excerpt

the end of the three-bar cycle: after leading the beat for the first two and a half bars of the cycle, the bass plays the last two chords of the cycle straight on the beat and "pops" the top octave, a common funk-bass technique that accents the off-beats.

Prince uses this three-bar phrase (i.e., the vocal melody, piano, and bass ostinati) to create a large-scale cycle of tension and release that corresponds to the structural alternation between verse and chorus. The rotational mismatch of the two-bar drum ostinato against the three-bar voice/piano/bass melody creates a subtle but pervasive tension that enacts the lover's quarrel described in the lyrics. (The easiest way to notice this tension is by listening to the high-tom note at the end of the drum machine's two-bar phrase, which punctuates the vocal melody at odd and seemingly random moments.) Prince relieves this tension by giving the piano, bass, and vocals a five-bar melodic phrase at the end of each verse: at the end of their fourth three-bar phrase, the pitched instruments hold on the E-major chord for two bars (with some rhythmic embellishment). This resolves the hypermetric tension but at the same time creates a harmonic tension—an implication, to use Leonard Meyer's language—that pushes the listener to anticipate the chorus (this prolonged E major resolves to an A minor chord at the chorus, revealing its dominant function).[90] During the chorus, the pitched instruments return to the two-bar ostinati that they played during the song's introduction (see example 26), rejoining the two-bar cycle of the drum machine, while the singers deliver the song's four-bar melodic hook, creating an even 4:2 ratio of hypermetric phrases.

Within the hermeneutic provided by the song's lyrics, this cycle of hypermetric tension and resolution enacts the tension between the lovers and/or the internal conflict in the principal character. Lyrically, Prince alternates between describing his devotion to his lover in each verse, and his disdain for her decision to leave in the chorus. However, the embodied metaphor that this phrase-level rhythmic dissonance creates enacts this emotional pull-push even more eloquently. As Mark Johnson points out in his theory of embodied metaphors, the "cycle schema" is cognitively embedded in our thinking by a host of natural physical cycles.[91] Both the drum machine and the pitched instruments are playing cyclic ostinati for the bulk of each verse in this song, cycles which the listener may subconsciously associate with the natural cycles of the body. But with the three-against-two hypermetric dissonance, Prince places these cycles in conflict with each other. However physically "natural" each cycle may feel in isolation, the two simply don't line up, just as the principal character is at odds with his lover and himself.

Prince builds on this structural cycle of hypermetric tension and resolution in two other ways that contribute to a large-scale sense of rhythmic teleology. First, as in "When Doves Cry," he progressively adds more rhythmic layers with each repetition of the verse section, building up the micro-level polyrhythmic density to create a macro sense of increasing tension as the song progresses. Second, after entraining the listener to expect the three-against-two-bar phrase-length mismatch over two repetitions of the verse section, Prince introduces a third verse-*like* section in which the uneven phrase-length ratio is resolved. This section is aberrant in another important way that I will discuss momentarily, but suffice it to say that, by creating a large-scale structural cycle of tension and resolution and then resolving that tension in the final verse, Prince creates a linear narrative out of cyclic rhythms.

Prince progressively elaborates the rhythmic texture of "Anotherloverholenyohead" over time by adding rhythmic layers to each successive verse section, creating a feeling of narrative teleology. For example: the song begins with an incomplete version of the drum-machine groove—only the kick drum, tom-toms, and tambourine play their parts—and only after eight bars (or four repetitions of the two-bar cycle) does Prince complete the drum-machine groove by adding in the snare drum and high-hat cymbal. The pitched instruments also contribute to this structural rhythmic elaboration: the eight-bar introduction features an angular solo melody played by a Roland GT-1 guitar-synthesizer (an electric guitar fitted with a MIDI tracking device that is used to play a synthesized timbre), but after the completion of that melody the bass and piano enter with their regular chorus ostinati, dispelling the structural tension engendered by that meandering, through-composed eight-bar melody with their clearly recognizable two-bar cyclic pattern (example 26).[92] This kind of additive rhythmic texture is a standard introductory trope: by withholding and then revealing the full polyrhythmic texture of the groove, producers like Prince create a localized sense of suspense and resolution. As Robert Fink argues, the technique of delaying the entry of the snare-drum backbeat on beats 2 and 4, a pattern that generations of rock and soul music listeners have been trained to expect, functions like the delayed arrival of the tonic (Fink calls it the "tonic rhythm") and creates a sense of structural tension and resolution.[93] Further, Mark Butler argues that this technique of beginning with an ungrouped beat and then adding other ostinati that move at higher rhythmic grouping levels, EDM producers construct the song's meter in full view of the listener.[94]

The song's verses provide an even more striking example of how Prince uses progressive rhythmic elaboration to create a sense of linear teleology. While the chorus remains more or less the same as the song goes on, providing a cyclic resolution to the hypermetric dissonance in the verses, Prince rhythmically changes the second and third verses in a way that creates a sense of forward narrative development. Most notably: in the second verse Prince fragments his own lead vocal rhythm and adds backup vocals that interact with the lead vocal melody to create a complex rhythmic interaction on top of the already rhythmically fraught texture (see example 28). As I mentioned, during the first verse Prince's lead vocal moves rhythmically with the bass, holding on one pitch and then moving upwards together with a sixteenth-note slide on the "and" of beats 2, 4, and 2 again (example 27). Having set up this pattern in the first verse Prince plays around with it in the second verse (example 28): the bass remains the same, but Prince fragments his vocal melody by inserting eighth-note rests where none were previously, and by breaking its rhythmic link with the bass, sometimes moving at the same time but more often not. This breakdown of the rhythmic link between lead vocal and bass heightens the drama of the rhythmic texture and, with it, the psychological tension of the song's lyrics.

Having chopped his lead vocal melody into rhythmic fragments in the second verse, Prince fills the gaps with a new rhythmic layer: the voices of band members Lisa Coleman and Wendy Melvoin, who enter into a call-and-response with the lead (see example 28). In each of the second verse's four melodic phrases, the unison backup singers occupy a slightly different rhythmic position relative to the lead singer. In the first, they begin simultaneously with the lead vocal but then introduce a distinctive and competing rhythmic pattern, made up of two eighth notes followed by an eighth rest ("we were *rest* bro-thers *rest* sis-ters *rest*") that fits into the newly introduced gap in the lead vocal's rhythm, drawing interest away from the lead vocal line. In the third and fourth phrases (beginning with the lyrics "even though we had big fun" and "sho' as there's a sun," respectively), the dominant/subordinate gender roles of the call-response pattern begin to switch. The lead vocal seems to grow hesitant: Prince leaves more eighth-note rests, delays the entry of some lines, and fails to sing the full lyric of others; meanwhile, the backup singers confidently deliver all of the lyrics for the third and fourth phrases in uninterrupted volleys of eighth and sixteenth notes. Indeed, in the fourth and final phrase the male singer deviates so far from his previously established rhythm that the female singers enter first, inverting their call/response relationship. Within the hermeneutic frame of the song's lyrics, these rhythmic transformations read as yet another ratcheting up of the tension within the lead character's psyche and/or as an enactment of an argument between the male and female characters, the latter interpretation being supported by the complicating presence of actual women's voices and the reversed gender roles in the call-and-response pattern. Furthermore, the mercurial, moment-by-moment changes that Prince makes in both his lead vocal's rhythm

Example 28. “Anotherloverholenyohead,” verse 2

and in the call-and-response pattern function in a manner analogous to the fragmentation and transformation that a melodic motive might undergo in a sonata-form development section: even a sophisticated listener might find themselves struggling to follow the transformations of the lead vocal's motivic rhythm amidst the complex back-and-forth of the vocal call-and-response.

By adding this new foreground layer of rhythmic complexity to the second verse, Prince combined a linear process of development with the already established hypermetric cycle of tension and resolution built into the verse-chorus structure. This combination gives the second verse a much greater feeling of dramatic conflict compared to the first and introduces a sense of uncertainty or expectation about what will follow the second chorus (will it be a third verse, and if so, will Prince continue to ramp up the rhythmic complexity as he did in the second?). He resolves this uncertainty by inserting a new, verse-*like* bridge section (with a consequential new rhythmic layer) immediately after that second chorus, where the listener would have expected either a verse or an instrumental solo (see example 29). During this bridge section, and continuing into the coda section beyond it, Prince resolves the hypermetric tension between two- and three-bar phrase lengths that he had previously introduced in the verses (by changing the three-bar keyboard/bass ostinati into two four-bar phrases), but adds a through-composed orchestral melody by Clare Fischer. While the resolution of the three-against-two-bar phrase-length dissonance does eliminate one layer of tension, the symphonic orchestration adds a new layer of rhythmic complexity to the texture and sonically enacts the juxtaposition of working-class African American and upper-class Anglo-European cultural values that motivate the movie's plot.

The symphonic arrangement in the bridge of "Anotherloverholenyohead" does not follow the established conventions of funk or soul orchestration. Instead of a harmonized countermelody along the lines of Marvin Gaye's "What's Going On," or the kind of sizzling harmonic padding heard on songs like Barry White's "Love's Theme," Clare Fischer's string arrangement occupies a strangely orthogonal space with regard to the song's harmony and rhythm (see example 29). The odd character of this string arrangement stems partly from its indifference to the underlying harmony: Fischer seems to hint at a B-major tonality, in contrast to the A-minor tonal center of the verses or the F♯ minor of the choruses (though more closely related to the latter). In fact, this juxtaposition of B and A tonal centers recalls the "bitonality" of Milhaud

Example 29. "Anotherloverholenyohead," bridge / string soli

or neoclassical-era Stravinsky (a musical influence Fischer and Prince shared). But it is rhythm, more than harmony, that really sets the orchestral arrangement askew from the funk band: the strings add another rhythmic layer, but this layer does not have a clear or consistent relationship with the underlying meter. At times they seem to be metrically shifted relative to the dominant pulse, as when the strings change notes on the off-beat in mm. 62–63 (see example 29), but this pattern does not hold. At other times they sound swung, as with the triplet pattern in m. 65, but this doesn't last either. Overall, there is no consistent rhythmic relationship between the orchestra and the funk band, recalling David Rivkin's quote about how Fischer's arrangements "cut across" the texture of Prince's songs.

The strings are tacet during the chorus that follows, only to return again with a similarly challenging arrangement during the chorus-like coda section that ends the album version of the song (at 3:02 and 3:19).

Though the strings in this coda section have a closer harmonic correspondence to the coda's A-minor tonic (as opposed to their weak harmonic match to the F♯ minor of the preceding bridge section), this relative consonance is overshadowed by the continuing sense of rhythmic disjunction. As in the bridge, the coda's orchestral arrangement has neither a clear rhythmic motive nor a regular phrase length, making it chafe against the now regularized four-bar phrase lengths of the drum machine and pitched instruments.

In fact, the relative lack of rhythmic and harmonic correspondence between the strings and the rest of the band may actually have been the result of tape manipulation on Prince's part. Though Fischer had a reputation for writing orchestral arrangements with extended harmonies and rhythmic ambiguity, evidence suggests he did not originally intend for this particular string arrangement to be used in this song. Saxophone player Eric Leeds informed me that Prince was in the habit of using multitrack tape to shift Fischer's arrangements temporally, to excerpt or rearrange them, and even to juxtapose arrangements onto wholly different songs: "I can't even say for sure that Fischer's strings on the song came from an arrangement specifically for this song. Prince would sometimes take string sections from arrangements for other songs and fly them into a completely different song. He was sending a lot of stuff to Claire at this time, so who knows."[95] When I examined Fischer's archives, I could find no sheet music for "Anotherloverholenyohead," and no mention of it in the fastidious list that his wife kept of his arranging work (though her list only included a general credit for the *Parade* album). Nor did Fischer himself have any memory of writing a string arrangement for this song when I interviewed him. This leads me to believe that Prince created the orchestral arrangements in the bridge and coda of this song by juxtaposing a section of a separate arrangement, a tape-splicing technique that the composer-musician Frank Zappa called "xenochrony," making the lack of rhythmic correspondence not just the arranger's choice but a principled decision on Prince's part.[96]

While I have no primary-source evidence for Prince's compositional intent for this orchestral arrangement, there is a tantalizing tidbit from a rehearsal bootleg that suggests he knew its disruptive potential. Recorded in February of 1986 and circulating under the title "An Honest Man," this bootleg includes recordings of Prince in rehearsal with his band for their upcoming "Hit and Run" tour of material from *Parade*.[97] Prince requests that saxophone player Eric Leeds write a horn arrangement to occupy the bridge section because, as Prince himself puts it, "We're gonna probably lose the strange strings 'cuz we'll be without orchestra." Removing the "strange strings" was a necessary practical concession for the live concerts, given the prohibitive expense of touring with an orchestra and Prince's principled refusal to use prerecorded backing tracks in live performance. Yet by calling them "strange," Prince shows his awareness of the odd and uncomfortable relationship that the orchestra has to the rest of the funk band in this song.

Furthermore, the arrangement that Prince ultimately commissioned from Leeds has an equally complex rhythmic relationship to the rest of the groove (this arrangement can be heard on the live bootleg of the August 25, 1986, show at Le Zenith in Paris, and also on the twelve-inch dance remix of "Anotherloverholenyohead," albeit in a truncated form). The melody line that Leeds wrote for the extended coda section—which is melodically angular and rhythmically syncopated—goes through a three-step process of rhythmic diminution. Starting at 2:53 in the bootleg recording, the horns play their melody in whole-note and syncopated half-note values; at 4:36, the melody reappears in half- and quarter-note values; and at 5:02 the horn line reappears in quarter-note and off-beat eighth-note durations. While this horn arrangement sounds nothing like the "strange strings" that originally occupied the bridge and coda of "Anotherloverholenyohead," it nonetheless fulfills a similar role by placing an independent linear rhythmic stratum on top of the already busy funk groove.

In both arrangements, the conflict that Prince stages between the song's normal funk groove and the new rhythmic layer in the bridge and coda—Fischer's "strange" strings or Leeds's horns—represents the apotheosis of a large-scale structural progression. Over the course of the first two verses and choruses, Prince established a cycle of phrase-length dissonance (during the verse) and resolution (during the chorus) but then ended that cycle in the following section (the bridge) by resolving the hypermetric dissonance. At the same time, he built a linear progression of rhythmic elaboration by adding the call-and-response backup voices in the second verse, raising the implication of further rhythmic complexity to come, which he answered by adding a new—but unexpected—rhythmic layer (the orchestra). These two rhythmic processes—hypermetric cycle and linear elaboration—both led to the bridge section, where Prince musically enacted the movie's conflict of African American street culture versus Anglo-European high culture by juxtaposing the incongruous symphonic orchestration onto the established funk groove. Prince then continued this interaction between funk band and symphony orchestra through the coda section until the song's conclusion (with a return to F♯ minor and an unexpected shift in the groove, which Prince fades out from 3:46 to 4:01 in the album version). The structural and rhythmic message is clear: this interaction between funk band and symphony orchestra is both the song's climax and denouement, and the fulfillment of a large-scale process of rhythmic development.

There are several interrelated conclusions that I want to tease out of this encounter with the "strange strings." The first is its temporal aspect. During the bridge section of "Anotherloverholenyohead," one might hear the rhythmic conflict between the four-bar funk ostinato and the through-composed strings as merely a confrontation between "cyclic" and "linear" modes of temporality, an interpretation that would fit squarely within the "hot rhythm" stereotype that portrays African-derived music as incapable of linear teleology. But Prince circumvented this reading: he demonstrated during the introduction and first two verses of this song that adding new cyclical layers to the groove could create a forward-moving syntax of tension and resolution, a technique used by earlier soul and funk artists like Norman Whitfield and Isaac Hayes.[98] Prince also added another through-composed layer to the song that was *not* supplied by a European-style symphony orchestra—namely the backup vocals in verse 2—that added yet more teleological drive towards the song's bridge. As Prince demonstrated throughout "Anotherloverholenyohead," the supposed opposition between cyclic and linear temporality is false.

The second conclusion I want to draw is that Prince, like soul and funk music producers before him, used the tension between rhythmic strata to dramatize the internal and external conflicts faced by the song's principal character. The most notable rhythmic tension that Prince created in this song is the two- and three-bar phrase-length dissonance between pitched and non-pitched instruments during the verses. As a listener, it's easy to hear this rhythmic mismatch as an enactment of the interpersonal tension between the main character and his soon-to-be ex-lover, given the "image schema" that links cyclicism with nature and the body; one can just as easily hear it as a depiction of his internal conflict as he vacillates between feelings of tenderness and anger, given the hermeneutic window provided by the lyrics.[99] The complicated call-and-response between male lead vocal and female backup vocals in the second verse enacts this conflict even more literally, as the listener hears the antiphonal complexity of their interaction and the main character's movement towards a subordinate role in the dynamic. By using rhythm both to enact the complicated mental state of his lead character and the push and pull of the lover's quarrel, Prince gives the lie to the epistemological opposition of mind and body upon which the discourse of hot rhythm relies.

The third conclusion that I want to draw from Prince's juxtaposition of symphonic strings and funk groove is that while it falsifies the oppositions between body and mind and between cyclic and linear temporality posited by the stereotype of hot rhythm, it *does* enact a confrontation between European and African American derived soundscapes, though not in the simplistic binary-oppositional sense. The timbres of Clare Fischer's string arrangement bring to mind their European pedigree, while their lack of rhythmic correspondence to the underlying funk groove portrays the orchestra as antagonistic, or at least indifferent. During the coda, the drum groove continues its regular four-bar ostinato, while the symphonic strings (among other layers) fade in and out, their harmonic and rhythmic cadences not *quite* corresponding to the rest of the instruments. Yet the rhythmic dissonance introduced by the orchestra in the bridge and coda sections is subtle rather than overpowering: the legato articulation and long note durations played by the strings allow them to fade into the rhythmic background, compared to the clear articulation, denser rhythmic grid, and embedded grouping dissonances of the drum machine and other electric instruments (or compared to the vocals' antiphonal complexity).

Prince's treatment of Fischer's string arrangement approaches literal pastiche through his use of xenochrony, yet it is far from postmodern blank parody or a cut-and-paste bricolage. Given the resources available to Prince he could easily have staged a far more dissonant collision of orchestra and funk band—such as the pastiche ending of the Beatles' "A Day in the Life"—*or* a far more lavish treatment, à la Barry White's "Love's Theme," but instead he chose to place the orchestra and funk groove at an angle to each, with the funk groove as the principal character. In so doing, Prince's use of strings in "Anotherloverholenyohead" evokes the cosmopolitanism experienced at mid-century by a generation of African American men in France. Rather than a confrontation, the rambling bridge and coda sections feel like scenes in which Prince has cast himself as Baudelaire's flâneur, strolling comfortably through the arcades of Paris as he observes the goods on offer.[100] Ultimately, if we allow the funk rhythm to stand in for African American culture and the strings for European, then we can hear this section not as an assimilation of one into the other, but rather a comfortable coexistence or conversation. Unlike earlier models of bourgeois Black subjectivity, such as Berry Gordy's early Motown hits, Prince does not use his string arrangement as a signal of conformity to European American middle-class ideals. Rather, Prince's ambivalent use of symphonic strings in "Anotherloverholenyohead"—with their avant-garde, almost aleatoric quality—presumes the value of the funk tradition without needing to make it a performance of hard work, or to dress it head to toe in European luxury. The cosmopolitan citizen recognizes the value of other cultures and peoples without abandoning his or her own, after all, and this is precisely what Prince signals with the pleasant coexistence—yet relatively weak harmonic and rhythmic correlation—between orchestra and funk band.[101] We do not hear a perfect synthesis of traditions, but rather two discrete entities occupying the same space, and though they create rhythmic (and other) dissonances, they do not collide, but remain stably superimposed.

Conclusions

By reducing funk's textural density while maintaining its core principle of polyrhythmic layering, Prince struck against the primitivist stereotypes of "hot rhythm," such as mindless physicality, sex, and violence. He did this by mapping the complex interactions of funk polyrhythm onto the internal subjectivity of his songs' characters while at the same time reducing the overall density to make those interactions more easily legible. With the help of the Linn LM1 drum machine, Prince created grooves replete with multilayered metrical dissonance yet whose relatively sparse textures made it easier for listeners to perceive the subtlety and precision of the foreground grooves as well as the interactions between cyclical and linear modes of temporality embedded in the middle-ground and background rhythms.

In so doing, Prince was part of a groundswell among Black artists of the 1970s and '80s whose music used the rhythmic tension and compound temporality of funk rhythm within austere musical textures to enact psychological interiority and social protest. This movement included producers such as Norman Whitfield, Grandmaster Flash, Juan Atkins, and a great many others, and their music falsified the stereotypes of "hot rhythm" by working against what Frantz Fanon called the "epidermalization" of racial inferiority.[102] As Fanon argued, the perpetuation of white supremacy is based on assigning an inferior, object status to people on the basis of certain skin colors, a status that makes the *external* surface of a person the schema that determines identity under the white gaze.[103] Paul Gilroy argued that this epidermalization led to the persistent stereotype of African American culture as being essentially rooted in the body rather than the mind.[104] Constructing funk grooves that enact psychological *interiority*, then, attacks not just the discursive identification of African American rhythm with the body and nature, as in "hot rhythm," it also attacks the epidermalization upon which such raciological thinking is built.

Prince staked his claim to this kind of stripped-down funk subjectivity with two big hits: 1984's "When Doves Cry" and 1986's "Kiss." The former of these songs had quite an impact at the time, but its starkly minimal sound was not representative of the guitar-rock style that characterized Prince's larger *Purple Rain* project. By contrast, Prince built his next movie soundtrack—*Parade/Under the Cherry Moon*, which included both "Kiss" and "Anotherloverholenyohead"—with the austere funk aesthetic at its core. By starting with a bare-bones instrumentation, Prince gave himself room to add the symphony orchestra as another layer of polyrhythm, and in so doing create a musical model of Black cosmopolitanism to accompany his cinematic turn as an outsider in France. Shana Redmond makes a related point in her article on Janelle Monáe (an artist who cites Prince as an influence), arguing that in Monáe's song and video "Cold War," and in Michael Jackson's "Stranger in Moscow" before it, both artists used images of international travel and outsider identity to reimagine "the relationship among blackness, space, and freedom, thereby upsetting discursive representations of the black body as literally and figuratively fixed," a project that Redmond positions within the history of Black artists' and writers' expatriate experiences in Europe.[105]

Prince's decision to set and film *Under the Cherry Moon* in France connected him with this same tradition of Black artists and writers—from Frederick Douglass and W. E. B. DuBois to Charlie Parker and Dizzy Gillespie—for whom the expatriate experience provided resources for the fight against American racism and international fascism. As Gilroy argues, at the same moment American forces fought against Nazi genocide in WWII, the racial-biological thinking Germany used to systematize that genocide (i.e., the equation of ethnic and national identity) remained part of America's legal framework in the form of "Jim Crow" segregation.[106] Because the transnational experiences of Black GIs during WWII—as well as the many African American artists and writers who made similar sojourns to Europe before and after—allowed them to temporarily step outside the American system of racial segregation, it thereby provided the moral resources for generations of activists to fight that racial segregation, and the "epidermalization" upon which it was built.[107] As such, "cosmopolitanism" provides not only an ethical rubric for living in the world, as Appiah postulates, but also a resource for fighting against the racists who refuse to follow that rubric.

In sum, by showing how the funk rhythm idiom can enact complex psychological interiority rather than violent exteriority, how it can incorporate multiple modes of temporality, and how it can flexibly accommodate the European orchestral idiom without sacrificing its own musical identity, Prince enacted a cultural model that opposes the equation of ethnicity and nationality that undergirds "hot rhythm" stereotypes and Western racism in general, and that erodes the longstanding cultural authority afforded to the European symphonic tradition.[108] In this sense, Prince's *Parade/Under the Cherry Moon* project continued the cultural work begun by the arrival of orchestrated ragtime in Europe during WWI and the popularity of swing jazz in Europe during WWII.[109] As historian Michael Kater has argued, the popularity of African American jazz music was an anti-fascist force in Europe, one that worked against the cultural authority of the German symphonic tradition and the closely related discourse of Aryan racial superiority.[110] Similarly, Prince's rhythmic superimposition of symphony orchestra and funk band provides a vision of the Black musical subject as expatriate, a position that throws into relief the myriad interior experiences that "Black" cultural forms can express when freed from the limiting discourses of raciological and nationalistic thinking. Prince's *Parade* enacts a Black expatriate in Europe experiencing cultural multiplicity in a way that resembles both the concept of "double consciousness," that experience of simultaneously being self and other that W. E. B. DuBois used as a metaphor for African American identity, and also Daphne Brooks's concept of "Afro-alienation," a technique by which Black performers use alterity or outsider identity as a source of critical perspective and self-making power.[111] In his use of funk rhythm, Prince enacted not just the interior conflict of a lovelorn subject, but a new identity that spans multiple continents, decades, and genres, negating the idea of a single cultural identity or racial essence.

FOUR | Ecstasy and Prophecy in Prince's Singing

In 1987, Prince experienced a crisis of faith. In late November 1986 he had completed and sequenced an ambitious triple album of material entitled *Crystal Ball* only to have the project's release vetoed by his label, Warner Brothers, over concerns that the high consumer price of a triple album would result in low sales.[1] This defeat came on the heels of two critically and commercially unsuccessful album releases, 1985's *Around the World in a Day* and 1986's *Parade*. According to Prince's biographers, the artist was particularly stung by the suggestion that his crossover success with the mainstream rock sound of *Purple Rain*, as well as forays into psychedelia and symphonic orchestration on *ATWIAD* and *Parade* (respectively), had put him out of touch with his African American audience.[2] According to some associates, Prince assembled his next album as a rejoinder to such criticisms: *The Black Album* contained funk and dance tracks spiked with a notable hip-hop influence and aggressive, sometimes violent lyrics.[3]

However, *The Black Album* precipitated Prince's crisis, and led him to a more overt engagement with religion in his work. On Tuesday, December 1, 1987, with *The Black Album*'s scheduled release just seven days away and copies already being loaded onto trucks, Prince took an advance pressing of the album to the suburban Minneapolis dance club Rupert's to test it on a live audience. On returning to his recently completed Paisley Park recording complex afterward, Prince reportedly experienced a divine vision in which *The Black Album* was revealed to him as a work of evil, motivated by spite and imbued with the Devil's influence.[4] While several associates have indicated that this vision may have been the result of Prince's first, unhappy experience with the psychotropic amphetamine Ecstasy, it nonetheless triggered a very real spiritual awakening that led Prince to cancel the release of *The Black Album* (which wasn't officially released until seven years later) and throw his energy into the religiously themed 1988 album *Lovesexy*, which he supported with a world tour.[5]

This spiritual awakening infused every aspect of the *Lovesexy* album and tour, from Prince's musical selections to the staging and set design. Prince described the spiritual crisis precipitated by *The Black Album* in the tour's souvenir program, referring to the December 1 date as "Blue Tuesday," to himself as a character named "Camille," and to the Devil as "Spooky Electric":

> Camille set out to silence his critics. "No longer daring"—his enemies laughed. "No longer glam, his funk is half-assed. . . . One leg is much shorter than the other one is weak. His strokes are tepid, his colors are meek."
>
> . . . Camille rocked hard in a funky place. Stuck his long funk in competition's face. Tuesday came. Blue Tuesday. His canvas full, and lying on the table, Camille mustered all the hate that he was able. Hate 4 the ones who ever doubted his game. Hate 4 the ones who ever doubted his name. "Tis nobody funkier—let the Black Album fly." Spooky Electric was talking, Camille started 2 cry. Tricked. A fool he had been. In the lowest utmostest. He had allowed the dark side of him 2 create something evil.[6]

Prince's program notes name many of songs on *The Black Album* and *Lovesexy* using images of darkness and light to portray the spiritual contrast between the two projects. Prince also used this dark and light spiritual dichotomy to structure the *Lovesexy* stage show: he played his more lascivious early material in the first act and his newer, divinely inspired *Lovesexy* songs in the second, with the song "Anna Stesia" as a bridge between the two, enacting his character's spiritual awakening, at the end of Act I.[7] On either side of that number, Prince placed two songs whose stark stylistic contrast made this spiritual transition from dark to light clear: before the transition, the hip-hop themed song "Bob George," and after, the gospel-tinged "Eye No."

The way that Prince used his voice across these three songs enacts his character's spiritual journey from darkness to light, and introduces the two main musical idioms that I explore in this chapter, that of the "prophetic" and the "ecstatic" religious voices, which derive respectively from the funk and gospel genres. The song "Bob George," the penultimate number in the first act, featured a technologically mediated low-bass voice accompanied by a hip-hop groove. The transformational song "Anna Stesia" featured primarily Prince's primary chest register, and relied on a subtly complex harmonic progression to enact his character's transformation. Then, following an intermission and a spoken-word poem entitled "Cross the Line," the second act began with the song "Eye No," a song that—on the album version—was sung entirely in a breathy high falsetto (though he used his chest voice in some live performances).

The first of these songs, "Bob George," is one of two songs from the aborted *Black Album* that Prince played live in the first, sinful act of the *Lovesexy* show (the other being "Superfunkycalifragisexy"). "Bob George" is one of the most overtly hip-hop styled songs on *The Black Album*, and the only song on that album in which Prince uses a technologically modulated low-bass voice. The song is a scathing parody of both rapping (as a vocal technique) and the violent, misogynistic lyrics associated with the then-new gangsta-rap subgenre. The song's musical background features a drum-machine beat reminiscent of the ascetic, Roland TR-808–dominated production style of early "hardcore" rap acts like Run-DMC. Over that beat, Prince—in character as a thuggish pimp—delivers a monologue in which he berates and threatens his girlfriend for her involvement with another man, Bob George. The monologue ends with the sounds of gunfire and a police standoff, both of which Prince portrayed onstage. The monologue is spoken, not sung, and Prince's rhythmic flow is lazy and off-the beat, mocking the gangsta-rap subgenre of hip-hop even as it participates in it. Adding menace to this monologue is the unnaturally low bass register in which Prince delivers it. Where Prince had previously used variable tape-speed technology in the recording studio to change the pitch of vocals, in these live performances he relied on a newer piece of audio technology known as a harmonizer to electronically lower the pitch of his voice without affecting the tape speed, creating a character rhythmically nimble enough to rap but with a ponderously, uncannily low voice.

It is telling that Prince chose to portray the main character of "Bob George," his most sinful and earthly character, using the medium of rap, a genre that, according to several associates, Prince had not yet accepted as artistically valid.[8] It is even more telling that for this song Prince used the unnaturally low quality of the pitch-shifted bass voice, giving the violent threats and sexist trash talk a toxically hyper-masculine quality that anticipated the early 1990s criticism of misogyny and homophobia in gangsta rap.[9] In the stage show, after the police chase and shootout, Prince's "Bob George" character ends the song by reciting the Lord's Prayer, leading into the spiritual transformation in Act I's closer, "Anna Stesia."

In contrast to "Bob George," Prince sang the bulk of "Anna Stesia" in his unaffected chest voice, comfortably within his tenor range. The song enacts a soul in crisis: the first verse and chorus find Prince singing a monotone vocal melody on E♭, the mediant of the song's C-minor tonic, over a repetitive and ambiguous chord progression. His lyrics obsess about a woman named Anna Stesia, playing on the double entendre of that character's name (read *anesthesia*) to imply that the character's dependence upon her is merely a way to numb his pain, the only true cure for which is God, as revealed near the song's end. In his analysis, musicologist Stan Hawkins points out that as the song unfolds Prince adds timbral density, melodic variation, and a final, dramatic harmonic change that marks the character's shift from sin to penitence—or, as Hawkins puts it, "from the carnal to the theological"—that climaxes at the line "Now my Lord I understand" and then subsides into a singalong chorus of "Love is God, God is Love, Girls and boys love God above."[10]

It's more than the lyrics or the change of harmony that enact the character's spiritual conversion in "Anna Stesia," though: Prince also shifted from his chest voice into his falsetto register, where he joined a multitracked group of male and female voices singing the "Love is God" chant for the song's final minute and a half. This vocal transference from the chest to the falsetto vocal register, combined with the choral harmony and repetitive nature of the chant, give this final section of the song a gospel quality that reinforces the sacred message of the lyrics. On the *Lovesexy* tour, Prince performed this pivotal song seated at a keyboard, and during the transformative section his chair and keyboard rose up above the stage as the artist was suffused by a bright white stage light, literally enacting the spiritual uplift and dark-to-light transformation portrayed in the song.

Prince continued this theme in the show's next song: following the intermission, Prince began the second act with the *Lovesexy* album's opening track, "Eye No." This song consists of a bright and polyrhythmic funk groove over which, on the album version, Prince sang entirely in a breathy falsetto register.[11] "Eye No" projects joy and happiness through its major-mode harmony, fast tempo, bouncy polyrhythm, and Prince's high vocal tessitura, while the song's lyrics detail the abundance of God's love and exhort the listener to cast off the Devil's influence. In this context, Prince's consistent and seemingly effortless use of his high falsetto both points to the influence of gospel music and enacts the transcendence of earthly boundaries that God's grace offers. In this three-song progression from "Bob George" to "Anna Stesia" and finally to "Eye No," Prince's vocal register enacts a pilgrim's progress, suggesting that by accepting God's love the listener—like the singer—can rise above the violence, sexism, and profanity portrayed in "Bob George," circumvent the struggle and confusion portrayed in "Anna Stesia," and enter the kingdom of spiritual and sensual bliss portrayed in "Eye No" and the rest of the second act's songs.

Prince went through numerous stylistic periods in his career, both musically and visually, and many journalists and scholars interpreted this fluidity as evidence of a quintessentially postmodern or poststructuralist approach. This was especially true when scholars considered Prince's use of the voice, which, as I hope my discussion of his *Lovesexy* album and tour shows, was similarly fluid. Musicologist Anne Danielsen argued that Prince's use of multiple vocal registers and personas disrupted the Romantic values of rock criticism—in which an artist's "authentic" true self is located within their singing voice—and functioned like a mask, enacting a postmodern version of selfhood that was fragmentary and performative rather than unified and organic.[12] However, if we read Prince's multiple personas solely as a Bowie-esque parody of rock's authenticity fetish, we risk overlooking the specificity and consistency of Prince's references to African American identity and religious faith in his work. In particular, Prince's use of these two voices—one so low you can't get under it, the other so high you can't get over it, to quote Funkadelic's "One Nation under a Groove"—come from two different strains of African American religious cosmology: the prophetic Afrofuturism of funk, and the ecstatic transcendence of gospel.

In this chapter I will focus on how Prince used these two vocal techniques, both of which are informed by the syncretic worship traditions of the Black church but with different historical resonances, and explore the intersecting vectors of racial, gender, religious, and class identity in Prince's work. Musicologist Stan Hawkins made a similar point in his analysis of Prince's song "Chelsea Rodgers," arguing that Prince's performative decisions as a vocalist (and producer) communicate intersecting aspects of identity, including gender and race, and that this was partly due to his use of idiomatic techniques drawn from Black-identified musical genres such as soul, funk, and disco.[13] But where Hawkins (following performance-studies scholars like Philip Auslander and Simon Frith) focused on Prince's construction of a "vocal presence" or "musical persona"—a performative character or image that attracts and mediates audience identification—I am focusing more narrowly on these two specific vocal idioms (the gospel falsetto and funk basso profundo), their historical connection to African American religious traditions, and how Prince used them in his recorded music, which remains my primary object of analysis (rather than his image or persona).[14]

Timbre is an important analytical consideration in the subfield of popular musicology, as Derek Scott points out, and vocal timbre is particularly important among pop-music scholars who focus on performance and gesture.[15] This subgroup includes many of the intersectional scholars I surveyed in this book's introduction, who are seeking to redress the historical biases against women, African American, and queer artists in the American culture industries. In this milieu, performance and gesture are important analytical considerations due to the limited control that marginalized artists historically had over other, more easily analyzed aspects of their music and careers such as song choice, genre, instrumentation, marketing, or copyright ownership. Faced with these limitations, marginalized artists have often relied on less rigidly policed parameters such as vocal timbre, fashion, and physical gesture, using them as avenues for resistance and personal expression. For example, in her analysis of Sister Rosetta Tharpe's recordings of the gospel song "Rock Me," Gayle Wald argues that Tharpe's performative decisions—including vocal timbre—helped her balance intersecting demands of racial, gender, and religious representation as she crossed over between gospel and pop genres.[16] Emily Lordi makes a related point about how the soul music genre provided a space where singers like Nina Simone, Aretha Franklin, and James Brown could use performative parameters such as "the sweat of the body, the strain of the voice, [and] the fabulous costumes" to articulate intersecting vectors of identity including race, sex, religion, and economic class.[17] Similarly, in her analysis of Janelle Monáe's "Cold War," Shana Redmond focuses on how Monáe's performative decisions regarding her voice and body are rooted in "black diasporic arts traditions" and work to articulate a Black feminist perspective that disrupts stereotypes of Black women's hypersexuality.[18]

The connection between vocality and identity—in particular racial and gender identity—is the topic of musicologist Nina Eidsheim's 2019 book *The Race of Sound.* Where many people think there's a stable or essential connection between voice and identity (as, in Danielsen's analysis, rock criticism's Romantic discourse would have it), Eidsheim argues instead for understanding vocality as a performative play of material and symbolic signifiers—styles and techniques—that singers and listeners learn.[19] Specifically, the fact that people often use the voice as an index of gender or racial identity is due to the processes of enculturation and entrainment through which we learn to vocalize and to listen, and *not* due to any essential, physiological quality of the voice.[20] Artists like Tharpe, Simone, Franklin, Brown, Monaé, and Prince learned certain vocal idioms—melodic gestures, vocal techniques, and/or production technologies—by listening to and practicing earlier musical genres such as R&B, soul, gospel, and funk, and the performative decisions they make regarding how and when to deploy these idioms—the "material and symbolic play"—convey meaning for listeners familiar with those genres.[21]

By analyzing how Prince used just two specific vocal idioms—the gospel and soul falsetto, and funk's electronic basso profundo—I am endeavoring to follow Eidsheim's model, in which "extracting the thread of technique and style"—i.e., reading the artist's performative decisions regarding vocal idiom—constitutes "a method of critical practice."[22] These two vocal techniques that I am tracing show up again and again in Prince's music through the years, and Prince used them in ways consistent with the cultural work that gospel and funk artists of the past did to foster African American pride and political empowerment. Yet these voices carry different associations in terms of gender representation—one androgynous, the other macho—and Prince's decision to use *both* shows an artist negotiating the complex way that gender and racial representation intersect with religious identity. Despite the theological differences represented by these two cultural practices—gospel singing and funk Afrofuturism—they are both expressions of African American religious cosmology, and I will illuminate how Prince brought religious faith into his work as a tool of liberation from gender- and class-based racial stereotypes.

Prince's Ecstatic Falsetto

Prince spent his first four albums—1978's *For You*, 1979's *Prince*, 1980's *Dirty Mind*, and 1981's *Controversy*—singing almost exclusively in his high falsetto register, which fit the genre aesthetics of disco and R&B of that era. As a representative example, consider the song "I Feel for You," from Prince's eponymously titled 1979 album, in which his vocal melody stays entirely within the range C♯^{4}–C♯^{5}. The upper limit of the male tenor range is generally set at A^4, a note which lies above the passaggio where most men's voices experience a break, and yet Prince's voice sounds effortless as he sails a fourth above it. His timbre is full-throated and warm, with no strain evident, and it is a clear example of what vocal pedagogues trained in the *bel canto* tradition of Western opera would call "second-mode phonation," a phrase that has replaced the value-laden term "falsetto" in the literature, though not in common parlance.[23]

By the early 1980s Prince had largely descended from second-mode phonation into his chest voice as he moved into the more rock-oriented sound of 1982's *1999* and 1984's *Purple Rain*. The double album *1999* features falsetto lead vocals on only three out of eleven tracks ("Free," "Let's Pretend We're Married," and "International Lover"), and three of the four radio singles that charted in the United States featured Prince singing in the so-called primary-mode musical registers of "chest" and "head" voice ("1999," "Delirious," and "Little Red Corvette").[24] 1984's *Purple Rain* continued this trend, with only one of its nine songs sung primarily in falsetto ("The Beautiful Ones"). Yet even as he decreased the overall quantity of songs sung in his high falsetto register, he continued to use it structurally to mark climactic moments in his tracks. For example, Prince sings the bulk of *1999*'s "Little Red Corvette" in his chest register but ascends to a brilliantly clear and sustained high F^5 during the song's final, repetitive vamp, some thirty seconds before the fade-out of a five-minute song. Or consider "When Doves Cry," the first single from 1984's *Purple Rain* soundtrack. Prince's lead vocal remains in his chest register throughout most of the song, where he used a disaffected monotone melody and narrow dynamic range to portray the alienated emotional state of the song's main character. Yet during the climactic coda section of this song, Prince ascended into his falsetto voice, soaring to the song's melodic zenith—a high G^5—as the rest of the band vamped on a repeated fragment from the song's chorus.

Several scholars have analyzed Prince's use of the high falsetto voice as a form of gender or sexual disruption. Notable in this literature are musicologist Robert Walser's 1994 reading of the song "Kiss" and feminist philosopher Nancy Holland's 1988 discussion of "When Doves Cry." While these analyses both rely in part on Prince's use of repetitive, cyclical musical structures (an argument that I feel has been superceded by Robert Fink's work on rhythmic teleology in African American popular music, as I discussed in chapter 3), both authors also point out that Prince's voice is an important part of why these songs enact non-heteronormative and/or non-patriarchal models of gender and sexual pleasure.[25] Specifically, Holland argues that Prince constructs a female model of sexual desire in "When Doves Cry" in part through the "vulnerability" of his voice.[26] Walser makes a similar argument about Prince's "Kiss," noting the feminine-sounding high vocal range that Prince occupies during this song: as Walser points out, Prince sings lyrics full of sexual come-ons in a light, vulnerable-sounding falsetto that bounces between A^4 and C^5.[27] Walser argues that when Prince finally does reach his climactic high A^5 during the song's final chorus, the high tessitura and melodic contour make a screaming melodic gesture that enacts a postmodern loss of centered subjectivity and a non-teleological model of sexual pleasure.[28]

Productive as these readings are, the gender disruption and sexual ambiguity in Prince's songs "Kiss" and "When Doves Cry" are informed by longstanding cultural associations between the male falsetto voice and sexual nonconformity. In Western society, a male singer crossing into a higher vocal register gets easily mapped onto gender or sexual boundary crossings because of the bio-deterministic association between testosterone and lower voices. Indeed, several musicologists have gone so far as to argue that the falsetto is an intrinsically poststructural vocal register: Joke Dame, following Judith Butler, argues that the high male falsetto shows that voices, like genders, "are not sexually fixed categories but prone to choice as well."[29] Thus, just as gender is a cultural construct, so too are our understandings of the male falsetto voice informed by social discourses.

I want to extend our understanding of the social discourses that inform our perceptions of Prince's falsetto by considering how those perceptions have been shaped both by the discourse of "classical" vocal pedagogy and by the modern pop-musical styles in which the male falsetto is most often used. As we now know, second-mode phonation (the proper name for the falsetto technique) is physically produced in a different way from so-called chest or head voices, which are known in the vocal pedagogy literature as primary-mode phonation. Specifically, secondary-mode phonation involves a different positioning of the laryngeal muscles that results in the vocal folds vibrating in a manner analogous to the way that string players can lightly touch a vibrating string (rather than fully pressing it down) to produce a harmonic upper partial rather than a fundamental tone. However, up until this discovery was made (thanks to the invention of fiber-optic laryngoscopy), classical vocal pedagogy distrusted the male falsetto voice. Borrowing the term "register" from pipe organs, voice teachers had named the two primary male registers for the subjective experience of singers, who feel the resonance of these registers either in their chest or their head, and debated whether the falsetto should be admitted as a true third register or dismissed as a weak alternative to the head voice.[30]

Another factor that contributes to the perception of high-voiced men as sexual outsiders is the male falsetto's association with the bygone figure of the castrato. This association is due in part to the similarity of range between the male falsetto and that of the castrato (though castrati did not need to use second-mode phonation to reach their high register, for obvious reasons), and to the fact that male falsettists have replaced castrati in the performance repertoire of Baroque opera. Katherine Bergeron has written of the historical reception of castrati, pointing out that their coveted vocal power—the range of a soprano with the lung capacity of an adult male—was yoked to discourses of sexual deviance and physical deformity that rendered the castrato a monstrous figure, simultaneously envied and pitied.[31]

If 1980s pop audiences were unaware of such antecedents, they were nonetheless familiar with falsettists in a number of popular musical styles, notably disco and heavy metal. Disco in particular lent a flavor of outsider sexuality to the falsetto voice, owing to that style's origins in the gay loft culture of post-Stonewall New York. Indeed, one of the biggest disco divas of the 1970s was the artist Sylvester, a man who performed in drag and sang almost solely using the falsetto technique.[32] Even when voiced by a biologically female diva, the ecstatic soprano register of disco retained its potential threat. Case in point is Donna Summer, "disco's Aphrodite": despite her positioning as an avatar of female (hetero)sexuality, anti-disco rock critics seized upon her somewhat awkward body (tall, lanky) and her supposed sexual voraciousness and portrayed her as a kind of female castrato, biologically female but nonetheless sexually monstrous.[33] When the steely male soprano voices of the Brothers Gibb helped disco cross over into straight middle-American popularity, their use of the falsetto voice seemed "excessive, compulsive, forced, [and] artificial," according to cultural theorist Anne-Lise François, and as such exemplified the very falseness and artificiality that for so many Americans disqualified disco as real music.[34] Disco never quite shed its associations with minorities and sexual outsiders, and as rock critic Dave Marsh and others have argued, the anti-disco backlash that culminated in Steve Dahl's "Disco Demolition" night on July 12, 1979, had more than a hint of homophobia to it.[35] Prince began his recording career in the late 1970s, at the height of disco's popularity among the white middle-class "mainstream" audience, and in that context Prince's use of the male falsetto register would have been strongly inflected by disco's outsider sexuality.[36]

Disco is not the only pop-cultural context in which we must consider Prince's use of the male falsetto, however. Heavy metal music is another genre that, in the late 1970s and early 1980s, featured prominent use of the male falsetto, including such singers as Robert Plant of Led Zeppelin, Ronnie James Dio of Black Sabbath, Rob Halford of Judas Priest, and Bruce Dickinson of Iron Maiden. Within that genre, two factors mitigated against audience reception of the heavy metal falsetto as a form of gender transgression. First, heavy metal is socially coded as a masculine space. In her discussion of the genre-defining hard-rock band Led Zeppelin, musicologist Susan Fast references Robert Plant's high vocal tessitura as a "feminine" coded element of his gender performance but argues that such androgyny was neutralized by the heterosexual framing provided by the hard-rock genre, which many music critics, sociologists, and musicologists have written about—rightly or wrongly—as overwhelmingly phallic and even misogynistic.[37] In his book on heavy metal, musicologist Robert Walser also notes that although the genre includes performative elements that transgress the rigid code of patriarchal masculine behavior, including the overtly androgynous makeup and gender-bending stage attire used by certain glam- or hair-metal bands, nonetheless these elements exist within a larger system that reinscribes patriarchal society's distrust of femininity.[38] The second factor that mitigates against hearing heavy metal falsetto as gender transgressive is the prevalence in heavy metal of what vocal pedagogues call the "reinforced falsetto." Second-mode phonation involves the vibration of a small portion of the vocal folds, yielding higher pitches at a lighter, breathier dynamic level. By contrast, the reinforced falsetto involves the additional compression of the supraglottis—the area of the larynx directly above the vocal folds—and constriction of the pharynx, as researcher Marco Guzman has demonstrated, and this technique adds dynamic power and timbral roughness to the falsetto sound, giving it a loud, gritty timbre well suited to metal and hard rock.[39] Setting aside the semantic debate over whether or not such adjustments are enough to warrant classification as a separate vocal tessitura (both types of falsetto rely on the same method of glottal adduction), the *perceptual* differences of the reinforced falsetto as raspy, gritty, and powerful correspond to the masculine-coded heavy metal genre. As Walser argues, "Human screams and shouts are usually accompanied by vocal distortion, as the capacities of the vocal chords are exceeded," and this communicates stereotypically masculine qualities of power and strength.[40]

Though Prince did use this "reinforced falsetto" technique in certain songs, such as the hard-rock styled "Bambi," and though he used a more hard-rock guitar style on his pre–*Dirty Mind* albums, as I discussed in chapter 1 of this book, he was not marketed as part of the heavy metal genre in the late 1970s or early 1980s and his music was not received as part of that style. Prince was famously booed off the stage when he first opened for the Rolling Stones on October 9, 1981, evidence that he was not accepted as part of the hard-rock genre by the Rolling Stones audience.[41] As such, it was the genre of disco music that cast its shadow over Prince's music when he first entered the American market in 1978, and it was barely half a year after the eruption of discophobia marked by Dahl's "Disco Demolition" event when Prince scored his first number one hit on the *Billboard* R&B Singles chart with the falsetto-voiced, disco-rhythmed "I Wanna Be Your Lover" in December 1979. Though Prince did certain things to avoid being associated with the disco genre in his early career—such as avoiding the use of horns in his music and declining to be produced by Maurice White, of the disco-funk band Earth, Wind & Fire—he didn't avoid using the falsetto technique.[42] In addition, he actively incorporated a sexual-outsider status into his own image, a status that was borrowed in equal parts from new-wave post-punk and from disco. Prince lined his eyes with black eyeliner and clothed his body in a succession of gender-bending looks that included high-heeled boots, leg-warmers with zebra-striped underpants, and the occasional piece of women's lingerie. In a 1983 *Rolling Stone* profile, writer Debby Miller pointed out that Prince was using sex and seduction as part of his act but in the reverse of the usual, macho manner of male R&B stars: "Prince seems to have been off studying with Mae West, learning high camp and low-rent vamping."[43] During this period, Prince's lyrical themes were salacious in the extreme, up to and including brother-sister incest.[44] Furthermore, his lyrical double-entendres in songs such as "Do Me Baby," "Jack U Off," and "I Love U in Me" suggested that the singer might enjoy a passive or polymorphous role in sex rather than the stereotypically dominant role demanded by phallocentric masculinity. In this context, Prince's heavy dependence on his high-range singing voice read as one more element of gender transgression.[45]

Yet there is another context outside of the *bel canto* vocal pedagogy literature *and* white middle-America's perceptions of hard rock and disco in which we should interpret the falsetto, and that is the gospel-influenced vocal idiom that undergirds many African American popular genres, including R&B and disco. There is a long history of falsetto singing in the rhythm-and-blues genre, in which context it tends to be used heteronormatively: Nina Eidsheim points out that for "African American male vocalists of the 1960s," the falsetto singing technique, deployed in the high register, "signaled hypermasculinity"; as musicologist Anthony Heilbut puts it, "an artfully cultivated falsetto, crooned by an Al Green or a Bee Gee, has become vocalized foreplay. That women swoon to such voices has long been apparent."[46] When Prince's first charting single, "I Wanna Be Your Lover," entered *Billboard*'s Hot Soul Singles chart on October 13, 1979, the list also included songs with male falsetto lead vocals by Ashford and Simpson, Earth, Wind & Fire, Curtis Mayfield, the Isley Brothers, and Raydio, not to mention the high voice of Michael Jackson with "Don't Stop 'til You Get Enough."[47] At the time, none of these artists was particularly associated with gender-bending or non-heteronormative constructions of sexuality. As such, white America's reception of Prince's falsetto voice as a kind of gender rebellion, as well as the discophobia of the late 1970s and early 1980s, are informed by mainstream ignorance of the performance codes of gospel, a genre that is at the root of much of the R&B vocal idiom. As musicologist Craig Werner points out in his discussion of Prince's music, "the problem came from his white audience's lack of cultural literacy. When many listeners heard a song 'about' sex, they heard a song about sex. Grounded in the gospel impulse. . . . Prince was (usually) testifying to sex and love and the power of the Lord."[48]

The male falsetto has an important place within the African American gospel music tradition, and it entered into the gestural lexicon of Black vernacular genres that developed out of gospel. Though Prince never belonged to any of the Christian denominations most closely associated with sanctified gospel singing, i.e., the Holiness/Pentecostal, COGIC (Church of God in Christ), or Baptist Churches, he nonetheless would have been familiar with gospel as a musical style through its saturation of Black vernacular pop styles from the 1960s onward, and he was a devout Christian for the entirety of his adult life.[49] As such, the melodic gestures and aesthetic values of gospel provide a key to understanding how Prince used the high falsetto voice, and the spiritual aspect of that work.

Contrary to the discourses of European vocal pedagogy, disco, or heavy metal discussed earlier, the male falsetto voice is well within the masculine norm for gospel music. Traditional gospel values not smooth transitions between chest, head, and falsetto registers, nor evenness of tone color (as does the European *bel canto* tradition), but what musicologist Horace Boyer calls a "strained, full-throated" sound, an ideal which conforms to Olly Wilson's concept of the "heterogeneous sound ideal" among African-diasporic musical cultures.[50] In a 1979 article, Boyer further described the vocal aesthetics of gospel music as follows:

> When one speaks of a beautiful voice among gospel singers, such technical components as a well-modulated "head" tone, stable pitch, and roundness of tone are given little consideration, for the important aspects of the gospel voice are its tone color, vocal agility, and range. Both tone color and agility are irrevocably linked to range; the wider the range, the more "beautiful" the voice. . . . Sallie Martin and Mahalia Jackson, for example, won special acclaim for their wide ranges, particularly their low registers, while such male singers as Herman Stevens, James Lee . . . and Alex Bradford have been given laurels for their extremely high falsettos.[51]

Because of the importance of range, gospel aesthetics privilege singers—male and female alike—whose voices defy the typical limits of gender. As if to rebuff the gender-normative discourse of monstrosity in the Western tradition, the sounds considered "beautiful" within the gospel aesthetic include the extreme low range of the female voice which crosses into the male tenor range, and the extreme high range of the male voice which crosses into the female soprano range.

In addition to valuing voices whose wide range defies the binary gender model, gospel music also includes characteristic melodic gestures that are linked to the genre's religious function. As Samuel Floyd recounts, when gospel music "crossed over" and became a form of popular entertainment in the 1960s (blending with elements of secular jazz and R&B as it did so), it retained certain idiomatic characteristics from the church, including "vocal embellishments," "subtle rhythmic treatments," as well as the "yea-saying" vocal interjections and "call-and-response patterns and phrasings."[52] Boyer provides an even more detailed discussion of gospel's definitive melodic gestures, allowing us to trace that idiom through its secular R&B descendants doo-wop, soul, and disco. First, there is the melismatic adornment of vocal melodies, especially when accompanied by glossolalic interjections ("Oh, Lord," "Mercy," or simply "Yeah!"); energetic double-time four-four, with the backbeats accentuated by handclaps and tambourine; call-and-response interaction between soloist and group; and perhaps most tellingly, moments when, in the midst of a "vamp" or "drive," when the group has been reiterating a phrase or fragment (often with increasing dynamic level and rhythmic activity), a single voice ascends to an extreme of range in an ecstatic release of emotion, a moment that musicologist Anthony Heilbut describes as "the climax we anticipate almost subliminally."[53]

Although these idiomatic gospel gestures have become commonplace in secular genres of soul and disco, arguably none of them by itself is enough to make a song "gospel" without the participation of a community of churchgoers fluent in the theology underlying these material practices. To understand why "gospel" gestures like the male falsetto ascending to a melodic climax remain powerful markers of African American cultural practice, we must understand the theology that suffuses them. Gospel music, originally called "sanctified singing," began with the rise of Pentecostalism in America and took root in a host of African American Holiness and Sanctified denominations in the first decades of the twentieth century.[54] In addition to the Holiness doctrine (an offshoot of Methodism), which allows any individual to be saved through the acts of conversion and sanctification, Pentecostals believe that another step, often called "baptism by fire" or "baptism in the Holy Spirit," is necessary for salvation. This extra step consists of a spiritual visitation in which the congregant's soul is filled with divine presence as described in the second chapter of the book of Acts, when Christ's disciples gathered for the feast of the Pentecost.[55] This baptism by the Holy Spirit is signaled by outward physical signs such as glossolalia, the ecstatic speaking-in-tongues, that, in the African American Pentecostal tradition, often takes the form of song. The ecstasy of this baptism has been known to take other forms, including dance, but what all Pentecostal sects share is the presence of an energetic physical manifestation that the Spirit is working within the individual congregant.[56]

"When Doves Cry" and "Kiss" as Gospel Transcendence

This doctrine of baptism in the spirit translates into a particular type of melodic gesture in the gospel genre, as enumerated by Heilbut and Boyer above, that involves melodic fragmentation, repetition with elaboration, and climactic high-register breakthrough. Consider the song "One Day," recorded by the Dixie Hummingbirds with the Angelic Singers in the mid-1940s. The song is structurally comprised of regular sixteen-bar strophes, and its harmony moves between tonic, dominant and subdominant, with male and female singers alternating vocal leads. During the last strophe, however, the singers interrupt the regular phrase length and delay the final cadence of the three-chord harmonic progression by repeating a fragment of the melody and harmony (the words "one day" and the motion from subdominant to dominant). They repeat this fragment with increasing melodic elaboration for nearly half a minute; the penultimate melodic elaboration comes when two singers execute a rapid-fire call-and-response figure by tossing the word "one" back and forth between them, which presages the climactic ascent of a lone female vocalist into her highest tessitura for a series of long, extended high notes, after which the song's final cadence quickly arrives.

As a second example of this gospel vocal idiom, consider the Swan Silvertones' 1959 recording "Mary Don't You Weep." This song shows the gradual interpenetration of sacred gospel and secular R&B that had happened over the course of the later 1940s and 1950s—timbrally, the male vocal quartet is now accompanied by a full rhythm section of drums, guitar, and bass rather than just piano—but the characteristic melodic gesture of fragmentation, repetition-with-elaboration, and registral climax remains the same as "One Day." "Mary" also uses a sixteen-bar strophic structure with three-chord harmony (I, IV, and V), and the lead singer begins the song comfortably in his chest register. On the third strophe, however, the structure is interrupted, and a fragment of the phrase is repeated (the harmonic motion from tonic to subdominant near the end of the strophe). This fragment is repeated for the entire second half of the song, from 1:30 until the end at 2:50. During this repetitive vamp, the lead vocalist begins a process of melodic elaboration, adding melismas and quasi-improvised lyrical interpolations exhorting the other singers to call down the Spirit. These calls are answered by the group's falsettist Claude Jeter, whose emotional interjections strain progressively higher and longer until he finally ascends to a gritty high F♯^{4} at the 2:31 mark, which he holds for six beats. After this spectacular climactic moment, the song quickly comes to an end (its final, plagal cadence coming only four bars later).

In both of these examples, the highest pitch range, grittiest tone color, and loudest dynamic level of the vocal melody are reserved for the ecstatic climax of the song. The climax is prepared by a "drive"—a repetitive ostinato based on a harmonic fragment of a larger strophe, during which the singers progressively elaborate the melody and build up rhythmic density, often through the use of call-and-response patterns between singers. The intense emotion built into the drive section pushes a lead singer to ascend to the extreme heights of their vocal range, an exertion marked by the gritty timbre that Boyer described above. These moments are important not only for the musical climax that they bring to these songs, but also for their religious function as an enactment of the entry of the Holy Spirit into the congregation.

This ecstatic gesture shows up many times in Prince's work, including "When Doves Cry." This is one of the songs in which, as scholar Nancy Holland argued, Prince constructed a non-heteronormative model of gender and sexual desire, a construction based in part on the vulnerability of the vocal melody. Holland is right to point out that the song's sparse texture and extremely constrained vocal melody create a feeling of non-teleological plateau that defies the typical single-climax model of male sexuality and thereby reads as feminine or queer.[57] But her reading is most likely based on the shortened version of this song released as the radio single, only 3:48 in length as compared to the full 5:54 of the album version. The longer version does include an ecstatic climax—one whose shape closely resembles the gospel model described above—that directly refutes the non-teleological model Holland proposes, along the same lines that Robert Fink demonstrated in his "Goal-Directed Soul" study.[58] Specifically, Prince uses a repeated fragment of the song's harmonic progression, over which he gradually adds layers of melodic embellishment, ultimately leading to an ecstatic moment when his lead vocal breaks through the song's pitch ceiling with a climactic high falsetto scream.

Structurally, "When Doves Cry" alternates between eight- or sixteen-bar verses, a sixteen-bar chorus, and an eight-bar interstitial vamp, with a progressive increase in rhythmic density (analyzed in detail in chapter 3 of this book). The moment of ecstatic transcendence comes during a coda-like section that begins at 3:20, after the third chorus, during which the song's normal structural cycle of vamp, verse, and chorus ceases, and Prince repeats a four-bar fragment of the song's vamp section. Prince then adds semi-improvised vocal embellishments, some of which are in his chest voice but an increasing number of which he sings in his high falsetto, that lead to a spectacular antiphonal interaction between Prince's lead vocal and the chorus of background singers. This choir (which is comprised of Prince's multitracked voice singing at different harmonic intervals) sings a terraced arpeggio in four short, offbeat bursts. The first time they sing this gesture it leads to a virtuosic keyboard solo, but on their second ascent the choir's "call" is answered

Example 30. "When Doves Cry," melodic transcendence (mm. 154–162, at 5:07)

by an ecstatic breakthrough from the lead vocal. At the downbeat of m. 158 (see example 30), Prince's solo vocal melody surpasses the song's previous pitch ceiling and ascends to a sustained high G^5, from which it descends in a series of melismatic embellishments.

Given the lyrics and instrumentation of "When Doves Cry," it's easy to hear this climactic moment as the volatile irruption of unwanted Oedipal feeling, in keeping with the theme of gender-play that Prince had established in his work. However, this high falsetto scream has precisely the "grain" that defines the sanctified gospel singer in Boyer's description, and this melodic gesture has precisely the same shape—fragmentation and repetition-with-elaboration leading to a high falsetto climax—that I demonstrated in the earlier gospel examples. By understanding the history and specific melodic idiom of the gospel genre, we can therefore hear this moment not only as a moment of sexual release but also as a moment of spiritual transcendence, in which Prince—like a Holiness/Pentecostal preacher—is singing down the Spirit with the antiphonal help of his congregation. Indeed, others have made this connection, most famously the popular 1990s rapper M.C. Hammer, whose Christian-themed song "Pray," on the 1990 album *Please Hammer, Don't Hurt 'Em*, loops a sample of this very moment in Prince's "When Doves Cry," relying on the gospel nature of this melodic gesture to construct a sanctified atmosphere for the song.[59]

Another of Prince's songs that shows the same slippage between constructions of sexuality and gospel-music religious ecstasy is the song "Kiss," from Prince's 1986 *Parade* album. The song uses a strophic structure, a modified blues form whose I-IV-V harmonic progression is slowed down to half speed so that each strophe lasts twenty-four bars with an interstitial four-bar vamp at the end, a modification that Robert Walser described as "a kind of suspended animation akin to an erotic trance."[60] Unlike "When Doves Cry," in which Prince sings mostly in his chest voice and ascends to the falsetto range only during the climactic coda section at the end, Prince spends the entirety of "Kiss" floating in his falsetto range, with a chorus of backing vocalists adding harmony at the end of each strophe. Walser argues that the sense of non-heteronormative sexuality comes in part from this vocal tessitura, which he describes as "an androgynous falsetto, trembling with desire and vulnerability," and he argues that when Prince ascends into falsetto screams near the end of the song it represents "the dissolution of his centered subjectivity in the face of desire," a moment in which his male-gendered self dissolves into oceanic, non-teleological sexual pleasure.[61]

This climactic moment also uses the same gospel vocal idiom of fragmentation, repetition-with-elaboration, and ecstatic falsetto breakthrough as "When Doves Cry" did, albeit with some differences. In "Kiss," Prince does not suspend the structural progression of the song during an extended coda section as he did in "When Doves Cry" (and as the earlier gospel examples did). But Prince's expansion of the strophic twelve-bar blues form into a slower twenty-four-bar structure—what Walser argued was a non-teleological enactment of libidinal plateau—makes the final eight bars of each strophe function like the drive section of a gospel song in miniature. Specifically, during the last eight bars of each strophe, the harmonic progression is arrested on a fragment of the normal twelve-bar blues pattern, the motion from V to IV that precedes the turnaround at the end of each strophe. These eight-bar sections contain the lyrical refrain of the song, "You don't have to be rich to be my girl," sung by a chorus of background vocalists, and as the song progresses through its three full strophes Prince adds more and more elaborate lead vocal melody embellishments in call-and-response patterns with the backing vocalists, lending further resemblance to the "drive" section of a typical gospel song. This process builds up to a registral and dynamic climax during the eight-bar drive portion of the song's third and final strophe. In this final refrain, the lead vocal's call-and-response melodic elaboration boils over: Prince's falsetto lead vocal melody ascends to higher and higher pitches until finally, with a loud dynamic and a tone rasping with exertion, it breaks away from the melody's previous minor-third E–G axis (5–♭7 against the tonic A) and slides up to a high B^4, an extremely high note for a male singer even with the falsetto technique. Underscoring this moment's climactic importance is the fact that the song ends almost immediately afterward. One can definitely hear this as a moment of sexual climax or subjective dissolution, as Walser suggests, but audience members familiar with the tropes of gospel music may also hear this as a moment of spiritual transcendence.

Ultimately, both readings of Prince's falsetto register work simultaneously—in "When Doves Cry" and "Kiss" we can hear the high falsetto as both an enactment of sexuality and as an expression of spiritual transcendence—and must be understood intersectionally. The soul music genre was founded by artists—from Ray Charles and Sam Cooke to Aretha Franklin and Marvin Gaye—who, fluent in the gospel tradition, chose to use its melodic tropes to depict the more earthly ecstasies of sex.[62] Indeed, as gospel songs like "Oh Happy Day" crossed over and became popular music, and as gospel vocal tropes migrated into vernacular genres such as jazz, R&B, soul, and rock, the original spiritual function—the "gettin' over" transcendence—of the melodic gesture that I've been discussing may well have been lost on many listeners, crossing over without bringing the cross over, as the saying goes.[63] Yet even with this long history, in Prince's work this sacred/sexual juxtaposition retained its ability to shock, a fact that, I argue, comes from his *combination* of the religious vocal idiom with non-heteronormative constructions of sexuality and/or gender.

Prince's queering of the by-then commonplace mode of Black musical sacred sexuality upset the detente that the two forces had reached, and it reactivated a longstanding tension over issues of class and gender representation in the Black community. On the one side, the transcendence of the "gettin' over" melodic trope links Prince to the campaign for Black liberation that has traditionally been fed by the Black church; on the other side, Prince's falsetto histrionics reminded some listeners of the effeminized "freakish man" stereotype that has been wielded against Black men since antebellum times. Indeed, a tension over its ecstatic worship style has marked the reception of Pentecostalism and gospel music since the very beginnings of the Holiness/Pentecostal movement in the Azusa Street Revival of 1906. Though Pentecostal denominations such as the Church of God in Christ (COGIC) are now considered by sociologists part of the established Black church, it was not until the 1920s and '30s that the ecstatic musical style of gospel was accepted into the older Black Baptist and Methodist-Episcopal worship practices, and not until Mahalia Jackson's appearance at John F. Kennedy's January 1961 inauguration that sanctified singing was publicly identified as the voice of the Black church.[64]

Class issues, and the attendant pressures to assimilate, likely played a factor in the initial reluctance of these mainstream African American denominations to accept the overtly physical and emotional displays of Pentecostal worship practice. During the Great Migration, the Holiness/Pentecostal movement gained followers from among the lower economic rungs of African Americans. The older and more established African American denominations—such as the African Methodist Episcopal and the National Baptist Convention—generally viewed the rise of storefront Pentecostal churches and the ecstatic worship style practiced therein as a regressive movement that played into the stereotype of African American people as uneducated, more emotional and physical than intellectual.[65] The ecstatic "whooping" of gospel music therefore marked a lower-class or "country" identity that ran counter to the assimilationist values of the Black bourgeoisie.[66] Indeed, when the COGIC denominations first petitioned the National Council of Churches for membership, they were roundly denied, largely "because they were regarded as a cult."[67]

The behavioral codes of the Anglo-American bourgeoisie at mid-century to which such Black parishioners aspired to assimilate included a strict code of heteronormative behavior, and Prince's mixture of gospel tropes with constructions of non-heteronormative sexuality has historical precedent in the "freakish man" archetype. Historian Marybeth Hamilton has detailed the history of gender-nonconforming male performers in working-class Black entertainment from the turn of the century's "minstrel shows, cabarets, tent shows, and Black vaudeville," through the rise of blues and R&B in the 1930s–50s.[68] Such gender-nonconforming male performers, both drag queens and high-camp singers like George Hannah and Little Richard, were often referred to with the term "freakish man," which queer theorist Tim Retzloff summarizes as "a flamboyant, sissified entertainer in African American vaudeville."[69] Retzloff and Hamilton both argue that and the freakish man was not merely tolerated but often celebrated in the working-class performing venues of the 1920s–1950s where, Retzloff argues, their bawdy humor helped to ameliorate the sexual tensions and family instability brought on by the process of urbanization that working-class African American people were experiencing as a result of the Great Migration.[70]

It is within this context that Black male performers like Little Richard and also the less well-known Detroit preacher Prophet Jones ascended to stardom, and the fates of these two performers demonstrate the linkage between class, religion, gender, and race that Prince utilized as a source of power. Prophet Jones was a preacher whose effeminate persona and whooping, Pentecostal-influenced preaching style earned him a devoted following among Detroit's working-class African American population (and access to white-controlled media outlets), but also criticism from the city's more established African American denominations on grounds that his fame was a setback for the cause of racial integration.[71] Retzloff concludes that Jones's eventual downfall, precipitated by an undercover sting that exposed his homosexuality, showed how the class division within the Black community played out in terms of gender and sexuality: Jones's working-class base of supporters remained loyal (perhaps due to the origins of the freakish man archetype in working-class Black entertainment), while members of the Black middle class "lauded" the morals charges against Jones.[72]

Scholars Marybeth Hamilton, Samuel Floyd, and Mark Tucker have made similar points about Little Richard, another African American performer who mixed Pentecostal ecstasy with an effeminate style of gender self-presentation and a barely concealed homosexual identity.[73] Richard cut his teeth performing drag and campy R&B numbers on the chitlin circuit, and Hamilton argues that Richard's flamboyant effeminacy is emblematic of the centrality of the "freakish man" to the formation of R&B in the 1940s and '50s. Hamilton describes Richard's gospel-soaked vocal melody on the chorus of the 1957 R&B hit "Lucille" in a way that echoes Walser's description of Prince's falsetto screams at the end of "Kiss": "his extraordinarily expressive cry of 'Lu-cille!', which turns hypermasculine growl into falsetto shriek, conveying in its vocal flamboyance the visual shock of drag itself."[74] As Tucker and Floyd have pointed out, the high emotional camp of this performance style and the intimations of Richard's homosexuality may have contributed to his crossover success by rendering him less threatening to white authority figures, allowing Richard to sidestep the fears of miscegenation that fueled the white backlash against rock 'n' roll during the early 1950s.[75] Yet Richard was not without his own critics in the Black religious community, not least himself: in 1958, Richard explicitly renounced rock 'n' roll, and implicitly renounced homosexuality, when he entered the ministry. Hamilton argues that it was not just the debauchery of the R&B world but also Richard's gay identity and gender-nonconforming appearance that he could not reconcile with his religiosity, pointing out that Richard dumped all his jewelry in a river and also gave up "his makeup and his pompadour, all the visual signs of his gay identity" before entering bible school to become a minister.[76]

The downfalls of Prophet Jones and Little Richard were symptomatic of the mounting pressure that middle-class African American people in the 1940s–1970s were under to distance themselves not just from their working-class country origins, but specifically from the "freakish man" archetype.[77] On one hand, homosexual panic (the so-called "Lavender scare") gripped America during the early 1950s as a result of the McCarthyist conflation of homosexuality and communism. On the other hand, white America has a long history of constructing effeminized caricatures of Black masculinity and wielding them as emblems of Black difference and white supremacy. As Eric Lott argued in his study of blackface minstrelsy, American minstrel shows included several stock characters that were based on grotesquely exaggerated gender and sexual characteristics, such as the "wench" character, an effeminized, cross-dressing male used for comic relief.[78] Lott argues that such constructions were used to buttress white male identity, and that such patterns of gendered racial stereotype remained active in American culture long after the disappearance of blackface minstrelsy. Black masculinity was thus politicized, and Hamilton points out that from the mid-1950s through the 1970s rejecting the "freakish man" stereotype was a component of both the civil rights movement, which "stressed respectability"—sexual and otherwise—and of the Black power movement, which emphasized "heterosexual machismo."[79]

As Hamilton points out, Richard's use of the "freakish man" persona may have seemed to many members of the African American community a politically regressive move that reinscribed the negative stereotype of the "sissified Sambo, an updated version of the feminized buffoon of blackface comedy."[80] Retzloff argues that while Prophet Jones's downfall was triggered by members of the white media, there were plenty of attacks from members of the middle-class Black community, attacks "that were intended to divorce homosexuality from the

African American body, with which it had been conflated in the popular imagination since the late nineteenth century."[81] Both Retzloff and Hamilton point out that it was during the early 1950s that drag balls, once a mainstay of Black performing venues that received coverage in prominent Black newspapers, went back underground, disappearing from middle-class visibility.[82] If the logic of white supremacy relied on constructing the Black body as essentially different, and if gender nonconformity served as an outward sign of difference, then we must consider the mincing, campy performance style associated with the "freakish man" archetype as a kind of third rail in African American gender politics, powerful but also potentially dangerous.

In this context, Prince's queering of the sacred-sexual trope—the link that he made between the high, whooping gospel falsetto, his androgynous self-presentation, and his musical constructions of non-heteronormative sexual desire—are politically ambivalent. On the one hand, they do have the power to liberate listeners from the structural boundaries of binary gender and phallocentric sex, as the postmodern arguments of Walser and Holland demonstrate. Indeed, both Hamilton and Tucker make similar points about Little Richard, arguing that Richard's non-heteronormative gender construction "forecast the sexual revolutions to come," paving the way for later, postmodern deconstructions of Otherness by artists like Grace Jones and Prince.[83] On the other hand, we cannot dismiss the possibility that Prince's use of the "freakish man" archetype may have been politically regressive, reigniting a century-old white stereotype of the emasculated Black man. Like Richard before him, Prince was accused of downplaying his heterosexuality and masculinity and pandering to white stereotypes in order to achieve crossover success: writer Nelson George suggested that both Prince and Michael Jackson "ran fast and far both from blackness and conventional images of male sexuality."[84] Sananda Maitreya (previously known as Terence Trent D'Arby), a popular recording artist in the 1980s and '90s, made a similar point while describing the double bind that African American artists such as himself and Prince faced during that time: "Any black act in the States who has been [a] massive quote-unquote crossover success has had to emasculate himself to some degree. Prince has had to play the bisexual image, cast aspersions as to his dominant heterosexuality, [Michael] Jackson's had to be asexual."[85] Literary critic Marjorie Garber, discussing this quote, argues that race, gender, and sexuality operate along correlated axes of power, with "white" and "male" as the favored poles (to which I would also add "heterosexual" and "cis-gendered"); the implication being that gaining privilege on one axis can come at the expense of privilege on another.[86] Setting aside Maitreya/D'Arby's tacit valuation of normative masculine heterosexual patriarchy, his bitterness is poignant evidence that the image of emasculated Black men promoted by the white-dominated media industry still has the power to wound.

I want to suggest a third reading for Prince's use of the falsetto voice and of the androgynous "freakish man" archetype. Rather than hearing it as either a postmodern deconstruction or a politically regressive stereotype, we can synthesize the two positions by focusing on the religious function of gospel's ecstatic falsetto melodies. Prince most certainly embodied the topos of Black sexual Otherness in his early career—one need only do a cursory internet image search to find myriad examples of Prince's gender-confounding stage outfits from his early career. Yet this was not the only sexual subject position Prince staked for himself: Prince also constructed traditional, heteronormative masculine subject positions in songs throughout the 1980s such as "Head," and explored a swaggering macho persona in hip-hop-influenced 1990s songs like "Gett Off." Furthermore, the ecstatic falsetto scream was just one of many colors in Prince's vocal palette. As I will discuss in the next section of this chapter, Prince often used an electronically affected deep-bass vocal range at particular moments in his music, a voice that projected a decidedly patriarchal subject position. This multiplicity, as Walser, Danielsen, and Holland have argued, allowed listeners to view the "freakish man" archetype from an ironic distance.

However, I do not agree with the conclusion that Prince's project was essentially a postmodern deconstruction of identity. Rather, the cosmological origins of Prince's high falsetto scream—the gospel trope of vocal transcendence—provide a context for hearing Prince's queering of that voice as a tool of *racial* disruption. As I have discussed, Prince's high falsetto wailing at the end of "When Doves Cry," "Kiss," "Little Red Corvette," and many other songs is part of a cosmological tradition that stretches back at least to the advent of glossolalia in the Holiness/Pentecostal movement, and likely even further to the ecstatic musicking of African American worshippers at camp meetings during the Great Awakening, what Albert Raboteau has described as the syncretic "slave religion" of early Black converts to Christianity.[87] As such, Prince's falsetto screams—just like those of Little Richard and Prophet Jones—get their liberatory power from a model of spiritual transcendence rooted in the Black church, an institution that has been central to the political liberation of African American people since antebellum days. Put another way, Prince's use of the sacred-sexual falsetto vocal trope comes from the African American sacred tradition, and while his queering of that trope reactivated a debate over gender representation in the Black community it nevertheless enacted his core belief (as a Christian) in the promise of transcending earthly categories of race, gender, and sexuality through faith in the kingdom of God. Unlike Little Richard, Prince did not seem (at this point in his career) to harbor feelings of contradiction between non-heteronormative sexuality and divinity, and he used the gospel falsetto to articulate Christian faith and Black identity in a way that freed them from restrictions based on class and gender, liberating Black masculinity by reaching toward divinity.

Prince and the Prophetic Voice

Prince's ecstatic high falsetto was just one of several different vocal techniques he employed throughout his career, and androgynous gender and non-heteronormative sexuality were by no means the only sexual subject positions that he constructed. The voice that sits at the opposite extreme from the sexual and gender fluidity enacted in songs like "Kiss" and "When Doves Cry" is a hyper-masculine basso profundo that Prince used in various projects. As I mentioned earlier in this chapter, this use of multiple voices led musicologist Anne Danielsen to argue that Prince was a fundamentally postmodern artist whose work undermined stable conceptions of gender and racial identity.[88] On the contrary, by examining Prince's use of the deep bass register we can see how this voice, much like the high falsetto gospel trope that Prince used, also has its roots in African American cosmological traditions, and that Prince used it as part of the same project of liberating Black masculinity from stereotypical representations.

The first appearance of the extreme low bass voice in Prince's oeuvre comes from the 1982 song "1999": a deep and somewhat threatening voice opens the track, slowly and deliberately intoning the line "Don't worry, I won't hurt you. I only want you to have some fun." The line is made ominous by the unnaturally low register, which Prince most likely achieved using the Varispeed recording technique (in which the track is recorded with the magnetic tape moving at a faster speed so that the pitch would sound lower when played back at standard speed). This particular instance of the low bass voice is also ominous because of its uncanny doubling: a second copy of the voice plays back simultaneously but at different, even lower pitch level. Within the framework of the song's lyrics, this voice portrays a kind of extraterrestrial presence, and as the song unfolds Prince treats the listener to a raucous party in the face of Armageddon, complete with a mid-tempo polyrhythmic dance groove, lyrics that reference the biblical book of Revelations, and sound effects of bombs exploding. Two albums later, the song "Temptation" from 1985's *Around the World In A Day* features a similar, electronically produced deep bass voice during the song's coda. The bass voice in "Temptation" differs from the one in "1999," but remains uncanny: it is *not* doubled, and has a much deeper register, which Prince most likely achieved using a harmonizer (a type of studio effect that can alter the frequency of an audio signal without affecting its speed). Within the lyrical framework of "Temptation," Prince used this voice to portray a punitive god: the song's protagonist, having confessed to the sin of lust, is reprimanded, and ultimately condemned to death, by this deep voice.

Prince continued to use this electronic low-bass voice sporadically up to and including the song "Revelation" from his final album, 2015's *HITnRUN Phase Two.* Sometimes Prince used the voice extensively within a song, sometimes only for a moment, but it is a recurring technique that runs parallel to Prince's use of the ecstatic high falsetto throughout his oeuvre. Yet it is not just the timbre and tessitura of this low bass voice that connects songs such as "1999," "Temptation," "Bob George," "The Exodus Has Begun," "The Rainbow Children," "Art Official Cage," "X's Face," and "Revelation": Prince also linked these songs with themes of high technology, cosmology, and masculinity, a mixture—commonly called Afrofuturism—that has deep roots in Black religious practice.

The theme of technology is ever-present in Prince's use of the low bass voice partly because it is only through the use of studio technology such as Varispeed tape recording, harmonizers, and multitracking that Prince is able to speak in this unnaturally low register in the first place. But technology also shows up as a lyrical topos in such songs. "1999" is one example of this, as I've already discussed; another example, "The Exodus Has Begun" from the 1996 album *Exodus* (released under the name of Prince's backing band, the New Power Generation) features the electronic low-bass voice as the emcee of an interstellar party taking place on a spaceship that the band has commandeered.

The theme of masculinity is also embedded in Prince's use of this deep bass voice, in part because of the long history of associating lower voices with masculine authority in Western culture, an association that goes back at least to the Rossinian codes of *bel canto* opera in which authority figures were cast as bass voices to contrast with the high tenor voices of the young male heroes. But as with technology, Prince extended the theme of masculinity into these songs' lyrics. On the one hand, Prince deployed his electronic basso profundo to portray toxically hyper-masculine characters such as the narrator of "Bob George," who threatens to kill his girlfriend and ends the song shooting at police officers. Prince also uses this model of thuggish masculinity in the song "New Power Day" from *Exodus*, in which he portrays an unnamed character engaged in a fight whose violence is brutal to the point of being cartoonish. On the other hand, Prince also used this hyper-masculine deep bass voice to articulate the proper limits of male behavior in the field of sex and courtship, as in songs like "The Sensual Everafter" and "1+1+1 Is 3" from *The Rainbow Children*, or the aforementioned "Temptation" from *Around the World in a Day*.

Prince also lyrically links his low bass voice to the theme of cosmology. This sometimes takes the form of extraterrestrial aliens and space travel, as in "1999" and "The Exodus Has Begun," and sometimes as the voice of a deity, as in the song "Temptation." Yet another way that Prince activates the theme of religion is to use this voice in conjunction with spoken-word interludes voiced by a talking computer character, a device that recalls the "talking book" archetype within Black religious history.[89] Prince used this device throughout 1995's *The Gold Experience* and 1999's *Rave Un2 the Joy Fantastic*, though without the techno-low-bass voice; 2001's *The Rainbow Children* mixes the two voices, with the low bass voice referring to the talking-computer voice as "the Akashic record." Toward the end of Prince's life, the talking computer showed up numerous times in close proximity to the low bass voice, including the songs "Affirmation" from 2014's *Art Official Age* and "Mr. Nelson" from 2015's *HITnRUN Phase One*.

Arresting though the electronic low-bass voice is, listeners may have been inclined to dismiss it as a special effect due to its sporadic appearance. Prince never used it to sing an entire song, nor did it show up on every album, nor did he use it consistently on the albums where it does show up. Furthermore, the thematic mixture of futuristic technology, gods and aliens, and masculinity may have seemed to many listeners as merely an example of Prince's idiosyncratic private beliefs, beliefs that Prince's own guitarist Dez Dickerson once described as "a mish-mash" and a "sort of new religion," and which biographer Per Nilsen characterized as a "self-made mythology."[90] Yet there was one album where these two elements—the low bass voice and the seemingly idiosyncratic blend of religion, futurism, and masculinity—were impossible to ignore, and that was 2001's *The Rainbow Children.*

Like a number of other Prince albums, *The Rainbow Children* has a unifying concept—the religious beliefs of the Jehovah's Witness faith, to which Prince had recently converted—that Prince conveyed through spoken vignettes, skits, and talking-computer monologues delivered in and between songs. Previous examples of such unifying interstitial material include Kirstie Alley's role as a newspaper reporter on Prince's so-called *Love Symbol* album of 1992, Prince's use of a female-voiced computer narrator on 1995's *The Gold Experience,* the "segue" tracks included on the New Power Generation album *Exodus,* and the aforementioned, omniscient computer narrator on *Art Official Age* and *HITnRUN Phase One.* But *The Rainbow Children* has the most extensive use of the electronic low-bass voice of any single project in Prince's career. The voice is impossibly low—one reviewer called it a "computer generated *basso-profundo,*" and another simply referred to it as "Darth [Vader]-like"—and it does not have the slurred quality that marks the use of Varispeed pitch shifting, meaning that Prince created it using a digital harmonizer, a fact that he confirmed by performing the songs live in concert during his 2002 world tour (Varispeed cannot be performed live).[91]

Not only is the low bass voice inescapable on *The Rainbow Children,* but Prince's thematic mixture of techno-futurism and religious cosmology pervades the album to a degree that few could ignore. Many reviewers were mystified by these themes, and critical reactions ranged from condescending to hostile. *Rolling Stone*'s Arion Berger complained that the album "offers church interludes that are too mystical to carry earthly convention."[92] Marc Weingarten of *Entertainment Weekly* heard it as "a muddled conflation of one-world utopianism, Christianity, and paganism."[93] Perhaps most dismissively of all, the *Onion A.V. Club* described the album's lyrical themes as "the rabbit hole of a private mythology," a statement that echoed Dez Dickerson's earlier critique of Prince's religious views.[94]

Afrofuturism as Manichaean Cosmology

What these reviewers missed was that Prince's seemingly idiosyncratic mix of futuristic technology, biblical prophecy, gnostic mysticism, humor, and machismo has a long history in the funk genre, and a name: Afrofuturism. Scholar Mark Dery, who first used the term analytically, provisionally defined it as a type of "African-American signification that appropriates images of technology and a prosthetically enhanced future," and identified it in the music of African American artists Jimi Hendrix, George Clinton, Bernie Worrell, Lee "Scratch" Perry, Sun Ra, and Herbie Hancock.[95] Building on Dery's work, several musicologists have explored how Black musicians have used the Afrofuturist trope to symbolically heal the fractured past and/or comment on the politically alienated present experienced by Black Americans by projecting the African diaspora into an imagined, techno-utopian future that is infused with elements of precolonial African cultures. Ken McLeod points out that musical Afrofuturism mixes "historical prophetic imagination, such as Egyptian theories of the afterlife" with utopian science-fiction futurism; in essence, allowing the African diaspora to return to "an imaginary utopian homeland" that is represented by outer space.[96] Griffith Rollefson argues that musical Afrofuturists such as funk artist George Clinton, jazz artist Sun Ra, and rapper Kool Keith "problematize the rigid binary of blackness / whiteness" by mixing the universalist (read *white*) topic of techno-futurism with specific tropes from African-diasporic culture and biblical stories such as exodus, a strategy of "anti-anti-essentialism" that transcends race while simultaneously "retaining a critical blackness."[97]

Prince's particular use of the electronically mediated low-bass voice and the Afrofuturist trope was strongly influenced by the work of George Clinton, and to understand the theological ramifications of Prince's low bass voice we need to examine this precedent. Clinton began using the device of the low bass voice, albeit without any technological interventions to lower the pitch, on Parliament's 1975 album *Chocolate City*, whose title song used a macho deep-bass voice—inspired by the deejay patter that had been common on Black radio in the 1950s and 60s—to celebrate the growing electoral power of African American communities in the seventies.[98] On the two albums that followed, *Mothership Connection* and *Clones of Dr. Funkenstein*, Clinton augmented this macho, low bass voice with a richly detailed Afrofuturist mythology embodied by the character of Dr. Funkenstein. Portrayed by Clinton himself, Dr. Funkenstein was both an interstellar traveler and a hyper-macho pimp who sported a (faux) ermine coat, wide-brimmed hat, and natty walking cane. Dr. Funkenstein spoke in the low bass voice that Clinton had established on the previous *Chocolate City*, and his lyrical patter presented the core elements of the P-Funk mythology. Consider Funkenstein's monologue from the song "Prelude" on the 1976 album *Clones of Dr. Funkenstein*, which includes numerous techno-futurist references: cloning, a spaceship called the "Mothership," astronauts, and extraterrestrial visitors. Yet Clinton mixes these with verbal and visual signifiers of inner-city Black life, such as Dr. Funkenstein's pimp swagger. Furthermore, Clinton adds references to ancient Egyptian pyramids and pharaohs, signifiers of a glorious African past. Lastly, Clinton subtly introduced the topic of religion and Christianity with references to the "chosen one" and the revelation of hidden, gnostic knowledge, not to mention through the preacherly quality of his monologue, which keyboardist Bernie Worrell augmented with a simulacrum of a church organ.

Clinton reinforced this thematic mixture of precolonial African past, impoverished inner-city present, futuristic technology, and gnostic biblical prophecy in the staging of his live shows during the 1977 P-Funk Earth Tour, during which the band literalized their Afrofuturist mythology with an elaborate deus ex machina device. The Mothership spaceship, in miniature, first traversed the auditorium on a wire and then "landed" onstage as a full-sized spacecraft descended from the theater rigging, after which the hatch opened in a puff of stage smoke to reveal Dr. Funkenstein, who then pimp-walked down the staircase to his microphone. This techno-futuristic moment was also infused with elements of traditional Black Christian worship: Specifically, the band performed an adaptation of the spiritual "Swing Low, Sweet Chariot"—transformed into "Swing Down, Sweet Chariot"—during this scene.[99] Thus prepared, the arrival of the Mothership took on a deeply spiritual significance for many audience members.[100] Scholar John Corbett describes the Funkenstein character and Mothership stage machinery as "a detailed myth-in-performance" that enacted the exodus of African Americans from inner-city impoverishment into their true extraterrestrial community of Afronauts. (And as Robin D. G. Kelley argues, Clinton also connected that Afrofuturist mythology to the biblical story of Exodus).[101] These references to exodus in Clinton's mothership performances highlight a deep theological link between Afrofuturism and older traditions of Black Christianity that Prince would later use.

In his book *Children of Ezekiel*, Michael Lieb argues that a common eschatology underlies African American religious movements, from the earliest syncretic Christian worship practices of antebellum slaves, to Millerite faiths like the Seventh-day Adventists and the Jehovah's Witnesses, to modern movements such as the Nation of Islam. According to Lieb, these diverse religious practices all treat the Christian Bible as a source of encoded prophecy, employing a nonlinear approach that samples and recombines biblical texts to produce a vision of the future in keeping with the concerns of the present, an approach that displays the same quality of intertextuality that, according to Henry Louis Gates Jr., is at the core of African American expressive culture.[102] In particular, Lieb argues that these end-time movements bring together two particular images or ideas from the Christian Bible: first, from the books of Prophets comes the vision of Ezekiel's wheel, a vision that represents the divine will made concrete as a techno-mechanical object that became equated with the symbol of the chariot; second, this divine chariot is connected to God's deliverance of the Israelites in the book of Exodus and God's retribution against the wicked described in the book of Revelations.[103] Lieb argues that this linkage originally represented Black Americans' impulse to symbolically escape the constraints of antebellum slavery and reconfigure Christian mythology to place themselves at the center, and that this textual strategy remained a key component of various Black power movements in the United States from Marcus Garvey's Ethiopianism of the 1920s, to the reclamation of the Egyptian pyramids by the Black Power movement of the 1970s.[104]

This intertextual focus on divine technology as a vehicle of deliverance and retribution suffuses the theology not only of the historical Black church[105] but of other end-time faiths that have had significant African American participation, such as the Seventh-day Adventists, Jehovah's Witnesses, and the Nation of Islam.[106] As religious historian Andrew Holden points out, "millenarianism is a form of resistance that serves to strengthen the conviction of a people who see themselves as persecuted . . . with the assurance that God will exact vengeance on evil."[107] Given the centuries of persecution that African Americans have endured, Holden's point suggests a connection between the millenarian theology of the Seventh-day Adventist and Jehovah's Witness faiths and the liberation theology of mainline African American Christian denominations. Indeed, such a connection is supported by sociological data: in their 2001 American Religious Identification Survey, sociologists Barry Kosmin, Egon Mayer, and Ariela Keysar statistically examined the relationship between ethnicity and religion in America, and their data (drawn from the 2000 decennial census) shows a pattern of high African American involvement in the aforementioned denominations.[108]

In this light, the Afrofuturism that infused the funk genre of the 1970s becomes just one more example of the particular theological construction that Lieb describes as linking various faith traditions.[109] It is this impulse that made the chariot a symbol of freedom in African

American spirituals like "Swing Low Sweet Chariot," and this same impulse that led George Clinton to transform it into the spacefaring Mothership as his band sang "swing *down* sweet Chariot."[110] This impulse deeply informs Prince's use of the electronic low-bass voice not only because of his obvious musical debt to funk pioneer George Clinton, but also because of Prince's own religious faith, which he foregrounded on 2001's *The Rainbow Children.*

Prince Rides the Chariot: *The Rainbow Children*

According to biographers, Prince was an adherent of two of the aforementioned end-time religious sects at various points in his life. Prince was raised by parents active in the Seventh-day Adventist church in North Minneapolis, which he sometimes attended; and after spending most of his adult life as a non-denominational Christian, he converted to the Jehovah's Witness faith around the time of his 1997–98 Jam of the Year tour.[111] These two churches have common origins in the Millerite "Great Disappointment" of 1843, when the world failed to end as predicted, and as such they are both founded on the belief that God's destruction of the world is both imminent and necessary.[112] Both sects believe that prophetic knowledge is encoded within the Bible and was revealed by their founders' selective interpretation and recombination of biblical texts.[113] Furthermore, the founders of both sects were obsessed with futuristic technology. Seventh-day Adventists, obsessed with medical technology, made the issue of health and hygiene paramount and raised the figure of the "doctor" above even the minister in importance.[114] Jehovah's Witness founder Charles Taze Russell focused on modern technology's potential to liberate the individual from work, and his successor, Joseph Rutherford, structured the Watch Tower Society—the governing body of the Jehovah's Witness faith—as a techno-theocracy whose hierarchical levels mirror the "wheels-within-wheels" of Ezekiel's vision.[115]

While we cannot know the full extent to which Seventh-day Adventist or Jehovah's Witness theology influenced Prince's private beliefs or worship practices, we do know that his 2001 album *The Rainbow Children* is suffused with Jehovah's Witness tenets. Furthermore, Afrofuturism resonates throughout the album, as does the technologically mediated low bass voice of the narrator. One of the album's central lyrical images, the "digital garden," is a futuristic techno-dystopian setting where the album's protagonists find themselves alienated and persecuted, a reverse of the normally utopian images of futurist technology in Afrofuturist literature, but one that is consistent with Afrofuturism's role as a political protest against alienation in the present.

In the tradition of Afrofuturism, Prince mixes technological themes with ideas of hidden or gnostic knowledge, ancient Egypt, and end-time biblical prophecy. At various times on the album, the low-bass narrator introduces the voice of a talking book or computer that it refers to as the "Akashic record," which plays recordings of various impossible-to-record historical events. This is a reference to the Theosophical Society, who posited the existence of "the Akashic record," a mystical document that, they imagined, contained all knowledge of past and future events.[116] The Theosophical Society was a mystical group formed in New York in 1875, around the same time that Charles Taze Russell founded what would later become the Jehovah's Witnesses, and both groups shared a belief in the importance of decoding occult knowledge modeled on the Greek concept of "gnosis." By referencing this book, then, Prince is imbuing his album with mystical religious secrets from the past, just as George Clinton's Afrofuturistic "Prelude" suggested extraterrestrial knowledge hidden among the pyramids of Egypt.

Biblically, *The Rainbow Children* takes the listener on an intertextual tour from original sin through apocalypse and beyond, into the rebuilding of God's kingdom on Earth that, in Jehovah's Witness theology, follows Armageddon. The title of the album and of its opening song refers to the rainbow covenant from the story of Noah in the biblical book of Genesis, a pact that the Jehovah's Witnesses interpret as a restriction against ingesting blood, from whence derives the common Jehovah's Witness practices of refusing transfusions and keeping a vegetarian diet, both of which Prince adopted in his own life.[117] During the verses of "The Rainbow Children" the low bass narrator retells a version of Adam and Eve's fall from grace, also from the book of Genesis, while in the chorus a different voice sings about the "new translation," a reference to the Jehovah's Witness proprietary version of the Christian bible, the *New World Translation.* Prince brings up the Jehovah's Witness dietary restrictions again during the song "She Loves Me 4 Me," in which he praises a woman for her meat-abstaining diet. The penultimate song on the album, "The Everlasting Now," is a polyrhythmic dance track that enacts a post-apocalyptic paradise on Earth, which is a reference to the belief—shared by several apocalyptic faiths, including the Jehovah's Witnesses—that the promised paradise that awaits the faithful after Armageddon is actually just a violently cleansed and rebuilt version of our existing Earth.

Alongside technology, esoteric mysticism, and biblical prophecy, Prince weaves themes of gender and race into *The Rainbow Children.* First, gender is an inescapable theme due to the hyper-masculinity of the low bass narrator: by delivering religiously themed lyrics in an inhumanly low tessitura and with a deliberate, unrushed pace, Prince gives these monologues a patriarchal weight that suggests the voice of Jehovah himself, or at the very least one of his earthly prophets. Second, lyrics in several of the songs sharply delineate male and female gender roles as prescribed by the Bible. For example, in "The Rainbow Children," the album's retelling of the Adam and Eve myth, the low-voiced narrator refers to the Adam character as the "wise one" and downplays his rebellion against Jehovah, and refers to the Eve character simply as "his woman" and describes how their ejection from paradise was entirely precipitated by her susceptibility to sin. Another example is the album's second song, "Muse 2 the Pharaoh," in which Prince uses ancient Egypt as background for an exploration of Proverbs 31:10, a Bible verse that describes the proper behavior for the wife of a king.

Race is another important theme of *The Rainbow Children,* and the component that makes this an Afrofuturistic album rather than simply a futuristic one. Throughout the album Prince sets his futuristic and biblical lyrics to music that references his funk forebears, placing African Americans at the center of the album's prophetic narrative. In the album's fourth song, "The Work, Pt. 1," Prince lyrically links the Jehovah's Witnesses' central occupation—door to door proselytizing—with funk godfather James Brown, the hardest-working man in show business, in whose unmistakable style Prince wrote the song. In the album's penultimate song, "The Everlasting Now," Prince links the cosmological event described in the lyrics—the deliverance of the chosen people to their post-apocalyptic paradise on Earth—to the funk pioneer Sly Stone by calling out the names of his songs "Everybody Is a Star" and "Everyday People" and using a bass line reminiscent of Larry Graham, bass player for the Family Stone and Prince's close collaborator in the early 2000s (Graham contributed bass lines to two of *The Rainbow Children's* songs).[118] In fact it was Graham himself who guided Prince on his conversion to the Jehovah's Witness faith, a faith in which Graham was a church elder. In the musical analysis that follows, I will trace the themes of religious prophecy and African American identity through one specific song on *The Rainbow Children,* "Family Name," in order to explore how Prince used the Afrofuturist trope and the technologized low-bass voice to liberate Black masculinity from limiting binary oppositions of race and gender.

"Family Name"

"Family Name" is over eight minutes long with three large-scale sections. The first, comprising mm. 1–68 of the song (from the beginning until 3:01) is a long introduction in which Prince uses the talking-book trope to introduce the song's themes. The second is a series of alternating verse and bridge sections, which Prince sings in his high falsetto, that spans mm. 69–123 (3:01–5:28). The third large-scale section is a coda, lasting from m. 124 to m. 178 (5:28–7:51), that features a series of spoken-word vignettes, including an interjection by the techno-low-bass voice, and concluding with a searing guitar solo and a recorded quote from Dr. Martin Luther King Jr. Though Prince reserves the electronically produced low bass voice of prophecy for one single line during the coda, the talking-computer voices in the introduction serve a similar cosmological purpose by activating both the talking-book trope and the Afrofuturist themes.

The introduction (mm. 1–68) establishes both the song's funk pedigree and its Afrofuturistic mix of themes. Prince sets the scene with a polyrhythmic groove comprised of a one-bar drum ostinato and a two-bar bass pattern on A minor, played by then-band members John Blackwell (drums) and Rhonda Smith (bass) (see example 31). Blackwell's drum pattern displays the polyrhythmic technique typical of funk drumming, including layers that move at different rhythmic densities—the sixteenth-note pulse of the high-hat against the eighth-note and implied quarter-note pulse of the bass and snare drums—as well as the presence of embedded rhythmic dissonance between the dominant four-four meter and the implied triplets of the snare drum. In keeping with funk's deemphasis of harmonic progression, Prince doesn't include any chord changes until mm. 53–54 (2:20), towards the end of the song's first large-scale section, when he first interrupts the A-minor ostinato with a brief harmonic turnaround.

During this introductory section Prince uses a talking computer—complete with the click-clack sounds of a computer keyboard—to establish the thematic mix of futurism, Afrocentrism, religious prophecy, and the decoding of hidden, esoteric information. Prince literalizes the talking-computer trope by using two different voice settings from a common text-to-speech computer application, one low and one high. The higher voice narrates the computer-menu navigation, after which the lower computer voice gives a rambling lecture that touches on the importance of names—which hold particular significance both in

Example 31. "Family Name," drum and bass ostinatio

African American history and in Jehovah's Witness theology—and critiques the structural binarism of terms like "Black" and "white," making clear the song's theme of racial identity. Following this lecture, the higher computer voice narrates another menu selection in the Akashic record, and the listener hears two "recordings" of historical events. The first brings up the issue of colonialism by portraying a group of British-accented legislators expelling an unnamed group of people from an unnamed colony. The second dramatic vignette portrays the arrival of African slaves in the colonies: the listener hears slaves disembarking from the Middle Passage and a slave owner giving an African man his new name. By dramatizing the theft of African American people's patrilineal names in the colonies, Prince both explicates the song's title—"Family Name"—and sets the moral stakes for the two large-scale sections of the song to follow, the next of which begins immediately after this moment, at the downbeat of m. 69 (at 3:01).

Only certain names have theological importance for the Jehovah's Witnesses, the greatest of which is the name for God from which the sect takes its name, but in the context of African American history all surnames names have an obvious significance. The loss of African Americans' names, which during the antebellum era were largely replaced by those of slaveowners, is irreparable. Indeed, the renunciation of these assigned surnames has been one of the signal issues for the Nation of Islam, which advocates that members drop their "slave names" in favor of a neutral marker, as made famous by Malcolm "X," or a revealed spirit name as in the case of Muhammad Ali, whom Prince names in the lyrics of "Family Name." Though never a member of the Nation of Islam, Prince himself famously renounced his own given name during the years 1993–2000, replacing it with a famous yet unpronounceable glyph often referred to as the "love symbol." Journalists at the time attributed this name change to a dispute over his contract with his then-label Warner Brothers and the ownership of his master recording. But Prince made the explicit connection between Black identity and artists rights by writing the word "slave" on his face in makeup pencil whenever he appeared in public during this period, and by declaring that "if you don't own your masters, your master owns you."[119] As legal scholar Twila Perry argues, the history of slavery gives particular importance to the ownership of one's work for Black Americans.[120] In this context, the thematic importance that Prince gives to names in this song carries both his personal history of artistic dispossession and the broader history of African American's alienation from their own labor under slavery.

Returning to the song: after the dramatic interlude depicting the theft of an African slaves' name, Prince begins the song's second large-scale section, the alternating verses and bridges that comprise the song proper, at m. 69 (at the 3:00 mark). The verses are based upon the same polyrhythmic drum and bass ostinato as the preceding section (see example 31), though the mode shifts from minor to major, and the texture is thickened by the addition of synthesizer and guitar. With this modal change comes a larger shift in harmony, as Prince introduces a chord progression—I–IV–I–IV–vi–V/V–V–I in A major (see example 32)—that adds a forward-moving layer of harmonic syntax on top of the already forward-leaning groove. The bridge section that alternates with this verse features an even thicker texture that includes choral-style harmonized backing vocals, and a chord progression that begins on the subdominant and moves through a slow plagal cadence (technically, it moves IV–I–IV–I–IV–vi–IV–♭VII–I–I, with each numeral representing one bar).

This second large-scale section (i.e., the verse-bridge alternation that goes from m. 69 to m.123, or 3:00–5:28) consists of two double verses with a bridge section at the end of each. Prince uses his falsetto register almost exclusively during this part of the song, which is particularly striking owing to the fact that the only voices heard in the song up until this point have been the computer-generated voices and historical vignettes ascribed to the Akashic record. The strophic repetition of Prince's falsetto vocal melody (see example 32) serves to juxtapose the different lyrical concerns of each verse, which move between Jehovah's Witness theology and examples of Black historical oppression. For example, in verse 1 Prince alludes to living in "the last days of the Devil's Deal," and in verse 2 he sings, "You've been here since 1914," both of which refer to the Jehovah's Witness belief that the year 1914 marked the beginning of the last days before Armageddon, when Satan infil-

Example 32. "Family Name," verse 1 vocals (mm. 69–77)

trated the Earth and Christ invisibly returned to do battle with him.[121] In Jehovah's Witness theology, the Earth and all institutions have been indelibly tainted by the Devil's influence since this event, from which belief derives the Jehovah's Witness policy of nonparticipation in elections, jury duty, military service, or any other governmental body.[122] This central belief in the world's inherent wickedness explains several other lyrical references in verses 2 through 4 of "Family Name" including corporations, the military, schools, and preachers of other denominations. Prince's lyrics then create a link between this devilish corruption and the issue of slavery, which Prince brings up in the third verse ("Did we really come over in a boat?"). This juxtaposition of themes suggests that legalized slavery was, like all governments and other earthly institutions, directed by the Devil, thus contextualizing institutional racism as a sin from which the faithful will be delivered at Armageddon. When the bridge sections come Prince further elaborates this racial-religious axis with a lyrical refrain about the theft of family names.

By declaiming all these lyrics in his high falsetto register and deploying a backing choir during the repeated bridge subsections, Prince aurally references the gospel and soul genres which, as I discussed earlier, use the falsetto voice at important spiritual and structural moments. Yet there is a crucial difference between "Family Name" and Prince's earlier falsetto songs such as "Kiss": in "Family Name" Prince *avoids* the distinctive melodic gesture of fragmentation, repetition-with-elaboration, and breakthrough that, as I argued earlier, musically links soul and gospel music to the ecstatic worship practices of the Black Pentecostal Church. Prince does not engage in *any* ecstatic vocal pyrotechnics during this second large-scale section of "Family Name." Instead, Prince lets the light articulation of his high falsetto voice and the strophic repetition of the vocal melody foreground the content of the lyrics, which recalls the falsetto-delivered social commentary of artists like Curtis Mayfield, whose song "(Don't Worry) If There's a Hell Below, We're All Going to Go" made a similar connection between demonic influence and racial oppression. This is not to say that Prince completely avoids high-falsetto screams during the song, throwing in two during the third large-scale section (at mm. 163 and 164). But as I will discuss, he does not use this gesture to signify ecstasy or transcendence, quite the opposite. Thus, while Prince's use of the male falsetto in this second large-scale section of "Family Name" provides an aural connection to the Black religious tradition, he avoids the distinctive melodic gesture that symbolizes spiritual salvation in gospel music.

Instead, during the third and final large-scale section of "Family Name," which I am calling a coda, and which stretches from m. 124 to m. 178 (i.e., 5:28 until the end at 7:51), Prince uses the gospel high-falsetto voice in conjunction with the Afrofuturist low bass to construct a narrative in which millenarian apocalypse, rather than ecstatic baptism in the Spirit, redeems America from the sin of racial oppression. Structurally, Prince marks this final section as a coda by abandoning the cyclic alternation of verse and bridge sections and moving into an episodic structure. This coda has seven discrete subsections arranged around a recapitulation of the bridge at the center (in subsection 4), with a rising action in the fifth subsection, and a climax and denouement in the sixth and seventh. Prince used this type of extended, episodic coda section in many previous songs—such as "When Doves Cry"—as a setup for gospel-derived ecstatic melodic gestures; indeed, an episodic structure based on a repeated fragment of the song's groove is endemic to much gospel music, in which an extended "vamp" section precedes the arrival of the Holy Spirit. Yet in "Family Name" Prince eschews this familiar gospel idiom; instead he teases the listener by suggesting but withholding an ecstatic melodic breakthrough, and instead deploying the technological low-bass voice to herald an apocalyptic musical confrontation.

In the first coda subsection (from mm. 124–132, or 5:28–5:52), Prince creates a break that makes the coda feel like a disruption of, rather than a mere appendage to, the verse-bridge structure of preceding large-scale section. Prince does this by dropping out the lead and background vocals and introducing an unfamiliar new bass and guitar riff, one that exploits the modal ambiguity of the blues scale by switching back and forth between the major and minor thirds of tonic A. The end of this first coda subsection creates an even greater feeling of disruption: at m. 130, the regular drum groove stops for three bars during which the bass and guitar play a series of furious thirty-second-note descending chromatic gestures in unison, accompanied by the drums. This moment not only ruptures the rhythmic flow of the groove but also destabilizes the harmony by shifting the tonal center from A down to E. If the disjunction between this coda and the preceding verse-bridge section of the song had not been clear at the start of the first coda subsection, it certainly is by its finish.

Prince uses the second coda subsection (mm. 133–141, or 5:52–6:16) to build a sense of mystery and foreboding. He does this by radically thinning out the instrumental texture (it includes little more than an ominous bass drone on E over a reduced drum groove) and delivering a short monologue, at a low volume and energy level, in his primary-mode speaking voice. The vocal register and spoken-word declamation of this monologue are particularly attention-grabbing owing to the fact that they provide a stark contrast to both the high falsetto voice of the song's second large-scale section *and* the computer-generated voices of the first, making it feel almost as though Prince himself is parting the curtain for a moment of direct communication. The lyrics Prince thus delivers are cryptic and ominous: Prince coyly suggests "maybe we should start all over" at one point, which in the context of Jehovah's Witness theology hints at the destruction and rebuilding of the earth at Armageddon. Prince's monologue also contains two specific historical references that buttress the song's racial-religious theme: the first, "put up a one-gloved fist," refers to the Black power salute given by Tommie Smith and John Carlos during the 1968 Olympic games; the second, "violet brown," refers to the two identifying colors forced upon Jehovah's Witnesses and Gypsies, respectively, in Nazi concentration camps.[123] This lyrical connection between two historical examples of ethnic and religious oppression parallels the juxtaposition of Jehovah's Witness beliefs and African American subjugation that Prince made during the earlier verse and bridge sections. Prince ends this second coda subsection at mm. 140–

41 with a brief return of the tonic A and the song's original drum and bass groove (see example 31). Despite this, the dip in energy, volume, and textural density of this second subsection, together with the lyrical references and the harmonic shift to E minor, creates a distinct sense of mystery or foreboding.

In the third coda subsection, mm. 142–150 or 6:16–6:40, Prince ratchets up this sense of tension by introducing an element of technological menace, symbolized by aggressive bass and guitar timbres (see example 33). The drums drop out entirely for the first seven bars of this subsection, creating a rhythmic vacuum that temporally disorients the listener. Harmonically, Prince moves from the tonic A down to the submediant F♯ minor. Timbrally, Prince drops out his vocals and adds a buzzing distortion effect to *both* the bass *and* guitar. Because of their particular melodic gestures—low, droning F♯s in the bass, and a wah-wah-inflected guitar solo that ends with a siren-like whammy-bar pitch bend (see example 33, m. 148)—this distortion effect lends a sense of power or menace to the bass and guitar that is aurally rooted in technology.

The fourth subsection (mm. 151–157, at 6:40) is a recapitulation of the song's familiar bridge section in the tonic A major, which momentarily dispels the tension and marks the structural midpoint of the coda. The familiar call-and-response interaction between lead vocalist and backing choir surrounds the listener with a sense of community rooted in the gospel tradition. Furthermore, the repetitive nature of the bridge's harmonic progression—which rocks back and forth between subdominant and tonic—combined with the gospel antiphony between lead singer and choir feels like the beginning of a repetitive vamp that will lead to an ecstatic falsetto breakthrough. Yet Prince does not allow the listener to remain in this gospel-informed interpretive frame for long: he truncates the bridge, interrupting it at m. 156 after only seven bars, as compared to its previous lengths of ten and nine bars. This cutoff is particularly jarring for two reasons: first, it happens on the bridge's only minor chord, the F♯ minor submediant; second, instead of resolving the harmony with the expected IV–V–I cadence, Prince interjects a furious descending melodic gesture from beat 3 of m. 156 to beat 3 of m. 157, played by the bass and guitar together, that transports the listener back to E minor while confounding the listener's rhythmic sense of where the barline is.

By ending the fourth subsection in such an abrupt manner, Prince frustrates the expectation of ecstatic transcendence and reactivates the sense of impending threat he had constructed in the preceding coda

Example 33. “Family Name,” coda subsection 3 (mm. 142–150, at 6:16)

subsections. Over the next two subsections, Prince constructs an apocalyptic version of salvation: in the fifth coda subsection (mm. 158–161, 6:59–7:09), Prince uses both the prophetic low-bass voice *and* a voice from the Akashic record to announce the return of a vengeful Jehovah, after which the sixth coda subsection (mm. 162–177, 7:09–7:51, see example 34) enacts Armageddon.

At the start of the fifth coda subsection (m. 158) the regular drum groove and tonic A return, momentarily dispelling the menace of the E minor turn that had interrupted the preceding bridge recap. However, any sense of a safe return to the home key is quickly dispelled by the entry of the technological basso profundo voice. This prophetic voice intones a simple introduction—"This is the voice of Thomas Jefferson"—after which the Akashic record plays one last recording: a high-pitched, chipmunk-like voice delivers the line "My fellow Americans, if there is a just God, we're gonna pay 4 this." The uncanny quality of this second voice aurally communicates its technological mediation—it was doubtless made with the same digital pitch-shifting technology as the low bass voice—and reinforces the thematic connection between technology and mystical knowledge symbolized by the Akashic record. At the same time, the lyrics that it delivers paraphrase a famous critique of slavery published by Thomas Jefferson in his *Notes on the State of Virginia*, in which he rhetorically asked, "Can the liberties of a nation be thought secure when we have removed their only firm basis, a conviction . . . that these liberties are the gift of God? That they are not to be violated but with his wrath? *Indeed I tremble for my country when I reflect that God is just: that his justice cannot sleep forever*" (emphasis mine).[124] As with Prince's spoken monologue, Jefferson's essay connects race and religion by identifying liberty as a gift from God, and suggesting that the violation of that gift would logically be punishable by God's wrath.

This historical revelation from the Akashic record spans the end of the fifth coda subsection and the beginning of the sixth, at which point Prince underscores the lyrics with the entry of a chromatic bass riff. The riff is heavily distorted, and it may be doubled by an electric guitar (the timbre is so thick that it's difficult to tell whether it contains multiple instruments playing in unison). The riff rocks back and forth between the tonic and its chromatic upper and lower neighbors (see example 34), and Prince repeats it as an ostinato through the rest of this subsection (ending at m. 177). The harmonic and timbral implications of this riff are both symbolically and musically destabilizing: its chromatic motion between A♯, A, and G♯, coupled with the fact that the lowest bass

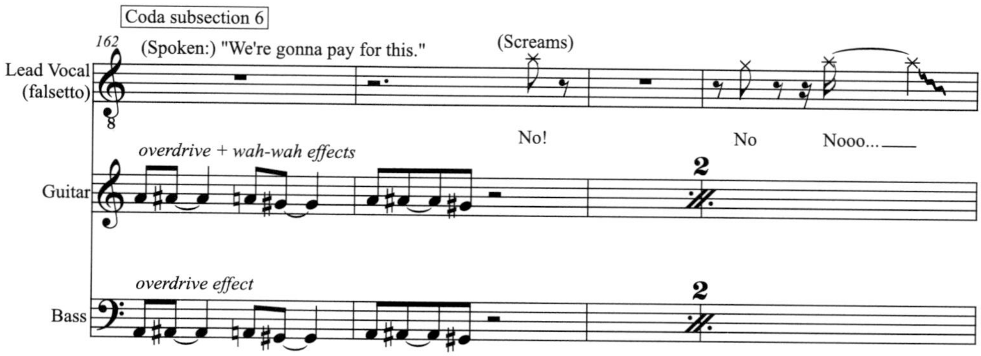

Example 34. "Family Name," coda subsection 6 excerpt (mm. 162–165, at 7:09)

instrument plays it, undermines the tonic, making it feel as though the ground itself is shifting and swaying. Timbrally, the growling distortion on the bass riff is reminiscent of crackling or tearing, suggesting the very earth under the listener's feet buckling and giving way. Above this unstable ground, Prince plays a high-register guitar solo, the longest and most aggressive of the entire album.

What Prince enacts during this sixth subsection, with the distorted bass moving chromatically around the tonic and his pyrotechnic guitar solo, is the sound of a technologically mediated Armageddon prophesied both by Jefferson and by the Jehovah's Witnesses. The guitar solo includes numerous gestures that suggest screaming and explosions: First, Prince begins the solo (at 7:25) by simply allowing his heavily overdriven guitar to feed back. Prince then interjects several furious sequences of tremolo picked descending thirty-second notes, punctuated by wah-wah-inflected upward leaps that sound like anguished cries, which then descend to notes so low that they sound like an unpitched burr. Amidst this destruction, the only vocal sound we hear are three falsetto screams of "no" at the very beginning of the subsection, in mm. 163–164 (see example 34). These falsetto screams are fleeting but fraught with meaning, given Prince's earlier decision to cut off the recapitulation of the gospel-tinged bridge (coda subsection 4) before it could achieve the kind of ecstatic melodic breakthrough that symbolizes transcendence in the sanctified singing tradition. Instead, Prince used this guitar solo as a musical analog for God's wrathful destruction of the wicked, and in the midst of this destruction he used a high falsetto whoop—the melodic gesture that normally symbolizes salvation through baptism in the Spirit—to portray the shrieks of sinners perishing amidst the lasers and bombs of God's techno-chariot as he cleanses the Earth in Armageddon.

Prince ends this sixth coda subsection with a brief chromatic turnaround (D♯-D-E-D♯-E) that deposits the listeners once again on a short-lived E minor tonic at the downbeat of m. 178. What follows in the seventh and final coda subsection at m. 178 (from 7:51 to the song's conclusion at 8:17) is an actual sample of a historical recording, unlike the earlier Akashic record "recordings." Here, Dr. Martin Luther King Jr., from his iconic "I Have a Dream" speech at the 1963 March on Washington, delivers the concluding sentence: "Black men and white men, Jews and Gentiles, Protestants and Catholics, will be able to join hands and sing in the words of the old Negro spiritual, 'Free at last, Free at last, Great God a-mighty, We are free at last.'"[125] Prince underscores this speech with an ambiguous synthesizer chord rooted on C, played at an extremely low volume, that does not harmonically resolve to any of the song's previous tonal centers (A, F♯, or E). By using this particular section of the "I Have a Dream" speech, Prince gives the song's apocalyptic conclusion a clear teleology: the paradise toward which we are moving is a place of freedom from divisions of race and religion, yet the path to get there leads through millenarian destruction. Indeed, this unresolved harmony suggests that paradise must still be earned, as in the Jehovah's Witness belief that the saved will be tasked with rebuilding the earth after Armageddon.[126] Prince makes this teleology clear by using the sound of a cheering crowd mixed with the prophetic low-bass voice to blur the end of "Family Name" into the beginning of the next song, "The Everlasting Now," in which he enacts the joyous rebuilding of Earth-as-Eden over a James Brownian groove.

To sum up, the seven subsections of the coda construct an apocalyptic narrative of religious salvation in which the destruction of the earth delivers the faithful simultaneously from religious persecution *and* from racial/ethnic division. Prince began the episodic coda section of the song by disrupting the preceding verse-bridge structure; in the second coda subsection he used a musically foreboding drone to underscore lyrics about racial and religious oppression; he introduced an element of technological menace in the third episode using the distorted bass timbre and guitar solo; and recapped the gospel-tinged bridge subsection in the fourth episode. Yet the model of salvation through ecstatic transcendence that was implied by the gospel melodic gesture of the bridge section proved illusory when Prince interrupted the bridge recap with the fifth coda subsection, in which the prophetic low bass voice and a historical "recording" of Thomas Jefferson delivered warnings of divine retribution. Subsequently, in the sixth subsection Prince aurally portrayed God's destruction of Satan and the oppressors of the faithful with a guitar solo accompanied by anguished screams, leading to the seventh and final subsection in which the listeners find themselves in a paradise free of racism and religious persecution yet with the harmony, and the work of rebuilding, still unresolved.

Conclusions

In closing, I would like to consider how Prince's vocal constructions of race and religious identity in "Family Name" intersect with issues of gender and sexuality. As I've discussed, the high falsetto whoop is an echo of gospel's Holiness/Pentecostal glossolalia filtered through secular soul and R&B music, while the low bass voice communicates millenarianism by way of funk's Afrofuturist tropes. These two cosmologies have some important differences: in the Holiness/Pentecostal tradition, salvation is achieved through baptism in the Holy Spirit, and the high falsetto breakthrough gesture serves as one embodiment of this. However, in millenarian sects like the Jehovah's Witnesses, salvation depends upon the destruction of Satan and all of his earthly institutions, followed by the rebuilding of Earth as a new Eden. Both religious strains are present in "Family Name."

These two voices also have very different resonances in terms of gender. Where the high falsetto voice may strike some listeners as androgynous or fey, the low bass voice is unavoidably masculine and patriarchal. Yet these two constructions both carry the historical freight of white supremacy: the former can be an uncomfortable reminder of the minstrel show "wench" or "sissy," while the latter may edge toward stereotypes of Black men as hyper-virile. Indeed, the low bass voice that Prince used carries a hint of the masculinist rhetoric of 1970s Black nationalism due to the influence of George Clinton, whose Dr. Funkenstein character resonated with the macho swagger of contemporaries like Huey Newton and Eldridge Cleaver.

How does this question of gender representation inflect Prince's construction of racial-religious identity in "Family Name"? By using both the high falsetto and technological low-bass voice, Prince set two distinct representations of African American cosmology *and* two constructions of Black masculinity in conversation with each other. In a religious sense, one can hear these two voices as representing the good news of the Gospels and the angry God of Revelations—one voice high, ecstatic, and promising transcendence; the other low, stern, heralding God's wrath—in a narrative arc that disrupts the gospel model of salvation to fulfill the apocalyptic futurist model of Prince's Jehovah's Witness faith. If we map these two voices onto the traditional gender binary of high-voiced feminine and low-voiced masculine then this narrative arc seems to privilege the patriarchy: Prince constrains his falsetto voice within a relatively circumscribed melodic ambit and does not allow it to slip into ecstasy, and he concludes the song by moving from his low bass voice into the recorded voice of Martin Luther King Jr. himself, the patriarch and moral lodestar of America's fight for racial equality.

America continues to struggle with the representational legacy of slavery and white supremacy in which Black men, caught in a double bind of desire and revulsion by white society, are portrayed alternately as hyper-masculine beasts and as cross-dressing buffoons. These constructions are ambivalent in the sense that they have been used both as tools of white oppression and of Black liberation. On one hand, the exaggerated masculinity of groups like the Black Panthers and of films like *Shaft* and *Superfly* were a reclamation of Black manhood as a political protest against the racism of the 1970s. On the other hand, as sociologists such as Andrea Hunter and James Earl Davis have argued, this equation of Black masculinity with violence and aggressive (hetero) sexuality became maladaptive and contributed to social ills in the 1980s such as the rise of gangs and the crack-cocaine economy in the inner city.[127] Indeed, it was this representation of Black masculinity as hyper-macho—violent, misogynistic, and homophobic—that garnered gangsta rap its main criticism in the 1990s.[128] Similarly, Black cross-dressing has been a tool of both oppression and resistance: as Marjorie Garber argues, the transvestite is a figure that "haunts images of African Americans in literature and culture" and often serves as "another mode of involuntary servitude."[129] Yet Garber also details the long history of African American artists such as Flip Wilson, Little Richard, and Prince who have reclaimed this effeminized representation of Black masculinity "as a vehicle for social and political empowerment."[130] The question of whether *any* specific representation of Black masculinity is repressive or liberatory comes down to the question of "who manipulates the image and whose pleasure or power it serves," in Garber's formulation.[131]

The two voices I have been discussing in this chapter map easily onto these two poles of gender representation. Prince used his low bass voice to enact various versions of hyper-masculinity, from the violent antihero of "Bob George" to the patriarchal prophet of *The Rainbow Children*, and he used his high falsetto on several prior occasions to explore non-heteronormative modes of sexual desire and gender identity as in "When Doves Cry" and "Kiss." In Prince's *Lovesexy* stage show, which I described at the beginning of this chapter, Prince's voice traced a career from low to high as an analogue for his spiritual journey from base and vulgar to transcendent and liberated. Yet in the song "Family Name" and in Prince's larger career, he seemed to follow a contrary trajectory, from high-voiced gender androgyny toward the low voice of patriarchal masculinity.

Prince made numerous changes in his later career that marked a more heteronormative conception of gender: he gave up the androgynous, body-displaying costumery of his early career for more traditionally masculine suits, a decision he characterized in the song lyrics of "Stare," from 2015's *HITnRUN Phase Two* by saying, "We used to go onstage in our underwear, [but] we changed up." He also gave up profanity and other explicit sexual language in his songs and live performances around the time of his conversion to the Jehovah's Witness faith, eschewing the Rabelaisian sexual liberation of his youth for a more conservative adulthood in which he hewed to a model of monogamous marriage. Prince even sparked a small controversy by hinting, in a *New Yorker* magazine interview, that he believed in a strictly heterosexual model of marriage: "When asked about his perspective on social issues—gay marriage, abortion—Prince tapped his Bible and said, "God came to earth and saw people sticking it wherever and doing it with whatever, and he just cleared it all out. He was, like, 'Enough.'"[132] Author Claire Hoffman elaborated on this moment in a follow-up article:

> I was a little surprised when he said it, because he has always seemed so unrestricted sexually. . . . Anyway, he walked me into his library and opened a Bible up to the Sermon on the Mount, and that's when he got to talking about trying to live biblically. For what it's worth, the way he said it wasn't hateful so much as sad and resigned. Prince is a true believer, and I think that's important to keep in mind in hearing his viewpoint.[133]

The disappointment in Hoffman's response to Prince's lack of support for marriage equality was shared by many fams, including myself. One possible way of reading this, and the narrative arc of "Family Name," is that Prince was moving away from the playful androgyny of his youthful work, and the equally playful sacred-sexuality of projects like *Lovesexy*, and toward a more conservative stance on both masculinity and theology in his mature years. I do not mean to imply that Prince abandoned the liberatory sexual politics of his earlier career—I cannot presume to speak to his beliefs—nor do I believe that making this argument diminishes the power of Prince's earlier constructions of non-heteronormative gender and polymorphous sexual desire. The music exists independently of the artist who created it, and Prince's musical message of gender and sexual liberation positively impacted many listeners in the 1980s and 1990s. Rather, I am suggesting that, in the context of *The Rainbow Children*, Prince subsumed questions of gender and sexuality within those of racial-religious identity: as Hoffman said, Prince was a "true believer," and focusing on his constructions of religious faith in "Family Name" can also yield a message of liberation, which is where I want to conclude this chapter.

By using the high falsetto *and* the techno-low-bass voices side by side in "Family Name" Prince exposed their commonalities of origin and purpose. The high falsetto in soul music carries with it the legacy of the Black Holiness/Pentecostal church tradition, and specifically the ecstatic model of worship known as baptism in the Spirit (an idiom that, as artists like Ray Charles demonstrated, maps easily onto sexual ecstasy). On the other hand, the low bass voice comes from the funk tradition (by way of George Clinton) and carries with it an Afrofuturism that overlaps the Manichaean apocalypticism of several faiths that have drawn significant African American participation, such as the Seventh-day Adventists, Jehovah's Witnesses, and the Nation of Islam. Both voices coexist in "Family Name" and in Prince's oeuvre in general, and both represent religious traditions that, despite their doctrinal differences, carry the liberatory theology of the Black church. We'll never know what he meant exactly, but perhaps Prince was simply pointing upward to God as the means of transcending all earthly burdens, including not only racism but also sexism and homophobia.

Where Prince's earlier works used the ecstatic falsetto voice to break down the binary oppositions between sacred and sexual, male and female, and/or straight and gay in songs like "When Doves Cry" and "Kiss," in later works like "Family Name" he subordinated the ecstatic voice (and its gender liminality) to a prophetic low voice and a vision of God's deliverance of the people of Earth from *all* division or persecution, presumably including those based on gender and sexual orientation as well as race. In this light, I would like to read Prince's shift away from the ecstatic voice and toward the prophetic voice not as a rejection of the gender and sexual liberation of his youth, but rather as a reflection of the millenarian focus of the church in which he spent the last years of his life, in which the destruction and rebuilding of the Earth is a necessary precondition for salvation and paradise. From this perspective, Prince's particular deployment of the low bass voice of prophecy, which cuts off the transcendent trajectory of the gospel-influenced bridge during the coda of "Family Name," is a wake-up call letting listeners know that a future free from racism, sexism, homophobia, war, and pain cannot be won without a final fight.

FIVE | Horns, Masculinity, and the Anxiety of Influence

It is New Year's Eve of 1987; Prince is performing his *Sign o' the Times* stage show on the new soundstage of his recently completed recording complex, Paisley Park. The event, a $200-a-plate benefit for a local charity, is one of only a handful of occasions on which Prince will perform this show in America. Nonetheless, the night will be remembered primarily as the only time that Prince and Miles Davis performed together, the zenith of their on-again, off-again collaboration.[1] Even though he is performing within a framework completely controlled by Prince—Prince's song, his stage show, his band, even his own building—Miles Davis's presence shifts the center of gravity for the short time he is onstage.[2] (This performance is available on the *Sign o' the Times: Super Deluxe Edition* boxed set).

Davis takes the stage only once, during a half-hour extended jam on the song "It's Gonna Be a Beautiful Night," and the two artists have a tense interaction. Davis begins tentatively: he strolls on without introduction and begins getting a feel for the groove (a harmonically static D-Dorian vamp) by repeating a simple two-bar motive, little more than the flat seventh, fifth, and root. Prince stands downstage, his posture conveying high energy—one of his legs nearly vibrates as he keeps the beat—and sharp concentration, as he faces away from the audience and toward his band. Davis paces back and forth across the upstage space between Prince and the band, his horn and eyes angled inscrutably downward. After twelve bars of his simple motive, Davis starts exploring, trilling in his middle register before breaking out some high notes, allowing a few to sound dirty and cracked as he pushes toward a breakthrough.

Throughout their time onstage together, Prince does not grant Davis enough time to develop an interesting solo. Just as Davis begins pushing into his upper register, Prince calls an audible, cuing a six-beat turnaround—one of several prearranged riffs that the band plays on Prince's cue—that interrupts both Davis's solo and the four-bar phrase structure of the song. Davis is silent for the next six bars, then reenters with a more aggressive version of his first motive, shifted off the beat and played at a higher intensity, full of cracked notes. Two bars later Prince cues a single hit on the downbeat of a measure, a trick he borrowed from James Brown's live show, and three bars after that Prince again cues the turnaround. This time Davis enters hard on the heels of the turnaround, playing the most aggressive phrase of his solo, sixteenth-note runs that thrust upward, then double back. But after four bars of what could be a spectacular display by Davis, Prince cues another downbeat hit and Davis breaks off his sixteenth-note ascent, returning to his original motive, during which Prince again cues the turnaround.

This stop-start interaction between Davis and Prince eventually turns into a call-and-response pattern, and they trade two- and four-beat riffs back and forth (starting at 7:38) for sixteen bars, before returning to their unspoken struggle. Whenever Davis tries to play longer phrases that build momentum slowly, or leaves one of his trademark pauses, Prince invariably cues the band to do something. At one point it seems clear that Prince has disrupted Davis in the middle of an interesting idea: the trumpeter reacts by peeling off a high squeak, dropping the horn momentarily from his lips and giving Prince a curt nod (at 8:49). Davis's solo, which began roughly five and a half minutes into the song, is over by nine minutes and twenty seconds. Prince thanks the old lion and Davis walks briskly offstage, where, according to Prince's manager Alan Leeds, he announced, "That little motherfucker tried to set me up!"[3]

While there is a risk of reading too much into this brief interaction—we can never know whether having been "set up" was a bad or a good thing—the video suggests conflict. As Prince's saxophone player Eric Leeds describes the night, Davis's presence called into question Prince's role as bandleader:

> Prince threw up one of his hand cues. . . . It could happen in any song: it was the same old thing, it didn't matter what key or what song. . . . We would have to play this little riff. And he gives one of the cues behind Miles's solo. . . .

> We ignored him, because everybody in the band was grooving on Miles. I mean, particularly for myself and [trumpet player] Matt [Blistan], more than anybody up there, this is like . . . this is the single most important music in my life. Bar none . . . any aspiration I've had, it all came through Miles.[4]

Miles Davis, a towering but restless figure in American jazz—he the father of cool, modal, and fusion jazz—was sharing the stage with Prince, and in doing so confused the issue of leadership. For a moment, the band didn't know whom to follow, though—as the audibles that interrupt Davis's solo attest—they soon remembered.

Offstage, Prince had an ambivalent history with Davis, alternately avoiding and courting the senior artist. They first met in late 1985, when they were both on the Warner Brothers record label, after Davis had expressed admiration for Prince's work. As George Cole tells the story in his book *The Last Miles*, the jazz legend asked to collaborate with Prince; while Prince was reportedly honored by this request, he never invited Davis into the studio, and instead recorded material and sent the tapes to Davis for overdubbing.[5] Prince's reluctance to work directly with Davis may have stemmed from a sense of awe or intimidation: as Eric Leeds related the story, "Miles had been wanting Prince to produce him, and Prince would not," and when Eric asked why, Prince replied, "I can't tell Miles what to do."[6]

Prince's push-pull interactions with Davis are emblematic of two interrelated tensions in his career. One is the question of how wind and brass instruments fit into Prince's music. Prince made his name in the early 1980s as a stylistic provocateur whose blend of rock guitar and new-wave synthesizers pushed the cutting edge of pop music. In his earlier career, Prince had avoided using horns entirely in an effort to distinguish himself from then-contemporary sounds in R&B music, embracing instead the emerging technology of synthesizers.[7] With Prince's help, synthesizers became ubiquitous: by the early 1980s, horn sections in pop music were a thing of the past, and by the early 1990s they were more likely to be heard as a sample in a hip-hop song than in a contemporary R&B or rock hit. Given this background, Prince's decision to give horns a central place in his 1980s and 1990s bands showed the same curious ambivalence as his relationship to Davis: what radioactive power did horns have that made them simultaneously attractive and repellent to Prince? Furthermore, after Prince brought horns into his band, he used them to reference not only old-school R&B and funk legends like James

Brown and Parliament-Funkadelic, but also jazz music from Dixieland to bebop. If Prince had been reluctant to be associated with R&B, why was he willing to risk being viewed as a jazz-fusion artist?

The second tension that Prince's onstage interaction with Davis demonstrates is the issue of patriarchy. Biographically, Prince had fraught relationships both with his biological father and with musical heroes like Davis, James Brown, Sly Stone, and George Clinton. Thematically, Prince had staked his claim to a kind of sexual polymorphism that, as Robert Walser argues, resisted patriarchal gender roles.[8] Yet where Prince spent the 1980s playing the part of androgynous satyr, the 1990s found him engaging the exaggerated machismo of hip-hop, and by the 2000s he was sporting natty suits, exploring jazz, and studiously avoiding discussions of queer identity.[9] These two spheres, the biographical and the musical—Prince's fraught relationships with masculinity and with the musical styles of his father's generation—all came together in the bell of Miles Davis's trumpet.

This chapter explores how Prince used horns to negotiate the intertwined tension between the musical past and present, and between competing versions of Black masculinity. Toward that goal, I present close readings of horn-heavy songs from two different phases of Prince's career. Prince's career divides roughly into four periods, based upon the configuration of his horn section and his position within the music industry. During the first period, from 1978's *For You* through 1984's *Purple Rain,* Prince was struggling to build his national reputation. Horns were still an established part of the R&B landscape in the late 1970s, and during this first phase of his career Prince did not use horns at all, ostensibly to avoid being pigeonholed as an R&B artist.[10] In their place, Prince used synthesizers to fill out his arrangements, developing a blend of rock guitar and new-wave synthesizer that became known as the "Minneapolis sound." Following the success of *Purple Rain,* Prince entered the second period his career, spanning the years 1985–1990. With his crossover success, Prince no longer had to worry about his label marketing him solely as an R&B artist, but with the sudden ubiquity of Minneapolis-sound-alike hits on the pop charts he *did* have reason to fear "being typecast as 'Mr. Purple Rain.'"[11] As a result, this second phase found Prince experimenting with new timbres and techniques, while building his own state-of-the-art studio complex in which to record. One of the experiments Prince made was bringing horns into his band, and he came to rely on the flexible two-piece section of Eric Leeds on saxophone and Matt Blistan on trumpet, a band perhaps best represented by the albums *Sign o' the Times* and *Lovesexy* and their respective tours.[12]

During these first two periods of his career Prince was not only crossing over in the sense of mixing traditionally Black and white musical styles, he was also crossing boundaries of gender and sexuality by cultivating a coyly androgynous persona. As Stan Hawkins and Sarah Niblock summarized, "Prince broke with the hyper-masculine conventions of the black soul star," and further, he "defied ideals of heteronormativity by not acting out his masculinity in the 'right way.'"[13] Yet by the early 1990s, Prince's Minneapolis sound and androgynous image began to seem passé as the popularity of hip-hop grew. Thus began the third phase of Prince's career, spanning 1991's *Diamonds and Pearls* through 1998's *Newpower Soul* and associated tours. During this period, Prince formed a new backing band called the New Power Generation that featured both a rapper and a five-person horn section—a Minneapolis-based ensemble called the Hornheads—consisting of two trumpets, alto and tenor sax, and trombone. If audiences had been surprised by the alacrity with which Prince integrated horns into his band after avoiding them for so long, they may have been equally surprised by the way Prince incorporated the exaggerated machismo of hip-hop into his music and stage act after playing the foppish dandy for so long. Though Prince enjoyed success with several albums during the 1990s, he had an acrimonious split from his record label and re-embarked on his career as an independent artist.

The fourth period of Prince's career began at the turn of the millennium with the jazz-influenced *Rainbow Children*, and includes 2004's *Musicology* and beyond. Prince abandoned rap and gave up the violent machismo of his hip-hop persona during this period, but he did not return to the gender-bending of his youth, moving instead toward a more mature identity of bespoke suits and jazz fusion. Prince stopped using profane language, began sporting ties and fedoras onstage, and mixed old-school R&B and jazz numbers into his act. During this period, Prince favored a middle-sized horn section of three players, two saxophones and one trombone, and two of his most consistent collaborators were highly pedigreed R&B players, former JB Horns bandleader Maceo Parker and former Parliament-Funkadelic trombonist Greg Boyer, marking a change from his early-career reluctance to work with senior artists like Miles Davis.

Though Prince's sound changed dramatically between these four periods, his musical commitment to rhythm-and-blues history remained constant, as did his thematic interest in gender, sex, and patriarchy. Horns were a sound out of the musical past by the time Prince picked them up, the flagship solo instruments of his musical progenitors Miles Davis and James Brown, and as such they enabled Prince to explore the interconnections between R&B history and Black masculinity. Wind and brass are also instruments that Prince, a famous musical polymath, never learned how to play. For an artist concerned with maintaining control over his artistic output, who had a fraught relationship to father figures, and who had made his early reputation by deconstructing traditional masculinity, the association of horns with Black music history and patriarchal masculinity gave them a radioactive power that Prince first avoided and later exploited, in songs like "Housequake" and "Sexy M.F."

In "Housequake," from *Sign o' the Times*, Prince signifies on the tradition of rhythm-and-blues dance songs like "The Twist" and "Hot Pants," using his two-person horn section to reference the older tradition and create a unified narrative even as the song's trickster narrator deconstructs traditional R&B and gender roles. "Sexy M.F.," from the *Love Symbol* album, again finds Prince engaging with the horn style of James Brown, using that older sound—and a mature, sophisticated masculinity—as a foil for gangsta rap's exaggerated machismo. In both of these songs, far from downplaying the implicit historicism of his horn sections, Prince used the musical and cultural history encoded in the sound of live horns to struggle against—and ultimately to reclaim—his place in the patriarchy of Black music.

Prince and Patriarchy

The whiff of intergenerational conflict between Prince and Miles Davis in their single onstage appearance together brings up the question of Prince's relationship to patriarchy. Davis (May 26, 1926—September 28, 1991) was of roughly the same generation as Prince's own father, John L. Nelson (June 29, 1916—August 25, 2001), and in many ways Prince's mixture of awe and avoidance regarding the senior artist mimicked that of a young man emerging from the shadow of his father. John L. Nelson was himself a musician, a piano player known in Minneapolis for his idiosyncratic jazz-fusion music, and whose group, the Prince Rogers Trio, included Prince's mother Mattie as a singer for a time.[14] Prince's given name—Prince Rogers Nelson—had been his father's stage name and, according to Prince's cousin Charles Smith, a name that Prince resented, insisting on being called "Skipper" until he was well into high school.[15] Prince had a fraught relationship with his father: a stern disciplinarian, John L. Nelson reportedly forbade young Prince to play his piano, and it was only after the elder Nelson abandoned the family—leaving the piano behind—that Prince taught himself to play it. Later, after Prince had left his mother's house and moved in with his father, John Nelson kicked him out for an infraction of curfew and refused to let him move back in, even after receiving Prince's tearful apology. This event forced Prince to move in with the family of a high-school friend and, according to a 1985 interview, left a psychological scar on the young artist.[16] After he became successful, Prince reportedly reconciled with his father, but until John Nelson's death in 2001 the two alternated between periods of closeness and estrangement. Though Prince generally eschewed self-revelation, his difficult relationship with his father became grist for his art: the movies *Purple Rain* and *Graffiti Bridge*, and the song "Papa" from the 1994 album *Come*, all portray fictional stories of an abusive father and a son who struggles to break the cycle of abuse.

Prince recapitulated this ambivalent dynamic with his musical progenitors, alternately avoiding and seeking out collaborations with senior artists. Often, his interactions with his heroes had a mixture of respect and humiliation worthy of a family drama. For example: though he publicly praised Prince's work, Davis mixed his affection with barbs. During a dinner party Prince was hosting in Davis's honor, the elder artist traded jibes with Prince's father, saying something to the effect of, "Now I know why that motherfucking son of yours is so crazy!"[17] When he did collaborate with senior musicians like Davis, Prince kept tight control over the results. Despite the fact that Davis added several of Prince's songs to his live playbook and recorded them for inclusion on his *Doo-Bop* album, none was included when the album was posthumously released, allegedly at Prince's insistence, and to this day Prince only allowed one of their collaborations to be released, the song "Sticky Wicked," on Chaka Khan's 1988 album *CK*.[18]

Prince also had the opportunity to meet Sly Stone while he was working on his first album at the Record Plant in Sausalito, California. Stone's blend of funk and psychedelic rock had a formative influence on Prince's music and image, yet the meeting produced nothing: Stone, who was sleeping in a spare room at the recording complex at the time, was either too strung out or too uninterested even to speak to Prince.[19] Despite such dismissive treatment, the younger artist remained invested in Stone's work, covering Sly and the Family Stone songs in concert, hiring former members of the Family Stone to play in his own band, and employing one of Stone's former managers, Steve Fargnoli. Prince even tried to sign Stone to his own Paisley Park record label years later in an attempt to revive the artist's moribund career, to no avail.[20]

Even where Prince had productive relationships with his musical heroes, the relationships often had unequal power dynamics. Prince signed Parliament-Funkadelic founder George Clinton to his proprietary Paisley Park label, releasing two albums by Clinton and featuring him in 1990's *Graffiti Bridge.* Yet by this point Prince's career success had eclipsed that of Clinton, who was at the time struggling with tax problems and drug-related legal issues: Clinton described his business relationship with Prince by saying, "I hollered 'help' and Prince came to the rescue."[21] Prince also had a longstanding relationship with former Family Stone member Larry Graham, whose innovative funk bass technique influenced Prince's own work. Not only did Prince sign Graham to his NPG record label in 1999, the senior artist moved his family from Atlanta to Minneapolis to play in Prince's band. Graham filled a paternal role in Prince's spiritual life, bringing Prince into the Jehovah's Witness faith, in which Graham is a church elder. Yet even their relationship had a whiff of competition: as *Bass Player* magazine's Carl Coryat pointed out, Prince all but stopped playing bass onstage during this period, thereby avoiding direct comparison to his elder; when asked why, Prince tellingly responded, "I hope it's out of respect for Larry, and not because I feel inadequate compared to him."[22]

James Brown has a towering reputation as the father of funk music, and Prince has struggled with his legacy perhaps more than that of any other elder Black musician. Around the time of *Purple Rain,* Brown invited both Prince and Michael Jackson to join him onstage during one of his concerts. Jackson went first, and the event ended in humiliation for Prince: unrehearsed, Prince took the stage and improvised for a short time on guitar, after which he made a gaffe by leaning on a stage-prop streetlamp which fell over; Prince left immediately after.[23] Not only had Prince been embarrassed in front of his chief rival at the time, his performance was damned by the faint praise of Brown himself, who wrote in his autobiography that "Prince played some guitar, but I think he was a little nervous because Michael fit into my thing a bit better since Michael had been studying me for years."[24]

After this ego-bruising experience, Prince never again appeared with Brown onstage, but continued musically emulating his hero, covering Brown songs in concert and finding proxy ways of claiming Brown's legacy. Prince hired Alan Leeds as his road manager "sight unseen" on the strength of Leeds's former job as Brown's road manager.[25] This relationship gave Prince access to the famous JB Horns, but he did not use any of them until years after Alan Leeds had left his employ, choosing instead to hire Alan's younger brother Eric to play tenor sax in his band because, as Eric Leeds argued, "he was scared to death of them."[26] Eric Leeds tells a story that makes Prince's position clear: one day when Prince and Eric were working in one of the studios at Paisley Park, several members of James Brown's band were in an adjoining studio being interviewed by a documentary film crew.

> Maceo was there, Fred Wesley, Clyde Stubblefield, you know, all these guys were there. All my idols you know, and I hadn't seen them in years. They were all in Studio A, working, filming. The same afternoon, I'm working with Prince in Studio B. And I asked Prince, I said, "Do you know who's over in Studio A? [JB Horns members] Pee-Wee, Fred, and Maceo. Why am I here alone?" Prince would not entertain the idea of having them come over and play. And I said, "Can I at least ask them to come over? They'd love to meet you." And Prince said, "Just be sure they know they're not going to play."[27]

It was not until 1999 that Prince would enter the recording studio with former Brown sax player Maceo Parker.

Prince's reluctance to work directly with his musical fathers, and his tendency to maintain strict control when he did, raises the question of how Prince's biographical and musical worlds connect. Harold Bloom's theory of influence gives us a framework for understanding the similarity between the psychological relationship of fathers and sons and the mechanics of artistic patrilineage.[28] Bloom's theory concerns the paradox of finding one's voice as a young artist: having been inspired by the work of previous generations, the young artist is at the same time penned in by that body of work. The young artist must find a way of escaping or devaluing the work of his progenitors ("misreading") in order to open up a space for new creation, or risk being viewed as a weak or derivative artist.[29] In light of Bloom's theory, Prince's fraught relationship with his own father provides a logical context for why he was reluctant to work directly with musical patriarchs like Miles Davis or James Brown, both men with reputations for aggressive and authoritarian behavior. Considering the formidable artistic legacy of artists like Davis and Brown, Bloom's theory also provides context for why Prince may have felt the need to maintain distance or control in his musical relationships with them or their proxies as he established his own artistic voice.

For Prince, one sonic way to distinguish himself from his musical fathers was by rejecting the instrumental timbres most closely identified with the Black music of his father's generation, the horns, and this is more or less what Prince did. As Eric Leeds remembers it, Prince was initially driven to define himself in opposition to the jazz and R&B traditions to which his icons belonged, regardless of how important that music was to him: "Prince had always been adamant about never wanting real horns in his band. Not because he didn't appreciate them, but he wanted to be the 'anti-.' You know, the antithesis; create a new sound, create a new texture."[30] In addition to the Bloomsian anxiety of influence, there is an inescapable racial component to Prince's decision. Horns were the flagship solo instruments of jazz and R&B, and remained defining timbral elements of 1970s soul and funk music, all genres that remained associated with the Black community even as the generically related genres of rock 'n' roll and rock became solidly identified with white America. As Krin Gabbard points out, Black jazz trumpeters of the early twentieth century found the instrument ideal not only for demonstrating their musical chops, but also for asserting "that they were men and not boys," a stance that linked trumpet virtuosity to Black masculinity in the American imagination.[31] Doug Miller argues that the saxophone became an important vector of African American aesthetic values in postwar rhythm-and-blues music—the "moan within the tone"—and that the honking saxophone idiom carried this history even into the 1980s and '90s.[32] As Prince began his career, horns were a sign not just of the jazz and R&B genres but also of Black male identity itself.

Prince's decision to avoid horns points to the marketing reality facing a Black artist in the 1970s and 1980s: avoiding the jazz and R&B legacy of his forefathers made it easier for Prince to pursue a crossover career on the guitar-dominated mainstream charts. Within a major label such as Warner Brothers, where artists working in Black-identified musical genres were managed by a separate department from mainstream pop artists, an African American artist like Prince could reasonably have expected that including horns in his band would have limited the number of media outlets in which his label would promote him. According to one Warner executive, this was precisely Prince's fear: "Prince was very concerned about being labeled a black artist or being segmented into the black department. He said to us, 'I'm not an R&B artist. I'm not a rock 'n' roller. I'm an artist and I do a wide range of music. If I deliver you rock 'n' roll, don't come back to me and say I can't do it because I'm black.'"[33] Yet picking up the guitar did not allow Prince to escape the anxiety of influence either: Prince at times bristled at being constantly compared to Jimi Hendrix, and as the members of the Black Rock Coalition would argue, Black artists working in the white-identified rock genre faced an uphill battle in the 1980s and '90s.[34] Nonetheless, his initial decision to eschew horns coupled with his later decision to incorporate them into his post-*Purple Rain* bands suggests a prodigal relationship between Prince and his Black musical patrimony. The question that remains is how, once Prince brought horns into his band, he dealt with this anxiety of influence—how he navigated the web of associations attached to horns, including musical genre, his African American heritage, and his relationship to patriarchal masculinity—and this is a question that only the music can answer.

"Housequake": Esu Does the Twist

Following the huge crossover success of *Purple Rain*, Prince had the industry clout and economic power to pursue nearly any project he wanted, and he quickly incorporated new influences and instruments into his music. The albums he recorded during this period—*Around the World in a Day*, *Parade*, *Sign o' the Times*, *Lovesexy* and the *Black Album*—show an increasingly experimental approach, highlights of which include the world-music-tinged "Around the World in a Day," the ten-minute orchestral piece "Crystal Ball," and Prince's first rap songs "Holly Rock" (performed by Sheila E. in the movie *Krush Groove*) and "Bob George." It seemed as though Prince were stepping away from his popular Minneapolis sound, an impression Prince himself confirmed in a 1985 interview:

> You know how easy it would have been to open *Around the World in a Day* with the guitar solo that's on the end of "Let's Go Crazy"? You know how easy it would have been to just put it in a different key? That would have shut everybody up who said the album wasn't half as powerful. I don't want to make an album like the earlier ones.[35]

It was during this time that Prince brought horns into his band. This change was tentative at first: Prince hired the alto saxophone player from Sheila E.'s band for one recording session on the *Around the World in a*

Day album before bringing in tenor sax player Eric Leeds on a more regular basis. Prince incorporated Leeds into two side projects, the Family and Madhouse, before adding him to his own backing band, the Revolution, for the recording of *Parade*. Prince subsequently hired Eric Leeds's colleague Matt Blistan on trumpet but stopped there, relying on this two-person horn section for his *Sign o' the Times* and *Lovesexy* albums.

For an artist with a reputation for early adoption of new music technology and a reluctance to be identified with the R&B genre, Prince's decision to incorporate horns might have seemed a step backward. Prince's own guitarist Wendy Melvoin complained that expanding the band had ruined what had been unique about it, turning them from an anomaly—a synthesizer-driven rock band with a Black lead singer—into "just an everyday funk band."[36] In fact, horns were something of an anachronism at that time: MIDI-equipped synthesizers and drum machines had, by the late 1980s, changed the economics of the recording industry, making synthesizers an affordable alternative to live horns. Ironically, Prince was exploring a sound that he himself had helped relegate to the past: as former James Brown horn arranger Fred Wesley points out, the popularity of Prince's early 1980s synthesizer sound had contributed to the twilight of live horns in R&B.[37] The most prominent saxophone soloist in 1980s pop music was Clarence Clemons, of rocker Bruce Springsteen's band (whom Prince had seen play on the *Born in the USA* tour in 1984), and even in that context the saxophone was widely regarded as a throwback.[38] Prince was not insensitive to the symbolic weight of his change in instrumentation: though his albums *Around the World in a Day*, *Parade*, *Sign o' the Times*, and *Lovesexy* all featured horns (as did the live shows he did in support of those albums), the radio singles he released during this period—such as "Raspberry Beret," "Kiss" and "Sign o' the Times"—did not. Prince did make one exception during this period, releasing the horn-laden song "Mountains" as the second single from the *Parade* album; but its lackluster chart performance—it reached number 23 on the *Billboard* Hot 100 chart as compared to the number one position achieved by "Kiss," the horn-less first single from the album—seems to prove the point that horns were no longer au courant in mainstream American pop music at the time.[39]

The reception of "Housequake" further illustrates the confluence of race and genre that horns represented. "Housequake" is a dance song that features the horn section in a lead role, and Prince opted against releasing it as a single, a decision motivated by "his on-going fear of being typecast as an R&B artist," according to his manager.[40] In its place, Prince and his label promoted the album's synthesizer-and-drum-machine title track and the rock-guitar fueled "U Got the Look," both of which entered the top ten of the mainstream *Billboard* Hot 100 chart. Nonetheless, "Housequake" gained so much popularity among Black listeners that R&B radio stations began playing it directly from the album. As Eric Leeds remembers, "Black radio was playing the hell out of 'Housequake,' but it was never a single."[41]

The fact that R&B radio DJs deviated from industry norms and played this particular album track highlights the Black music history embedded in the song. As one reviewer described it, "The uproarious 'Housequake' is a virtual survey of thirty years of Black performance styles: the title apparently refers to house music, which erupted out of Chicago last year; the singer's boastful persona is borrowed from rap; the wicked beat and machine-gun horn lines are pure James Brown; and the goofy exhortation that brackets the track—'Shut up, already! Damn!'—is lifted from Little Richard."[42] In "Housequake," Prince signifies on old-school R&B dance songs like "The Twist" by interpolating the traditional sound of horns into a modern sonic landscape of synthesizer and drum machine, assuaging the anxiety of influence with postmodern irony. Yet what prevents the song from being either blank parody or nostalgic kitsch is the way Prince deploys the horns. Rather than being a static signifier of the past, the horns are a protagonist within the song, and what begins as a campy parody of a dance song with a capricious narrator and some horns tacked on for color ends as a melodic triumph for the horns.

Throughout "Housequake," Prince throws in cues that the savvy listener can trace back to the tradition of 1960s R&B dance-craze songs such as "Walking the Dog" or "The Twist." Like those songs, "Housequake" features a master-of-ceremonies who tells the audience how to perform the eponymous dance. At one point (2:16), Prince quotes the lyrics to "The Twist," an intertextual reference that would not have been out of place during the genre's heyday, when artists routinely recorded follow-up and answer songs to previous dance hits.[43] Adding to the feeling of genre reference is Prince's use of his two-piece horn section, whose first motive is almost identical to the hook from James Brown's 1971 dance hit "Hot Pants" (see example 36 and example 37).

Prince places these old-school genre references in a dance song recognizably of its era—the late 1980s—in terms of timbre and structure. The backing track is a stark-yet-funky polyrhythmic dance groove (see example 35) built out of the same bare-bones instrumentation—Linn drum machine, bass, sparsely placed synthesizer lines and jangling, non-distorted electric guitar—as Prince's earlier hits "When Doves Cry" and "Kiss." Prince relies on funk- and dance-music techniques of the 1970s and 1980s to create a sense of structural progression: the harmony remains static, and Prince's arrangement adds and subtracts elements of the groove to create discrete formal sections.[44] Specifically, Prince brings the synthesizer, guitar, and horn parts in and out of the mix to create alternating thin- and thick-textured sections that function like verse and chorus (terms that I will use for the sake of clarity). This groove serves as the sonic backdrop to a drama that Prince creates between two main characters: the first is an androgynous narrator, whose playful tricks threaten to turn the song into a parody of the dance genre; the second is his horn section, which conveys the song's retro-R&B pedigree and ultimately provides the song's narrative conclusion.

It bears remembering that two other artists had hits in 1988 with covers of 1960s dance-craze songs: the Fat Boys, a novelty rap act, rerecorded "The Twist," while the queen of European dance-pop, Kylie Minogue, scored with her updated version of "The Loco-Motion." "Housequake" could have fallen into this same category of nostalgic kitsch, were it not for the narrator, an androgynous trickster identified as "Camille" in the album's liner notes, whose playful mockery tilts the song towards postmodern irony. The song begins with Camille abusing the listener, shouting "Shut up already! Damn!" before a note has been played. This upbraiding continues throughout the song: for example, during the chorus Camille mocks the audience's call-and-response participation, pronouncing it "bullshit." Prince-as-Camille delivers these lines in a voice that is high-pitched, reedy, and preternaturally fast, giving it an uncanny power. Prince achieved this vocal persona by varying the speed of the tape during recording, a technique that George Clinton had previously used to create the similarly mischievous character "Lollypop Man" in the 1976 hit "P-Funk (Wants To Get Funked Up)." In addition to this audible debt to George Clinton, Prince hinted that he took the name Camille from the nineteenth-century hermaphrodite whose diaries were discovered and published by Michel Foucault, a reference that suggests Prince intended Camille's androgyny as a destabilizing critical tool.[45]

With his mixture of intertextual references—encompassing Hank Ballard, the JB Horns, and George Clinton alongside the darling of 1980s post-structuralism—Prince was signifyin(g) on the tradition of R&B dance-craze songs.[46] Camille's destabilizing antics present a negative critique of the genre in a way that calls to mind both Henry Louis

Gates Jr.'s concept of motivated signification—repetition with a signal difference—and Harold Bloom's idea of "misreading" as an artistic means of distancing oneself from one's predecessors. For every R&B dance-song convention the song references, there is a moment when Camille upends it. Not only does Camille mock the audience's call-and-response participation, s/he refuses to provide clear instructions or any narrative buildup: there is no progression from introduction to mastery of the dance, no moment of "now that you can do it, let's make a train." When Camille teaches the audience the steps of the Housequake dance (at 0:52), s/he does so in reverse order, singing "U put your foot down on the 2 / U jump up on the one," an offhand line that makes it hard to understand the dance without benefit of the concert video.[47] There is no mention of courtship: Camille neither invites the listener to find a partner nor acknowledges romantic interaction of any kind. Indeed, there is something childlike and sexless to Camille: alongside "The Twist," Camille quotes the children's author Dr. Seuss, rhyming "green eggs and ham" with "damn." This, coupled with Camille's androgynous vocal timbre and sing-song declamation—which sits somewhere between rapping and singing—projects the mischievousness of a playground taunt. Even judged against the playful quality of many 1960s dance songs, Camille is a parody of a traditional emcee: "Do the Funky Chicken" may have been silly, but it had clear instructions. Furthermore, for a Black artist who had successfully crossed over onto the mainstream charts, Prince's implied critique of an earlier wave of R&B crossover artists seems like patricide. Is Prince using Camille as a mask to distance himself from his R&B predecessors?

The instrumentation and rhythm that Prince constructs for "Housequake" works against any feeling of nostalgic kitsch by reinforcing Camille's puckish, mercurial character. Instead of filling the texture with a retro-R&B sound, the groove is stark and modern with an undercurrent of ambiguity, characteristics that Prince communicates in a couple of ways. First, "Housequake"'s groove pushes the defining feature of funk rhythm—implied metric conflict—to the point of instability (see example 35).[48] The drum machine's two-bar ostinato is more or less typical of the funk genre, with a modified clave pattern (played by a de-tuned tom-tom drum) adding polyrhythmic spice to a straight sixteenth-note high-hat pulse, heavy kick-drum downbeat, and snare-drum backbeat. Yet as the other instruments add their rhythmic patterns, they emphasize the off-beats—synthesizer bass on the "and" of beat 1, guitar on the "and" of beat 2, for example—to a degree that

Example 35. "Housequake," thick chorus section (mm. 17–25, 0:36), concert pitch

threatens to overwhelm the normalizing duple meter. Furthermore, the bass drum reverses the typical accent pattern in the second half of each two-bar ostinato, playing on beats 2 and 4 instead of the downbeat. This kick-drum reversal, coupled with the buildup of off-beat accents, creates a funky yet disorienting lacuna in every second bar, one that upends the funk expectation of a heavy "one."

Second, the instrumental background is austere and harmonically ambiguous. The synthesized bass plays the same two-bar pattern throughout the song, yet despite its regularity, it pulls between two competing tonal centers, beginning on F but ending on B♭. Furthermore, the bass slides between A and A♭, a move that sounds alternately like a blue-note on scale degree three and like a leading tone to B♭. The guitar doesn't clarify this ambiguity—its jangling timbre acts more as rhythm than as harmony—and the harmonic padding added by the synthesizer (see Synth 2 in example 35) obscures more than it reveals of the song's true tonal center, owing to its timbre, which has wide vibrato and an ambiguous pitch that sounds like two oscillators tuned a fourth apart. According to Eric Leeds, "The song is in F (and) the bass slides between the major and minor third."[49] Heard in this context, the bass's regular shift between major and minor modes creates a subtle but insistent feeling of instability, especially when added to the drum machine's shifting kick-drum pattern. This metrically and modally shifting ground is both a fitting environment for Prince's puckish narrator and a good embodiment of the dance's title: not as unstable as an earthquake, but shaky enough to rock the house.

In this funhouse landscape, it is the horns that provide a narrative teleology. The song has two main horn motives (see example 36 and example 38): though introduced in isolation, these lines ultimately combine into one cohesive unit that provides thematic closure. The horns enter with their first motive at the first thick-textured chorus section, at 1:10 (motive A, example 36). Motive A echoes Camille's sing-song mockery with its concise open-and-shut melodic shape: its opening half features an ascending melodic leap in a short-long rhythm—a "ta-dah" gesture—while its closing gesture is a flutter of sixteenth notes whose half-step lower-neighbor motion sounds like the childish "nee-ner-nee" of a playground taunt (and concludes with another "ta-dah"). Structurally, this horn entry comes right after Camille has "taught" the dance, and then yelled "bullshit" at the audience's participation, creating a strong association between the horns and Camille's mocking approach to R&B dance crazes. Furthermore, the lower-neighbor motion in the "response" half of motive A echoes a horn lick used often by James Brown's arranger Fred Wesley (e.g. "Hot Pants," example 37), making the reference to R&B history even clearer. According to Eric Leeds, Prince was explicit in what he wanted from the horns first entry in the song, and dictated this first melody to them during the song's recording session on October 18 1986.[50] With its combination of insouciance and historical resonance, Motive A reinforces the feeling of genre parody introduced by Camille, and after deploying it during the first chorus at 1:10, Prince repeats Motive A in the following verse (at 1:26) and chorus (at 1:43), fixing it in the listener's memory.

Prince introduces a contrasting horn motive in the song's third chorus (at 2:00), setting in motion a hero's narrative of struggle and triumph for the horns. Motive B is a unison soli line (see example 38) with an open, unresolved melodic shape that contrasts the neat symmetry—the good gestalt, to use Leonard Meyer's formulation—of motive A.[51] Motive B opens with an ascending minor third from D to F, hinting at a B♭-major triad, and ends with a descending A♭-major triad, concluding a tritone below motive B's starting pitch. The motive suggests harmonic motion but doesn't specify a destination: one can hear the two note-groupings as implied B♭-major and A♭-major chords (thus moving IV to ♭III); alternately, one can hear them against the implied F tonic as an Fadd6 resolving to an Fmin7 chord. Eric Leeds advocates the latter: "The texture of the horns is based on a minor sixth chord. The second line starts on the sixth, hits the major seventh before landing on the minor third. If there's anything remotely unique about the sonority of

Example 36. "Housequake," horn motive A (mm. 33–34, 1:10), concert pitch

Example 37. "Hot Pants," second horn motive, concert pitch

the song it's that."[52] As Leeds points out, this gesture gives motive B a distinctive harmonic profile, one that is melodically open and harmonically unresolved.

Prince also imbues motive B with an added layer of rhythmic conflict, which further reinforces the overall affect of changeability and caprice that Camille's lyrics introduced. Where motive A stayed within the duple-meter accent pattern, motive B has two 6/8 groupings that are offset from the song's main meter. As Anne Danielsen argues, it is the evanescent quality of polyrhythm that defines funk rhythm, and motive B shows the truth of this: by momentarily hinting at another metric possibility, motive B rebels against the duple grid and, in so doing, makes this section even funkier than those preceding it.[53]

Over the next few sections, the horns begin to rebel against Camille, as the song structure loosens. In the fourth verse-like section, at 2:16, Prince reverses the hypermetric placement of the horns' A motive by moving it from the first to the second half of each four-bar phrase. This is a subtle shift, yet it makes motive A seem more like an equal and independent response to each of Camille's lines. Following this verse,

Example 38. "Housequake," horn motive B (mm. 49–50, 2:00), concert pitch

Prince inserts an anomalous ten-bar vamp section at 2:33 that blurs the qualities of a thin verse and a thick chorus section: the synthesizer plays its chorus padding, but the guitar is silent, and Camille's voice is mostly absent. In this ambiguous section, Camille and the horns have a pointed exchange: Camille delivers one throwaway line, which the horns answer immediately with their more assertive B motive. Camille remains silent, and the horns repeat motive B, this time with the backup vocalists answering them. With this, it is as though the horns have circumvented Camille for the moment and initiated a more direct relationship with the backup singers and, by extension, the listener. By the end of the following chorus section, Camille him/herself acknowledges that a shift has taken place, shouting "the saxophone is the fault" as a lead-in to a brief saxophone solo (at 3:09). Though it passes quickly, the moment is significant. Not only does the saxophone get the solo, rather than the guitar or synthesizer, Camille's lyric also contradicts a pattern from earlier in the song: in each of the previous chorus sections, Camille shouted "the kick drum is the fault." By shifting focus from kick drum to saxophone, Camille has symbolically shifted the song's focus away from the electronic sound of contemporary dance music and toward the acoustic saxophone sound of earlier R&B.

At the end of the song, Prince ratchets up the dynamic intensity with two repeated chorus sections (at 3:43 and 4:00) that culminate in a triumphant coda for the horns. The climax of the song arrives in the chorus section beginning at 4:00, as each instrument increases its rhythmic activity and dynamic level: Camille delivers a rapid string of lyrics, filling the rhythmic matrix at the sixteenth-note level; the wobbly, vibrating synthesizer pad sounds an octave higher; and both the rhythm guitar and the second synthesizer play more varied and active rhythms. Against this backdrop, the horns make a dramatic and dialectical move. Having previously moved motive A to the second half of each four-bar phrase (in verse 4), the horns move motive B into the now-empty first half of each phrase, fusing the two motives into a self-sufficient four-bar whole (see example 39). By reversing the order of these two motives—with the funkier, melodically inconclusive B motive answered by the

Example 39. "Housequake," unified A/B horn motive (mm. 115–122, 4:00), concert pitch

melodically and rhythmically closed A motive—the horns resolve motive B's questioning shape and turn motive A from a playground taunt into a stabilizing cadence, creating a call-and-response loop that plays twice. Further, the united B/A motive has a much stronger harmonic implication—it feels like an Aeolian cadence (♭VII-I) on B♭—which subtly but firmly shifts the harmonic landscape.

The horns' motivic unification brings the song to its conclusion. At the end of this chorus section, at 4:16, Camille yells out "everybody shut up, listen to the band," and all instruments drop out except the horns, who play a new C motive (example 40). Motive C is clearly related to the unresolved downward gesture at the end of motive B: in unison, the horns play a descending arpeggio on straight quarter notes, which they then repeat twice in rhythmic diminution. Motive C also echoes motive B's harmonic ambiguity—the pitch content, D♭, B natural, G, E natural, implies either a D♭half-dim7 chord in first inversion or, more likely, an E-minor add6 chord—while the sixteenth-note rhythms momentarily shift the metric emphasis to 6/8, echoing the polyrhythmic tension of motive B as well. The horns then repeat motive C on a second, equally unresolved chord (an A half-dim7, built in descending order from the G).

Having created a moment pregnant with harmonic and rhythmic tension, the horns themselves resolve motive C by recapitulating the A motive, concluding the song. At this, Camille once again shouts "Shut up, already! Damn!," but by this time the horns have taken the breath out of Camille's bluster: Prince slows the tape-speed down as Camille speaks, revealing his/her fast, androgynous patter for the studio trickery that it is, and making Camille sound like a toy whose battery has run out.

With "Housequake," Prince created an intertextual dialogue between two different eras of dance music while walking a fine line between mockery and homage. This ambivalence toward the past is in keeping with the double-voiced nature of the signifyin(g) trope and is what allowed Prince to sonically forge a meaningful connection to

Example 40. “Housequake,” horn motive C (mm. 123–128, 4:16), concert pitch

the past—incorporating horns into his band—while sidestepping the anxiety of influence. With its lyrical and formal connection to past R&B dance-craze songs, “Housequake” is a talking text, to use Gates’s term, that allowed Prince/Camille to use the 1960s R&B dance-craze topos while simultaneously keeping it—and the binary, every-guy-grab-a-girl mode of gender embedded within it—at a critical distance, and it is this critical attitude that banishes the anxiety of influence.

At the same time, Prince was signifyin(g) on a second, unmotivated level, to use Gates’s term for uncritical pastiche. For all Camille’s taunting, the horns have a triumphant narrative teleology in “Housequake”: starting as isolated motives that merely echo Camille’s playful nastiness, the fragmentary horn motives become a unified melodic statement that provides its own good gestalt of call and response. That Prince builds this melodic narrative of fragmentation and unification on what is essentially a James Brown quote makes the aspect of homage even clearer.

By putting on the mask of Camille, Prince gave himself permission to pay tribute to an older style of Black dance music while at the same time holding it at a distance, an ambivalence that also extends to the song's gender representation. On one hand, Prince used his Camille persona to step outside of binary gender and look back at it critically, a project that reached its culmination in another song on *Sign o' the Times*, the funky yet poignant meditation on gender "If I Was Your Girlfriend." On the other hand, with his horns, Prince invoked the founding patriarch of funk music, James Brown, and even Camille's androgynous voice is a call-back to another founding patriarch of funk, George Clinton. Ultimately, "Housequake" serves *both* as a mockery of the older generation of R&B and its simplistic binary gender roles, *and* at the same time as a sincere expression of filial debt to those artists: to paraphrase Gates, Prince played the dozens on James Brown, Rufus Thomas, and Little Eva as he dodged past them.[54] Furthermore, when we consider Prince's use of horns in light of his early-career skittishness toward them—skittishness borne partly of the marketing double standard facing Black crossover artists in the 1980s, and partly of Prince's problematic history with biological and musical father figures—we can hear the horns in "Housequake" as a clarion call connecting Prince to the long lineage of R&B.

Race and Gender

"Housequake" shows how horns allowed Prince to open up a new dialogue with the musical past. Yet "the past" was a territory ruled by Prince's artistic fathers, and if Prince was growing more comfortable publicly embracing the R&B side of his artistic legacy, he was not necessarily comfortable with traditional gender roles, and Camille was just one among many examples from this period of how Prince created characters that critiqued the patriarchy. As the 1980s faded into the '90s, the landscape of popular music shifted, and the rise of rap and hip-hop forced white America to engage with a more confrontational archetype of Black masculinity. Prince's popularity waned during this era, as his Minneapolis sound was eclipsed by hip-hop. At the same time, his model of gender-bending critique was increasingly at odds with the dominant discourse of Black male identity, which came to be dominated by what Mark Anthony Neal calls the archetype of the "hip-hop thug."[55]

In order to understand how Prince constructed a new, hip-hop-influenced sound and gender image in the 1990s—a sound that, I will show, looked back to R&B of the past—we must first understand how Prince's deconstruction of traditional gender roles sat within the larger discourse of Black masculinity. Prince's role models—James Brown and Miles Davis especially—were not only musical giants, but also icons of Black power and exemplars of masculinity. When Davis first made his name as a bebop trumpeter, his cool demeanor, defiant machismo, and refusal to pander to white audiences made him a hero to Black power intellectuals like Amiri Baraka.[56] No less an icon of masculinity, James Brown was hot where Davis was cool, bringing all the athleticism and showmanship of a boxing match to his stage act. Not only did Brown onstage embody the traditional masculine values of hard work, virility, and control, he also used his lyrics and public appearances to spread messages of Black pride and economic empowerment, explicitly linking economic and political power with masculine power. As Brown put it during a tense exchange on the Mike Douglas show in 1969, "You call yourself a man, knowing that I pay taxes same as you, stayed right here and used my sweat and blood to help build this country, and I got to be a second- or third-class citizen? Do you call that a man?"[57]

From the beginning of his career through the 1980s, Prince embodied a very different model of Black manhood from the combative virility of Davis and Brown, making his name as a sexual provocateur who pushed not only boundaries of middle-class taste but also of heteronormative gender. His lyrics were sexually explicit, but it was his queering of gender roles that grabbed attention: wearing stage outfits that mixed male and female clothing and exposed Prince's body to the audience's gaze, he sang songs—such as "Do Me, Baby," "When Doves Cry," and "Kiss"—that embodied a receptive rather than active sexual role.[58] This gender-bending persona was not only popular with audiences in the 1980s, it also struck a chord with academics. Several scholars argued that Prince's androgyny—like that of his elder Little Richard and his contemporary Michael Jackson—was empowering, critiquing mainstream ideas about race and gender by disrupting the stereotype of Black men as violent hyper-masculine brutes, as well as giving Black artists more mobility in the mainstream marketplace.[59] On the other side, critics like Nelson George called into question the political efficacy of Prince's androgyny, viewing it as a betrayal of the struggles that artists like Davis and Brown had gone through to claim traditional masculinity, a role that had for too long been denied Black men in America.[60]

George's critique taps into a vein of masculinist rhetoric within Black nationalism: from Eldridge Cleaver to Louis Farrakhan, Black leaders have demanded their manhood in the same breath as racial equality.[61] As hip-hop grew in popularity over the 1990s, with its sometimes violent and/or misogynistic depictions of Black masculinity, this equation of Black power with male heterosexual privilege reentered the American conversation.[62] Hip-hop, and more specifically gangsta rap, polarized the debate over Black masculinity: as Mark Anthony Neal argues, popular depictions of thuggish Black masculinity associated with the hip-hop generation prompted a backlash not only in the white media but also from Black religious and educational leaders, who revived a masculine archetype of respectability that Neal calls the "strong black man" to counteract the "hip-hop thug."[63] With this dichotomy at the center of America's conversation about race, Prince's binary-disrupting gender play seemed less and less relevant. At the same time, as hip-hop and new jack swing came to dominate the R&B and pop charts, he began to experience a slump in album sales.

Prince struggled to find his place in the new commercial and political landscape of the nineties, in which he was neither the most popular Black crossover artist nor the most sexually scandalous. In so doing, he remade his sound and image in a way that took cues from hip-hop and engaged more directly with the traditional masculinity he had previously deconstructed or avoided. Yet rather than adopting a hip-hop sound similar to the aggressive, sample-based production style of late 1980s and early 1990s hip-hop (exemplified by groups like Public Enemy or N.W.A.), Prince redoubled his commitment to the older, more traditional sound of horns. Indeed, this mirrored a "jazz" moment that hip-hop had in the early 1990s, when a cadre of artists including A Tribe Called Quest and De La Soul self-consciously incorporated jazz samples into their sound as a way to distinguish themselves from the prevailing sound and image of 1990s hip-hop.[64] The question I want to consider in the following analysis, is what did Prince get from expanding his horn section, and how did it help him in the arena of popular culture, where gangsta rap was the dominant sound of Black masculinity?

When Horns Met Hip-Hop: "Sexy M.F."

In the 1990s, as hip-hop music moved from an urban niche market into the mainstream of the music industry, America's simmering debate over race and representation boiled over. The subgenre of gangsta rap seemed to confirm white America's worst fears, igniting a moral panic with its lyrical depictions of the gangster lifestyle of South Los Angeles and the violence, misogyny, and homophobia of its practitioners. Rappers like Ice-T and groups like N.W.A. also sparked discussions within the African American community over the political ramifications of rap's thuggish representation of Black identity.[65] *Newsweek* magazine devoted its March 19, 1990, issue to "decoding" rap music, with articles that alternately contextualized gangsta rap as a harmless safety valve for underprivileged teenagers and dismissed it as the nihilistic fantasy of social outcasts.[66] As Neal argues, educational and religious leaders from the Black community pushed hard against gangsta rap on the grounds that its sexism, violence, and "minstrel-show" overtones threatened women, the family, and the progress made by the Black middle class in the post–civil rights era.[67] Yet the backlash did nothing to dull hip-hop's luster: by 1993, gangsta rap artists Dr. Dre and Snoop Dogg topped both *Billboard*'s R&B and mainstream album charts, and when *Newsweek* again put rap on its cover, it was as much to announce the genre's cultural ascendance as to bemoan its negative influence on America's youth.[68]

Prince came late to hip-hop. According to longtime manager Alan Leeds, Prince initially viewed rap as a fad, and bristled at sharing the charts with performers who "do nothing but talk."[69] By 1993 Prince had revised this position, but by that time incorporating rap meant engaging with a thuggish mode of masculinity that was at odds with the androgyny of his previous image. As critic Nelson George put it, when hip-hop came into play, "the whole level of masculinity was different. There was no room for ambiguity. . . . A lot of people suddenly said, 'Prince? He's a sissy.'"[70] The 1993 arrests of Snoop Dogg and Tupac Shakur—on charges of murder and sexual assault, respectively—made this point clear and set the new standard of authenticity for Black men in the music industry.[71] Musically, this aggressive, thuggish masculinity was expressed both in gangsta rap lyrics and also in a louder and busier production style built upon dense layers of digital sampling, a far cry from the austere drum-machine-and-vocals style of earlier East Coast rap music as well as from Prince's own Minneapolis sound. As R&B and pop producers began incorporating this hip-hop influence into new styles—new jack swing, for example—Prince's electro-symphonic funk began to seem as dated as his androgyny.[72]

Concurrent with hip-hop's rise was a dip in Prince's record sales: where *Purple Rain* sold around 12 million units domestically in its week of release in 1984, *Lovesexy* sold only 750,000 upon release in 1988.[73] Whether or not he was trying to follow trends in Black music, the early 1990s saw Prince integrate hip-hop into his sound, a period I characterized in a 2020 article as his "Gangsta Glam" phase.[74] During this phase, he formed a new backing band, the New Power Generation, which included a deep-voiced rapper, Tony Mosley, and a record-scratching DJ. Prince also began using samples and drum loops, and as he made these changes he abandoned the synthesized timbres and austere textures of the Minneapolis sound for fuller arrangements that resembled the dense, noisy soundscapes of hip-hop producers like Dr. Dre and the Bomb Squad.[75] One only need compare Prince's song "The Flow," from the *Love Symbol* album (1992) to "Night of the Living Baseheads" or "Bring the Noise" from Public Enemy's *It Takes a Nation of Millions to Hold Us Back* to hear the similarity.

Music critics noticed, interpreting Prince's new hip-hop-influenced style as either a fresh reinvention or a crass attempt to follow new trends in Black music. *Entertainment Weekly* writer Greg Sandow concluded that "This [the *Love Symbol* album] is Prince's blackest (meaning most African American) record since the never released but widely bootlegged *Black Album* of 1988."[76] On the other hand, *Rolling Stone* was dismissive of "the attempts to integrate rap into Prince's pop universe," and *Minneapolis Star Tribune* writer Jon Bream opined, "Prince used to be hip; now he's just another hip-hopper."[77]

If Prince's rap did not convince the music critics—to say nothing of his lack of street credibility—they may have been responding to a stylistic ambivalence built into his music. Prince never seemed entirely at home within the genre conventions of hip-hop: where most rappers used samples in the studio and DJs in performance to provide their backing music, Prince doubled-down on his live band, expanding it to include a five-piece horn section. This ambivalence in Prince's sound symbolized a deeper conflict over the gender politics of hip-hop: how could Prince, whose *Lovesexy* album cover had featured him reclining, naked and vulnerable, against oversized orchid blooms, compete with rappers who carried guns and/or served jail time? During his "Gangsta Glam" phase, Prince put on an aggressive stage persona: wearing chains, toting a gun-shaped microphone, and delivering raps laced with profanity and violent images. But ultimately, the five-piece horn section was Prince's most effective weapon. By creating grooves that recalled the heyday of James Brown, Prince claimed musical precedence over hip-hop, while his lyrics and sartorial style communicated elite rather than street status.

Horns had been a part of Prince's sound since 1985's *Around the World in a Day*, but in 1991 he began collaborating with an established five-piece brass ensemble called the Hornheads, which included Steve Strand on lead trumpet, Dave Jensen on second trumpet, Kenni Holmen on tenor and soprano sax, Kathy Jensen on baritone and alto sax, and Michael Nelson on trombone. Nelson, the group's arranger, explained to me that Prince first hired the Hornheads with the idea of arranging several songs by Madhouse—Prince's jazz-oriented side project with Eric Leeds—for a larger horn section.[78] Prince scrapped this idea, and instead put the Hornheads to work on what was to become 1992's *Love Symbol* album. The five-piece Hornheads was larger and more traditional to R&B than Prince's former tenor-and-trumpet two-piece, a fact that was not lost on Prince's former sax player Eric Leeds: "When I first heard that section, with Prince's [band] . . . it sounded, to me, so corny. Not because of what Mike was doing, but just the whole idea of a big, fat, traditional [horn] section being utilized. I said, 'This is the antithesis to what horns should be in Prince's music.' There is no way a five-piece horn section can sound other than traditional."[79] Music critics also noted the retrospective quality of Prince's new sound, comparing it to funk icons of the past, as in the "jabbing brass and jangling guitar" of 1970s groups like Tower of Power, and "the glory days of James Brown and the JB's."[80]

This debate over whether Prince's new 1990s horn sound was cliched or not demonstrates the three-way tug-of-war in which Prince was engaged, between his own previous Minneapolis style, the R&B styles of his forefathers, and the contemporary hip-hop sound that was swallowing them both. By reaching backward to a more traditional five-piece horn section, Prince was claiming stylistic primacy over his hip-hop contemporaries; at the same time, adopting hip-hop's youthful swagger allowed him to assuage the Bloomsian anxiety of influence that had motivated him to avoid horns in the first place. "Sexy M.F.," from Prince's 1992 *Love Symbol* album, is a prime example of this tension: it was the first commercially released song that Prince himself entirely rapped, rather than sang, yet the musical arrangement features his five-piece horn section playing a groove based on James Brown's "Super Bad." As the following analysis shows, Prince uses this stylistic tension between old and new as the backdrop for a story about a man split between two different versions of masculinity, one refined and sophisticated, the other crude and rough.[81] As Neal points out, this was a common rhetorical strategy at the time (he calls it the "hip-hop thug versus the new talented tenth"): for some leaders in the African American community, the upstart genre of hip-hop—and the violence and sexism of gang culture—represented a threat to the hard-won gains that the respectable, church-going Black middle class had made in the civil rights era.[82] In "Sexy M.F.," Prince's horn section enacts the main character's interior struggle between these two poles but ultimately refuses to resolve the tension, instead allowing the swagger and violence of hip-hop to coexist with the timbres and techniques of an older man's R&B.

Throughout the song, Prince's tight, forceful vocal flow conveys a swagger and aggression that is at odds with many of the lyrics, in which he boasts of his restraint, refinement, and elegance. Prince's rapping is indebted to the aggressive flow of Chuck D or Ice Cube: he uses a relatively monotone voice pitched low in his register; his diction is clipped, and for the most part his rhythmic delivery sits right on top of the beat. His lyrics mix images of refined pleasures—a villa on the French Riviera, cooking, spiritual discussions—with vulgar sexual terms, conveying his character's internal struggle over what kind of masculinity he wants to project. Furthermore, the song's profane hook—"sexy motherfucker"—is the only lyric that gets sung rather than rapped, a hip-hop technique that Prince uses to invest this lyric with soul and emotion, creating an almost comic level of irony. To be sure, this tension between sophistication and street language had a strong precedent in gangsta rap at the time. High-class gangsters were popping up all over, from Ice-T's 1991 "Lifestyles of the Rich and Famous" to the Wu-Tang Clan's rhymes about Cristal champagne and Lexus luxury sedans, and gender theorist Cynthia Fuchs argues that Prince's performance of this macho gangsta archetype was so hyperbolic as to constitute a camp parody of it.[83] Yet if we focus on the musical decisions Prince makes in this track and set aside whatever ridiculousness we may perceive in the song's lyrics and music video, we hear a character struggling with the tension between thuggish id and mature superego.

Prince's rapping is a firm genre reference to early 1990s hip-hop, against which the sound of the horns and live band is an anachronous juxtaposition: instead of using samples or other hip-hop production techniques, Prince's band plays a groove, on live instruments, that is recognizably derived from a James Brown song. From the first bar, the song's harmonic and timbral profile clearly mark it as old-school funk: the band consists of a five-piece horn section, drums, bass, and a clean (non-distorted) electric guitar; each instrument stays in its rhythmic pocket, and the harmony is static on the tonic A chord, moving only when Prince cues a prearranged turnaround. In fact, Prince's rapping, and the sexually explicit lyrics, are the only signifiers of modern hip-hop. This was a curious decision for an artist at the time: as Robert Walser has shown, hip-hop producers of the 1990s had well-developed techniques for musically enacting tension and chaos, involving layered

Example 41. "Sexy M.F.," principal groove (mm. 1–2, 0:01), concert pitch

samples, drum machines and sequenced synthesizer lines that enact the noise and violence of a modern urban landscape.[84] Prince used these techniques on other tracks, but on "Sexy M.F." he uses only his live band, foregrounding his horns.

As Prince's lyrics ping-pong between vulgarity and sophistication, his horns convey a sense of tight control. Specifically, the horns play two precise hits per measure on the tonic A chord in time with the snare drum, one hit on the downbeat and the second on the "and" of beat two (see example 41). This horn/snare motive is, in fact, identical to the one James Brown used in his 1970 hit "Super Bad," and Prince fills out the rest of the musical texture with a groove similar to this precursor. Not only is Prince's groove just as tightly disciplined as the James Brown original—with each instrument playing a unique and unchanging ostinato that interlocks precisely with all the others to create a funky, polyrhythmic matrix—the retrospective allusion to Brown adds to the feeling of patriarchal authority.

At the same time, the horn section and snare drum are explosive, hinting at a repressed violence lurking below the veneer of maturity. This feeling of violence comes from several things. First, the placement of the two horn/snare hits creates an uneven rhythmic pattern: with the first hit squarely on the "one" (the beat that is traditionally emphasized in funk music), the second hit anticipates beat 3 by an eighth note; this is followed by a relatively empty space in the second half of each bar, creating an asymmetry that shoves the listener forward. The second hint of aggression comes from the sheer sound-force of Prince's horn and snare combination: the horns have a sharp attack, loud dynamic, play a widely voiced chord, and occupy a wall of sound spanning from the far left to the far right sides of the stereo spectrum. Third, there is harmonic tension built into the horn chord, whose five voices spell out an A7#9 chord, which contains *both* the major and the minor third (see example 41). Though they are separated by an octave, the C♯ third and enharmonic C-natural ninth clash against each other, an internal conflict that Prince hammers into the listener's ears twice per bar for the duration of the song. As Michael Nelson remembers it, Prince was specific in his desire for this particular sonority:

> I remember "Sexy Motherfucker," he asked us play an A7 and to hit that [Nelson sings the snare drum rhythm, then plays the horn chord on the piano] like the chord he was playing on guitar. I recognized it as a stock funk voicing: it was actually an A7 sharp nine, so it has the major and minor third, and they're split [he plays the chord A–C♯–G–A–C-natural]. So you have that dissonance [plays diminished octave]. I immediately played him that voicing, and he goes, "Yeah, that's it."[85]

With its combination of ferocity and discipline, this main horn groove enacts the very essence of Freudian patriarchal masculinity, a fact made more poignant by its close resemblance to a James Brown song. As John Mowitt argues, drumming is an analogue to physical beating, and both activities have disciplinary overtones: it was a drum that regulated the earliest Western military cadences, and it is the father's disciplinary slap that, Freud argued, ends the infantile Oedipal stage and ushers in manhood.[86] Prince closely identifies the horn section with the snare drum's rhythm in this song, keeping the horns in unison with the beating drum during the normal groove; by rapping, Prince also identifies his main character with the beating drums. In so doing, the horns and snare together provide the regularized "beating" that gives the groove its discipline and, by extension, the male protagonist his mature masculine identity.

Prince punctuates this groove with a raucous turnaround, led by the horns, that expands on this balance between violence and control (example 42). On Prince's verbal cue of "Come here, baby," the horns move to a widely voiced D7 chord which they play with a crisp forte-piano and crescendo; they follow with a short, three-note cadential figure that descends chromatically to a C chord on the downbeat and then rests, leaving a bar of silence. This turnaround is lightning in a jar, giving motion and excitement without resolution: it is the only harmonic change in the song, but it ends on an unresolved chord (the flat mediant, funky but not functional); the rhythm consists of one long sustained note followed by three short, sharp ones, a pattern that implies there will be another long note at the end, which the horns do not deliver.[87] By allowing the horns off their leash to snap and snarl for a moment, Prince reminds us of their power, yet by denying them a satisfying rhythmic or harmonic cadence, Prince's main character demonstrates his hold on the leash; the irregular intervals at which he deploys this turnaround only add to the feeling that a mature discipline keeps this power in check.

The structure of "Sexy M.F." creates a narrative in which the main character's mature side—the superego, to use Freud's term, or the "strong black man," to use Neal's—appears to triumph, only to be overtaken in the end by its raucous, hedonistic urges. Having established the disciplined main groove during the first verse (example 41) and introduced the raucous horn turnaround and lyrical refrain that takes the place of a chorus (example 42), Prince repeats this verse-refrain structure twice more—another touch of discipline—before allowing any solos. Following the precedent of James Brown, Prince verbally cues each solo section, and the order in which he calls them out—first the horn soli, then Hammond organ, followed by guitar—moves from the loudest and most turgid timbre to the cleanest and quietest. Yet after tracing this pathway of increasing sophistication, Prince unleashes his backup rapper and deploys the horn soli again, ending the song with a raucous shout-chorus and an unannounced saxophone solo that explode

Example 42. "Sexy M.F.," turnaround / hook (mm. 5–6, 0:10), concert pitch

the carefully cultivated air of control with an over-the-top expression of male sexual bravado.

This narrative begins and ends with a muscular horn soli (example 43), a section that demonstrates the horns full power and symbolically enacts the main character setting aside his mature restraint. This soli is neatly symmetrical: a six-beat call and six-beat response followed by a one-bar tacet, played twice. The "call" is a modified version of the normal horn-snare groove—two hits on an A7♯9 chord—with the chord respelled, placing the trumpets a third higher and pushing them into their loudest dynamic range. Prince augments this phrase with a honking baritone-saxophone response after every horn hit, a low "ba-rump" that adds tension by increasing the rhythmic asymmetry of the gesture and emphasizing the two conflicting notes of the A7♯9 chord (C-natural and C♯). After establishing this rhythmic and harmonic tension, Prince uses the subsequent six-beat "response" phrase to display the power that results when that tension is released.

Example 43. "Sexy M.F.," horn soli (mm. 44–51, 1:38), concert pitch

On the next eighth note following the last bari sax "ba-rump," the horns play three ascending notes and then land on an accented A9 chord just before the next downbeat. They hold this pealing chord for two and a half beats and then resolve downward to a short, off-beat F9 chord. After the first statement of this horn call-response gesture, Prince mutters "I like it" in a low voice; after the second, the horns add a two-note resolution to the tonic A chord that is almost pornophonic in its turgid timbre and smeared pitches.

This horn soli is a display of carefully governed power: even as the horns erupt into overlapping voice-leadings and passing dissonance, they remain in perfect rhythmic unison with identical dynamics throughout, and they stop neatly after their two symmetrical statements. After the first horn soli, Prince begins rapping immediately (there is no turn-around, making it unique among all the other solo sections), creating a strong identification between the horns and the man. Indeed, when Prince reenters, his lyrics dovetail perfectly with the phallic horn line that has just subsided: he raps luridly about how "hard" he is, but in the same breath brags about his ability to resist the temptations of the body. According to horn arranger Michael Nelson, Prince was very specific in what he wanted out of the soli, going so far as to dictate certain lines on his guitar. During the "call," Prince was so determined to have a very low baritone sax "ba-rump" that, after recording the horn players, he ran Kathy Jensen's original baritone sax notes of G♯ and A through a harmonizer to create the low C-natural and C♯ notes, which fell below the range of the standard baritone sax with which she had recorded. During the "response," Prince dictated this horn smear to the players note for note by bending the notes on his guitar.[88]

In another display of restraint, Prince didn't take an instrumental solo himself. Following the controlled explosion that is the horn soli, Prince cues two more instrumental solos—a Hammond organ at 2:28, followed by a jazz guitar at 3:00—whose timbres, dynamics and overall affect move from cool to cooler. If the virtuoso electric guitar solo is the phallic climax of a typical rock song (which Prince literalized with his water-squirting guitar in the movie *Purple Rain*), then Prince structured "Sexy M.F."'s solos as a performance of self-denial, moving away from the eruptive horn soli and toward a quiet jazz guitar meditation performed by the backup guitarist in his band. Prince added to the feeling of maturity by using instrumental timbres that are strongly indexed to previous decades of Black music. In addition to the horns, an obvious nod to the Godfather of soul, keyboardist Tommy Barbarella's Hammond B3 organ timbre immediately calls to mind 1960s organ-led R&B groups like Booker T and the MGs, while guitarist Levi Seacer uses a clean, unaffected guitar sound that recalls jazz players like Wes Montgomery and George Benson, contrasting Prince's usual overdriven rock guitar sound.[89]

Having structured these soli/solo sections into a timbral and dynamic progression from brassy to mellow, it seems as though Prince's character has mastered his Freudian id, rejecting the hip-hop thug's violence and sexual aggression in favor of the mature model of patriarchal masculinity.This narrative trajectory, together with the muscular yet disciplined horn groove, resonates with the importance that Black nationalist leaders have placed on traditional masculinity throughout American history.[90] Not coincidentally, this masculine archetype was being revived by Black leaders in the 1990s as a corrective to the perceived thuggery of the hip-hop generation, as Minister Louis Farrakhan's Million Man March demonstrated scarcely two years after Prince's release of "Sexy M.F."[91]

What happens next complicates this narrative arc: Prince shatters the cool maturity of the jazz guitar solo by following it with a raucous shout-chorus, the whole band chanting "sexy motherfucker shakin' that ass," releasing the main character's violence and sexuality. The men sound like a mob, and their chant rhythmically unites with the snare/horn hits on the words "sexy" and "shakin'," emphasizing the repressed sexual threat within the main groove. In the middle of this shout-chorus, Prince's backup rapper Tony Mosley delivers a fast-paced verse whose delivery is rhythmically aggressive, full of triplets, syncopation, and unexpected pauses. Mosley's lyrics have the same mix of vulgarity and sophistication as Prince's, but the polarity is reversed: rather than a vulgar display sublimated, the main character happily offers to throw away his decorum for a chance with the woman in question. The overall affect is less comic than it is predatory, owing mostly to the fact that Prince juxtaposes a second statement of the eight-bar horn soli onto Mosley's rap. This soli—its syncopated stabs answered by the guttural grunt of the baritone sax, followed by the turgid rise to the trumpet's clarion high ninth capped by the smeared A9 resolution—now sounds like an illustration of the lurid thrusting that Mosley's lyrics insinuate.

After the nexus of Mosley's rap with the horn soli and shout-chorus, Prince enacts the end of his main character's sexual sublimation—and the song—with an exuberant tenor saxophone solo at 4:21, juxtaposed against the horns by-now familiar soli (see example 43). The tenor sax takes advantage of the instrument's full range and throaty, overblown timbre, soloing for a full twenty-eight bars, ignoring structural boundaries: when the horn section inserts a turnaround after sixteen bars of sax solo, the tenor continues to honk and bray, even through the full-bar rest that follows the turnaround, and even after an unprecedented second statement of the turnaround. The tenor saxophone's refusal to stay within the disciplined phrase structure of both the horn soli *and* the turnaround not only signals its escape from the Freudian discipline of the regularized groove, it also puts the sax in the position of emcee: the saxophone solo puts an end to the rapping once and for all—neither Prince nor Mosley raps again for the duration of the song. At the conclusion of "Sexy M.F.," it is not the rapper but the saxophone that has the best "flow" (as theorized by Tricia Rose, hip-hop artists "create and sustain rhythmic motion, continuity, and circularity via flow"), a fitting conclusion for a song in which the horn section has so eloquently enacted the main character's conflicted masculinity.[92]

In the 1990s, Prince had to find his own distinctive voice in a commercial soundscape dominated by hip-hop. In "Sexy M.F.," he combined rap with old-school funk in a way that allowed him to participate in hip-hop's macho one-upmanship while simultaneously critiquing the genre and its exaggerated masculinity. What's more, the song's narrative trajectory leaves the tension between the "hip-hop thug" and the "strong black man" unresolved: Prince begins the song with the tightly controlled power of the main horn groove and follows it with increasingly sophisticated solos, only to explode the calm with raucous energy at the end. This lack of resolution is a canny bit of undercoding that allows the listener to draw their own conclusions about which brand of manhood Prince was championing. Yet both are, in their own way, traditional modes of masculinity, unmarked by the androgyny of Prince's earlier career. Whether Prince was rapping about epicurean delights and rarified conversation or about his tireless appetite for sex and violence, it was bragging either way. If Prince was setting out a vision of sophisticated masculinity as a corrective against the vulgarity of the hip-hop generation, he was merely trading one kind of machismo for another, one invested with the rhetorical weight that elite Black leaders such as W. E. B. DuBois, Martin Luther King Jr., and Louis Farrakhan had already poured into it.[93]

Is "Sexy M.F." a celebration of old-school funk and traditional masculinity, or of hip-hop and thuggish violence? In the end, it can only be both: in "Sexy M.F.," Prince uses old-school funk and patriarchal Freudian masculinity to beat the wild young gangstas at their own macho game. The song is a tightrope stretched between old-school funk and nineties hip-hop, and by keeping his balance Prince was able to traverse the chasm—of obscurity, or of forever being associated with the Minneapolis sound—and remain a competitive force on the R&B and pop charts. As with all tightropes, Prince depended upon both ends to hold him up. When Prince expanded his horn section from two to five, his band sounded more like the funk of yesteryear, making it that much harder for him to escape the Bloomsian anxiety of influence. Yet the more Prince rapped and used samples, the more he was accused of chasing trends rather than setting them: in this respect, Prince's reliance on the funk genre and his live horn section was a bulwark of tradition erected against the fickle winds of fashion.

In the end, Prince's stylistic fusion favors old-school funk: whether we hear the song as a triumph of thug or mature man, the song's conclusion is a clear victory for the horns over hip-hop. Prince's horn section carries the symbolic freight of the character's manhood, both in the disciplinary beating with which the main groove demonstrates the internalized Freudian conflict that is the core of traditional masculinity, and the explosive release of id at the song's end. The horns give a virtuoso performance of masculinity, of one sort or another, from the first to the last bar of the song: this, more than the rapping, is the most hip-hop aspect of the song. It is also an implicit boast of musical superiority: by favoring live horns, the sound of an earlier generation, Prince locates himself at the root of a tradition—old-school funk—that his hip-hop contemporaries were at the time merely sampling. As Prince moved into the next phase of his career in the new millennium, he seemed less concerned with the anxiety of influence, and the horn section became a more and more important aspect of his work. Hip-hop all but disappeared from Prince's music, and the influence of jazz increased, as Prince became more comfortable wearing the mantle of Black musical patriarch.

Prince the Prodigal: Reclaiming Black Music History

It is Sunday, February 8, 2004, and Prince is playing an after-show at the House of Blues on L.A.'s Sunset Strip. He has dubbed it his "After Grammy Jam," in honor of the appearance he made earlier that day at the forty-sixth annual NARAS award ceremony (taped downtown at the Staples Center), where he performed a duet with the reigning crossover star Beyoncé Knowles. The band backing him up is virtually the same as the one from his 2002 One Nite Alone tour. Though Prince plays little of the material from his jazz-inflected *Rainbow Children* album, he nonetheless allows the band to stretch out in long jams, and prominently features his three-person horn section. This section—trombone, and tenor and alto saxophone—is the centerpiece of Prince's band, even on songs he did not originally record with reeds and brass. On early hits like "Controversy" and "D.M.S.R.," the horns play along with the synthesizer hooks and weave in soli lines from other songs. Prince interpolates the horn riff from Sam and Dave's 1967 R&B hit "Soul Man" into his own 1986 hit "Kiss." In so doing, Prince creates arrangements that—to a longtime listener—sound like reunification, an echo of the prelapsarian funk we might have heard in the 1980s had Prince not decided to exclude horns.

If one had looked over the shoulders of the horn players that night, or at any time during the 2002 tour, one would have gotten a quick lesson in funk horn history. Given the changing lineup of reed and brass players Prince was using, he allowed music stands onstage, especially during his loose, free-form after-show jams. The job of music director fell to trombonist Greg Boyer, who prepared lead sheets for the horns that included a numbered list of famous horn melodies (according to Eric Leeds, who performed during the Japanese leg of the 2002 tour).

> Some of the horn lines we would play included JB's "Get on the Good Foot," I believe we may have quoted "Ain't It Funky Now" also; we might also play a line from Kool and the Gang (maybe "Who's Gonna Take the Weight," and perhaps some others). We also would reference some lines from P-Funk songs . . . "Get Up for the Down Stroke" or "Tear the Roof Off," occasionally. We might also throw in some lines from earlier Prince songs such as "Housequake," "Girls and Boys," etc.[94]

Prince was clearly no longer concerned about appearing too closely associated with the music of his father's generation. Boyer's conveniently numbered lead sheets, presumably made with Prince's approval, canonized horn riffs from across the spectrum of R&B and jazz irrespective of the genre or decade in which they were originally marketed. On Boyer's lead sheet, and subsequently in Prince's aftershows, founding fathers of funk like James Brown and George Clinton rubbed elbows with jazz standards from Dixieland to bebop—Prince quoted both Charlie Parker's "Now's the Time" and "Down by the Riverside" in concert—who in turn made space for younger artists like Tower of Power and Prince himself. Boyer's list reifies the history of horns, interpolates Prince's work into that history, and puts them all into a free-flowing intertextual dialogue. What's more, Prince no longer balked at sharing the stage with his pedigreed elders: alongside Greg Boyer, longtime horn arranger for Parliament-Funkadelic, stood none other than Maceo Parker, famously of the JB Horns as well as P-Funk (to say nothing of the bass player Larry Graham, who had routinely performed with Prince since the turn of the millennium). Here at last was all of the influence and none of the anxiety.

Given Prince's early resistance to working directly with the patriarchs of funk and jazz, it is easy to cast him in the role of prodigal son. In a 2004 interview on the Prince fan website Housequake.com, Greg Boyer made a similar point. When asked if the One Nite Alone tour was an anomaly in Prince's career, Boyer responded:

> It was totally different than any other tour he had done up to that point. . . . People had gotten used to Prince changing the music, as long as it was within the guise of the funk-rock-punk-sexy-etc. scope

> that they were used to. But it seemed nobody braced themselves for the inevitable—that Prince would get older! And if you're blessed enough to get "up in the years," or smart enough not to get yourself killed over stupid stuff, your outlook will change. He went headfirst into a jazz thing and, in my humble opinion, it was electrifying. I was glad to be a part of the whole thing, since I too am a lifelong funk guy with jazz running through my veins.[95]

Boyer hints that Prince's audience, though accustomed to Prince's mutability of sound and image, was nonetheless unprepared for the *traditional* direction the star had taken. Gone were the revealing costumes and the simulated sex acts onstage, gone was the androgyny, and gone was any hint of profanity in the song lyrics. In place of the former enfant terrible, Prince's post-millennial audiences encountered a deeply religious artist whose statements of faith no longer conflated the spiritual and the sexual. They also encountered an artist who, while still playful, was much more gender-normative in his self-presentation, and whose sound had turned toward the jazz canon.

In actuality, Prince had been exploring jazz long before he rubbed elbows with Miles Davis in the middle 1980s, but he typically released that material through side projects like Madhouse. His first notable quotations from the jazz canon were in his concert appearances: in the 1987 theatrical release of his *Sign o' the Times* concert, Prince's band quotes Duke Ellington's "Take the ATrain" and Charlie Parker's "Now's the Time." By the 1990s, his use of jazz expanded alongside his horn section: 1991's *Diamonds and Pearls* included "Strollin'," a gently swung ballad with walking bass and Wes Montgomery–style guitar work; by 1995's *The Gold Experience*, Prince was comfortable with his horn section quoting Thelonious Monk's "Well, You Needn't" over the coda of his song "Billy Jack Bitch," though this experiment did not survive onto the finished album.[96] After the turn of the millennium came three albums and one tour of original but clearly jazz-influenced material. On 2001's *The Rainbow Children*, Prince incorporated the smooth-jazz soprano saxophone player Najee on several tracks, alongside his old collaborators the Hornheads. Distributed solely through Prince's website, 2002's *Xpectation* was an all-instrumental album that combined funk slow-jam grooves with angular, exploratory solos; the four instrumental tracks on 2003's *N.E.W.S.* took this a step further by using multi-section structures created through a process of directed group improvisation. Even if one dismisses these albums as boutique material not meant for the mass market, it was hard to overlook One Nite Alone, Prince's most extensive tour of the United States since 1997–98 and one of his few tours to deviate from a greatest-hits set-list. One Nite Alone found Prince avoiding his best-known material and instead leading his band through jazzier territory drawn principally from *The Rainbow Children*, and giving his horn and piano players ample time for long improvised solos. Even the restaurant that Prince briefly opened in Las Vegas, during a four-month residency at the Rio hotel that he and his band played in 2007, was named "Jazz Cuisine."

For those attending Prince's 2002 One Nite Alone tour or his 2007 Las Vegas run and expecting a recap of Prince's greatest hits, hearing a trombone solo over the chord changes for "When the Saints Go Marching In" may have been jarring. One possible reason why lies in the unspoken value judgments implicit in Boyer's allusion to Prince as getting "up in the years." Could it be that Prince's increased interest in jazz was, like his interest in suits, the expression of a man who had outgrown his youthful gender/genre bending and wanted to stake his claim to Black musical patriarchy? If so, Prince could not have picked a better musical strategy: first, because jazz is strongly identified with its origins in the African American musical community, and second, because jazz was still a man's world. As musicologist David Ake points out, jazz has not only remained "an overwhelmingly male domain," it is also among "the few areas of the popular imagination in which Black males have been perceived to be superior to their white counterparts" (an association that retains more than a whiff of the primitivist association of Blackness with supernatural potency in music and sex).[97] Thirdly, jazz has become "respectable," a symbol of both high culture and upward class mobility.[98]

Based on these cultural associations, Prince may well have been using jazz—and his pedigreed horn players and tailored suits—to burnish his image, helping him appear more mature, more masculine, and/or more Black. However, in his musical (and even sartorial) references, Prince resisted the canonic constructions of both "jazz" and "masculinity." Prince's use of jazz was markedly different from the sentimental nostalgia of reflected prestige displayed by other late-career artists who released albums of jazz standards in the 2000s, such as Rod Stewart or Paul McCartney. As any music student knows, the jazz genre is anything but monolithic, and Prince used an eclectic range of jazz references that undercut what musicologist Tom Perchard called the "conservative Marsalisite jazz history" of traditional jazz.[99] Furthermore, as

Stan Hawkins and Sarah Niblock have argued, even the more conservative tailoring of Prince's post–*Purple Rain* suits contained a degree of dandyism (or "self-aestheticization") that queered the conventions of traditional masculinity.[100]

The history of jazz is a web of diverging styles, each with a distinct combination of musical techniques and identity politics, from the dance floor functionality of Ellington's big-band arrangements, to the after-hours exclusivity of bebop; and from to the radical freedom of Ornette Coleman's harmolodics to the populist accessibility of Cannonball Adderley's hard-bop. Bearing this in mind, it's illuminating to consider what specific jazz references Prince actually made, and how the eclecticism of these references reflects on his (similarly catholic) admixture of R&B, funk, and soul genres. Prince referenced bebop jazz in his *Sign o' The Times* tour by quoting Charlie Parker, but his backing band played it while he was offstage doing a costume change. On his 2004–05 *Musicology* tour, Prince's horn section would routinely include a traditional Dixieland number, but here again it was an interlude in which Prince did not participate. The jazz technique in which Prince seems most at home is group improvisation: according to Eric Leeds, Prince's facility at improvisation may have been the thing that most closely allied him with the "jazz sensibility."[101] Prince was famous for running his rehearsals as extended jam sessions, and he used the technique of directed improvisation to create 2003's *N.E.W.S.* album, which was the product of one night's live recording with a full band (drums, bass, keyboard, saxophone, and himself on guitar) and nothing written in advance.

The technique of group improvisation reaches all the way back to traditional New Orleans style jazz, but more recently it recalls the Coleman-led "free jazz" movement of the 1960s. Like bebop, free jazz was a style born of the desire to bring jazz back into the Black community by creating an idiom inaccessible to outsiders and infused with recognizably African American tropes. In particular, free-jazz practitioners sought to break down the divisions, propagated by the white-controlled music industry, between jazz and more popular genres like funk and R&B.[102] Yet what separates Prince's group improvisation from free jazz is Prince's use of tonal harmony and danceable funk rhythms. Despite Prince's use of group improv and his reference to bebop, the music that results from that process sounds neither like the free-jazz explorations of Ornette Coleman nor like the breakneck small-group jazz of Charlie Parker.

For Prince, jazz keeps a firm grasp on its "Saturday night" function, and his jazz-oriented albums like *The Rainbow Children* and *N.E.W.S.* sound more like the déclassé styles of smooth or fusion jazz than anything one might hear at Jazz at Lincoln Center.[103] Bebop, free jazz, and even the culturally conservative Ken Burns–Albert Murray–Wynton Marsalis claim that jazz is "America's classical music" are all predicated on the idea of jazz as an art not accessible to everyone (either on the basis of race or of social class). As a mainstream pop musician, Prince was never part of these discourses of exclusivity. Prince's forays into jazz may be angular and atonal at times, or conservatively retrospective at others, but he mostly strove for a recognizably contemporary and accessible jazz-funk sound. By putting "Pass the Peas" alongside "Down by the Riverside," and P-Funk next to Charlie Parker and Miles Davis, Prince constructed a canon that defied the high and low distinctions of concert hall and dance hall that has crept into the jazz world. Even at his jazziest, Prince's work had the rhythmic underpinning of funk, and in that respect sounds closest to the fusion-era Miles Davis of *Bitches Brew*, Weather Report, or even the smooth jazz of David Sanborn, George Benson, and Najee. Whatever the soloist or the horn section was up to, Prince kept his rhythm section playing a consistent groove, with common chord changes and regular four- and eight-bar phrases, all of which invite the listener to get up and dance.

It seems more appropriate to consider Prince in relation to the populist side of jazz history that encompasses soul jazz, hard-bop, jazz fusion, and smooth jazz. Bandleaders like Cannonball Adderley and Miles Davis rebelled against the canonization of jazz and in the 1960s and '70s and made music—variously labeled hard-bop and fusion—with the goal of selling records, reaching audiences for whom soul and rock were the new norm, and generally reconnecting jazz with its function as entertainment rather than art music. At the same time, rock and soul keyboard players like Ray Charles, Booker T. Jones, and the Meters' Art Neville released instrumental jams that blended the beat of funk with the extended improvised solos of jazz, creating the subgenre of soul jazz. Musicologist David Rosenthal has argued that these fusions of jazz—music that blended the jazz tradition of improvised solos with the rhythmic foundation of funk and R&B—were the lingua franca of Black musicians and listeners alike in the 1970s, attracting large audiences and getting radio airplay on R&B stations at a time when "jazz" was in the process of moving out of the nightclub and into the concert hall.[104] This was, arguably, the idiom in which Prince's musician father would have worked in the 1960s and '70s. In the ensuing decades, as neo-traditionalists reinforced the boundary between "true" jazz and jazz debased by fusion with popular genres, Prince's work looked back to a time before such divisions were in place, when the common origins and cross-fertilization of jazz and other genres of Black music produced "a consensus image of the black professional musician," equally at home in a variety of styles.[105]

Through the horns of Maceo Parker, Greg Boyer, and Miles Davis, Prince connected himself musically to the founding fathers of funk and jazz fusion and also with the musical language of his own late father. Referencing jazzmen like Duke Ellington, Charlie Parker, and Miles Davis, Prince may well have been looking for the reflected prestige and masculinity that the label "jazz" had acquired. But Prince put these "fathers" on equal footing with less lofty ones like James Brown, George Clinton, and Sly Stone, and less manly ones like Little Richard, Mavis Staples, and Chaka Khan. By allowing his horns to bounce from Dixieland to Birdland to the Mothership, Prince performed a subtle historiographic coup. We hear him rewriting the history of popular music, imagining an America in which Black masculinity was not made into a fetish object and Black music was not split into separate marketing categories. We can hear this project in the mixture of references on the live recordings from the One Nite Alone and *Musicology* tours; we can also hear it in how "Sexy M.F." mixed hip-hop and horns, and how "Housequake" queered 1960s revivalism. When Prince invited Miles Davis onstage with him that long-ago New Year's Eve, the consonance was perhaps greater than the young artist could have imagined. In his career's final phase, Prince's work was marked by a more conservative approach to sexuality and gender and a curatorial attitude toward Black music, but leavened by an inclusive continuity between jazz, R&B, and pop: not the nostalgia of neo-traditionalist jazz purists like Wynton Marsalis, but a position closer to Davis's own assertion that jazz was never meant to become "a museum thing locked under glass."[106] In the end, Prince refused to respect the division between high and low art, refused to acknowledge the historical divisions between musical genres, and refused to pander to audience or industry expectations of what a "real" Black man should sound like.

Conclusion

"Piano & a Microphone" and Prince's Legacy

Near the end of his life, Prince took on three unexpectedly revealing projects. These included his first ever solo tour without a backing band, 2016's Piano & a Microphone; opening his Paisley Park recording complex for public tours; and an autobiography titled *The Beautiful Ones*, announced in 2016 but published posthumously. All three of these projects shared a quality of retrospection and self-revelation that surprised fams and journalists, who had grown accustomed to Prince's desire for privacy and reluctance to discuss his own past. Although music journalists had for years mined Prince's biography for clues to help decode his music, this marked the first period when Prince spoke publicly about his life and creative process, and willingly revisited his past. Indeed, Prince's career-long disinclination to talk about his past or analyze his own work had given him aura of inscrutability—Stan Hawkins and Sarah Niblock describe Prince as having a "mysterious and ambiguous pop identity unlike anything or anyone else"—and the timing and content of these three projects suggested a late-career shift: an urge to open up, perhaps even a crisis of self-representation.[1] But I argue that Prince's late-career retrospection and self-revelation were the logical next steps for an artist who had long fought to control every aspect of his own work and image, as I hope the analyses presented in the preceding chapters have shown. Though this book has not been a chronological survey of Prince's work, nonetheless these three interconnected projects provide a perfect end point, because in each of them Prince constructed a narrative of his own career—in words, with *The Beautiful Ones*; in music, with his Piano & a Microphone tour; and in the physical space of his

Paisley Park complex-cum-museum. As such, I will spend this concluding chapter briefly describing each of these, and exploring what they say about Prince's legacy and how he wanted to represent it.

The Beautiful Ones

On March 17, 2016, Prince convened an invitation-only audience at the Avenue nightclub in Manhattan, where he announced his plan to release his memoir the following year on an imprint of Random House, with the help of coauthor Dan Piepenbring, before performing a short concert. According to the *New York Times*, Prince's stated goal for the book was to start from "the beginning—my first memory—and hopefully we can move all the way to the Super Bowl," meaning his famous 2007 Superbowl halftime performance.[2] This announcement thrilled those of us in the Prince fam community, as we had been subsisting on unauthorized biographies and magazine interviews up to that point. Prince had always been reluctant to talk candidly about his life, and most biographers ascribed this to a combination of a shy personality and a decision to use mystery and obfuscation as part of his art and image.[3] Indeed, for many years Prince refused most interview requests from print magazines and, on the rare occasion he granted them, would place conditions on the interviewers that made it difficult to capture his exact words. For example, for most of Prince's career, print journalists were forbidden to use audio recording devices to augment their note-taking (possibly motivated by the experience of having a 1981 interview recording bootlegged and released, to embarrass him for years afterward).[4] During a particularly fraught period during 1994 and '95 Prince went so far as to forbid journalists from writing down any notes at all during their interviews.[5] His treatment of television and radio hosts during this period was equally recalcitrant, including one infamous 1995 interview with BBC's *The Sunday Show* where Prince refused to speak directly to interviewer Veronica Webb, insisting instead on whispering his answers to his then-bandmate and girlfriend Mayte Garcia.[6] Given this history, Prince's announcement that he was writing his autobiography fell like manna from heaven, which made it all the more heartbreaking when Prince passed just over one month later, having left the project unfinished.

The book that Spiegel and Grau ultimately released in 2019 is a far cry from the comprehensive memoir that Prince had announced. Prince only authored twenty-eight handwritten pages before passing, and Piepenbring filled out the remainder of the book with his own reflections on working with Prince, amounting to a long-form interview article (part of which was published in the *New Yorker*), as well as reproductions of Prince's old photo albums, handwritten lyrics, and an early treatment of the *Purple Rain* movie.[7] Nonetheless, the book still sheds light on how Prince wanted his story to be told. The pages that Prince authored trace his childhood and adolescence, starting with his earliest memories and ending with his sexual awakening in early high school. Piepenbring's introductory chapters and sidebar comments create a framing device around Prince's words and draw attention to several themes that came up in his conversations with Prince and that carry through the memoir itself. Family is one obvious theme: in their conversations, Prince made it clear to Piepenbring that his first priority was to write about his mother, and Prince began his first handwritten chapter discussing the formative influence of his mother's gaze and the sound of his father's piano; later, Prince wrote about the trauma of their divorce.[8] Imagination and the power of music are the obvious second theme: Piepenbring says that Prince gave him the phrase "music is healing" as a guiding principle for the book. In the course of their conversations it became clear that racial justice was the most pressing issue that needed healing: in an early conversation, Prince set the audacious goal of writing "a book that solves racism."[9] Throughout the chapters that Prince wrote, he returns again and again to descriptions of the inner life of his imagination and how central it was to his personal identity—he connects his "overactive" brain with the blackouts and epileptic seizures he had as a small child—and to his professional output.[10] The third central theme that emerges in Prince's memoir is the importance of cultural creation and ownership, especially within the context of the music industry: he wanted the book to be "a handbook for the brilliant community," to provide useful information about how the music industry worked, and that its core message was about "the freedom to create autonomously."[11] Piepenbring points out that even a decade after Prince's fight with the Warner Brothers label, "chains of distribution and questions of ownership" were on his mind, and that Prince wanted to continue to spread the message that artists—especially artists of color—should retain ownership of their master recordings as a means of keeping generational wealth within the community.[12]

For students of Prince's life and career, none of these themes was surprising, though it was nice to hear it written in Prince's own distinctive voice. I was left wondering—along with Piepenbring himself—what kind of book Prince would have written had he lived.[13] Perhaps my dominant takeaway from the project is simply that Prince was, in the last year of his life, finally interested in seizing control of his own narrative, an interest that may have been motivated at least in part by thoughts of mortality: Piepenbring wrote, "According to one friend, several of the people [Prince] loved and admired were falling ill, making him conscious of his own mortality."[14] What we see in the pages that Prince wrote before passing is a narrative about the family and community in which he grew up, and about the inner life of his creative imagination; what we learn from the candid pictures and captions from Prince's photo album, included in facsimile, is that Prince was a keen observer whose eye was focused on the music industry and how to navigate it as a young artist. As it happened, these were largely the same themes that I had observed in Prince's Piano & a Microphone show in 2016, to which I now turn my attention. Piepenbring himself made the same point in his introduction to *The Beautiful Ones*, writing that "the book coincided with an inward turn in Prince's music-making," and that the Piano & a Microphone show "gave an idea of what was on his mind at the time. He was processing his past. Only when I saw the footage more than a year later did I see how this performance dovetailed with his ideas for [the memoir]."[15]

"Piano & a Microphone," January 21 2016, 8 p.m.

During the time I lived in Minnesota—from 1991 to 1999, and again from 2005 to 2016—I myself was a member of the Prince "fam" community ("fam," short for "family," because Prince disliked the word "fan," short for "fanatic"). Fams would congregate at Paisley Park on nights when Prince opened the venue for public parties and events; I was not the most hard-core fam by any metric, but I estimate that I spent between twelve and fifteen evenings at Paisley Park during Prince's lifetime, and it was always meaningful. My first ever visit was probably September 16 of 1995, when Prince was performing with his New Power Generation band, and I distinctly remember him playing covers of Little Richard's "The Girl Can't Help It" and Sly Stone's arrangement of "Que Sera Sera" late in the set.[16] My second visit was on October 10 of that same year, when Prince filmed the video for his song "Gold" from the *Gold Experience* album—ask anyone who was there that night about the huge chunks of gold mylar glitter that fell from the ceiling, which I was still finding in my car half a year later.[17] The very last time I saw Prince at Paisley Park was on January 21, 2016, at the first (8 p.m.) performance of the Piano & a Microphone tour's opening night gala (and I still regret not also buying a ticket to the second, 11 p.m., show that night).

As we now know, Piano & a Microphone was Prince's final tour; after that January 21 opening gala, the tour stretched from Febuary 16 in Melbourne, Australia, to his last-ever public performance on April 14 at Atlanta's Fox Theatre. But that night in January felt like the auspicious start of a new, less guarded phase in Prince's performing career. The two gala-night performances were held in Paisley Park's cavernous main soundstage, where I had seen Prince perform many times. While every opportunity to see Prince perform at Paisley Park felt intimate, this show was particularly so: first, Prince had recently renovated the soundstage, laying carpet, installing a small platform for his piano in front of the loading-dock door on the west wall (a 90-degree turn from the previous location of the stage, which was on the south wall), and putting in several risers with couches for VIP audience members. This renovation was announced prior to the show in a promotional video on the Paisley Park After Dark social-media channel, under the name "Paisley Park—The Remodel for *Piano & a Microphone* Gala Event—21st January 2016."

Second, and more importantly, this show felt intimate because Prince gave a stripped-down performance that was, quite literally, revelatory. To be sure, this was not the first time he had appeared solo during a public performance. His *Musicology Live 2004ever* tour shows included a multi-song encore section during which he appeared by himself onstage, seated, with an acoustic guitar, playing truncated versions of some of his hits. I saw that tour at the Staples center in Los Angeles on Wedsnesday, May 26, and Saturday, June 5, 2004, and the unplugged segment did create a wonderful sense of intimacy, but that intimacy was mitigated by the hugeness of the set, the arena, and the knowledge that it would likely only last for a few minutes before the full band returned. All that was gone during Piano & a Microphone: Prince made himself more vulnerable by playing theaters (not arenas) and appearing solo for the entire show (not just a segment); the only other things onstage were a piano, a microphone, and a few candles—no backing musicians, no guitar to hide behind, not even a set, only a kaleidoscopic light projection that bathed Prince and the backdrop in color. In fact the "piano" was an electronic keyboard housed inside a purple-painted, hollowed-out baby-grand piano shell; Prince later collaborated with Yamaha on the creation of a bespoke purple grand piano, an acoustic instrument with MIDI and a built-in sound module (similar to a Disklavier), but he passed away before having the chance to take the instrument on tour with him.[18] The second thing that made these shows much more intimate was, of course, the content: Prince's solo piano arrangements stripped each song to its chassis, and he spoke directly to the audience, telling stories about his childhood and career not in the showman's patter he had used in the *Musicology* tour segments, but more off the cuff. He didn't say much—even at his Piano & a Microphone shows Prince preferred to let the music speak for him—but he did talk about his own life, in particular about the music and people that had influenced him as a young songwriter.

Prince began his 8 p.m. show ambiguously: entering the stage without fanfare, Prince waited for the raucous crowd to stop cheering, then played one note and walked away; returning to the piano, he played a single minor chord and sang a snippet of a song I didn't recognize—"My name is [inaudible], my only mission is to make you cry happy tears of joy." The volume of the piano was thunderously loud and was doubled by a string-synth timbre; Prince's vocal microphone had a delay mod on it that caused each line to descend in pitch as it echoed. These uncanny touches quieted the crowd, and the introduction slowly revealed itself as a biographical sketch about Prince's earliest encounters with his father's piano. Minneapolis journalist Jon Bream succinctly described this portion of the show in his review:

> Prince, at 57, was about to present a conceptual musical autobiography. He was a 3-year-old who wanted to play the piano but his dad, a musician, wouldn't let him touch the instrument. So little Prince watched TV, which he indicated by jumping atop the purple piano and miming like he was munching chips while transfixed by the tube. His parents divorced when he was 7, he said, and thereafter he could play piano anytime he wanted. So he offered a passage and then proclaimed, "I can't play piano like my dad. How does Dad do that?" Then he whipped off a blues-jazz boogie segment and announced: "I wish I could sing." The audience of 1,200 laughed.[19]

John L. Nelson, Prince's father, was a musician in North Minneapolis's vibrant jazz community who played under the stage name "Prince Rogers," and many biographers have commented on the anxiety of influence that Prince must have felt growing up in his father's shadow, with his father's name. Immediately after this segment, Prince played two 1960s television theme songs on the piano, "Batman" (which aired

1966–68) and "The Man from U.N.C.L.E." (on television 1964–68), completing the audience's mental picture of a seven-year-old Prince alone in his living room in 1965, with the piano that his father had left behind.[20]

As the concert went on, Prince widened his biographical sketch to include other voices in his community who had influenced him. He talked about radio personalities such as Jack Harris, a DJ on KUXL, Minneapolis's only R&B-formatted radio station in the sixties and seventies, and immediately followed this with two cover songs by R&B artists that he had presumably heard on those radio shows, the Miracles' "I Second That Emotion" and the Jackson 5's "Who's Loving You." Prince also talked about artists from outside the Black community that he heard on Minnesota's rock and pop radio stations, notably Joni Mitchell—Prince played her song "A Case of You" later in the evening—and David Bowie, whom Prince briefly eulogized right before that (and whose song "Heroes" he played at some of his other Piano & a Microphone shows).[21] With these and a few other spoken-word segments, Prince vividly but judiciously sketched out his emotional and creative development in a way that contextualized it first within his nuclear family, then in his North Minneapolis neighborhood, and then in the larger musical community that he became part of through listening and recording.

Prince didn't only talk about his life that night; he also talked about his songs. His was nothing like the approach of the VH1 *Storytellers* show, where songwriters would spill their guts about the meanings of their songs. Prince didn't reveal the origins or meanings of his own songs, in keeping with his lifelong habit, instead preserving an open-ended, polysemous quality that allowed his listeners to create their own interpretations. (In the past, Prince had often said, "My songs are my children," and "My fans are my children's friends," implying that he wanted to give his listeners space to have their own relationships to the songs.[22]) Instead, when Prince talked about his songs that night, he talked about the act of writing them—the work itself. For example, when Prince played his first original song of the night, "Baby" (right after the TV themes and R&B covers), he introduced it in the voice of his younger self by saying, "Now I gotta write me some songs," and then dramatized the process of trying to write the short melodic flourish at the song's turnaround, with all the false starts and hesitations of a young songwriter. Some of his vignettes revealed truths about both his songwriting and the community that nurtured it, as when he talked about cowriting the song "Raspberry Beret" with one of his early collaborators, the classically and jazz trained keyboard player Lisa Coleman, whose chord voicings Prince came to rely on, and through whom he discovered Miles Davis and Bill Evans (as he told us that night).[23]

All told, Prince played twenty-nine songs (in whole or in part) at the 8 p.m. show on January 21, and in so doing he constructed a musical narrative of his life and career. Specifically, he played twenty-two of his own songs and seven cover songs (including the TV themes). The originals he played were drawn from across his catalog, from his first album, 1978's *For You,* to his final album, 2015's *HITnRUN Phase Two,* but with notable omissions: though he included at least one song from each of his first ten and his last three albums, he played virtually no songs that he had recorded during the 1990s: nothing from 1989's *Batman* soundtrack through 1999's *The Truth,* with just one song, from the 1999 album *Rave Un2 the Joy Fantastic,* representing that decade ("Eye Love U, But Eye Don't Trust U Anymore"). Although this set list did not stay the same from show to show—part of the concept for the Piano & a Microphone tour was that each concert would be different—his song choices at the other shows displayed a similar retrospective quality, a similar mix of originals and covers, and a similar underrepresentation of his 1990s material (according to user-submitted setlists available online).[24] Of the sixteen original songs that Prince played most frequently on the Piano & a Microphone tour (i.e., those that he played in at least eleven of the twenty-two total shows on that tour), eleven were originally recorded or released in the 1980s, one from the 2000s ("Black Sweat" from 2006's *3121* album), and only two from the 1990s ("Cream" and "Diamonds and Pearls," both from his hit 1991 album *Diamonds and Pearls*).[25] Looking over all the songs that he played on the tour, one-hundred twenty-one in toto, eighteen were cover songs (including R&B, funk, reggae, rock, folk, TV theme songs, gospel, and spirituals), leaving 103 of Prince's original songs. Of those originals, Prince played 56 songs (over half) from his 1970s and 1980s releases, 29 songs (roughly 28 percent) from his 2000s and 2010s releases, and only 18 songs (roughly 17 percent) from his 1990s releases, making that decade the least-represented category of songs on the tour.[26]

Though we can never know what momentary whim motivated Prince to select or skip certain songs on any given night, it is telling that he generally avoided songs from what was perhaps the most difficult time in his career and his life. The 1990s encompassed Prince's bitter fight against Warner Brothers Records, the death of his infant son, and the dissolution of his first marriage. Notably, most of the 1990s songs that he played on his Piano & a Microphone tour were from albums he released either *before* these troubles had begun (e.g., 1990's *Graffiti Bridge,* 1991's

Diamonds and Pearls, and 1992's *Love Symbol* album) or *after* he was liberated from his Warner Brothers recording contract (e.g., from 1996's *Emancipation* to 1999's *Rave Un2 the Joy Fantastic*). Regardless of how one parses these numbers, it seems clear that Prince was constructing a narrative primarily about the ascending trajectory of his early career and secondarily about his post–Warner Brothers career revival, while avoiding the period of his personal and professional nadir.

This is not to say that Prince avoided sad topics: at the January 21 performance that I attended, Prince spoke about his difficult relationship with his father and touched on the theme of mortality, though in a typically Princean way. This spoken-word segment came between the utopian "Paisley Park" and the somber "Sometimes It Snows in April" (these were the nineteenth and twentieth songs of the evening, putting this vignette about two-thirds of the way through his set):

> I thought I would never be able to play like my dad, and he never missed an opportunity to remind me of that. But we got along good. He was my best friend. How many of you have lucid dreams? I like dreaming now more than I used to. Some of my friends have passed away and I see them in my dreams. So it's like they are here, and the dreams are just like waking sometimes. You know?

Looking back at Prince's Piano & a Microphone performance that night, the retrospective impulse is very clear, as is the shape of the narrative he constructed. Through his song choices and his spoken reminiscences, he traced the upward arc of his creative journey from childhood to the full flowering of his songwriting powers in the mid-1980s and on into his mature triumphs from the 2010s, largely jumping over the most difficult years of his adulthood. He confronted mortality, though obliquely, and mostly dwelled on the formative relationships—in his family and in his community—that nurtured him. At the very end of the concert, Prince extended that circle of community to include us, the audience: after leading a singalong during the song "Anna Stesia," he concluded by saying "This is the first. You were here, and so was I," before leaving the stage.

The Paisley Park Museum and Celebration

This retrospective narrative impulse is equally on display in Prince's Paisley Park museum. During Prince's lifetime, Paisley Park was a contradiction, in that it was both a tightly guarded vault and also a semi-public commercial space. The facility itself opened on September 11, 1987, and booked external clients in its recording studios and soundstages from the very beginning: the first were Kool and the Gang, who used the soundstage to rehearse for their 1987 tour.[27] In 1996 Paisley Park stopped booking outside clients, but around that time Prince began opening Paisley Park for semi-public concerts and parties.[28] I myself attended a few secret Paisley Park parties and concerts in late 1995, though the official Paisley Park tour book lists Prince's November 12, 1996, release party for *Emancipation* as the beginning of the "late-night party" era at Paisley Park.[29] This openness became more regular in 1997–98 with a series of parties and concerts under the name "Love4OneAnother" that served as fundraisers for Prince's charity of the same name (a 501c3 nonprofit that Prince founded in 1996 with his first wife, Mayte Garcia).[30] After relocating to Los Angeles for much of the early 2000s, Prince's 2009 return to full-time Minnesota residency was marked by the return of these late-night parties, this time under the name "Paisley Park After Dark," which were promoted through Prince's official social media accounts.[31]

In addition to opening Paisley as a performance space, Prince started showing broader curatorial plans. This began in June 2000, when he hosted the first multiday "Celebration" at Paisley Park, an event that he ostensibly threw to celebrate the end of his publishing contract with Warner Brothers, at which point he reclaimed his birth name.[32] Prince enjoyed this event enough to host it twice more, in June of 2001 and 2002, although in 2002 he changed its name, ironically, to "Xenophobia." These three multiday events included panel discussions, tours, and concerts, featuring Prince and other associated musicians. Although he stopped holding these events after 2002, in 2015 he began hosting public tours of Paisley Park. These would happen on nights when a Paisley Park after Dark event was already scheduled: at one such event I myself saw the queue of fams waiting in line for a tour, although I foolishly skipped the line and remained in the soundstage in the hopes of seeing Prince, not realizing that he himself often participated in these tours.[33] After Prince's death, his estate was able to use the plans and ideas he had already shared with staff to quickly open Paisley Park as a museum in October 2016, a mere six months after his passing.[34] The estate also reestablished the multiday Celebration gatherings starting in June 2017, and these Celebrations are now a yearly moneymaker for the Prince estate and pilgrimage for his fam community (with the exception of 2021, when it was canceled due to the pandemic).

Paisley Park remains an environment designed by and for Prince, reflecting his priorities and aesthetics. His priorities centered around the creative work that he and his associates did there, as evidenced by the recording studios, editing suite, soundstage, and offices that comprise the first floor of the facility. Aesthetically, Prince had made several renovations that added color and a sense of historical narrative to the otherwise industrial-looking building, curatorial decisions that showed his consideration for the fam community and that facilitated Paisley's quick transition from home studio to museum. While the tour has evolved over time—at first, fams would pay their respects at the actual urn containing Prince's cremains, in the main atrium, until the family requested the urn be moved—and the museum staff periodically adds new rotating exhibits (such as Prince's car collection or shoe collection), the bones of the tour have remained largely the same, and revolve around the plans laid down by Prince during his lifetime. As of this writing I myself have taken two official guided tours of the Paisley Park museum (July 8, 2019, and July 29, 2022) and attended two events there (a Paisley Park after Dark party on July 23, 2022, and a Celebration fam convention on June 8–11, 2023), and I'll describe several key elements of the tour and discuss what they show about Prince's legacy and how he wanted to present it.

Just like Prince's Piano & a Microphone song choices, the Paisley Park museum tour takes visitors on a carefully guided pathway through Prince's career—a pathway that, the docents tell us, Prince himself plotted out. The tour includes only the first-floor areas of Paisley Park that were at least semi-public during his lifetime: beginning in the foyer, museumgoers spend time in the main atrium, whose adjoining storage rooms and offices have been converted into displays, then move through the work rooms where Prince and his associates created—Studios A, C, and B, and an editing suite—as well as two semi-private rooms off the atrium, the so-called "little kitchen" where Prince would prepare snacks, hang out, and watch basketball games on TV, and Prince's study, still stacked with books and CDs that had he'd left there. The tour then moves through the hangar-like soundstage and its adjoining "prestige area," which Prince had branded the NPG Music Club Room, and concludes in the soundstage's external foyer, which has been converted into the gift shop. What is excluded from the tour, just like at Elvis's Graceland, is the upstairs suite of rooms that included Prince's private residence; nor do tours include the basement, which houses Prince's famous Vault of unreleased recordings.

What this all foregrounds is the centrality of *work* in Prince's life, which should come as no surprise. Prince's work ethic has long been an important part of his public persona, like that of James Brown before him and Beyoncé Knowles after him (as Emily Lordi points out).[35] But Prince's commitment to work, as laid out at Paisley Park, seems singular: many artists have built home studios, but Paisley Park is primarily a studio—a light-industrial compound designed for commercial content creation, packed with state-of-the-art audio and video equipment—that Prince secondarily made into his home. Specifically, Prince made it into a home starting in 1996: the building was originally an antiseptic white, and in 1996 Prince expressed his exuberance over the impending birth of his son and his negotiated release from his Warner Brothers recording contract by undertaking an extensive renovation of Paisley Park (and closing the facility to outside rentals at the same time).[36] This included the addition of colorful murals, displays of gold and platinum albums recorded there, and historical photos and artwork throughout the first floor. Throughout that period Prince maintained separate residences nearby, but over time he eliminated them: his purple-painted house on Kiowa Trail (where his father lived from 1986 until his death in 2001) was demolished in 2003, and his Galpin Boulevard house (where Prince moved in 1985) was demolished in 2006, making Paisley Park his primary Minnesota residence.[37] Yet even after he moved back to Minneapolis from Los Angeles in 2009, Prince continued welcoming the public into Paisley Park, meaning that a space which was already two things—a production complex and a home—was also a third thing, a performance and museum space for the community, suffused with Prince's creative work.

You may take the museum tour yourself one day, so I'll spare you my detailed description of its entirety, but "dig if u will" three pictures of exhibits that Prince himself curated during his lifetime. First, the atrium: this light-filled room features a large open floor plan below a second-story balcony, topped by pyramid of windows. In the 1990s fams were allowed in this space, but around 2001 Prince closed it to the public, treating it as his own private living room (according to the docents) and the adjoining "little kitchen" as his television watching hangout spot. Prince's 1996 renovations surround the visitor here: Prince had the upper walls painted sky blue with clouds, with a mural of doves on one side (opposite the little kitchen), taking inspiration from the cages where Prince's pet doves were and are kept on a second-floor balcony (their cooing fills the room in quiet moments). The docent explains the symbolism of the atrium's design: the sky-blue walls and skylight are meant to instill a sense that there is no ceiling, or limit, on creativity inside these walls. On one side of the atrium, colored columns flank doorways to offices and storage closets, each decorated with a picture of Prince that was chosen by the artist himself (according to the docents). The other hallway walls lining the atrium are lined with gold and platinum albums. Given these design elements, the atrium gives the visitor a simultaneous impression of boundless, celestial creativity (the skylight and murals) and its earthly, record-industry measure (the RIAA sales plaques), with Prince's images linking the two realms.

Second, the history hallway. This is the farthest hallway from the foyer, at the terminus of the main atrium hallway and the soundstage foyer; it runs alongside the soundstage's north wall, past the production offices and the back door to Studio B, and empties onto the exterior lobby of the soundstage, which is now the museum gift shop. The wall along the north side of this "history hallway" includes a timeline display of Prince's career, with mounted photos illustrating each year from 1978 to 1996. According to the museum staff, Prince had this history hallway installed, most likely as part of his 1996 renovation, and chose the photos himself. All are staged photos, with no candids or behind-the-scenes images on display: many are familiar images used in album art or tour posters, though some are less well-known to American audiences, such as a triptych of Prince in red patent leather with his blue cloud-guitar and a mirrored Batman symbol that Prince used for his European "Nude" tour poster, which marks the year 1990. The story this hallway tells is of Prince's style evolution, an aspect of his creative output into which he put a great deal of thought and effort, and one that, Hawkins and Niblock argue, was a central component of Prince's subversive image.[38]

After Prince's death, the museum staff extended the history hallway by installing a wall dividing the soundstage foyer from the main atrium hallway (with a locking access door), adding photos from 1997 onward, and turned the soundstage foyer into a gallery called the Emancipation Room. Though Prince himself did not design this display, I think it's worth mentioning as part of his legacy because of Prince's public fight for ownership of his own work. On display in this room are Prince's handwritten notes regarding the December 31, 1999, expiration of his publishing contract with Warner Brothers, which was the event that precipitated his reclamation of his birth name after the "symbol" era of the late 1990s. This publishing-contract expiration date was the second of three important dates in the history of Prince's fight for control of his own work: the first was Prince's negotiated release from his recording contract with Warner Brothers, on April, 26, 1996 (which inspired the title for his album *Emancipation* from that year); the third was when Prince regained ownership of his master recordings from Warner Brothers, which was not until 2014.[39] Paisley Park, with its audio and video recording facilities, represented Prince's dream of unfettered creativity: in the reception foyer, a placard announces that Paisley Park represented Prince's goal of being able to create multiple media—music, film, fashion, and technology—under one roof. Yet the ability to create—owning the means of production—ultimately proved an insufficient guarantor of Prince's control of his own legacy. As his 1990s struggles with Warner Brothers revealed, ownership of the copyright and the sound rights to the master recordings proved equally if not more important, and one of Prince's important legacies is his advocacy for artists to maintain (or regain) their intellectual property rights and their independence from corporate contracts, which can be summed up by his oft-repeated slogan from the late 1990s, "If you don't own your masters, your masters own you."[40] Though Prince may have seemed like an outlier for this stance in the 1990s, and he certainly weathered criticism for it at the time, it proved prescient: since 2013, which was the first year that artists could buy back the rights to their master recordings under the 1976 Copyright Act, numerous other legacy recording artists have been pursuing this same strategy.[41] As *Billboard* magazine pointed out in a 2002 article predicting this 2013 sea change in the industry, legally reclaiming master-recording rights is particularly important—and fraught—for African American artists, who were historically excluded from the lucrative royalty streams that stem from catalog ownership. Prior to 2013 only a handful of prominent Black artists (including Ray Charles, Quincy Jones, Sam Cooke, and Curtis Mayfield) had been able to gain ownership of their masters.[42] As the music industry has increasingly turned to sync licensing and online streaming as means of realizing the value of back-catalog recordings in the post-Napster era, owning the rights to master recordings has become an important portfolio investment, one that can guarantee an annuity to an artist's family or estate after their passing, thus representing not just an artistic legacy but an important financial one as well.

The last element of the Paisley Park museum that I want to mention, the "Influence Wall," also speaks to Prince's legacy, although this time in an artistic rather than a financial sense. The Influence Wall is a large mural spread across the north wall of the first perpendicular hallway off the main atrium walkway, which includes the main entrances to Studios A (on its north wall) and C (on its south wall) and terminates in an external door to the courtyard parking lot. The mural is dedicated to the artists that influenced Prince and those that he, in turn, influenced. Prince originally commissioned it to adorn a hallway in the Rio hotel where he had a residency from November 2006 to April 2007 at a venue that he rechristened *3121*; after the end of the residency that year, Prince had the mural moved to Paisley Park and expanded.[43] Both the original Rio mural and the second iteration at Paisley Park were done by artist Sam Jennings, with specific instructions from Prince on which artists to include. The version at Paisley Park depicts Prince in the center of a right-to-left flow of history. On Prince's right are the artists who influenced him, including Sly Stone, James Brown, Miles Davis, Earth Wind & Fire, Grand Funk Railroad, Joni Mitchell, Stevie Wonder, Tower of Power, Rufus with Chaka Khan, Larry Graham, Jimi Hendrix, and Carlos Santana. On Prince's left are a select list of artists whom he influenced: this includes Wendy & Lisa, Vanity, Appolonia, the Time, Jam & Lewis, the Revolution, André Cymone, Kat Glover, Mazarati, Martika, the Family, and the Deele. Notably, all but one of these are artists with whom Prince worked directly—his celebrated protégés—for whom he wrote, recorded, and produced the backing tracks of their "original" recordings, making them de facto Prince releases but for the vocals (the exception being the Deele, a short-lived Prince sound-alike group that included producers LA Reid and Babyface).

The meaning of this mural is transparent—any biography of Prince you read will mention at least a subset of those same influences and protégés—and what it shows is not just Prince's awareness of his place in history but also his interest in controlling that historical narrative, especially pertaining to the artists whom he influenced. Admittedly, a full list of artists inspired by Prince would likely be too long to include in the hallway, but nonetheless his decision to exclude obvious choices like Beyoncé Knowles, Janelle Monáe, and Lizzo—artists whom he mentored but did *not* produce—and instead to include artists for whom he wrote and recorded the bulk of their material (giving him a much higher degree of control over their output) is telling. One might see, in these exclusions, a shadow of anxiety about Prince's legacy: by not featuring Beyoncé, Monáe, or Lizzo, Prince ensured that his wall of influences would not include any artist that could overshadow him. On the other hand, one might also see Prince's decision to include only his protégés as a sign of humility: Prince gave songs to many other artists whom he didn't include on the wall, such as the Bangles and Kenny Rogers (for whom he wrote "Manic Monday" and "You're My Love," respectively, though the latter was under a pseudonym), and his generosity extended beyond the music industry into a variety of philanthropic efforts.[44] Regardless of which view one takes of this cherry-picking, Prince's Influence Wall is a fairly circumscribed, even cautious version of his place in history.

To sum up what Prince's Paisley Park museum tells us about how he wanted to present his own legacy: first and foremost is the central importance of work and creativity, and Prince's desire to do that creative work in an environment of his own design, far from the meddling influence of Los Angeles label executives. Second is the care and thought he put into every aspect of his work, as symbolized by the atrium artwork and history hallway. Though I myself have never toured the Bayreuth Festspielhaus, Paisley Park puts me in mind of Richard Wagner's concept of the *gesamtkunstwerk* because of the way that Prince treated everything within his reach—from his music and choreography, to his makeup and wardrobe, to the color of Paisley Park's walls and the layout of its rooms—as part of a total work of art. Third is the ownership of this work, as demonstrated by the documents on display in the Emancipation Room and the decade-plus struggle for control of his publishing rights and master recordings that those documents represent. Fourth is the awareness of his own place in history, and the selective way that he chose to represent it in the hall of influences.

Conclusion: Celebration, and Prince's Legacy

These lessons about Prince's legacy came to life for me at Celebration, the annual fam gathering at Paisley Park, which I attended in 2023. According to the event announcement, this was an event explicitly dedicated to "uplifting Prince's legacy and carefully preserving his prolific artistic output and his creative sanctuary," and it is here that I will conclude my discussion.[45] On Saturday June 10, journalist Reg Chapman moderated two consecutive panels: the "Fam Panel" at 11 a.m., which included scholars, journalists, and media influencers discussing Prince's ongoing fan community; and a "7 Panel" at noon, including former members of Prince's NPG band. At each, Chapman asked a version of the same question: what are you doing to enhance Prince's legacy? The answers—both from the fam community panelists and the band members—all shared a theme of positivity and inclusiveness wrapped around a core message of "teach the children" proselytizing: in essence, our job is to spread Prince's message and to welcome younger listeners into the fold. This is the kind of anodyne message that anyone might expect at an event dedicated to a deceased celebrity, and after those panels concluded, another attendee expressed to me her frustration that none of the panelists had said *why* we need to be spreading the word about Prince's message, or what that message even is. What *is* the core of Prince's legacy that we are paying forward? For her, the answer was obvious: "Prince's music can heal the world."[46] What I took from her answer was that we (the fams and former band members) all believe that Prince's music has the power to heal, both in terms of personal trauma (which had been a theme of the panel) and in terms of community-building. This simple idea—that Prince's music has the power to heal, and to connect—resonated with me at Celebration that weekend, surrounded as I was by an incredibly diverse group of people who had become a community through our shared love for Prince's work and grief over his loss. Further, it brought back memories of all the other times that I had experienced this power in Prince's music and his live performances firsthand, such as the May 2015 "Dance Rally 4 Peace" concert that I discussed in this book's introduction.

So, what can we learn from Prince's three late-career projects—his unfinished memoir, his solo tour, and his personal museum? For me, the answer comes down to two word-pairs: community and family, work and ownership. Prince's *Beautiful Ones* autobiography allowed him to open up about his early life within the protective structure of a published book whose rights he owned and whose narrative voice he controlled, rather than in the context of a magazine or television interview edited and owned by someone else. The pages that Prince finished before his untimely passing spanned only his childhood and early musical career, but what we see is the interdependence of Prince's family and community identities—growing up small and bullied but also loved and nurtured in Minneapolis's Black Northside neighborhood in the 1960s and '70s—with his early creative work and his quest for a recording contract, i.e., mortgaging the ownership of that creative work in order to gain the capital necessary to launch his career.

Like the memoir, Prince's Piano & a Microphone shows gave him the opportunity to revisit his childhood and his development as a songwriter in a format where he was uniquely in control. Prince used these performances to narrate—and even dramatize—his early life and creative work. This included family revelations in the literal sense, as when he discussed the almost Oedipal experience of playing his father's piano, and also in the sense of chosen family or community, as when he played songs by other artists that had influenced him (and particularly when he imitated the piano playing style of his early bandmate Lisa Coleman). The theme of work was built into this narrative of family and community: Prince referenced his childhood frustration at not being able to play piano as well as his dad; he acted out his false starts as a songwriter trying to come up with a good melody for "Baby," and he played cover songs that had meant a lot to him in his youth and informed his later work.

Last but not least, opening up his Paisley Park inner sanctum for tours and fam conventions gave him the opportunity to curate his own museum and legacy, an operation that has only expanded since his passing. These tours and Celebrations literally bring together Prince's work *and* his community under one roof (a roof that he designed and owned). Paisley Park's original purpose was as a place of creative freedom for Prince and his chosen family of artists and collaborators to do their work. Later, Prince began to open up the space to his fams, and around the same time he began displaying a curatorial impulse that ultimately led to the building's designation as a museum, a gathering place for the ever-expanding community of people who have been or will be touched by his work. As the Prince estate continues to operate the museum and host these events, and as they continue to rerelease his work in ever more expanded editions, containing previously unreleased material, this fam community will continue to study and proselytize about the work that Prince did, work which his estate and heirs own in perpetuity, linking community and family to work and ownership for as long as Paisley Park stands. This is a community to which I will always belong, and a body of work whose power—to move hearts, change minds, and transform identities—I will always respect and study.

Notes

Introduction

1. Knowles-Carter, foreword, ix.
2. Nilsen, *Vault*, 85.
3. Chapman, "Prince's Countless Charitable Activities."
4. Walsh, *Gold Experience*, 45, 112.
5. Riemenschneider, "Paisley Park to Re-open."
6. Wenger and Case, "Thousands Turn Out."
7. Kreps, "Hear Prince's Dance Rally 4 Peace Paisley Park Concert."
8. Dan Stubbs, "Prince Covers the Waterboys"; Hasted, "Making of . . ."
9. Cole, *Last Miles*, 227.
10. Vail, *Synthesizer*, 158.
11. McAdams, "Perspectives on the Contribution of Timbre."
12. Gore, *Raising PG Kids*, 17.
13. Hawkins and Niblock, *Prince: The Making of a Pop Music Phenomenon*, 2–3.
14. Kornhaber, "Prince: Gay Icon"; Smith, "Queer Legacy of Prince."
15. Williams, "Black Muse 4 U," 296; Williams, "Prince was Not 'Biracial'"; Grow, "Prince, the Secret Philanthropist."
16. Hawkins, *Settling the Pop Score*, 174.
17. Woodworth, "Synthesizers as Social Protest," 235.
18. Perry, "Prince: Double-Consciousness in Expressing the Value of Work," 203.
19. George, *Death of Rhythm and Blues*, 174.
20. Nilsen, *Dance Music Sex Romance*, 244.
21. Nilsen, *Dance Music Sex Romance*, 15. Hahn, *Possessed*, 5.
22. Nilsen, *Dance Music Sex Romance*, 23–24.
23. Hahn, *Possessed*, 10; Hill, *Prince: A Pop Life*, 15–16.
24. Goetting, *Joined at the Hip*, 43–48.
25. Matos, *Sign 'O' The Times*, 36. Parke, 50.
26. Nilsen, *Dance Music Sex Romance*, 23. Hill, *Prince: A Pop Life*, 11.
27. Bream, *Prince: Inside the Purple Reign*, 26. Hahn, *Possessed*, 11–12; "Stations by Format: Minneapolis-St. Paul," *Billboard*, July 10, 1965, 38.

28. Hahn, *Possessed*, 11–12.

29. Nilsen, *Dance Music Sex Romance*, 22.

30. Andrea Swensson, *Got to Be Something Here*, xiii.

31. Bream, *Prince: Inside the Purple Reign*, 32. Protzman, "From the Archives."

32. Nilsen, *Dance Music Sex Romance*, 34.

33. Hill, *Prince: A Pop Life*, 82.

34. Hahn, *Possessed*, 32.

35. Karlen, "Prince Talks," *Rolling Stone*, Sept 12, 1985, 30.

36. MTV News, "Prince's Debut TV Interview from 1985."

37. Seifert, "Prince Tweets to You."

38. Hoskyns, *Prince: Imp of the Perverse*, 82.

39. Kerman, *Contemplating Music*, 146; Scott, "Introduction," 17.

40. Adorno, *Aesthetic Theory*, 85–86; Leppert, "Commentary," 108.

41. Kramer, *Interpreting Music*, 8.

42. Kramer, *Music as Cultural Practice*, 9–10. Scott, "Introduction," 18.

43. Scott, "Introduction," 18.

44. Scott, "Introduction," 28.

45. Scott, "Introduction," 20; Warner, *Pop Music*, 19; Prince, *Beautiful Ones*, 98.

46. Zak, *Poetics of Rock*, 62.

47. Scott, "Introduction," 18.

48. Scott, "Introduction," 30.

49. Lipsitz, *American Studies in a Moment of Danger*, 24–25, 83–85, 93, 97.

50. Grossberg, "Rockin' with Reagan," 139–40; Goodwin, "Popular Music and Postmodern Theory," 82, 86, 95.

51. Danielsen, "His Name Was Prince," 278–79; Walser, "Prince as Queer Poststructuralist," 84–85.

52. Holland, "Prince: Postmodern Icon," 322.

53. Brooks, "Everybody Still Wants to Fly," 8–11.

54. Crenshaw, "Demarginalizing the Intersection of Race and Sex," 139–40.

55. Carbado et al., "Intersectionality," 304.

56. Wald, "From Spirituals to Swing," 391; Brooks, "'This Voice Which Is Not One'"; Lordi, "Surviving the Hustle"; Redmond, "This Safer Space"; Brooks, "Write to Rock," 55.

57. Mahon, *Right to Rock*, 146–47.

58. Lordi, "Surviving the Hustle," 132, 136.

59. Perry, "Prince: Double-Consciousness in Expressing the Value of Work," 203.

60. Redmond, "This Safer Space," 401; Brooks, "'All That You Can't Leave Behind,'" 180; Wald, "From Spirituals to Swing," 387; Wald, "Soul Vibrations," 689.

61. Lordi, "Souls Intact," 57; Redmond, "This Safer Space," 400; Brooks, *Bodies in Dissent*, 7.

62. Lordi, "Souls Intact," 57.

63. Brooks, "Everybody Still Wants to Fly,"10.

64. Parke, *Picturing Prince*, 50, 160.

65. Wald, "From Spirituals to Swing," 392.

66. Lordi, "Souls Intact," 66–67.
67. Lordi, "Souls Intact," 65.
68. Daphne Brooks, *Bodies in Dissent*, 5.
69. Ro, *Prince: Inside the Music and the Masks*, 4.
70. Nilsen, *Dance Music Sex Romance*, 19.
71. Prince, *Beautiful Ones*, 80, 83.
72. Middleton, *Studying Popular Music*, 174–75; Tagg, "Analysing Popular Music," 47; Brackett, *Categorizing Sound*, 7, 11.
73. Negus, *Music Genres and Corporate Cultures*, 3.
74. Tagg, "Analysing Popular Music," 47–48. Brackett, *Categorizing Sound*, 4.
75. Nanni et al., "Ensemble of Deep Learning," 383, 391; Tzanetakis and Cook, "Musical Genre Classification of Audio Signals"; Brackett, *Categorizing Sound*, 4.
76. Middleton, *Studying Popular Music*, 175. Brackett, *Categorizing Sound*, 18.
77. Tagg, "Analysing Popular Music," 47.
78. McClary, *Conventional Wisdom*, 5.
79. Steve Waksman, "Reading the Instrument," 255.
80. Waksman, "Reading the Instrument," 253–54, 257.
81. Wilson, "Black Music as an Art Form."
82. Wilson, "Significance of the Relationship"; Olly Wilson, "Heterogeneous Sound Ideal"; Floyd, *Power of Black Music*, 5.
83. McClary, *Conventional Wisdom*, 6.
84. Lordi, " Souls Intact," 66–67; Radano, *Lying Up a Nation*; Small, *Music of the Common Tongue.*
85. George, *Death of Rhythm and Blues*, xii, 8–11; Negus, *Music Genres and Corporate Cultures*, 86–90; Sanjek, "Tell Me Something I Don't Already Know"; Garofalo, "Black Popular Music," 237–39.
86. Negus, *Music Genres and Corporate Cultures*, 86–87.
87. NAACP Economic Development Department, "The Discordant Sound of Music," 56.
88. Hahn, *Possessed*, 31–32.
89. Stewart, "'Funky Drummer'"; Agawu, "Structural Analysis or Cultural Analysis?"; Radano, "Hot Fantasies."
90. Radano, "Hot Fantasies," 459–61.
91. Walser, "Prince as Queer Poststructuralist"; Holland, "Purple Passion."
92. Miller, "Moan within the Tone."
93. Bloom, *Anxiety of Influence*, xxiii.
94. Minnesota Historical Society, "Minneapolis Music Collection"; Dean, "MHS Collections."
95. Haimo, "Atonality, Analysis, and the Intentional Fallacy," 198.
96. Nilsen, *Dance Music Sex Romance*, 101. Browne, "Prince's Legacy."

Chapter 1

1. Nilsen, *Vault*, 555–56.
2. Dickerson, *My Time with Prince*, 168.
3. Nilsen, *Vault*, 32.

4. Dickerson, *My Time with Prince*, 172.

5. Hilburn, "Renegade Prince."

6. Echols, *Hot Stuff*, 210.

7. Jim Mason, *Richmond News Leader*, quoted in Nilsen, *Dance Music Sex Romance*, 65; Carr, "Prince: Dirty Mind," 39.

8. Waksman, *Instruments of Desire*, 5, 11.

9. Sanjek, "Tell Me Something I Don't Already Know."

10. Wald, "From Spirituals to Swing," 391. Mahon, *Right to Rock*, 148. Garofalo, "Crossing Over," 122.

11. Vincent, *Funk*, 103.

12. Murray, *Crosstown Traffic*, 103.

13. Mahon, *Right to Rock*, 173.

14. George, *Death of Rhythm and Blues*, 147–70.

15. Walker, *Rebels on the Air*, 124–25.

16. Hill, *Prince: A Pop Life*, 17. George, *Death of Rhythm and Blues*, 160, 173, 184.

17. Mahon, *Right to Rock*, 146–47.

18. Brooks, "Write to Rock," 56–57.

19. Vincent, *Funk*, 103–4, 111–19.

20. Vincent, *Funk*, 119.

21. Day and Ritz, *On Time*, 19.

22. Keller, "Portrait of the Artist as a Native Son."

23. Nilsen, Dance Music Sex Romance, 33–34.

24. Nilsen, *Dance Music Sex Romance*, 32–33; Badeaux, *Moments . . . Remembering Prince*, 18.

25. Middleton, *Studying Popular Music*, 174

26. *Billboard*, "Prince: Chart History."

27. Joki, interview with the author.

28. Walser, *Running with the Devil*, 46–47.

29. Walser, *Running with the Devil*, 43.

30. Cateforis, *Are We Not New Wave?*, 10–12.

31. Dickerson, *My Time with Prince*, 149, 170.

32. Nilsen, *Vault*, 29–31.

33. Hahn, *Possessed*, 43.

34. Hilburn, "Renegade Prince."

35. Halambos, *Soul Music*, 11, 62.

36. Swensson, *Got To Be Something Here*, ix–x.

37. Osgood, interview with the author.

38. Riemenschneider, *First Avenue*, 13–15.

39. Riemenschneider, *First Avenue*, 45–50.

40. Riemenschneider, *First Avenue*, 62, 66, 105, 108.

41. Joki, interview with the author.

42. Osgood, interview with the author.

43. Osgood, interview with the author.

44. Dickerson, *My Time with Prince*, 95–96.

45. Nilsen, *Dance Music Sex Romance*, 22.

46. Lordi, "Souls Intact," 61; Lordi, "Surviving the Hustle," 135.
47. Echols, *Hot Stuff*, 209; Frank, "Discophobia"; Marsh, "Flip Side of '79," 28.
48. Nilsen, *Vault*, 338.
49. Salewicz, "Strutting with the New Soul Monarch."
50. Schwartz, "Prince: A Dirty Mind Comes Clean."
51. Quoted in Nilsen, *Dance Music Sex Romance*, 61.
52. Barry Walters, "Prince Leads Black Pop through the Back Door," 116.
53. Cateforis, *Are We Not New Wave?*, 2, 37, 56.
54. Lordi, "Souls Intact," 57, 67.
55. Shin and Judson, "Beneath the Black Aesthetic," 248.
56. Brooks, "Write to Rock," 55.
57. Waksman, *Instruments of Desire*, 191–93; Christgau, *Grown Up All Wrong*, 92.
58. Waksman, *Instruments of Desire*, 192–206.
59. Andy Gill, "Ten Questions for Little Richard," 2–3.
60. Cateforis, *Are We Not New Wave?*, 20–44.
61. Cateforis, *Are We Not New Wave?*, 36.
62. Hill, *Prince: A Pop Life*, 83.
63. Nilsen, *Vault*, 24–47.
64. Nilsen, *Dance Music Sex Romance*, 115.
65. Cateforis, *Are We Not New Wave?*, 37.
66. Bream, "Stevie Nicks' New Whirl"; Light, *Let's Go Crazy*, 81.

Chapter 2

1. Kirby, "Something in the Water."
2. Mills, "Princelings."
3. Duffy, *Prince: The First Illustrated Biography*, 24–25.
4. Schwartz, "Prince: A Dirty Mind Comes Clean"; Salewicz, "Strutting with the New Soul Monarch."
5. Husney, *Famous People Who've Met Me*, 147.
6. Cateforis, *Are We Not New Wave?*, 162–63, 179–80.
7. Woodworth, "Synthesizers as Social Protest."
8. Spencer, "Numero Group's Jon Kirby on Purple Snow."
9. Brooks, *Bodies in Dissent*, 5.
10. Nilsen, *Dance Music Sex Romance*, 39–40.
11. Carr, "Prince: A One-Man Band and a Whole Chorus, Too."
12. George, *Death of Rhythm and Blues*, 147–170.
13. Rob Bowman, *Soulsville, U.S.A.*, 222.
14. Waksman, *Instruments of Desire*, 5.
15. Mahon, *Right to Rock*, 146–47, 173.
16. Pinch and Trocco, *Analog Days*, 308.
17. Brooks, *Bodies in Dissent*, 5.
18. Moog, "Minimoog," 145.

19. Fink, interview with the author.
20. Cateforis, *Are We Not New Wave?*, 2011, 158.
21. Théberge, *Any Sound You Can Imagine*, 52.
22. Cateforis, *Are We Not New Wave?*, 2011, 161.
23. Moog, "Oberheim SEM Module," 153.
24. Dumas, interview with the author, August 10, 2005.
25. Moog, "Oberheim SEM Module," 151–52.
26. Dumas, interview with the author, August 26, 2005; Moog, "Oberheim SEM Module," 153.
27. Fink, interview with the author; Bob Moog, "Oberheim SEM Module," 154.
28. Dumas, interview with the author, August 26, 2005.
29. Wesley, *Hit Me, Fred*, 250.
30. Dumas, interview with the author, August 26, 2005.
31. Dumas, interview with the author, August 26, 2005.
32. Dumas, interview with the author, August 26, 2005.
33. Wesley, *Hit Me, Fred*, 250.
34. Dumas, interview with the author, August 26, 2005.
35. Dumas, interview with the author, August 26, 2005.
36. Fink, interview with the author.
37. Kovarsky, "Art of Synth Soloing," 30; Doerschuk, "Bernie Worrell: Burning Down the House," 176.
38. Walser, *Running with the Devil*, 62–63; Cateforis, *Are We Not New Wave?*, 156–57.
39. Fink, interview with the author.
40. Dumas, interview with the author, August 26, 2005.
41. Bowman, "Stax Sound."
42. Bowman, "Stax Sound," 301, 306–7.
43. Bowman, "Stax Sound," 307.
44. Waksman, *Instruments of Desire*, 184.
45. Nilsen, *Dance Music Sex Romance*, 65.
46. Pinch and Trocco, *Analog Days*, 148.
47. Walser, *Running with the Devil*, 130.
48. Walser, *Running with the Devil*, 107–8; Cateforis, *Are We Not New Wave?*, 156.
49. Frith, "Art Versus Technology," 264–267; Théberge, *Any Sound You Can Imagine*, 111–12.
50. Pinch and Trocco, *Analog Days*, 132, 208, 248; Cateforis, *Are We Not New Wave?*, 156–158, 204; Vail, "Keith Emerson's Moog," 107–15.
51. Théberge, *Any Sound You Can Imagine*, 195.
52. Fink, *Repeating Ourselves*, 26, 35–37.
53. Huyssen, "Vamp and the Machine," 233.
54. Cateforis, *Are We Not New Wave?*, 93, 166, 176.
55. Fink, *Repeating Ourselves*, 45.
56. Lawrence, *Love Saves the Day*, 378. Echols, *Hot Stuff*, 209.
57. Cateforis, "Are We Not New Wave? Nostalgia, Technology and Exoticism," 201.
58. Lull, "Popular Music: Resistance to New Wave," 125.

98. Huyssen, "Vamp and the Machine," 226–28.

99. Haraway, "Cyber Manifesto," 149, 176; Halberstam, "Automating Gender," 440; Brooks, *Bodies in Dissent*, 3.

100. Brooks, *Bodies in Dissent*, 3.

101. Brooks, *Bodies in Dissent*, 6, 5.

102. Brooks, *Bodies in Dissent*, 4–6.

103. Théberge, *Any Sound You Can Imagine*, 75. Pinch and Trocco, *Analog Days*, 132.

104. Dumas, interview with the author, August 26, 2005.

105. Covino, "Grammars of Transgression," 355.

Chapter 3

1. Nilsen, *Dance Music Sex Romance*, 176.

2. Nilsen, *Dance Music Sex Romance*, 176.

3. Nilsen, *Vault*, 616–17.

4. Baltake, "Batty Prince on the Riviera," 47; *Detroit Free Press*, "Nervy Prince Returns with a Stylistic Smash," FTR 13A; Lovell, "This Star Needn't Be Borne Underneath Prince's New Clothes."

5. Hill, *Prince: A Pop Life*, 179.

6. Thorne, *Prince: The Man and His Music*, 130; Hill, *Prince: A Pop Life*, 184.

7. Baker, *Blues, Ideology, and Afro-American Literature*, 157, 184–98; Gates, *Signifying Monkey*, 5.

8. Guralnick, *Sweet Soul Music*, 13–14.

9. Radano, "Hot Fantasies," 459.

10. Radano, "Hot Fantasies," 459–63.

11. Southern, *Music of Black Americans*, 206–9; Wilson, "Significance of the Relationship," 6–8; Danielsen, *Presence and Pleasure*, 43–46; Stewart, "'Funky Drummer.'"

12. Chernoff, *African Rhythm and African Sensibility*; Waterman, "African Influence on the Music of the Americas."

13. Faulkner, "Does Jazz Put the Sin in Syncopation," 34.

14. Martin and Segrave, *Anti-Rock: The Opposition to Rock'n'Roll*, 41.

15. Radano, "Hot Fantasies," 462.

16. Agawu, "Structural Analysis or Cultural Analysis," 39–40.

17. Fink, "Goal-Directed Soul?"

18. Nilsen, *Dance Music Sex Romance*, 33–34.

19. Dickerson, *My Time with Prince*, 62.

20. Duffy, *Prince: The First Illustrated Biography*, 20–23; George, "Too Much 'Rain' Clouds Prince Show," 36; Swensson, *Prince: Guitar & Bass*, 41; Tucker, "Love and Lust in Minneapolis," 54.

21. Hill, *Prince: A Pop Life*, 174; Duffy, *Prince: The First Illustrated Biography*, 23.

22. Jeff Jensen, "Weird, Wonderful Return of Prince," 31.

23. Nilsen, *Dance Music Sex Romance*, 94.

24. Duffy, *Prince: The First Illustrated Biography*, 85.

25. Appiah, *Cosmopolitanism,* xiii, xvii–wviii.
26. Fabre, *From Harlem to Paris,* 2.
27. Muyumba, *Shadow and the Act,* ix–xi; Gilroy, *Against Race,* 287.
28. Muyumba, *Shadow and the Act,* 24; Neal, "'A Man Without a Country,'" 409.
29. Muyumba, *Shadow and the Act,* 5.
30. Giddins and DeVeaux, *Jazz,* 255–56, 318; Gillespie, "To Be or Not . . . to Bop," 157.
31. Spicer, "(Ac)Cumulative Form in Pop-Rock Music," 33.
32. Nilsen, *Vault,* 47–48, 341.
33. Nilsen, *Dance Music Sex Romance,* 170; Hahn, *Possessed,* 65, 113; Brown, *Prince in the Studio,* 89; Fink, interview with the author; Tudahl, *Prince and the Purple Rain Era Studio Sessions,* 273–75.
34. Nilsen, *Dance Music Sex Romance,* 135; Hahn, *Possessed,* 65.
35. Nilsen, *Dance Music Sex Romance,* 135; Tudahl, *Prince and the Purple Rain Era Studio Sessions,* 270–71.
36. Walser, "Prince as Queer Poststructuralist," 80.
37. Wilson, "Significance of the Relationship," 6–9, 11.
38. Stewart, "'Funky Drummer,'" 297–99, 313.
39. Danielsen, *Presence and Pleasure,* 73.
40. Butler, *Unlocking the Groove,* 106–7; Krebs, "Some Extensions," 103–5.
41. Danielsen, *Presence and Pleasure,* 44. Stewart, "'Funky Drummer,'" 293, 309.
42. Danielsen, *Presence and Pleasure,* 73–91, 115–18.
43. Danielsen, *Presence and Pleasure,* 61; Vincent, *Funk,* 13; Tudahl, 273.
44. Krebs, "Some Extensions," 101.
45. Butler, *Unlocking the Groove,* 85.
46. Butler, *Unlocking the Groove,* 82–84.
47. Mowitt, *Percussion,* 16, 150.
48. Butler, *Unlocking the Groove,* 88.
49. Agawu, "Structural Analysis or Cultural Analysis," 40; Fink, *Repeating Ourselves,* 183; Spicer, "(Ac)Cumulative Form in Pop-Rock Music," 33.
50. Danielsen, *Presence and Pleasure,* 71. Stewart, "'Funky Drummer,'" 311.
51. Danielsen, *Presence and Pleasure,* 155–56, 180.
52. Danielsen, *Presence and Pleasure,* 172–74, 194.
53. Danielsen, *Presence and Pleasure,* 147–49, 155.
54. Danielsen, *Presence and Pleasure,* 144–49. Fink, *Repeating Ourselves,* 185.
55. Butler, *Unlocking the Groove,* 221–24.
56. Nilsen, *Dance Music Sex Romance,* 135.
57. Agawu, "Invention of 'African Rhythm,'" 380.
58. Radano, "Hot Fantasies," 461.
59. Carr, "Prince: Dirty Mind," 38–39; Tucker, "Love and Lust in Minneapolis," 54.
60. Sigerson, "Prince Strips Down," 55.
61. Kelley, *Race Rebels,* 170.
62. Fink, *Repeating Ourselves,* 224.
63. Rose, *Black Noise,* 39.

64. Chernoff, *African Rhythm and African Sensibility*, 28.
65. Radano, "Hot Fantasies," 462.
66. Johnson, *Body in the Mind*, 119–20.
67. Mowitt, *Percussion*, 6–7.
68. Karol Berger, *Bach's Cycle, Mozart's Arrow*, 7–9.
69. McClary, *Conventional Wisdom*, 65, 67.
70. Fink, *Repeating Ourselves*, 180–81, 227.
71. Karlen, "Prince Talks," September 12, 1985, 30; Nelson George, "Rhythm & the Blues," 53.
72. Hahn, *Possessed*, 74–75.
73. Hahn, *Possessed*, 75–77; Hill, *Prince: A Pop Life*, 185–86; Takiff, "Album of Reasons to Rain on Prince's *Parade*," 39; Sigerson, "Prince Strips Down," 53, 55.
74. Gilroy, *Against Race*, 7.
75. *New Orleans Times-Picayune*, "Location of 'Jass,'" 8.
76. Lemke, *Primitivist Modernism*, 70; Ernst, "The Man Who Made a Lady out of Jazz (Paul Whiteman)," 39.
77. Early, *One Nation Under a Groove*, 4, 58.
78. Bowman, *Soulsville U.S.A.*, 151–52; Brewer, "String Musicians," 204.
79. Brewer, "String Musicians," 209–11.
80. Neal, "Sold Out on Soul," 123.
81. Fischer, interview with the author.
82. Fischer, interview with the author.
83. Hahn, *Possessed*, 93; Nilsen, *Dance Music Sex Romance*, 169–70.
84. Hahn, *Possessed*, 99; Leeds, interview with the author; Michael Bland (Ebonyrhythmbuddha), "interesting thesis, but i'm not sure i totally agree . . . [Reply no. 46, posted 05/09/06 5:36 a.m.]," comment on *Prince.org* thread "Bland is Back Part 2," April 16, 2006, http://prince.org/msg/5/185602
85. Fischer, interview with the author.
86. Butler, *Unlocking the Groove*, 169–70.
87. Krebs, "Some Extensions," 101–3.
88. Walser, "Rhythm, Rhyme, and Rhetoric," 214n20; Butler, *Unlocking the Groove*, 170.
89. Butler, *Unlocking the Groove*, 166.
90. Leonard Meyer, *Emotion and Meaning in Music*, 83–94.
91. Johnson, *Body in the Mind*, 119–21.
92. Nilsen, *Dance Music Sex Romance*, 188.
93. Fink, *Repeating Ourselves*, 199.
94. Butler, *Unlocking the Groove*, 115.
95. Eric Leeds, email message to author, August 24, 2008.
96. Kelly Fisher Lowe, *Words and Music of Frank Zappa*, 6.
97. Nilsen, *Vault*, 562, 704.
98. Fink, *Repeating Ourselves*, 186.
99. Johnson, *Body in the Mind*, 119–20.
100. Benjamin, *Arcades Project*, 10.
101. Appiah, *Cosmopolitanism*, xvii.
102. Fanon, *Black Skin, White Masks*, xiv–xv.

103. Fanon, *Black Skin, White Masks*, 92.
104. Gilroy, *Against Race*, 23, 46.
105. Redmond, "This Safer Space," 401.
106. Gilroy, *Against Race*, 281–82.
107. Gilroy, *Against Race*, 32.
108. Gilroy, *Against Race*, 280–81.
109. Gilroy, *Against Race*, 290, 294.
110. Kater, "Forbidden Fruit," 13, 38; Gilroy, *Against Race*, 298.
111. DuBois, *Souls of Black Folk*, 3; Redmond, "This Safer Space," 400; Brooks, *Bodies in Dissent*, 3–4.

Chapter 4

1. Nilsen, *Vault*, 76.
2. Hahn, *Possessed*, 72.
3. Nilsen, *Vault*, 86–88; Hahn, *Possessed*, 122; Nilsen, *Dance Music Sex Romance*, 243.
4. Hahn, *Possessed*, 123; Nilsen, *Dance Music Sex Romance*, 247–48.
5. Hahn, *Possessed*, 123; Nilsen, *Dance Music Sex Romance*, 247–48.
6. Prince, "Lovesexy 88 tour program," 4, 10.
7. Hawkins, "Prince: Harmonic Analysis of 'Anna Stesia,'" 325–35.
8. Hahn, *Possessed*, 164; Nilsen, *Dance Music Sex Romance*, 243–44.
9. Adler, Foote, and Sawhill, "Rap Attitude," 56; Gates et al., "Decoding Rap Music," 60; Rose, *Black Noise*, 15, 103–4.
10. Hawkins, "Prince: Harmonic Analysis of 'Anna Stesia,'" 332–34.
11. In one recorded performance of the Lovesexy tour from 1988, Prince sings most of "Eye No" in his chest voice, but his audience would have been aware of the album version of this song in which Prince sings entirely in falsetto.
12. Danielsen, "His Name Was Prince," 279.
13. Hawkins, "'Chelsea Rodgers' Was a Model," 296–97, 300–301, 304.
14. Hawkins and Niblock, *Prince: The Making of a Pop Music Phenomenon*, 161; Auslander, "Musical Personae," 103; Frith, *Performing Rites*, 212.
15. Scott, "Introduction," 27.
16. Wald, "From Spirituals to Swing," 399–400.
17. Lordi, "Souls Intact," 62–64.
18. Redmond, "This Safer Space," 401, 405–6.
19. Eidsheim, *Race of Sound*, 6–9, 11, 27, 30.
20. Eidsheim, *Race of Sound*, 6–7, 30.
21. Eidsheim, *Race of Sound*, 30.
22. Eidsheim, *Race of Sound*, 33.
23. Giles, *History and Technique of the Counter-Tenor*, 168.
24. Nilsen, *Vault*, 363; *Billboard*, "Prince: Chart History."
25. Fink, "Goal-Directed Soul?"
26. Holland, "Purple Passion," 92–93.
27. Walser, "Prince as Queer Poststructuralist," 86.

28. Walser, "Prince as Queer Poststructuralist," 86.

29. Dame, "Unveiled Voices," 140.

30. Large, Iwata, and von Leden, "Male Operatic Head Register," 26; Large, "Towards an Integrated Physiologic-Acoustic Theory," 19.

31. Bergeron, "Castrato as History," 172–73.

32. François, "Fakin' It / Makin' It," 446–47; Hughes, "In the Empire of the Beat," 153–54.

33. Fink, *Repeating Ourselves*, 42, 245n56.

34. François, "Fakin' It / Makin' It," 443.

35. Echols, *Hot Stuff*, 209.

36. Echols, *Hot Stuff*, 39–41.

37. Fast, *In the Houses of the Holy*, 45, 47, 160–67.

38. Walser, *Running with the Devil*, 108, 128–36.

39. Guzman et al., "Laryngoscopic, Acoustic, Perceptual, and Functional Assessment of Voice in Rock Singers," 253.

40. Walser, *Running*, 42.

41. Nilsen, *Vault*, 32.

42. Nilsen, *Dance Music Sex Romance*, 32–33, 35. Hahn, *Possessed*, 21.

43. Miller, "Prince's Hot Rock," 23.

44. Hahn, *Possessed*, 33.

45. Hill, *Prince: A Pop Life*, 3; Hahn, *Possessed*, 33.

46. Eidsheim, *Race of Sound*, 107; Heilbut, *Fan Who Knew Too Much*, 253.

47. *Billboard*, "Hot Soul Singles."

48. Werner, *Change Is Gonna Come*, 278.

49. Boyer, *Golden Age of Gospel*, 12–26; Lincoln and Mamiya, *Black Church in the African American Experience*, 363–64.

50. Boyer, "Contemporary Gospel Music," 23; Wilson, "Heterogeneous Sound Ideal in African-American Music"; Floyd, *Power of Black Music*, 78.

51. Boyer, "Contemporary Gospel Music," 24.

52. Floyd, *Power of Black Music*, 197.

53. Boyer, "Contemporary Gospel Music," 23–31. Heilbut, *Gospel Sound*, 10.

54. Synan, *Holiness-Pentacostal Movement*, 165–68; Floyd, *Power of Black Music*, 63; Boyer, *Golden Age of Gospel*, 5–58.

55. Acts 2:3–4: "And there appeared unto them cloven tongues like as of fire, and it sat upon each of them. And they were all filled with the Holy Ghost, and began to speak with other tongues, as the Spirit gave them utterance" (Authorized King James Version).

56. Synan, *Holiness-Pentacostal Movement*, 105, 122.

57. Holland, "Purple Passion,"92–3.

58. Fink, "Goal-Directed Soul."

59. Hammer, *Please Hammer, Don't Hurt 'Em.*

60. Walser, "Prince as Queer Poststructuralist," 86.

61. Walser, "Prince as Queer Poststructuralist," 86.

62. Garofalo, *Rockin' Out*, 116–21.

63. Boyer, "Contemporary Gospel Music," 8.

64. Boyer, "Contemporary Gospel Music," 22; Lincoln and Mamiya, *Black Church in the African American Experience*, 378.

65. Weekes, "This House, This Music," 45; Synan, *Holiness-Pentacostal Movement*, 166, 177.
66. Boyer, "Contemporary Gospel Music," 9; Synan, *Holiness-Pentacostal Movement*, 177.
67. Lincoln and Mamiya, *Black Church in the African American Experience*, 223, 335.
68. Hamilton, "Sexual Politics and African-American Music," 168.
69. Retzloff, "'Seer or Queer?,'" 287.
70. Retzloff, "'Seer or Queer?,'" 287.
71. Retzloff, "'Seer or Queer?,'" 274, 281.
72. Retzloff, "'Seer or Queer?,'" 286.
73. Hamilton, "Sexual Politics and African-American Music," 174.
74. Hamilton, "Sexual Politics and African-American Music," 173.
75. Floyd, *Power of Black Music*, 180; Tucker, "'Tell Tchaikovsky the News,'" 286.
76. Ward, *Just My Soul Responding*, 190. Hamilton, "Sexual Politics and African-American Music," 174.
77. Hamilton, "Sexual Politics and African-American Music," 174.
78. Lott, *Love and Theft*, 26, 51–55.
79. Hamilton, "Sexual Politics and African-American Music," 174.
80. Hamilton, "Sexual Politics and African-American Music," 173.
81. Retzloff, "'Seer or Queer?,'" 286–87.
82. Retzloff, "'Seer or Queer?,'" 288; Hamilton, "Sexual Politics and African-American Music," 174.
83. Tucker, "'Tell Tchaikovsky the News,'" 286; Hamilton, "Sexual Politics and African-American Music," 173.
84. George, *Death of Rhythm and Blues*, 174.
85. Quoted in Garber, *Vested Interests*, 273–74.
86. Garber, *Vested Interests*, 271, 274.
87. Raboteau, *Slave Religion*, 59–61, 64–65.
88. Danielsen, "His Name Was Prince," 279.
89. Gates, *Signifying Monkey*, 127–169.
90. Quoted in Hill, *Prince: A Pop Life*, 100; Nilsen, *Dance Music Sex Romance*, 248.
91. Greenman, "Prince: *The Rainbow Children*," 112; Gundersen, "R&B Stars Pump Out New Disks," D05.
92. Berger, "*Rainbow Children*," 50.
93. Weingarten, "The Week: Prince," 82.
94. Phipps, "Prince: *The Rainbow Children*."
95. Dery, "Black to the Future," 180–182.
96. McLeod, "Space Oddities," 341–42.
97. Rollefson, "'Robot Voodoo Power' Thesis," 104–5.
98. Mills, *George Clinton and P-Funk*, 88.
99. Bowman, "On the One," 273.
100. Reed, *Holy Profane*, 141–42; Mills, *George Clinton and P-Funk*, 98, 101.
101. Corbett, *Extended Play*, 7, 17; Kelley, *Freedom Dreams*, 16, 31–32.
102. Lieb, *Children of Ezekiel*, 75; Gates, *Signifying Monkey*, 60.

103. Lieb, *Children of Ezekiel*, 1–4, 11, 13, 148.

104. Kelley, *Freedom Dreams*, 23–24; Szwed, *Space Is the Place*, 64, 71.

105. According to religious historians Eric Lincoln and Lawrence Mamiya, the seven major denominations that constitute the historical "Black Church" are "the African Methodist Episcopal (A.M.E.) Church; the African Methodist Episcopal Zion (A.M.E.Z.) Church; the Christian Methodist Episcopal (C.M.E.) Church; the National Baptist Convention, U.W.A., Incorporated (NBC); the National Baptist Convention of America, Unincorporated (NBCA); the Progressive National Baptist Convention (PNBC); and the Church of God in Christ (COGIC)." Lincoln and Mamiya, *Black Church in the African American Experience*, 1, 389.

106. Lieb, *Children of Ezekiel*, 147–48.

107. Holden, *Jehovah's Witnesses*, 11.

108. Kosmin, Mayer, and Keysar, *American Religious Identification Survey*, 12; Grieco and Cassidy, *Overview of Race and Hispanic Origin*, 3.

109. Lieb, *Children of Ezekiel*, 11.

110. Levine, *Black Culture and Black Consciousness*, 175.

111. Hahn, *Possessed*, 221; Nilsen, *Vault*, 583–84.

112. Bloom, *American Religion*, 71.

113. Lieb, *Children of Ezekiel*, 75.

114. Bloom, *American Religion*, 152.

115. Lieb, *Children of Ezekiel*, 81.

116. Greenman, "Prince: *The Rainbow Children*," 112.

117. Shemo, "Prince of a Guy"; Jean Hopfensperger, "'We Lost a Spiritual Brother' in Prince."

118. Danielsen, *Presence and Pleasure*, 11–12, 144–50.

119. DeCurtis, "Free at Last," 63.

120. Twila Perry, "'Let's Work!'"

121. Holden, *Jehovah's Witnesses*, 151, 187.

122. Holden, *Jehovah's Witnesses*, 26, 44.

123. Reynaud and Graffard, *Jehovah's Witnesses and the Nazis*, 92.

124. Jefferson, *Notes on the State of Virginia*, 170.

125. King, "I Have a Dream."

126. *Watchtower*, "Truth About Armageddon."

127. Hunter and Davis, "Constructing Gender," 468.

128. Samuels, "Rap on Rap," 147–53.

129. Garber, *Vested Interests*, 267–268.

130. Garber, *Vested Interests*, 267–268.

131. Garber, *Vested Interests*, 274.

132. Hoffman, "Home Visit," 44.

133. LaForce, "Behind the Scenes."

Chapter 5

1. Nilsen, *Dance Music Sex Romance*, 251.

2. Cazares, "Flashback."

3. Cole, "Interview: Alan Leeds"; Cole, *Last Miles.*
4. Leeds, interview with the author.
5. Cole, *Last Miles,* 226–31.
6. Eric Leeds, interview with the author.
7. Nilsen, *Dance Music Sex Romance,* 31, 39–40.
8. Walser, "Prince as Queer Poststructuralist," 80.
9. Hoffman, "Home Visit," 42–44.
10. Nilsen, *Dance Music Sex Romance,* 25.
11. Hahn, *Possessed,* 85–86; Mills, "Princelings," E3; Nilsen, *Dance Music Sex Romance,* 158.
12. Nilsen, *Vault,* 335–426. Leeds, interview with the author.
13. Hawkins and Niblock, *Prince: The Making of a Pop Music Phenomenon,* 39, 41.
14. Hahn, *Possessed,* 6.
15. Nilsen, *Dance Music Sex Romance,* 15.
16. Karlen, "Prince Talks," September 12, 1985, 26.
17. George Cole, "Interview: Alan Leeds."
18. Hahn, *Possessed,* 175; Cole, *Last Miles,* 230, 319–21, 403.
19. Nilsen, *Dance Music Sex Romance,* 38.
20. Jones, *Purple Reign,* 41.
21. Nilsen, *Dance Music Sex Romance,* 276.
22. Coryat, "His Highness Gets Down," 42.
23. Nilsen, *Dance Music Sex Romance,* 131.
24. Brown and Tucker, *James Brown,* 264.
25. Leeds, "James Brown and His First Family of Soul," 299.
26. Leeds, interview with the author.
27. Leeds, interview with the author.
28. Bloom, *Anxiety of Influence,* xxii, 8.
29. Bloom, *Anxiety of Influence,* xxiii, 3–18.
30. Leeds, interview with the author.
31. Gabbard, *Hotter Than That,* 62; McLeod, "Construction of Masculinity," 16.
32. Miller, "Moan within the Tone," 156–58.
33. Nilsen, *Dance Music Sex Romance,* 33–34.
34. Karlen, "Prince Talks," 30; Mahon, *Right to Rock,* 173.
35. Karlen, "Prince Talks," 30.
36. Hahn, *Possessed,* 95.
37. Wesley, *Hit Me, Fred,* 250–51.
38. Nilsen, *Dance Music Sex Romance,* 169.
39. Ro, *Prince: Inside the Music and the Masks,* 146.
40. Nilsen, *Dance Music Sex Romance,* 237.
41. Leeds, interview with the author.
42. Loder, "Prince's Baffling Brilliance," 146.
43. Bowman, "Stax Sound," 303.
44. Danielsen, *Presence and Pleasure,* 172–73; Butler, *Unlocking the Groove,* 203, 221–22.
45. Nilsen *Dance Music Sex Romance,* 216–17; Foucault, "Introduction," xi–xiii.

46. Gates, *Signifying Monkey*, xxvii–xxviii.

47. Prince, liner notes to *Sign 'O' The Times*, Warner Bros. 9 25577-2.

48. Danielsen, *Presence and Pleasure*, 71, 88–91.

49. Leeds, interview with the author.

50. Eric Leeds, email to the author, November 18, 2007.

51. Meyer, *Emotion and Meaning in Music*, 87, 151.

52. Leeds, interview with the author.

53. Danielsen, *Presence and Pleasure*, 71.

54. Gates, *Signifying Monkey*, 121.

55. Neal, *New Black Man*, 3, 41–42.

56. Gray, "Black Masculinity and Visual Culture," 401; McLeod, "Construction of Masculinity," 213.

57. Smith, *One: The Life and Times of James Brown*, 221.

58. Walser, "Prince as Queer Poststructuralist," 85; Holland, "Purple Passion," 91; Hawkins, *Settling the Pop Score*, 169.

59. Garber, *Vested Interests*, 295–96; Fuchs, "'I Wanna Be Your Fantasy,'" 143, 145; Hawkins and Niblock, *Prince: The Making of a Pop Music Phenomenon*, 3.

60. George, *Death of Rhythm and Blues*, 174; Garber, *Vested Interests*, 273–74.

61. Shin and Judson, "Beneath the Black Aesthetic," 250; Reid-Pharr, "It's Raining Men," 36, 38.

62. Gilroy, *Against Race*, 178, 196–97.

63. Neal, *New Black Man*, 3, 8, 41–42.

64. Perchard, "Hip Hop Samples Jazz," 283–84.

65. Kelley, *Race Rebels*, 183–228.

66. Gates et al., "Decoding Rap Music," 60; Adler, Foote, and Sawhill, "Rap Attitude," 56.

67. Neal, *New Black Man*, 15–16.

68. Leland et al., "Gangsta Rap and the Culture of Violence," 60; Quinn, "'Never Shoulda Been Let out the Penitentiary.'"

69. Hahn, *Possessed*, 164; Nilsen, *Dance Music Sex Romance*, 243–44.

70. Touré, "You Can Call Him Prince," 262.

71. Sims, "Gangster Rappers," A3.

72. George, *Hip Hop America*, 114–18; Browne, "Fade to 'Black,'" 70–71.

73. Hahn, *Possessed*, 128.

74. Woodworth, "'Rapping Done Let Us Down,'" 282.

75. Walser, "Rhythm, Rhyme, and Rhetoric."

76. Sandow, "Prince Mix-A-Lot," 62.

77. Light, "*Diamonds and Pearls*: Prince and the New Power Generation," 92; Bream, "Prince Album Is a Royal Disappointment," 1F.

78. Nelson, interview with the author.

79. Leeds, interview with the author.

80. Considine, "[*Love Symbol Album*], Prince and the N.P.G.," 70–71; Takiff, "Prince Is Still King," 35.

81. Neal, *New Black Man*, 3.

82. Neal, *New Black Man*, 3.

83. Fuchs, "'I Wanna Be Your Fantasy,'" 143.

84. Walser, "Rhythm, Rhyme, and Rhetoric," 199–203.

59. Cohen, "Human League."

60. Snowden, "Moog on the State of the Synthesizer," 22, 26, 32.

61. Freud, *Civilization and Its Discontents*, 42; Jain, "Prosthetic Imagination"; Theweleit, *Male Fantasies*, 257.

62. Huyssen, "Vamp and the Machine," 226.

63. Halberstam, "Automating Gender," 444–45.

64. Jentsch, "On the Psychology of the Uncanny."

65. Freud et al., "Fiction and Its Phantoms," 536.

66. Mori, "Uncanny Valley," 99–100.

67. Brooks, *Bodies in Dissent*, 3.

68. Hawkins and Niblock, *Prince: The Making of a Pop Music Phenomenon*, 41.

69. Hawkins and Niblock, *Prince: The Making of a Pop Music Phenomenon*, 41, 42.

70. Penman, "Prince: Lyceum, London."

71. Miller, "Prince's Hot Rock," 23; Hoskyns, "Prince: A Second Coming thru Purple Haze."

72. McLeod, "Space Oddities," 348. Cateforis, "Performing the Avant-Garde Groove," 565.

73. Vincent, *Funk*, 4.

74. Salewicz, "Strutting with the New Soul Monarch."

75. Haraway, "Cyborg Manifesto," 149–81.

76. McLeod, *Driving Identities*, 34, 64–65.

77. Fink, interview with the author.

78. Mowitt, *Percussion*, 150.

79. Dumas, interview with the author, November 29, 2005.

80. Fink, interview with the author.

81. Cateforis, *Are We Not New Wave?*, 171–76.

82. Tucker, "Love and Lust in Minneapolis," 54.

83. McClary, *Feminine Endings*, 12.

84. Nilsen, *Dance Music Sex Romance*, 62.

85. Hahn, *Possessed*, 38; Tucker, "Love and Lust in Minneapolis," 54–55; Holden, "Sex and Society," 51–52.

86. Walser, "Prince as Queer Poststructuralist."

87. Deleuze and Guattari, *Anti-Oedipus*, 1–8. Theweleit, *Male Fantasies*, 211–12, 256.

88. Theweleit, *Male Fantasies*, 256.

89. Cateforis, "Performing the Avant-Garde Groove," 566–68.

90. Wilson, "Black Music as an Art Form," 3.

91. Brown, *Prince in the Studio*, 71, 73.

92. Fink, interview with the author.

93. McLeod, *Driving Identities*, 35.

94. Mori, "Uncanny Valley," 99.

95. Spicer, "(Ac)Cumulative Form in Pop-Rock Music," 33; Luis-Manuel Garcia, "On and On," 7; McClary, *Feminine Endings*, 12.

96. Walser, "Prince as Queer Poststructuralist," 83–85. Fink, *Repeating Ourselves*, 45.

97. Theweleit, *Male Fantasies*, 208.

85. Nelson, interview with the author.
86. Mowitt, *Percussion*, 9, 138, 140–43.
87. Narmour, *Analysis and Cognition of Melodic Complexity*, 3–4.
88. Nelson, interview with the author.
89. Waksman, *Instruments of Desire*, 14–15; Nelson, interview with the author.
90. Neal, *New Black Man*, 21–22.
91. Reid-Pharr, "It's Raining Men," 36.
92. Rose, *Black Noise*, 39.
93. Neal, *New Black Man*, 9–10, 17–18.
94. Eric Leeds, email to the author, September 22, 2007.
95. *Housequake*, "Interview with Greg Boyer."
96. Nelson, interview with the author.
97. Ake, *Jazz Cultures*, 64.
98. Nicholson, *Is Jazz Dead?*; DeVeaux, "Constructing the Jazz Tradition"; Walser, *Keeping Time*, 332.
99. Perchard, "Hip Hop Samples Jazz," 295–96.
100. Hawkins and Niblock, *Prince: The Making of a Pop Music Phenomenon*, 47, 53.
101. Leeds, interview with the author.
102. Baskerville, "Free Jazz," 486.
103. Baskerville, "Free Jazz," 295; Johnson, "Hear Me Talkin' to Ya."
104. Rosenthal, "Jazz in the Ghetto," 52–53.
105. Ramsey, *Race Music*, 74.
106. Davis and Troupe, *Miles: The Autobiography*, 205.

Conclusion

1. Hawkins and Niblock, *Prince: The Making of a Pop Music Phenomenon*, 15.
2. Coscarelli, "Prince Announces Memoir Planned for 2017," C3.
3. Hill, *Prince: A Pop Life*, 71–73; Nilsen, *Dance Music Sex Romance*, 7; Ro, *Prince: Inside the Music and the Masks*, 69.
4. Nilsen, *Vault*, 30.
5. Deevoy, "Pleased to Meet You . . . ," 54. Baumgold, "Glitter Slave," 100.
6. Wall, *Prince: Purple Reign* (New York: Hachette, 2016), 151.
7. Piepenbring, "Beautiful One," 28–34.
8. Prince, *Beautiful Ones*, 16, 79, 97.
9. Prince, *Beautiful Ones*, 32, 18.
10. Prince, *Beautiful Ones*, 94.
11. Prince, *Beautiful Ones*, 32, 117.
12. Prince, *Beautiful Ones*, 17.
13. Prince, *Beautiful Ones*, 47.
14. Prince, *Beautiful Ones*, 16, 7.
15. Prince, *Beautiful Ones*, 7, 9.
16. Nilsen, *Vault*, 187.
17. Nilsen, *Vault*, 188.

18. Robair, "Rhapsody in Purple," *Keyboard,* 12.

19. Bream, "Prince Gets Personal."

20. Terrace, "692 *Batman,*" 77; Terrace, "5725 *The Man from U.N.C.L.E.,*" 650.

21. Setlist.fm, "Songs Played by Tour: Piano & a Microphone."

22. Guerrasio, "Secret Letter Prince Wrote."

23. Harris, "Prince Stuns."

24. Setlist.fm, "Songs Played by Tour: Piano & a Microphone."

25. Setlist.fm, "Songs Played by Tour: Piano & a Microphone."

26. Setlist.fm, "Songs Played by Tour: Piano & a Microphone."

27. Swensson, *Prince Paisley Park Archives,* 23.

28. Nilsen, *Vault,* 193

29. Swensson, *Prince Paisley Park Archives,* 63.

30. Garcia et al., "Who We Are."

31. Swensson, *Prince Paisley Park Archives,* 77.

32. Andrea Swensson, "Brief History of Paisley Park's Celebrations."

33. Swensson, *Prince Paisley Park Archives,* 89.

34. Swensson, *Prince Paisley Park Archives,* 89.

35. Lordi, "Surviving the Hustle," 132.

36. Clerc, *Prince: All the Songs,* 298, 300, 306; Nilsen, *Vault,* 193, 195.

37. Nilsen, *Vault,* 288. Iman Jafri, "House and Studio Are Gone"; Gabler, "200 Homes to Be Built."

38. Hawkins and Niblock, *Prince: The Making of a Pop Music Phenomenon,* 43–44.

39. Nilsen, *Vault,* 193–94; Perry, "Prince: Double-Consciousness in Expressing the Value of Work," 208; Ed Christman, "Prince's Revolution," 4.

40. Perry, "Prince: Double-Consciousness in Expressing the Value of Work," 205–6; Pareles, "Re-Inventor of His World and Himself," H34.

41. Christman, "Prince's Revolution," 4.

42. Mitchell, "Black Artists," 89–90.

43. Jennings, "Story Behind Prince's Influence Wall."

44. Cummings, "Prince: Introduction of a New Breed Leader," 171.

45. Estate of Prince Rogers Nelson, "Celebration 2023."

46. Blair, interview with the author.

Bibliography

Adler, Jerry, Jennifer Foote, and Ray Sawhill. "The Rap Attitude." *Newsweek*, March 19, 1990, 56.

Adorno, Theodor. *Aesthetic Theory*. Edited by Gretel Adorno and Rolf Tiedermann. Translated by Robert Hullot-Kentor. Minneapolis: University of Minnesota Press, 1997.

Adorno, Theodor, and Max Horkheimer. "The Culture Industry: Enlightenment as Mass Deception." In *Dialectic of Enlightenment*, translated by John Cumming, 120–67. New York: Herder and Herder, 1972.

Agawu, Kofi. "The Invention of 'African Rhythm.'" *Journal of the American Musicological Society* 48, no. 3 (Autumn 1995): 380–95.

Agawu, Kofi. "Structural Analysis or Cultural Analysis? Competing Perspectives on the 'Standard Pattern' of West African Rhythm." *Journal of the American Musicological Society* 59, no. 1 (Spring 2006): 1–46.

Ake, David. *Jazz Cultures*. Los Angeles: University of California Press, 2002.

Appiah, Kwame Anthony. *Cosmopolitanism: Ethics in a World of Strangers*. New York: W.W. Norton, 2006.

Auslander, Philip. "Musical Personae," *The Drama Review* 50, no. 1 (Spring 2006): 100–119.

Badeaux, Marylou. *Moments . . . Remembering Prince*. Marylou Badeaux, 2018.

Baker, Houston A., Jr. *Blues, Ideology, and Afro-American Literature: A Vernacular Theory*. Chicago: University of Chicago Press, 1984.

Baltake, Joe. "A Batty Prince on the Riviera." *Philadelphia Daily News*, July 3, 1986, 47.

Baskerville, John. "Free Jazz: A Reflection of Black Power Ideology." *Journal of Black Studies* 24, no. 4 (June 1994): 484–97.

Baumgold, Julie. "Glitter Slave." *Esquire Gentleman*, Fall 1995, 100–105.

Benjamin, Walter. *The Arcades Project*. Translated by Howard Eiland and Kevin McLaughlin. Cambridge, MA: Harvard University Press, 1999.

Berger, Arion. "*The Rainbow Children*." *Rolling Stone*, January 17, 2002, 50.

Berger, Karol. *Bach's Cycle, Mozart's Arrow: An Essay on the Origins of Musical Modernity*. Los Angeles: University of California Press, 2007.

Bergeron, Katherine. "The Castrato as History." *Cambridge Opera Journal* 8, no. 2 (July 1996): 167–84.

Billboard. "Hot Soul Singles." October 13, 1979, 50. Available at: https://books.google.com/books?id=FCQEAAAAMBAJ&lpg=PP1&dq=billboard%20magazine%20oct%2013%201979&pg=PP1#v=onepage&q=billboard%20magazine%20oct%2013%201979&f=false

Billboard. "Prince: Chart History." N.d. https://www.billboard.com/music/prince/chart-history, accessed June 19, 2019.

Billboard. "Stations by Format: Minneapolis-St. Paul." July 10, 1965, 38–39.

Blair, Paula. (Of Winnipeg, Manitoba). Interview with the author. Chanhassan, MN, June 10, 2023.

Bloom, Harold. *The American Religion: The Emergence of the Post-Christian Nation.* New York: Simon & Schuster, 1992.

Bloom, Harold *The Anxiety of Influence: A Theory of Poetry.* New York: Oxford University Press, 1997.

Bowman, Rob. "On the One: Parliament/Funkadelic, the Mothership, and Transformation." In *Music Traditions, Cultures, and Contexts,* edited by Robin Elliott and Gordon E. Smith, 271–80. Waterloo, ON: Wilfrid Laurier University Press, 2010.

Bowman, Rob. *Soulsville U.S.A.: The Story of Stax Records.* New York: Schirmer, 1997.

Bowman, Rob. "The Stax Sound: A Musicological Analysis." *Popular Music* 14, no. 3 (October 1995): 285–320.

Boyer, Horace Clarence. "Contemporary Gospel Music." *Black Perspective in Music* 7, no. 1 (Spring 1979): 5–58.

Boyer, Horace Clarence. *The Golden Age of Gospel.* Chicago: University of Illinois Press, 1995.

Brackett, David. *Categorizing Sound: Genre and Twentieth-Century Popular Music.* Los Angeles: University of California Press, 2016.

Bream, Jon. "Prince Album Is a Royal Disappointment." *Minneapolis Star Tribune,* October 11, 1992, 1F.

Bream, Jon. "Prince Gets Personal in his First-Ever Solo Show." *Minneapolis Star Tribune,* Jan. 22, 2016. https://www.startribune.com/prince-gets-personal-in-his-first-ever-solo-show/366176091/

Bream, Jon. *Prince: Inside the Purple Reign.* New York: Collier, 1984.

Bream, Jon. "Stevie Nicks' New Whirl." *Minneapolis Star Tribune.* August 23, 2011. http://www.startribune.com/stevie-nicks-new-whirl/128097743/, accessed June 20, 2019.

Brewer, Roy. "String Musicians in the Recording Studios of Memphis, Tennessee." *Popular Music* 19, no. 2 (April 2000): 201–15.

Brooks, Daphne. "'All That You Can't Leave Behind': Black Female Soul Singing and the Politics of Surrogation in the Age of Catastrophe." *Meridians* 8, no. 1 (2008): 180–204.

Brooks, Daphne. *Bodies in Dissent: Spectacular Performances of Race and Freedom, 1850–1910.* Durham, NC: Duke University Press, 2006.

Brooks, Daphne. "Everybody Still Wants to Fly." Program book for *Sign o' the Times (Super Deluxe Edition).* NPG Records / Warner Records B08BMSF4XT, 2020, 8 CDs and 1 DVD.

Brooks, Daphne. "'This Voice Which Is Not One': Amy Winehouse Sings the Ballad of Sonic Blue(s)face Culture." *Women & Performance* 20, no. 1 (March 2010): 37–60.

Brooks, Daphne. "The Write to Rock: Racial Mythologies, Feminist Theory, and the Pleasures of Rock Criticism." *Women & Music,* no. 12 (2008): 54–62.

Brown, Jake. *Prince in the Studio (1975–1995): Volume One.* Los Angeles: Colossus, 2010.

Brown, James, and Bruce Tucker. *James Brown: The Godfather of Soul.* New York: Da Capo Press, 2003.

Browne, David. "Fade to 'Black.'" *Entertainment Weekly,* December 2, 1994, 70–71.

Browne, David. "Prince's Legacy: Inside the Messy Battle." *Rolling Stone,* September 20, 2016, http://www.rollingstone.com/music/news/princes-legacy-inside-the-messy-battle-w440966

Butler, Mark. *Unlocking the Groove: Rhythm, Meter, and Musical Design in Electronic Dance Music.* Bloomington: Indiana University Press, 2006.

Carbado, Devon W., Kimberlé Williams Crenshaw, Vickie M Mays, and Barbara Tomlinson. "Intersectionality: Mapping the Movements of a Theory." *DuBois Review* 10, no. 2 (2013): 303–12.

Carr, Roy. "Prince: Dirty Mind." *New Musical Express,* November 29, 1980, 38–39.

Carr, Tim. "Prince: A One-Man Band and a Whole Chorus, Too." *Minneapolis Tribune,* April 30, 1978, 1D, 7D, 8D.

Case, Wesley. "Prince Touched Baltimore with Concert, Song after Freddie Gray's Death, Unrest." *Baltimore Sun,* April 21, 2016, https://www.baltimoresun.com/2016/04/21/prince-touched-baltimore-with-concert-song-after-freddie-grays-death-unrest/, accessed May 22, 2019.

Cateforis, Theo. *Are We Not New Wave? Modern Pop at the Turn of the 1980s.* Ann Arbor: University of Michigan Press, 2011.

Cateforis, Theo. "Are We Not New Wave? Nostalgia, Technology, and Exoticism in Popular Music at the Turn of the 1980s." PhD diss., SUNY Stony Brook, May 2000.

Cateforis, Theo. "Performing the Avant-Garde Groove: Devo and the Whiteness of New Wave." *American Music* 22, no. 4 (Winter 2004): 564–88.

Cazares, Simone. "Flashback: When Miles Davis Played with Prince at Paisley Park." *The Current (blog),* February 8, 2018, https://blog.thecurrent.org/2018/02/flashback-when-miles-davis-played-with-prince-at-paisley-park/, accessed June 13, 2019.

Chapman, Reg. "Prince's Countless Charitable Activities Come to Light After his Death." *CBS Minnesota,* April 26, 2016, https://minnesota.cbslocal.com/2016/04/26/prince-charity-donations/, accessed May 20, 2019.

Chernoff, John Miller. *African Rhythm and African Sensibility.* Chicago: University of Chicago Press, 1979.

Christgau, Robert. *Grown Up All Wrong: 75 Great Rock and Pop Artists from Vaudeville to Techno.* Cambridge, MA: Harvard University Press, 1998.

Christman, Ed. "Prince's Revolution." *Billboard,* May 3, 2014, 4.

Clerc, Benoît. *Prince: All the Songs.* London: Mitchell Beazley, 2022.

Cohen, Mitchell. "The Human League: Dare." *Creem,* June 1982, available at https://www.rocksbackpages.com/Library/Article/the-human-league-idarei, accessed May 20, 2014.

Cole, George. "Interview: Alan Leeds." *The Last Miles: The Music of Miles Davis, 1980–1991*, n.d., http://thelastmiles.com/interviews-alan-leeds.php, accessed May 3, 2008.

Cole, George. *The Last Miles: The Music of Miles Davis, 1980–1991*. Ann Arbor: University of Michigan Press, 2005.

Considine, JD. "[*Love Symbol Album*], Prince and the N.P.G." *Rolling Stone*, November 26, 1992, 70–71.

Corbett, John. *Extended Play: Sounding Off from John Cage to Dr. Funkenstein*. Durham, NC: Duke University Press, 1994.

Coryat, Karl. "His Highness Gets Down." *Bass Player*, November 1999, 36–37, 40–44, 46, 74.

Coscarelli, Joe. "Prince Announces Memoir Planned for 2017." *New York Times*, March 21, 2016, C3.

Covino, William A. "Grammars of Transgression: Golems, Cyborgs, and Mutants." *Rhetoric Review* 14, no. 2 (1996): 355–73.

Crenshaw, Kimberlé. "Demarginalizing the Intersection of Race and Sex: A Black Feminist Critique of Antidiscrimination Doctrine, Feminist Theory, and Antiracist Politics." *University of Chicago Legal Forum* 1989, no. 8 (1989): 139–67.

Cummings, Kamilah. "Prince: Introduction of a New Breed Leader." In *Prince and Popular Music: Critical Perspectives on an Interdisciplinary Life*, edited by Mike Alleyne and Kirsty Fairclough, 161–74. New York: Bloomsbury, 2020.

Dame, Joke. "Unveiled Voices: Sexual Difference and the Castrato." In *Queering the Pitch: The New Gay and Lesbian Musicology*, edited by Philip Brett, Elizabeth Wood, and Gary C. Thomas, 139–53. New York: Routledge, 1994.

Danielsen, Anne. "His Name Was Prince: A Study of *Diamonds and Pearls*." *Popular Music* 16, no. 3 (October 1997): 275–91.

Danielsen, Anne. *Presence and Pleasure: The Funk Grooves of James Brown and Parliament*. Middletown, CT: Wesleyan University Press, 2006.

Davis, Miles, and Quincy Troupe. *Miles: The Autobiography*. New York: Simon & Schuster, 1989.

Day, Morris, and David Ritz. *On Time: A Princely Life in Funk*. New York: Da Capo Press, 2019.

Dean, Patty. "MHS Collections: PunkFunkRockPop." *Minnesota History* 58, no. 1 (2002): 29–39.

DeCurtis, Anthony. "Free at Last." *Rolling Stone*, November 28, 1996, 61–63, 148.

Deevoy, Adrian. "Pleased to Meet You . . ." *Q Magazine*, July 1994, 54, 93–94.

Deleuze, Gilles, and Felix Guattari. *Anti-Oedipus: Capitalism and Schizophrenia*. Translated by Robert Hurley, Mark Seem, and Helen R Lane. Minneapolis, MN: University of Minnesota Press, 1983.

Dery, Mark. "Black to the Future: Interviews with Samuel R. Delany, Greg Tate, and Tricia Rose." In *Flame Wars: The Discourse of Cyberculture*, edited by Mark Dery, 179–222. Durham, NC: Duke University Press, 1994.

Detroit Free Press. "Nervy Prince Returns with a Stylistic Smash." July 3, 1986, FTR 13A.

DeVeaux, Scott. "Constructing the Jazz Tradition: Jazz Historiography." *Black American Literature Forum* 25, no. 3 (Autumn 1991): 252–60.

Dickerson, Dez. *My Time with Prince: Confessions of a Former Revolutionary*. Nashville, TN: Pavilion Press, 2003.

Doerschuk, Robert. "Bernie Worrell: Burning Down the House." In *Keyboard Presents: Synth Gods*, edited by Ernie Rideout, 172–79. Milwaukee: Backbeat, 2011.

DuBois, W.E.B. *The Souls of Black Folk*. Edited by Brent Edward Hayes. New York: Oxford University Press, 2007.

Duffy, John. *Prince: The First Illustrated Biography*. New York: Omnibus Press, 1992.

Dumas, Roger. Interview with the author. Minneapolis, MN, August 10, 2005.

Dumas, Roger. Interview with the author. Minneapolis, MN, August 26, 2005.

Dumas, Roger. Interview with the author. Minneapolis MN, November 29, 2005.

Early, Gerald. *One Nation Under a Groove: Motown and American Culture*. Ann Arbor: University of Michigan Press, 2004.

Echols, Alice. *Hot Stuff: Disco and the Remaking of American Culture*. New York: W.W. Norton, 2010.

Echols, Alice. *Shaky Ground: The '60s and Its Aftershocks*. New York: Columbia University Press, 2002.

Eidsheim, Nina. *The Race of Sound: Listening, Timbre, and Vocality in African American Music*. Durham, NC: Duke University Press, 2019.

Ernst, Hugh C. "The Man Who Made a Lady out of Jazz (Paul Whiteman)." In Walser, *Keeping Time*, 39–40.

Estate of Prince Rogers Nelson. "Celebration 2023." Paisley Park (website). 2023. https://www.paisleypark.com/celebration2023, accessed June 24, 2023.

Fabre, Michel. *From Harlem to Paris: Black American Writers in France, 1840–1980*. Chicago: University of Illinois Press, 1991.

Fanon, Frantz. *Black Skin, White Masks*. Translated by Richard Philcox. New York: Grove Press, 2008.

Fast, Susan. *In the Houses of the Holy: Led Zeppelin and the Power of Rock Music*. New York: Oxford University Press, 1993.

Faulkner, Anne Shaw. "Does Jazz Put the Sin in Syncopation?" In Walser, *Keeping Time*, 32–36.

Fink, Matt. Interview with the author. Savage, MN, November 8, 2005.

Fink, Robert. "Goal-Directed Soul? Analyzing Rhythmic Teleology in African American Popular Music." *Journal of the American Musicological Society* 64, no. 1 (Spring 2011): 179–238.

Fink, Robert. *Repeating Ourselves: American Minimal Music as Cultural Practice*. Los Angeles: University of California Press, 2005.

Fischer, Clare. Interview with the author. Studio City, CA, April 4, 2006.

Floyd, Samuel A. *The Power of Black Music: Interpreting Its History from Africa to the United States*. New York: Oxford University Press, 1995.

Foucault, Michel. "Introduction." In *Herculine Barbin: Being the Recently Discovered Memoirs of a Nineteenth-Century French Hermaphrodite*, by Herculine Barbin, translated by Richard McDougall, vii–xvii. New York: Pantheon, 1980.

François, Anne-Lise. "Fakin' It / Makin' It: Falsetto's Bid for Transcendence in 1970s Disco Highs." *Perspectives of New Music* 33, no. 1/2 (Winter–Summer 1995): 442–57.

Frank, Gillian. "Discophobia: Antigay Prejudice and the 1979 Backlash against Disco." *Journal of the History of Sexuality* 15, no. 2 (May 2007): 276–306.

Freud, Sigmund. *Civilization and Its Discontents*. Translated by James Strachey. New York: W.W. Norton, 1962.

Freud, Sigmund, James Strachey, Hélène Cixous, and Robert Dennomé. "Fiction and Its Phantoms: A Reading of Freud's *Das Unheimliche* (The "Uncanny")." *New Literary History* 7, no. 3 (Spring 1976): 525–48, 619–45.

Frith, Simon. "Art Versus Technology: The Strange Case of Popular Music." *Media, Culture, and Society* 8, no. 263 (1986): 263–79.

Frith, Simon. *Performing Rites: On the Value of Popular Music.* Cambridge, MA: Harvard University Press, 1996.

Fuchs, Cynthia. "'I Wanna Be Your Fantasy': Sex, Death, and The Artist Formerly Known as Prince." *Women & Performance* 8, no. 2 (1996): 137–51.

Gabbard, Krin. *Hotter Than That: The Trumpet, Jazz, and American Culture.* New York: Faber and Faber, 2008.

Gabler, Jay. "200 Homes to Be Built on Former Prince Residential Property in Chanhassan." *The Current* (blog), July 12, 2018. https://www.thecurrent.org/feature/2018/07/12/200-homes-to-be-built-on-former-prince-residential-property-in-chanhassen, accessed July 21, 2023.

Garber, Marjorie. *Vested Interests: Cross-Dressing and Cultural Anxiety.* New York: Routledge, 1997.

Garcia, Luis-Manuel. "On and On: Repetition as Process and Pleasure in Electronic Dance Music." *Music Theory Online* 11, no. 4 (October 2005): 1–19.

Garcia, Mayte, Tyka Nelson, Kirk Johnson, and Marieke Pot. "Who We Are." *Love 4 One Another*, https://l4oa.org/, accessed June 22, 2023.

Garofalo, Reebee. "Black Popular Music: Crossing Over or Going Under?" In *Rock and Popular Music: Politics, Policies, Institutions,* edited by Tony Bennett, Simon Frith, Lawrence Grossberg, John Shepherd, and Graeme Turner, 231–48. New York: Routledge, 1993.

Garofalo, Reebee. "Crossing Over: From Black Rhythm & Blues to White Rock 'n' Roll." In *Rhythm and Business: The Political Economy of Black Music,* edited by Norman Kelley, 112–37. New York: Akashic, 2002.

Garofalo, Reebee. *Rockin' Out: Popular Music in the U.S.A.* Boston: Allyn and Bacon, 1997.

Gates, David, Vern Smith, Patrice Johnson, Jennifer Foote, and Andrew Murr. "Decoding Rap Music." *Newsweek,* March 19, 1990, 60.

Gates, Henry Louis, Jr. *The Signifying Monkey: A Theory of African-American Literary Criticism.* New York: Oxford University Press, 1988.

George, Nelson. *Hip Hop America.* New York: Penguin, 1998.

George, Nelson. *The Death of Rhythm and Blues.* New York: Pantheon, 1988.

George, Nelson. "The Rhythm & the Blues: An Ear-Witness Account of the New Prince LP." *Billboard,* February 1, 1986, 53.

George, Nelson. "Too Much 'Rain' Clouds Prince Show." *Billboard,* November 17, 1984, 36.

Giddins, Gary, and Scott DeVeaux. *Jazz.* New York: W.W. Norton, 2009.

Giles, Peter. *The History and Technique of the Counter-Tenor: A Study of the Male High Voice Family.* Burlington: Ashgate, 1993.

Gill, Andy. "Ten Questions for Little Richard." In *Rip it Up: The Black Experience in Rock 'n' Roll,* edited by Kandia Crazy Horse, 1–4. New York: Palgrave Macmillan, 2004.

Gillespie, Dizzy. "To Be or Not . . . to Bop." In Walser, *Keeping Time,* 143–57.

Gilroy, Paul. *Against Race: Imagining Political Culture Beyond the Color Line*. Cambridge, MA: Harvard University Press, 2000.

Gilroy, Paul. *The Black Atlantic: Modernity and Double Consciousness*. New York: Verso, 1993.

Goetting, Jay. *Joined at the Hip: A History of Jazz in the Twin Cities*. St. Paul: Minnesota Historical Society Press, 2011.

Goodwin, Andrew. "Popular Music and Postmodern Theory." In *The Postmodern Arts: An Introductory Reader*, edited by Nigel Wheale, 80–100. New York: Routledge, 1995.

Gore, Tipper. *Raising PG Kids in an X-Rated Society*. Nashville, TN: Abingdon Press, 1987.

Gray, Herman. "Black Masculinity and Visual Culture." *Callaloo* 18, no. 2 (Spring 1995): 401–5.

Greenman, Ben. "Prince: *The Rainbow Children*." *New Yorker*, December 10, 2001, 112–13.

Grieco, Elizabeth M., and Rachel C Cassidy. *Overview of Race and Hispanic Origin. Census 2000 Brief*. Washington, DC: US Census Bureau, 2001. https://www2.census.gov/library/publications/decennial/2000/briefs/c2kbr01-01.pdf

Grossberg, Lawrence. "Rockin' with Reagan, or the Mainstreaming of Postmodernity." *Cultural Critique*, no. 10 (Autumn 1988): 123–49.

Grow, Kory. "Prince, the Secret Philanthropist: 'His Cause Was Humanity.'" *Rolling Stone*, April 25, 2016, https://www.rollingstone.com/culture/culture-news/prince-the-secret-philanthropist-his-cause-was-humanity-157700/, accessed May 31, 2019.

Guerrasio, Jason. "A Secret Letter Prince Wrote to His Fans Explains Why He Changed His Name to a Symbol in the '90s." *Business Insider*, May 16, 2016, https://www.businessinsider.com/prince-secret-letter-2016-5

Gundersen, Edna. "R&B Stars Pump Out New Disks: Prince, *The Rainbow Children*." *USA Today*, November 27, 2001, D05.

Guralnick, Peter. *Sweet Soul Music: Rhythm and Blues and the Southern Dream of Freedom*. New York: Little, Brown, 1986.

Guzman, Marco, Macarena Barros, Fernanda Espinoza, Alejandro Herrera, Daniela Parra, Daniel Muñoz, and Adam Lloyd. "Laryngoscopic, Acoustic, Perceptual, and Functional Assessment of Voice in Rock Singers." *Folia Phoniatrica* 65, no. 5 (2013): 248–56.

Hahn, Alex. *Possessed: The Rise and Fall of Prince*. New York: Billboard, 2003.

Haimo, Ethan. "Atonality, Analysis, and the Intentional Fallacy." *Music Theory Spectrum* 18, no. 2 (Autumn 1996): 167–99.

Halambos, Michael. *Soul Music: The Birth of a Sound in Black America*. New York: Da Capo Press, 1974.

Halberstam, Judith. "Automating Gender: Postmodern Feminism in the Age of the Intelligent Machine." *Feminist Studies* 17, no. 3 (Autumn 1991): 439–60.

Hamilton, Marybeth. "Sexual Politics and African-American Music; or, Placing Little Richard in History." *History Workshop Journal* 46, no. 1 (Autumn 1998): 161–76.

Hamm, Charles. "Genre, Performance, and Ideology in the Early Songs of Irving Berlin." In *Reading Pop: Approaches to Textual Analysis in Popular Music*, edited by Richard Middleton, 297–306. New York: Oxford University Press, 2000.

Hammer, M.C. "Please Hammer, Don't Hurt 'Em." *Please Hammer, Don't Hurt 'Em.* Capitol Records, 7 92857 2, 1990, CD.

Haraway, Donna. "A Cyborg Manifesto: Science, Technology, and Socialist-Feminism in the Late Twentieth Century." In *Simians, Cyborgs and Women: The Reinvention of Nature,* 149–181. New York: Routledge, 1991.

Harris, Keith. "Prince Stuns at Emotional 'Piano and a Microphone' Solo Show." *Rolling Stone,* January 22, 2016, http://www.rollingstone.com/music/live-reviews/prince-stuns-at-emotional-piano-and-a-microphone-solo-show-20160122, accessed January 22, 2016.

Hasted, Nick. "The Making of . . . The Waterboys' *The Whole of the Moon.*" *Uncut,* May 3, 2013, https://www.uncut.co.uk/features/the-making-of-the-waterboys-the-whole-of-the-moon-23109, accessed May 22, 2019.

Hawkins, Stan. "'Chelsea Rodgers' Was a Model—Vocality in Prince of the Twenty-First Century." In *The Ashgate Research Companion to Popular Musicology,* edited by Derek Scott, 295–305. New York: Routledge, 2016.

Hawkins, Stan. "Prince: Harmonic Analysis of 'Anna Stesia.'" *Popular Music* 11, no. 3 (October 1992): 325–35.

Hawkins, Stan. *Settling the Pop Score: Pop Texts and Identity Politics.* Burlington, VT: Ashgate, 2002.

Hawkins, Stan, and Sarah Niblock. *Prince: The Making of a Pop Music Phenomenon.* Burlington, VT: Ashgate, 2011.

Heilbut, Anthony. *The Fan Who Knew Too Much: Aretha Franklin, the Rise of the Soap Opera, Children of the Gospel Church, and Other Meditations.* New York: Alfred A. Knopf, 2012.

Heilbut, Anthony. *The Gospel Sound: Good News and Bad Times.* New York: Simon & Schuster, 1971.

Hilburn, Robert. "The Renegade Prince." *Los Angeles Times,* November 21, 1982, http://documents.latimes.com/remembering-prince-robert-hilburns-1982-la-times-feature-capturing-all-eccentricities-and-ambitions-/, accessed June 19, 2019.

Hill, Dave. *Prince: A Pop Life.* New York: Harmony, 1989.

Hoffman, Claire. "Home Visit: Soup with Prince." *New Yorker,* November 24, 2008, 42–44.

Holden, Andrew. *Jehovah's Witnesses: Portrait of a Contemporary Religious Movement.* New York: Routledge, 2002.

Holden, Stephen. "Sex and Society: Controversy, Prince." *Rolling Stone,* January 21, 1982, 51–52.

Holland, Nancy. "Prince: Postmodern Icon." *Journal of African American Studies* 21, no. 3 (September 2017): 320–36.

Holland, Nancy. "Purple Passion: Images of Female Desire in 'When Doves Cry.'" *Cultural Critique,* no. 10 (Autumn 1988): 89–98.

Hopfensperger, Jean. "'We Lost a Spiritual Brother' in Prince." *Minneapolis Star Tribune.* May 4, 2016, http://www.startribune.com/prince-s-death-puts-spotlight-on-jehovah-s-witnesses/377972981, accessed June 13, 2019.

Hoskyns, Barney. "Prince: A Second Coming thru Purple Haze." *New Musical Express,* April 2, 1983, available at https://www.rocksbackpages.com/Library/Article/prince-a-second-coming-thru-purple-haze/, accessed July 21, 2022.

Hoskyns, Barney. *Prince: Imp of the Perverse.* London: Virgin, 1988.

Housequake. "Interview with Greg Boyer." February 28, 2004, https://www.housequake.com/2004/02/28/greg-boyer-interview/, accessed June 18, 2019.

Hughes, Walter. "In the Empire of the Beat: Discipline and Disco." In *Microphone Fiends: Youth Music and Youth Culture*, edited by Andrew Ross and Tricia Rose, 147–57. New York: Routledge, 1994.

Hunter, Andrea G., and James Earl Davis. "Constructing Gender: An Exploration of Afro-American Men's Conceptualization of Manhood." *Gender and Society* 6, no. 3 (September 1992): 464–79.

Husney, Owen. *Famous People Who've Met Me*. Los Angeles: Rothco Press, 2018.

Huyssen, Andreas. "The Vamp and the Machine: Technology and Sexuality in Fritz Lang's *Metropolis*." *New German Critique*, nos. 24–25 (Autumn 1981–Winter 1982): 221–37.

Jafri, Iman. "The House and Studio Are Gone, but You Can Now Live on the Land Where Prince Recorded Some of *Sign o' the Times*." *The Current* (blog), September 2, 2020, https://www.thecurrent.org/feature/2020/09/02/the-house-and-studio-are-gone-but-you-can-now-live-on-the-land-where-prince-recorded-some-of, accessed July 21, 2023.

Jain, Sarah. "The Prosthetic Imagination: Enabling and Disabling the Prosthesis Trope." *Science, Technology, & Human Values* 24, no. 1 (Winter 1999): 31–54.

Jefferson, Thomas. *Notes on the State of Virginia*. Boston: Lilly and Wait, 1832.

Jennings, Sam. "The Story Behind Prince's Influence Wall." *Medium*, October 19, 2016, https://medium.com/@samjennings3000/the-story-behind-princes-influence-wall-e930c9cf5686, accessed June 24, 2023.

Jensen, Jeff. "The Weird, Wonderful Return of Prince." *Entertainment Weekly*, April 23, 2004, 26–32.

Jentsch, Ernst. "On the Psychology of the Uncanny (1906)." *Angelaki: Journal of the Theoretical Humanities* 2, no. 1 (1997): 7–16.

Johnson, Bruce. "Hear Me Talkin' to Ya: Problems of Jazz Discourse." *Popular Music* 12, no. 1 (January 1993): 1–12.

Johnson, Mark. *The Body in the Mind: The Bodily Basis of Meaning, Imagination, and Reason*. Chicago: University of Chicago Press, 1987.

Joki, Errol. Interview with the author. St. Paul, MN, March 19, 2011.

Jones, Liz. *Purple Reign: The Artist Formerly Known as Prince*. Seacaucus, NJ: Citadel Press, 1997.

Karlen, Neal. "Prince Talks." *Rolling Stone*, April 26, 1985, 24–30, 84–86.

Karlen, Neal. "Prince Talks." *Rolling Stone*, September 12, 1985, 24–30, 84–86.

Kater, Michael. "Forbidden Fruit? Jazz in the Third Reich." *American Historical Review* 94, no. 1 (February 1989): 11–43.

Keller, Martin. "Portrait of the Artist as a Native Son." *Minnesota Monthly*, March 1997, https://www.minnesotamonthly.com/arts-entertainment/princes-1997-minnesota-monthly-cover-story/, accessed Nov 11, 2021.

Kelley, Robin D. G. *Freedom Dreams: The Black Radical Imagination*. Boston: Beacon Press, 2002.

Kelley, Robin D. G. *Race Rebels: Culture, Politics, and the Black Working Class*. New York: Free Press, 1994.

Kerman, Joseph. *Contemplating Music: Challenges to Musicology*. Cambridge, MA: Harvard University Press, 1985.

King, Martin Luther, Jr. "I Have a Dream." Speech, Washington, DC, August 28,

1963. *National Archives*, https://www.archives.gov/files/social-media/transcripts/transcript-march-pt3-of-3-2602934.pdf

Kirby, Jon. "Something in the Water." Program book for *Purple Snow: Forecasting the Minneapolis Sound*. The Numero Group 050, 2013, 2013, 2 CDs.

Knowles-Carter, Beyoncé. Foreword to *Prince: A Private View*, by Afshin Shahadi, ix–x. New York: St. Martin's Press, 2017.

Kornhaber, Spencer. "Prince: Gay Icon, Whether He Wanted to Be or Not." *Atlantic*, April 22, 2016, https://www.theatlantic.com/entertainment/archive/2016/04/prince-gay-homophobia-conservative-liberal-progress/479502/, accessed May 31, 2019.

Kosmin, Barry, Egon Mayer, and Ariela Keysar. *American Religious Identification Survey*. New York: Graduate Center of the City University of New York, 2001.

Kovarsky, Jerry. "The Art of Synth Soloing: Tony Banks—Prog Rock's Masterful Composer and Arranger." *Electronic Musician*, February 2022, 30–31.

Kramer, Lawrence. *Interpreting Music*. Los Angeles: University of California Press, 2011.

Kramer, Lawrence. *Music as Cultural Practice, 1800–1900*. Los Angeles: University of California Press, 1990.

Krebs, Harold. "Some Extensions of the Concepts of Metrical Consonance and Dissonance." *Journal of Music Theory* 31, no. 1 (Spring 1987): 99–120.

Kreps, Daniel. "Hear Prince's Dance Rally 4 Peace Paisley Park Concert." *Rolling Stone*, May 13, 2015, https://www.rollingstone.com/politics/politics-news/hear-princes-dance-rally-4-peace-paisley-park-concert-69714/, accessed May 22, 2019.

LaForce, Thessaly. "Behind the Scenes: Glamorous Life." *New Yorker*, November 17, 2008, https://www.newyorker.com/culture/goings-on/behind-the-scenes-glamorous-life, accessed August 12, 2019.

Large, John W. "Towards an Integrated Physiologic-Acoustic Theory of Vocal Registers." *NATS Bulletin* 28, no. 3 (February 1972): 18–25.

Large, John W., S. Iwata, and H. von Leden. "The Male Operatic Head Register versus Falsetto." *Folia phoniatrica* 24, no. 1 (1972): 19–29.

Lawrence, Tim. *Love Saves the Day: A History of American Dance Music Culture, 1970–1979*. Durham, NC: Duke University Press, 2003.

Leeds, Alan. "James Brown and His First Family of Soul." In *The James Brown Reader: 50 Years of Writing about the Godfather of Soul*, edited by Nelson George and Alan Leeds, 297–302. New York: Plume, 2008.

Leeds, Eric. Interview with the author. Bloomington, MN, September 19, 2007.

Leland, John, Stanley Holmes, Tim Pryor, Mark Miller, and Charles Fleming. "Gangsta Rap and the Culture of Violence." *Newsweek*, November 29, 1993, 60.

Lemke, Sieglinde. *Primitivist Modernism: Black Culture and the Origins of Transatlantic Modernism*. New York: Oxford University Press, 1998.

Leppert, Richard. "Commentary." In *Essays on Music*, by Theodor Adorno, edited by Richard Leppert, translated by Susan Gillespie, 85–112. Los Angeles: University of California Press, 2002.

Levine, Lawrence. *Black Culture and Black Consciousness: Afro-American Folk Thought from Slavery to Freedom*. New York: Oxford University Press, 1977.

Lieb, Michael. *Children of Ezekiel: Aliens, UFOs, the Crisis of Race, and the Advent of End Times.* Durham, NC: Duke University Press, 1998.
Light, Alan. "*Diamonds and Pearls*: Prince and the New Power Generation." *Rolling Stone*, October 17, 1991, 92.
Light, Alan. *Let's Go Crazy: Prince and the Making of Purple Rain.* New York: Atria, 2014.
Lincoln, C. Eric, and Lawrence H. Mamiya. *The Black Church in the African American Experience.* Durham, NC: Duke University Press, 1990.
Lipsitz, George. *American Studies in a Moment of Danger.* Minneapolis: University of Minnesota Press, 2001.
Loder, Kurt. "Prince's Baffling Brilliance." *Rolling Stone*, April 23, 1987, 145–46.
Lordi, Emily. "Souls Intact: The Soul Performances of Audre Lorde, Aretha Franklin, and Nina Simone." *Women & Performance* 26, no. 1 (2016): 55–71.
Lordi, Emily. "Surviving the Hustle: Beyoncé's Performance of Work." *Black Camera* 9, no. 1 (Fall 2017): 131–45.
Lott, Eric. *Love and Theft: Blackface Minstrelsy and the American Working Class.* New York: Oxford University Press, 1993.
Lovell, Glenn. "This Star Needn't Be Borne Underneath Prince's New Clothes, 'Cherry Moon' Is the Same Old Song." *San Jose Mercury News*, July 3, 1986, Living 1G.
Lowe, Kelly Fisher. *The Words and Music of Frank Zappa.* New York: Praeger, 2006.
Lull, James. "Popular Music: Resistance to New Wave." *Journal of Communication* 32, no. 1 (Winter 1982): 121–31.
Mahon, Maureen. *Right to Rock: The Black Rock Coalition and the Cultural Politics of Race.* Durham, NC: Duke University Press, 2004.
Marsh, Dave. "The Flip Side of '79." *Rolling Stone*, December 27, 1979, 27–30.
Martin, Linda, and Kerry Segrave. *Anti-Rock: The Opposition to Rock 'n' Roll.* Boston: Da Capo Press, 1993.
Matos, Michaelangelo. *Sign 'O' the Times.* New York: Continuum, 2004.
McAdams, Stephen. "Perspectives on the Contribution of Timbre to Musical Structure." *Computer Music Journal* 33, no. 3 (Autumn 1999): 85–102.
McClary, Susan. *Conventional Wisdom: The Content of Musical Form.* Los Angeles: University of California Press, 2000.
McClary, Susan. *Feminine Endings.* Minneapolis: University of Minnesota Press, 1991.
McLeod, Ken. "The Construction of Masculinity in African American Music and Sports." *American Music* 27, no. 2 (Summer 2009): 204–26.
McLeod, Ken. *Driving Identities: At the Intersection of Popular Music and Automotive Culture.* New York, NY: Routledge, 2020.
McLeod, Ken. "Space Oddities: Aliens, Futurism, and Meaning in Popular Music." *Popular Music* 22, no. 3 (October 2003): 337–55.
Meyer, Leonard B. *Emotion and Meaning in Music.* Chicago: University of Chicago Press, 1961.
Middleton, Richard. *Studying Popular Music.* Philadelphia: Open University Press, 1990.
Miller, Debbie. "Prince's Hot Rock: The Secret Life of America's Sexiest One-Man Band." *Rolling Stone*, April 28, 1983, 18–23, 73.

Miller, Doug. "The Moan within the Tone: African Retentions in Rhythm and Blues Saxophone Style in Afro-American Popular Music." *Popular Music* 14, no. 2 (May 1995): 155–74.

Mills, David. *George Clinton and P-Funk: An Oral History.* Edited by Dave Marsh. New York: Avon Books, 1998.

Mills, David. "Princelings: Minneapolis New Magnet for Young Black Musicians." *Washington Times,* October 11, 1988, E3.

Minnesota Historical Society. "The Minneapolis Music Collection." 2002, http://www.mnhs.org/collections/mplsmusic/, accessed June 13, 2019.

Mitchell, Gail. "Black Artists Struggle to Regain Ownership of Master Recordings." *Billboard,* March 2, 2002, 1, 89–90.

Moog, Bob. "Minimoog: The Ultimate in Antique Analog?" In *Vintage Synthesizers,* edited by Mark Vail, 143–50. San Francisco: Miller Freeman, 1993.

Moog, Bob. "Oberheim SEM Module: Building Block of an Early Polyphonic Synth." In *Vintage Synthesizers,* edited by Mark Vail, 151–56. San Francisco: Miller Freeman, 1993.

Mori, Masahiro. "The Uncanny Valley." Translated by Karl F. MacDorman and Norri Kageki. *IEEE Robotics & Automation Magazine,* June 2012, 98–100.

Mowitt, John. *Percussion: Drumming, Beating, Striking.* Durham, NC: Duke University Press, 2002.

MTV News. "Prince's Debut TV Interview from 1985." *MTV News,* April 21, 2016, https://www.mtv.com/movie-and-tv-awards/video-clips/ev9cwl/prince-s-debut-tv-interview-from-1985, accessed September 25, 2024.

Murray, Charles Shaar. *Crosstown Traffic: Jimi Hendrix and the Rock 'n' Roll Revolution.* New York: St. Martin's Press, 1989.

Muyumba, Walton M. *The Shadow and the Act: Black Intellectual Practice, Jazz Improvisation, and Philosophical Pragmatism.* Chicago: University of Chicago Press, 2009.

NAACP Economic Development Department. "The Discordant Sound of Music: A Report on the Record Industry." In *Rhythm and Business: The Political Economy of Black Music,* edited by Norman Kelley, 44–58. New York: Akashic, 2002.

Nanni, Loris, Yandre Costa, Rafael Aguiar, Carlos Silla Jr., and Sheryl Brahnam. "Ensemble of Deep Learning, Visual and Acoustic Features for Music Genre Classification." *Journal of New Music Research* 47, no. 4 (2018): 383–97.

Narmour, Eugene. *The Analysis and Cognition of Melodic Complexity: The Implication-Realization Model.* Chicago: University of Chicago Press, 1992.

Nash, Jennifer C. "Re-thinking Intersectionality." *Feminist Review* 89, no. 1 (2008): 1–15.

Neal, Mark Anthony. "'A Man Without a Country': The Boundaries of Legibility, Social Capital, and Cosmopolitan Masculinity." *Criticism* 52, nos. 3 & 4 (Summer & Fall 2010): 399–411.

Neal, Mark Anthony. *New Black Man.* New York: Routledge, 2005.

Neal, Mark Anthony. "Sold Out on Soul: The Corporate Annexation of Black Popular Music." *Popular Music and Society* 21, no. 3 (Fall 1997): 117–35.

Negus, Keith. *Music Genres and Corporate Cultures.* New York: Routledge, 1999.

Nelson, Michael. Interview with the author. Minneapolis, MN, June 1, 2007.

New Orleans Times-Picayune. "The Location of 'Jass.'" In Walser, *Keeping Time,* 7–9.

Nicholson, Stuart. *Is Jazz Dead?: Or Has It Moved to a New Address.* New York: Routledge, 2005.

Nilsen, Per. *Dance Music Sex Romance.* London: Firefly, 1999.

Nilsen, Per. *The Vault: The Definitive Guide to the Musical World of Prince.* Linghem, Sweden: Uptown, 2004.

Osgood, Chris. Interview with the author. Eden Prairie, MN, July 19, 2011.

Pareles, Jon. "Recordings: Sonic and Sexual Updates from Prince." *New York Times,* Aug 19, 1990, H31.

Pareles, Jon. "A Re-Inventor of His World and Himself." *New York Times,* November 17, 1996, H1, 34.

Parke, Steve. *Picturing Prince.* London: Cassell Illustrated, 2017.

Parliament. *Clones of Dr. Funkenstein.* Casablanca NBLP 7034, 1976, LP.

Penman, Ian. "Prince: Lyceum, London." *New Musical Express,* June 13, 1981, available at https://www.rocksbackpages.com/Library/Article/prince-lyceum-london, accessed June 6, 2014.

Perchard, Tom. "Hip Hop Samples Jazz: Dynamics of Cultural Memory and Musical Tradition in the African American 1990s." *American Music* 29, no. 3 (Fall 2011): 277–307.

Perry, Twila. "'Let's Work!': The Racial and the Universal in Prince's Fight for Artist's Rights." Paper presented at the Prince from Minneapolis symposium, Minneapolis, MN, April 18, 2018.

Perry, Twila. "Prince: Double-Consciousness in Expressing the Value of Work." *Howard Journal of Communications* 30, no. 2 (2019): 202–10.

Phipps, Keith. "Prince: *The Rainbow Children.*" *Onion A.V. Club.* November 20, 2001. https://www.avclub.com/prince-the-rainbow-children-1798192821, accessed September 24, 2019.

Piepenbring, Dan. "The Beautiful One: Prince Had Grand Plans for his Autobiography, but Only a Few Months to Live." *New Yorker,* September 19, 2019, 28–34.

Pinch, Trevor, and Frank Trocco. *Analog Days: The Invention and Impact of the Moog Synthesizer.* Cambridge, MA: Harvard University Press, 2002.

Plasse, Marie A. "'Joy in Repetition'?: Prince's *Graffiti Bridge* and *Sign o' the Times* as Sequels to *Purple Rain.*" *Journal of Popular Culture* 30, no. 3 (Winter 1996): 57–65.

Prince. *The Beautiful Ones.* Edited by Dan Piepenbring. New York: Spiegel & Grau, 2019.

Prince. *Controversy.* Warner Bros. Records 3601-2, 1981, CD.

Prince. *Dirty Mind.* Warner Bros. Records 3478-2, 1980, CD.

Prince. *For You.* Warner Bros. Records 3150-2, 1978, CD.

Prince. *Graffiti Bridge.* Warner Bros. Records 9 27493-2, 1990, CD.

Prince. *Lovesexy.* Warner Bros. Records 7599-25720-2, 1988, CD.

Prince. "Lovesexy '88 tour program." 1988.

Prince. *1999.* Warner Bros. Records 9 23720-2, 1982, CD.

Prince. *Prince.* Warner Bros. Records 3366, 1979, CD.

Prince. *The Rainbow Children.* NPG Records 70004, 2001, CD.

Prince. *Under the Cherry Moon.* 1986; Burbank, CA: Warner Bros. Pictures. 2004; Burbank, CA: Warner Home Video 33538. DVD.

Prince and the New Power Generation, *Diamonds and Pearls.* Warner Bros. Records 9 25379-2, 1991, CD.

Prince and the New Power Generation. *Love Symbol.* Warner Bros. Records 9 45037-2, 1992, CD.

Prince and the Revolution. *Around the World in a Day.* Warner Bros. Records 9 25286-2, 1985, CD.

Prince and the Revolution. *Parade.* Warner Bros. Records 9 25395-2, 1986, CD.

Prince / The Artist (Formerly Known as Prince). *The Gold Experience.* Warner Bros. Records 9 45999-2, 1995, CD.

Protzman, Bob. "From the Archives: 18-Year-Old Prince Signs First Record Deal." *Twin Cities Pioneer Press,* April 21, 2016, https://www.twincities.com/2016/04/21/prince-signs-first-record-deal/, accessed June 7, 2019.

Quinn, Michael. "'Never Shoulda Been Let out the Penitentiary': Gangsta Rap and the Struggle over Racial Identity." *Cultural Critique,* no. 34 (Autumn 1996): 65–89.

Raboteau, Albert. *Slave Religion: The Invisible Institution in the Antebellum South.* New York: Oxford University Press, 1978.

Radano, Ronald. "Hot Fantasies: American Modernism, and the Idea of Black Rhythm." In *Music and the Racial Imagination,* edited by Ronald Radano and Philip V. Bohlman, 459–80. Chicago: University of Chicago Press, 2000.

Radano, Ronald. *Lying Up a Nation: Race and Black Music.* Chicago: University of Chicago Press, 2003.

Ramsey, Guthrie. *Race Music: Black Cultures from Bebop to Hip-Hop.* Los Angeles: University of California Press, 2003.

Redmond, Shana. "This Safer Space: Janelle Monáe's 'Cold War.'" *Journal of Popular Music Studies* 23, no. 4 (2011): 393–411.

Reed, Teresa. *The Holy Profane: Religion in Black Popular Music.* Lexington: University Press of Kentucky, 2003.

Reid-Pharr, Robert. "It's Raining Men." *Transition,* no. 69 (1996): 36–49.

Retzloff, Tim. "'Seer or Queer?' Postwar Fascination with Detroit's Prophet Jones." *GLQ: A Journal of Lesbian and Gay Studies* 8, no. 3 (2002): 271–96.

Reynaud, Michel, and Sylvie Graffard. *The Jehovah's Witnesses and the Nazis: Persecution, Deportation, and Murder, 1933–1945.* Translated by James A. Moorhouse. New York: Cooper Square Press, 2001.

Riemenschneider, Chris. *First Avenue: Minnesota's Mainroom.* St. Paul, MN: Minnesota Historical Society Press, 2017.

Riemenschneider, Chris. "Paisley Park to Re-open 'After Dark' to Celebrate New Prince Album Friday." *Minneapolis Star Tribune,* Artcetera Blog, September 17, 2018, http://www.startribune.com/paisley-park-to-re-open-after-dark-to-celebrate-new-prince-album-friday/493515811/, accessed May 20, 2019.

Ro, Ronin. *Prince: Inside the Music and the Masks.* New York: St. Martin's Press, 2011.

Robair, Gino. "Rhapsody in Purple: Prince's One-of-a-Kind Concert Grand." *Keyboard,* July 2016, 12.

Rollefson, J. Griffith. "The 'Robot Voodoo Power' Thesis: Afrofuturism and Anti-Anti-Essentialism from Sun Ra to Kool Keith." *Black Music Research Journal* 28, no. 1 (Spring 2008): 83–109.

Rose, Tricia. *Black Noise: Rap Music and Black Culture in Contemporary America.* Middletown, CT: Wesleyan University Press, 1994.

Rosenthal, David. "Jazz in the Ghetto: 1950–1970." *Popular Music* 7, no. 1 (January 1988): 51–56.

Russolo, Luigi. "The Art of Noises: Futurist Manifesto." In *Audio Culture: Readings in Modern Music,* edited by Christopher Cox and Daniel Warner, 10–14. New York: Continuum, 2006.

Said, Edward. *Orientalism.* New York: Vintage Books, 1979.

Salewicz, Chris. "Strutting with the New Soul Monarch." *New Musical Express,* June 6, 1981, available at https://www.rocksbackpages.com/Library/Article/prince-strutting-with-the-new-soul-monarch

Samuels, David. "The Rap on Rap: The 'Black Music' That Isn't Either." In *That's the Joint: The Hip-Hop Studies Reader,* edited by Murray Forman and Mark Anthony Neal, 147–53. New York: Routledge, 2004.

Sandow, Greg. "Prince Mix-A-Lot." *Entertainment Weekly,* October 23, 1992, 62.

Sanjek, David. "Tell Me Something I Don't Already Know: The Harvard Report on Soul Music Revisited." In *Rhythm and Business: The Political Economy of Black Music,* edited by Norman Kelley, 59–76. New York: Akashic, 2002.

Schwartz, Andy. "Prince: A Dirty Mind Comes Clean." *New York Rocker,* June 1981, available at http://www.rocksbackpages.com/article.html?ArticleID=6116, accessed June 21, 2019.

Scott, Derek. "Introduction." In *The Ashgate Research Companion to Popular Musicology,* edited by Derek Scott, 16–30. New York: Routledge, 2016.

Seifert, Dan. "Prince Tweets to You: The Artist Makes his Debut on Twitter." *The Verge,* August 14, 2013, https://www.theverge.com/2013/8/14/4620554/prince-tweets-to-you-the-artist-makes-his-debut-on-twitter, accessed December 30, 2020.

Setlist.fm. "Songs Played by Tour: Piano & a Microphone." N.d., https://www.setlist.fm/stats/prince-13d6b9ed.html?tour=5bd6937c, accessed June 22, 2023.

Shemo, Catherine Censor. "A Prince of a Guy." *Vegetarian Times,* October 1997, 78–83.

Shin, Andrew, and Barbara Judson. "Beneath the Black Aesthetic: James Baldwin's Primer of Black American Masculinity." *African American Review* 32, no. 2 (Summer 1998): 247–61.

Sigerson, Davitt. "Prince Strips Down." *Rolling Stone,* April 24, 1986, 53, 55.

Sims, Calvin. "Ganster Rappers: The Lives, the Lyrics." *New York Times,* November 28, 1993, A3.

Small, Christopher. *Music of the Common Tongue: Survival and Celebration in African American Music.* Middletown, CT: Wesleyan University Press, 1998.

Smith, Nathan. "The Queer Legacy of Prince." *Out,* June 7, 2016, https://www.out.com/music/2016/4/22/queer-legacy-prince, accessed May 31, 2019.

Smith, R. J. *The One: The Life and Music of James Brown.* New York: Gotham, 2012.

Snowden, Don. "Moog on the State of the Synthesizer." *Los Angeles Times,* June 7, 1981, 22, 26, 32.

Southern, Eileen. *The Music of Black Americans.* New York: W.W. Norton, 1971.

Spencer, Jack. "Numero Group's Jon Kirby on Purple Snow: Everybody Deserves to be Celebrated." *City Pages,* December 2, 2013, http://www.citypages.com

/music/numero-groups-jon-kirby-on-purple-snow-everybody-deserves-to-be-celebrated-6627590, accessed June 21, 2019.

Spicer, Mark. "(Ac)Cumulative Form in Pop-Rock Music." *Twentieth-Century Music* 1, no. 1 (2004): 29–64.

Stewart, Alexander. "'Funky Drummer': New Orleans, James Brown, and the Rhythmic Transformation of American Popular Music." *Popular Music* 19, no. 3 (2000): 293–318.

Stubbs, Dan. "Prince Covers the Waterboys at Tiny Ronnie Scott's Show." *NME*, February 18, 2014, https://www.nme.com/news/music/prince-164-1235848, accessed May 22, 2019.

Swensson, Andrea. "A Brief History of Paisley Park's Celebrations." *The Current* (blog), April 13, 2017, https://www.thecurrent.org/feature/2017/04/13/a-brief-history-of-paisley-parks-celebrations, accessed June 24, 2023.

Swensson, Andrea. *Got to Be Something Here: The Rise of the Minneapolis Sound*. Minneapolis: University of Minnesota Press, 2017.

Swensson, Andrea. *Prince: Guitar & Bass*. Minneapolis: P Park Management LLC, 2017.

Swensson, Andrea. *Prince Paisley Park Archives: Paisley Park*. Exhibition Tour Book Series. Minneapolis: P Park Management LLC, 2017.

Synan, Vinson. *The Holiness-Pentecostal Movement in the United States*. Grand Rapids, MI: William B. Eerdmans, 1971.

Szwed, John. *Space Is the Place: The Lives and Times of Sun Ra*. New York: Pantheon, 1997.

Tagg, Philip. "Analysing Popular Music: Theory, Method, and Practice." *Popular Music* 2 (1982): 37–67.

Takiff, Jonathan. "An Album of Reasons to Rain on Prince's *Parade*." *Philadelphia Daily News*, April 15, 1986, 39.

Takiff, Jonathan. "Prince Is Still King." *Philadelphia Daily News*, October 13, 1992, 35.

Terrace, Vincent. "5725 *The Man from U.N.C.L.E.*" Vol. 2 of *Encyclopedia of Television Shows, 1925–2010*, 2nd ed., by Vincent Terrace, 650. Jefferson, NC: McFarland, 2011.

Terrace, Vincent. "692 *Batman*." Vol. 1 of in *Encyclopedia of Television Shows, 1925–2010*, 2nd ed., by Vincent Terrace, 77. Jefferson, NC: McFarland, 2011.

Théberge, Paul. *Any Sound You Can Imagine: Making Music / Consuming Technology*. Middletown, CT: Wesleyan University Press, 1997.

Theweleit, Klaus. *Male Fantasies, Volume 1: Women, Floods, Bodies, History*. Translated by Stephen Conway. Minneapolis: University of Minnesota Press, 1987.

Thorne, Matt. *Prince: The Man and His Music*. Chicago: Bolden, 2016.

Touré. "You Can Call Him Prince." In *Never Drank the Kool-Aid*, 248–69. New York: Picador, 2006.

Tucker, Bruce. "'Tell Tchaikovsky the News': Postmodernism, Popular Culture, and the Emergence of Rock 'n' Roll." *Black Music Research Journal* 9, no. 2 (Autumn 1989): 271–95.

Tucker, Ken. "Love and Lust in Minneapolis: Prince, *Dirty Mind*." *Rolling Stone*, February 19, 1981, 54–55.

Tudahl, Duane. *Prince and the Purple Rain Era Studio Sessions: 1983 and 1984*. New York: Rowman & Littlefield, 2018.

Tzanetakis, George, and Perry Cook. "Musical Genre Classification of Audio Signals." *IEEE Transactions on Speech and Audio Processing* 10, no. 5 (2002): 293–302.

Vail, Mark. "Keith Emerson's Moog: The World's Most Dangerous Synth." In *Vintage Synthesizers,* edited by Mark Vail, 107–15. San Francisco: Miller Freeman, 1993.

Vail, Mark. *The Synthesizer.* New York: Oxford University Press, 2014.

Vincent, Rickey. *Funk: The Music, the People, and the Rhythm of the One.* New York: St. Martin's Griffin, 1996.

Waksman, Steve. *Instruments of Desire: The Electric Guitar and the Shaping of Musical Experience.* Cambridge, MA: Harvard University Press, 1999.

Waksman, Steve. "Reading the Instrument: An Introduction." *Popular Music and Society* 26, no. 3 (2003): 251–61.

Wald, Elijah. *Escaping the Delta: Robert Johnson and the Invention of the Blues.* New York: Amistad, 2004.

Wald, Gayle. "From Spirituals to Swing: Sister Rosetta Tharpe and Gospel Crossover." *American Quarterly* 55, no. 3 (Sept. 2003): 387–416.

Wald, Gayle. "Soul Vibrations: Black Music and Black Freedom in Sound and Space." *American Quarterly* 63, no. 3 (Sept. 2011): 673–96.

Walker, Jesse. *Rebels on the Air: An Alternative History of Radio in America.* New York: New York University Press, 2001.

Wall, Mick. *Prince: Purple Reign.* New York: Hachette, 2016.

Walser, Robert, ed. *Keeping Time: Readings in Jazz History.* New York: Oxford University Press, 1999.

Walser, Robert. "Prince as Queer Poststructuralist." *Popular Music and Society* 18, no. 2 (1994): 79–89.

Walser, Robert. "Rhythm, Rhyme, and Rhetoric in the Music of Public Enemy." *Ethnomusicology* 39, no. 2 (Spring–Summer 1995): 193–217.

Walser, Robert. *Running with the Devil: Power, Gender, and Madness in Heavy Metal Music.* Middletown, CT: Wesleyan University Press, 1993.

Walsh, Jim. *Gold Experience: Following Prince in the '90s.* Minneapolis: University of Minnesota Press, 2017.

Walters, Barry. "Prince Leads Black Pop through the Back Door." In *Rip It Up: The Black Experience in Rock 'n' Roll,* edited by Kandia Crazy Horse, 115–19. New York: Palgrave Macmillan, 2004.

Ward, Brian. *Just My Soul Responding: Rhythm and Blues, Black Consciousness, and Race Relations.* Los Angeles: University of California Press, 1998.

Warner, Timothy. *Pop Music: Technology and Creativity: Trevor Horn and the Digital Revolution.* Burlington, VT: Ashgate, 2003.

Watchtower. "The Truth About Armageddon." February 1, 2012, https://www.jw.org/en/publications/magazines/wp20120201/The-Truth-About-Armageddon/, accessed June 13, 2019.

Waterman, Richard. "African Influence on the Music of the Americas." In *Acculturation in the Americas,* edited by Sol Tax, 207–18. Chicago: University of Chicago Press, 1967.

Weekes, Melinda E. "This House, This Music: Exploring the Interdependent Interpretive Relationship between the Contemporary Black Church and

Contemporary Gospel Music." *Black Music Research Journal* 25, nos. 1/2 (Spring–Fall 2005): 43–72.

Weingarten, Marc. "The Week: Prince." *Entertainment Weekly*, November 23, 2001, 82.

Wenger, Yvonne, and Wesley Case. "Thousands Turn Out for Prince's 'Rally 4 Peace' Benefit Concert." *Baltimore Sun*, May 10, 2015, https://www.baltimoresun.com/entertainment/music/bs-md-prince-concert-20150510-story.html, accessed May 22, 2019.

Werner, Craig. *A Change Is Gonna Come: Music, Race, and the Soul of America.* New York: Plume, 1999.

Wesley, Fred. *Hit Me, Fred: Recollections of a Sideman.* Durham, NC: Duke University Press, 2002.

Williams, James Gordon. "Black Muse 4 U: Liminality, Self-Determination, and Racial Uplift in the Music of Prince." *Journal of African American Studies* 21, no. 3 (Sept. 2017): 296–319.

Williams, Stereo. "Prince Was Not 'Biracial.' He Loved His Blackness—and Yours." *Daily Beast*, April 24, 2016, https://www.thedailybeast.com/prince-was-not-biracial-he-loved-his-blacknessand-yours, accessed May 31, 2019.

Wilson, Olly. "Black Music as an Art Form." *Black Music Research Journal* 3, no. 1 (1983): 1–22.

Wilson, Olly. "The Heterogeneous Sound Ideal in African-American Music." In *Signifyin(g), Sanctifyin', & Slam Dunking: A Reader in African American Expressive Culture*, edited by Gena Dagel Caponi, 157–71. Amherst, MA: University of Massachusetts Press, 1999.

Wilson, Olly. "The Significance of the Relationship Between Afro-American Music and West African Music." *Black Perspective in Music* 2, no. 1 (Spring 1974): 3–22.

Woodworth, Griffin. "'Rapping Done Let Us Down': Prince's Hip-Hop Ambivalence." *Popular Music and Society* 43, no. 3 (2020): 281–300.

Woodworth, Griffin. "Synthesizers as Social Protest in Early-1970s Funk." In *The Relentless Pursuit of Tone: Timbre in Popular Music*, edited by Robert Fink, Melinda Latour, and Zachary Wallmark, 233–52. New York: Oxford University Press, 2018.

Zak, Albin. *The Poetics of Rock: Cutting Tracks, Making Records.* Los Angeles: University of California Press, 2001.

Index